WITHDRAWN
UTSA LIBRARIES

Controlling Government Spending

Controlling Government Spending
The Ethos, Ethics, and Economics of Expenditure Management

A. Premchand

OXFORD
UNIVERSITY PRESS

OXFORD
UNIVERSITY PRESS

YMCA Library Building, Jai Singh Road, New Delhi 110 001

Oxford University Press is a department of the University of Oxford. It furthers the University's objective of excellence in research, scholarship, and education by publishing worldwide in

Oxford New York
Auckland Cape Town Dar es Salaam Hong Kong Karachi
Kuala Lumpur Madrid Melbourne Mexico City Nairobi
New Delhi Shanghai Taipei Toronto

With offices in
Argentina Austria Brazil Chile Czech Republic France Greece
Guatemala Hungary Italy Japan Poland Portugal Singapore
South Korea Switzerland Taiwan Thailand Turkey Ukraine Vietnam

Oxford is a registered trade mark of Oxford University Press
in the UK and in certain other countries

First Published in India
by Oxford University Press, New Delhi, 2005

© Oxford University Press 2005

The moral rights of the author have been asserted
Database right Oxford University Press (maker)

All rights reserved. No part of this publication may be reproduced, stored in a retrieval system, or transmitted, in any form or by any means, without the prior permission in writing of Oxford University Press, or as expressly permitted by law, or under terms agreed with the appropriate reprographics rights organization. Enquiries concerning reproduction outside the scope of the above should be sent to the Rights Department, Oxford University Press, at the address above

You must not circulate this book in any other binding or cover
and you must impose this same condition on any acquiror

ISBN-13: 978-0-19-567387-6
ISBN-10: 0-19-567387-5

Typeset in AGaramond 10.5/12 by
Excel Publishing Services, New Delhi 110067
Printed by Roopak Printers, Delhi 110032
Published by Manzar Khan, Oxford University Press
YMCA Library Building, Jai Singh Road, New Delhi 110 001

Contents

Tables	*viii*
Figures	*ix*
Abbreviations	*x*

INTRODUCTION	1
1. FINANCIAL MANAGEMENT	4
Perceptions	4
Differences Between Developing and Industrial Countries	5
Anatomy of Financial Management	7
Ground-level Realities	10
Revitalizing the System for the Future	12
2. EXPENDITURE CONTROL: EVOLUTION AND PRACTICE OF AN IDEA	15
Recent Trends	15
Seeds of Transformation	19
Evolution: A Stylized View	25
Serving Royalty	26
Growth of Legislative Traditions	29
Wars, Debt, Depression, and Management of the Economy	34
Reconstruction, Development, and the Welfare State	36
Post-Welfare State, Civic Society, and Improved Governance	40

3. ADVANCING STRUCTURAL REFORMS: THEMES AND ISSUES 88

Changing Ideas and Institutions 88
Evaluation 91
Factors Contributing to Stagnation or Failure 98
Allocative Mechanisms and Rigidity 144

4. ETHICAL DIMENSIONS OF EXPENDITURE MANAGEMENT 164

Public Policy Making 167
Alternative Proposals 181
Towards Improvement and Sustainability 189

5. FISCAL TRANSPARENCY 191

History of Fiscal Transparency 191
Objectives 193
Content of Fiscal Information 194
Uses and Limitations 194

6. PUBLIC FINANCIAL ACCOUNTABILITY 204

Evolution and Practice of the Idea of Accountability 206
Financial Accountability 212
Factors Hindering Financial Accountability 220
Moving Ahead: Recent Developments 228
Towards a Constructive Agenda 232
Conclusions 235

7. EXPENDITURE MANAGEMENT AND LIFE SUPPORT PROGRAMMES 237

Introduction 237
Scope of Life Support Programmes 239

Differences Between Industrial and
Developing Countries 242
Financial Management Cycle 243
Issues in Practice 247
Tasks Ahead 254

8. PUBLIC EXPENDITURE
   MANAGEMENT IN SUB-NATIONAL
   GOVERNMENTS: STATUS AND ISSUES 255

   Preliminary Considerations 257
   Instruments of Management 259
   Issues and Approaches 264

9. PREPARING ANNUAL BUDGETS:
   A PRAGMATIC APPROACH 276

   Strengthening Expenditure Management 276
   Resource Allocation: Policy Framework 290
   Budget Management 302
   Supporting Infrastructure 350

References 357

Index 363

Tables

Table 1.1: Financial management framework—instruments and techniques — 8
Table 3.1: Transforming the expenditure management process—themes and implementation — 93
Table 3.2: Legislative control of expenditures — 112
Table 3.3: Measures taken to restrain growth of public expenditures — 135
Table 5.1: Fiscal transparency—components, instruments, and features — 196
Table 6.1: Instruments of financial accountability—features and limitations — 213
Table 7.1: Life support programmes and fiscal instruments — 240
Table 7.2: Financial management cycle — 244
Table 8.1: Instruments of public expenditure management — 260
Table 9.1: Different perspectives and common themes — 277
Table 9.2: Levels and instruments of public finance — 278
Table 9.3: Management structures, styles, and outcome — 279
Table 9.4: Types of expenditures — 293
Table 9.5: Objectives and instruments of expenditure management — 300
Table 9.6: Estimating changes in revenue and expenditure — 301
Table 9.7: Formulation of expenditure estimates — 309
Table 9.8: Fragmentation of expenditure control — 312
Table 9.9: Budget calendar — 316
Table 9.10: Budget execution—role of Ministry of Finance and spending agencies — 320
Table 9.11: Nexus between ministry of finance and spending agencies — 328
Table 9.12: Resource-use accounting — 340
Table 9.13: Scope of audit — 348

Figures

Figure 3.1:	Objective–allocation nexus	156
Figure 6.1:	From conventional to enhanced accountability	210
Figure 6.2:	Contents of accountability	211
Figure 6.3:	Financial accountability chain	212
Figure 9.1:	Medium-term fiscal framework and medium-term expenditure framework	296
Figure 9.2:	Stages of the budget—conventional approaches	304
Figure 9.3:	Stages of the budget—recent approaches	306
Figure 9.4:	Types of ceilings	307
Figure 9.5:	Portfolio of government expenditures	318

Abbreviations

APRM	African Peer Review Mechanism
EBRD	European Bank for Reconstruction and Development
EDP	Electronic data processing
EU	European Union
GAAP	Generally accepted accounting principles
GDP	Gross domestic product
IFI	International financial institution
IMF	International Monetary Fund
MTEF	Medium-term expenditure framework
MTFF	Medium-term fiscal framework
NATO	North American Treaty Organization
NEPAD	New Partnership for African Development
NGO	Non-governmental organization
OECD	Organization for Economic Cooperation and Development
PAC	Public Accounts Committee
PEM	Public expenditure management
PIPs	Public investment plans
SNG	Sub-National Government
UTI	Unit Trust of India
ZBB	Zero-based budgeting

Introduction

Governments in industrial countries and in the developing world continue to face major systemic and operational problems in controlling government expenditures inspite of the series of management reforms introduced and implemented during recent years. Despite the perceived failures in restraining the growth of expenditure, and relatively poor performance in the provision of public services within specified cost, time, and quality estimates and consequent steady erosion in the credibility of governments, there is, paradoxically, a growing demand for an extended range of services to be provided by governments. The emerging pressures to resist demands for expenditure increases are straining the management capacity of governments. Even as governments are endeavouring, either because of domestic or international compulsion (as a part of resource use agreements concluded with international and regional financial institutions) to implement management reforms, results have been less than substantial and what has been achieved is minuscule relative to the progress that remains to be made.

Meanwhile, the agenda of reform is being expanded to accommodate new demands made for more concrete steps towards the establishment of a civic society. Although the goal and the concept remain to be clarified, issues are being raised whether the role of fiscal transparency is to keep the public informed of the actions taken and results obtained, or to inform the public prior to the formulation of policies so that the public is empowered to play a constructive role in public management. Similarly, how should the channels of public accountability be designed to meet the growing appetite of the public and the legislators?

More important is the fundamental design of expenditure management itself and its capacity to meet the desire of a democratic society for participation while seeking to reconcile the macroeconomic requirements of fiscal stability and sustainability with the demands for more services, on the one hand, and building appropriate bridges with the legislatures while accommodating the autonomy requirements of the bureaucracy to be flexible in implementing policies on the other hand; J.M. Keynes observed nearly seven decades ago that before constructing relevant guidelines and formulating relevant theories to address the issues of the present and the future, there may be a good deal to be unlearnt from the theories and agendas pursued by the country's authorities, at the national and sub-national levels (where despite unanimous agreement on the imperative of providing autonomy in expenditure management, much remains to be done), and the agendas of the international financial institutions in this respect. Shedding the old, as Keynes noted, could be more difficult than building the new.

All the above factors stress the importance of undertaking an in-depth review of the designs of recent reforms, their content and adequacy to address the dominant concerns, and their contribution to date so that the direction of the much-needed transformation of expenditure management may be clearerly considered. In undertaking this detailed review, there is also an imperative to deal with pivotal areas such as ethics and related areas. This book aims to meet this urgent need. While some of the chapters included in the book have been published before, the two main chapters (2 and 3) are among those that have been essentially written as a part of this book; they also form the bulwark of the book. Chapter 1 was included in the *Handbook on Policy Development and Management,* Edward Elgar, Northampton MA (2002). Chapter 4 was published in *Economic and Political Weekly* (Vol. 39), February 2004. Chapter 5 was published in the *Encyclopedia of Public Administration and Policy,* Marcel Dekker, New York, 2003. Chapter 6 was written at the request of the Asian Development Bank and the World Conference on Governance for a conference held in Manila in 1999, and has been included in Salvatore Schiavo-Campo (ed.), *Governance, Corruption and Public Financial Management,* Asian Development Bank, Manila, 1999. Almost all chapters draw on lectures delivered by the author at the Duke University, Kennedy School of Government, Georgia State University (Andrew Young School of Public Policy), and presentations at seminars conducted by the Asian Development Bank, National Institute of Public Finance and Policy (New Delhi), and the United Nations. Their kindness in encouraging the author, and in permitting the reproduction of the referred printed material is gratefully acknowledged. The participants at the seminars and workshops were generous in providing comments and in raising important issues that needed further consideration. A vote of thanks to them too. Arthur Monteiro is responsible for transforming the author's increasingly illegible handwriting into an electronic form; his patience proved to be an admirable asset.

The main conclusion of this book is that the expenditure management system is in the throes of a serious crisis and in the absence of immediate efforts to address the contributing factors, the situation is bound to deteriorate further. In each functional area of expenditure management, the factors contributing to the ongoing crisis are different, and require a highly nuanced strategy. To facilitate this task, each chapter describes in detail, the instruments of control, their limitations and strengths. Given the commonality of instruments, however, there is inevitably some overlap among the chapters; each chapter is self-contained and provides abundant material to formulate policy packages that can lead to strengthened expenditure management systems.

1. Financial Management

PERCEPTIONS

Financial management has been perceived in different ways by practitioners, accountants, economists, and management experts; the differences in their perceptions are discernible in the design and content of financial management systems. In most developing countries, following the colonial legacy, financial management was essentially viewed as a process that enabled the central agencies (such as the treasury and its modern equivalent, the ministry of finance) to keep the 'wickedness' of the administrative or spending agencies under control through a continuous review and specification of inputs and verification of documents submitted for payments. As an extension of this approach, financial management was viewed as being restricted to budget implementation, administration of payment systems, accounting and reporting on the status of funds received and spent. This approach, with a long lineage, continues to be prevalent even now, although on a declining scale.

Over the years, however, the traditional view has yielded place to other approaches. In the 1950s, there was an attempt to incorporate forms of management accounting into government practices, reflecting the influence of accountants. Later, with the emergence of development planning as an important instrument of economic and fiscal policies, economists tended to view financial management essentially as an allocative mechanism. Subsequent reforms in financial management focused on the use of government budget as a vehicle of economic development through the application of cost–benefit analysis techniques and through improved budget classification systems. From the 1970s, economists moved from allocative issues to the need for containment of fiscal deficits through, among others, tightened financial management, aimed at ensuring a budget outcome congruent with intent. A decade later, their attention moved to the broader issue of the proper role of the state and the tasks that could be undertaken by the corporate sector independently or in collaboration with government. Meanwhile, the management schools of thought, which had hitherto concentrated on corporate matters, turned their attention to public bodies with a view to examining why governments were not effective in providing client-orientated services. Their view of the overall management of the public sector included a corporate type of financial management revolving around cost centres, and management autonomy for managers within an overall framework of accountability.

The result of these diverse approaches has been a periodic identity crisis, and a chequered history of attempts to rejuvenate financial management in the developing world. Segments of financial management, not the totality, were addressed periodically, leaving a highly uneven landscape. To identify the current issues therefore, a broader view of financial management is in order. For analytical purposes, it includes the functional areas of budget making, budget implementation, the macroeconomic framework governing the preceding two areas, and accounting, reporting, and evaluation. It is thus concerned with resource allocation, resource utilization, and resource use accounting. Moreover, financial management cannot be looked at in a disembodied way; it needs to be considered within the overall context of the macroeconomic framework.

DIFFERENCES BETWEEN DEVELOPING AND INDUSTRIAL COUNTRIES

In most industrial countries, the use of information technology is extensive and most payments to and from government as well as accounting systems today benefit from these applications. Information technology has also facilitated the application of accrual accounting and contributed to a reduction in the costs of financial management systems. Although the extended application of technology bears risks, it has enabled governments in industrial countries to develop better oversight of financial matters. The developing world shows a diverse picture. In Asia and Latin America, some countries have made significant advances in the application of electronic technology, gaining from the benefits of technology and reduction in administrative costs, while other countries have used technology primarily for mechanical processing of documents rather than an abridgement of the administrative process. In sub-Saharan African countries, even the maintenance of computerized payrolls continues to be problematic as the basic records are found to be wanting.

A second major difference relates to the sources of innovation. In the industrial world, most innovations in the area of financial management had their origins in legislative discontentment, and the high level of public debate—facilitated partly by the exchange of professionals between governments and universities and other independent institutions. In the developing world, most legislative institutions have been more acquiescent and less interested in building effective financial management in governments. More recently, some countries in Latin America and Eastern Europe have shown interest in the replication of the oversight machinery seen in Western democracies. The sources of innovation in the developing world have, for the most part, been aid donors and international financial institutions. Countries that are dependent on foreign aid find that fiscal decision making is a joint and shared exercise and that international financial institutions (IFIs) play a decisive role in policy making as well as in the design of the supporting infrastructure of institutions, systems, and operational procedures. Some innovations such as rolling expenditure planning, medium-term investment plans, computerization of accounting and payment systems, and management of internal and external debt have been made possible through the generous stimulus provided by the IFIs.

Third, there is a major difference in the use of corporate and non-governmental organizations (NGOs) in the delivery of government-funded programmes. In the industrial world, the range of social services provided by the state has grown substantially and a stage was reached where it was not organizationally feasible for governments to sustain them any longer. This led to the emergence of an extensive network of NGOs for the delivery of government-funded programmes. From a financial management point of view, this contributed to a separation of funding from the payment of services, and to the emergence of a third-party payment system. In developing countries, developments in this area are highly uneven; although contracting is extensively resorted to in defence, education, and economic infrastructure sectors, reliance on NGOs or individuals (for example, medical practitioners) for provision of services is not as yet a prominent feature.

Notwithstanding the above differences, the credibility of government financial management systems in both industrial and developing countries continues to be very low; there is a perception of considerable waste in the use of public money and the dominating influence of vested interests on budget allocations. Additionally, there is the view, for which there is considerable evidence, that in the developing world even the most routine financial management operations are intensely politicized.

ANATOMY OF FINANCIAL MANAGEMENT

The experience of financial management shows that there are broadly four successive stages in which various types of controls are applied in an effort to identify and measure the financial implications of current and proposed policies; and once measured, to ensure that the estimates are adhered to and implemented and that the expected benefits have accrued. Thus, controls administered as a part of the system seek to determine the goals of policies and their financial implications, and once the policies are approved, they seek to verify the compliance of laws and rules established for the purpose of maintaining financial rectitude and discipline. Control structures also provide opportunities to selectively revoke previous decisions, where appropriate. The four stages, which have evolved over the years are best viewed as a composite management framework in which each step of the process adds value towards the achievement of policy goals (see Table 1.1). The controls may be administered internally by the administrative agencies or by the central agencies; each pattern has its own share of anomalies and issues.

Policy controls reflect the first and most important step in financial management. This step forces agencies to estimate financial implications with care. Although, until recently, the focus of this estimation has been the fiscal year, estimates are now being made over the life cycle of the proposed policy (which may have its own sunset provisions) or over the medium term. Most developing countries hitherto concentrated their efforts on the formulation of development plans, but are gradually moving, partly at the instance of IFIs, to a medium-term rolling fiscal framework and associated expenditure planning.

Ideally, controls that are judiciously utilized during the policy formulation stage should pave the way for a smooth functioning of the financial management system through the fiscal year. In practice,

Table 1.1
Financial Management Framework—Instruments and Techniques

	Policy controls	Process controls	Regulatory tasks	Efficiency controls
Resource allocation	**Instruments** • Medium-term fiscal framework • Development plans **Techniques** • Balanced budget approaches • Deficit reduction strategies • Planning, programming performance budget techniques • Output budgets • Accrual budgets • Target-based budgeting	• Budget calendar • Review of estimates • Consultative procedures with stockholders and stakeholders	• Specification of processes for client consultation • Specification of norms for staff increases and related aspects of running costs	• Formulation of performance indicators through the use of performance, output and target-based or zero-based budget
Resource utilization	**Instruments** • Formulation of quantitative targets for costs and delivery of services • Efficiency and economy targets • Contingency reserves • Strategic revisions **Techniques** • Time-sliced release of funds • Policy embargoes • Efficiency dividends • Flexible use of resources	• Quarterly or monthly apportionment of budgets • Tendering, competitive bidding, and contracting • Monitoring of commitments • Pre-audit of payment claims • Organization of payments	• Specification of contracting procedures • Specification of terms and conditions for government lending	• Monitoring operations to ascertain conformity with efficiency goals
Resource-use accounting	**Instruments** • Specification of goals relating to assets and liabilities of governments over the medium term **Techniques** • Preparation of financial statements showing the asset and liability position at periodic intervals	• Maintenance of preliminary and final accounts • Analysis of cost variations	• Specification accounting standards	• Specification of process and procedures for internal and external evaluation

however, there are a number of factors which contribute to the complexity and frequent ineffectiveness of the system. More often than not, financial implications are consistently underestimated to gain a foothold in the budget. Some policies are based on the recognized 'need' and have to be carried out regardless of the financial implications. Some policies have built-in norms for personnel and so on. These policies generate supply-driven increases in expenditures. Then there are policies emanating from permanent legislation (entitlement programmes and social safety nets) which contribute to demand-driven increases in expenditures. In countries where the judiciary is taking an active role, its interventions and awards also contribute to increases in expenditures. Foreign aid plays its own role in this process; the pulls and pressures exercised by IFIs leave their imprint on the process as well as on policies. In general, governments tend to make over–optimistic assumptions about revenue growth and underestimate expenditure growth. Inevitably, what emerges is an annual budget which, with all the window-dressing it entails, becomes a putative one, frequently updated throughout the year. When budget activity ceases to be seasonal and becomes an ongoing activity throughout the year, it adds to the prevailing uncertainty, and erodes the credibility of the budget process as well as the effectiveness of the instruments used.

The process controls acquire importance during the budget implementation phase (resource utilization, shown in Table 1.1). This phase was equated with financial management by those belonging to the accounting profession as their activities assumed importance during this and the concluding phase of resource-use accounting. When policies are not formulated with care, the controls exercised during this phase could have a negative impact. In many developing countries, when a shortfall in revenues is experienced, governments resort to limiting their contractual commitments to available cash so that ceilings on domestic credit can be honoured. This practice, common to most developing countries and former centrally planned economies, has contributed to significant additions to arrears in payments and associated liquidity problems. These aspects reveal the limitations of the existing practices of policy formulation.

The regulatory tasks form part of the responsibilities of the central agencies and reflect more of what needs to be done rather than what has been done. These tasks relate to consultative procedures, specification of contracting procedures, and accounting and performance standards. With respect to contracting procedures, comprehensive standards remain to be specified for service provision by NGOs and other voluntary organizations. Similarly, accounting is an area where standards still need to be formulated. In their absence some data—particularly on assets and liabilities and external debt—tend to be misleading.

Performance standards, where available, imply the pursuit of efficiency and economy in the use of resources. The experience in this regard reveals a mixed picture. Some developing countries in Asia and Latin America sought to introduce variations of performance budgeting in the early 1960s and 1970s. In some cases they were utilized on a supplementary basis, more to convey additional information, and rarely replaced the existing systems. In a few cases these experiments were withdrawn as disillusionment, which was partly the result of ineffective implementation, set in. While there has been a revival of performance-oriented budgeting since the early 1990s, more remains to be done in this area. The pursuit of efficiency and economy remains to be explicitly delineated in the operational financial management framework of many developing countries.

GROUND-LEVEL REALITIES

The stages in Table 1.1 are not given equal emphasis in practice. There is a disproportionate dependence on process controls. Apart from the apparent absence of performance-oriented financial management and related pursuit of economy and efficiency, the system has several soft constraints and perverse incentives that lead to contrary results. In the understanding of the spending agencies, budget estimates for a fiscal year are only an initial step that can be ratcheted up during the fiscal year through intense political pressure; if that gambit is not successful, excess expenditures can always be incurred; and if that option is also not available, arrears in payment can be incurred. Rules prohibiting such practices are rarely invoked and failure to observe them does not entail any penalties. Moreover, spending agencies have little incentive to search for economies as there are no rewards for such efforts. Medium-term rolling expenditure planning provides them with a false sense of security in that they seem to assume the continuation of policies (without any change) over the medium-term. Meanwhile, the resource shortfall contributes to an all-round underfunding of projects and programmes.

Further, financial management processes in many developing countries dependent on foreign aid show a diarchical approach, in that foreign-aided projects are operated through systems insisted upon by the donor (which may include earmarking, double-entry bookkeeping, and compilation of annual financial statements including balance sheets), while other sectors are operated through conventional systems. The former are viewed as isolated cases with the consequence that there is an enclave mentality in their administration. The modernization implicit in their administration is rarely extended to other areas of governmental administration. This diarchical approach has had the effect of eroding the basic strengths of the existing systems and diminishing their credibility.

The experience of developing countries shows that they face considerable difficulty in making short-term adjustments in expenditures when shortfalls in revenue demand such adjustments. From the point of view of the spending departments, medium-term expenditure plans on a rolling basis are a kind of informal contract between the central and spending agencies. From the point of view of central agencies, they are a part of the exercise to examine medium-term trends and such estimates and projections do not by themselves provide any assurance that funds would be available. When confronted with revenue shortfalls, governments have resorted to tactical measures such as across-the-board cuts or embargoes on the filling of posts. However, these measures had little effect as spending agencies did not undertake any fundamental adjustment in their spending portfolios. This failure contributed to a situation where the effectiveness of financial management as an instrument of fiscal policy has become moot. In addition, fiscal slippages have raised questions about the basic strengths of financial management, particularly at a time when they are expected to assume additional responsibilities in ensuring service delivery, rendering accountability, and moderating the rate of growth of expenditures.

The experience also reveals the weaknesses in expenditure management. The conventional method of expenditure control was the ceiling on personnel and the number of posts that could be created during a budget year. This approach proved to be of limited use in a context where norms of personnel began to be developed as a part of development plans. Control over personnel yielded place to control of running costs and, in course of time, to specification of global ceilings. But having lost control of the components in the previous stages, control of the aggregate appeared to be arbitrary and, more significantly, without a rationale other than that it facilitated the task of keeping within resource realities.

Yet another facet of expenditure control administered in most developing countries has been the lack of ability to distinguish among categories of expenditure or among agencies. A one-size-fits-all approach was adopted, but this became increasingly inappropriate as the portfolio of expenditure changed. A major part of government outlays is now devoted to transfers to other levels of government, to autonomous agencies and to individuals, as well as third-party payments and contractual payments. Each of these categories requires a different approach to control, but the machinery of financial management has yet to reflect this.

The machinery of financial management also reveals an excessive degree of centralization in the responsibilities of ministries of finance. The underlying belief is that the spending agencies are not to be trusted in financial matters, that they do not have a financial conscience, therefore, centralization is justified. This has led to the emergence of a situation where ministries of finance are not only engaged in steering but also in extensive rowing. Experience shows that they have not been very successful in these endeavours.

The working of the other components of the financial management machinery shows that they are not equipped to compensate for these shortcomings. Audit, as organized in many developing countries, is still oriented to the process of financial control and is not entitled to review policy matters or to examine the books of contractors or NGOs. Nor is it yet fully equipped to undertake efficiency reviews. Legislatures, too, have become less effective as day-to-day economic decision making has shifted to the executive. In many countries, a major percentage of total expenditures is exempt from legislative voting and there are fewer opportunities for the legislature to contribute inputs into the crucial aspects of economic policy making.

In summary, the financial management machinery in developing countries has been generally slow in adapting itself to changing requirements and growing needs. There is a mismatch between the needs of fiscal policy and the responses of the financial management processes, exacerbated by the segmented approach of reform-oriented accountants, economists, and management consultants. A fundamental review of systems and operational techniques is in order.

REVITALIZING THE SYSTEM FOR THE FUTURE

The fiscal turbulence experienced during the last decades has severely tested the financial management system in most developing countries.

There has been a steady increase in the demands made on the system. Admittedly, the system does not have the capacity to pursue all the objectives at the same time in view of the built-in conflict among some of the objectives which is yet to be resolved. Emphasis on performance requires the backing of fully assured resources. Pursuit of macroeconomic stability may, however, require short-term changes in the resources provided for the purpose. Prudence and orderly fiscal management requires governments to make strategic choices for the fiscal year and to devise supporting financial management systems that would facilitate the fulfilment of the specified goals. This requires, as a first step, specification of the fiscal strategy for the medium term and an indication of the improvements being sought in the supporting systemic infrastructure.

The much-needed revitalization of the financial management system comprises four components: (i) strengthened policy formulation; (ii) accountability framework; (iii) greater application of information technology; and (iv) peer review of the infrastructure facilities.

Policy formulation is the Achilles' heel of the financial management system, notwithstanding the introduction of a medium-term rolling fiscal and expenditure framework. This is largely because rolling planning is undertaken at an aggregate level and as a linear extrapolation of previous trends. Initially, planning signified a departure from the previous practice. However, more needs to be done if planning is to serve as an instrument that can illuminate expenditure trends and the underlying factors contributing to variations, and act as a major contributory factor to policies. High-risk programmes need to be highlighted, and programmes that lead to efficiency gains as well as those with the potential of moderating the rate of expenditure growth, should be identified. To facilitate public debate on future expenditure policies, the medium-term and the annual forecasts—together with a management strategy that would support the policy goals—should be announced about midway through the financial year. Such a process would promote public choice and, more important, a greater understanding of the costs and benefits of the programmes.

Accountability has so far been limited to the narrower aspects of accounting for money collected and utilized. This has contributed to a culture where compliance with the rules has become more important than the achievement of goals. This has to yield to a management culture based on trust and accountability for results. In view of the growing gap between funding and the provision of services, an accountability framework covering government agencies and other service providers needs to be developed.

The potential yields from greater investment in the application of technology are significant. Technology has reduced the gap between the controller and controlled through simultaneous access to information. Governments also have the option of buying services from the corporate sector without engaging in investment in technology for their own operations. Payroll management, payment of pensions, loan repayments, and the collection of taxes can now be contracted out to the banking system and to other companies.

Most systems in government, including financial management, remain moribund largely because of a lack of a peer review of the operations of the systems. It is essential that government financial management systems, as well as audit and legislative control systems, are subject to periodic review to examine whether their approaches and practices remain relevant in view of the changing requirements.

2. Expenditure Control
Evolution and Practice of an Idea

The system of expenditure control in government is once again in the domain of public discussion, not for any notable achievements but for failures. It is an issue that is common to industrial and developing countries, oil-producing and importing countries, emergent economies and economies which have been in transition during the last decade (and more)—moving from central planning to market-oriented systems. The difference among these countries is primarily one of degree and each one is trying to address the issue in its own way. Given the commonality of the issue, however, a number of similar features are discernible in their efforts.

RECENT TRENDS

The role of governments and the range of services they provide, and the economy, efficiency, and effectiveness with which services are provided became major public policy issues in the wake of large fiscal deficits over a prolonged period. Inevitably, these aspects led to serious enquiries into the nature and effectiveness of expenditure control systems in governments, and as will be discussed later, a series of reforms were introduced aimed at moderating the rate of growth of expenditure. Although the results of these efforts varied among groups of countries, there was, by the mid-1980s, a small reduction in the rate of general government expenditure. As a consequence, fiscal deficits came to be contained, and by the early 1990s, a few industrial countries, and some developing countries (including Korea and Thailand which were to face major crises later for different reasons) had even recorded fiscal surpluses. This helped restore the public confidence in the system, and the view emerged that although it was a complex and formidable task, expenditure growth could be contained within the limits of growth of resources. However, the success achieved had too short a life, and by the mid-1990s and later, pressures for additional expenditure came to be felt severely. By the end of the century, many fiscal surpluses had disappeared and there was a recrudescence of deficits, in turn necessitating a whole range of new efforts to control expenditure growth and to contain fiscal deficits. Implicit in this effort is the need for a search for more durable expenditure management solutions.

Some of the issues relating to expenditure growth during the 1980s and 1990s were sought to be achieved through a containment of the role of the state, and more important, through a readjustment in the form of steady withdrawal from some sectors. As a part of this effort, state-owned assets were sold and policies were introduced that aimed at private provision of services. Some of these services were publicly funded, while in a few cases they were funded totally by the corporate sector, and most of these public–private partnerships envisaged a total recovery of costs from the users. Elsewhere too, the full recovery of user charges became an important policy tenet. It was expected that this process of detachment and divestment would endure for a relatively long period. However, this expectation too was short-lived, with two types of pressures accumulating in both industrial and developing countries. Several years ago, the German social philosopher Wagner proposed a theory to the effect that public expenditure would tend to grow as the state extended some of its traditional functions, and undertook more intensive efforts to provide the conventional sources. Although propounded as a law, it had many limitations; the general underlying truth was, however, considered tenable. Some governments in the West are now facing increasing pressure to go beyond the services that have been hitherto provided, and to address the more important core issue of 'life satisfaction'. Research undertaken in various fields, including the medical sciences, has revealed what makes people satisfied with their lives. A major part in this is played by mental health scales. In addition to the conventionally recognized factors such as income, work, nature of employment, and inequality of incomes, it is now acknowledged that improved health services, more leisure, and societal relationships, including the quality of governance, have a definitive, if not always precisely measurable, impact on democratic involvement and self-improvement of the community. In turn, these major issues of public policy raise fundamental questions about the expenditure programmes of governments, the evaluation of the likely benefits, and the implementation of programmes in such a way as to ensure a consistent, economic provision of benefits. Associated with this is the issue of how to contain the rate of expenditure growth when such pressures for growing expenditures are being increasingly encountered by governments everywhere. To the extent that these form a part of minimum governance, it is only natural that this issue is gaining importance.

Surveys of existing policy commitments, let alone the new ones that are likely to be made in response to changing economic requirements, show that there are enormous pressures on governments to increase the range of their services. These are built into the policy making approaches and apparatus and to that extent cast long shadows on the claims and need for medium-term fiscal sustainability. Several factors, including the following, are common to all groups of countries. First, there has been a change in the demographic features of many societies. In general, people are living for long periods, requiring in turn, payment of benefits that are likely to contribute to additional burdens on the future generations of workers. This feature is already abundantly clear in advanced economies, and is becoming clearer by the day in developing countries and transition economies which have been making efforts to introduce variations of the social security system in the form of social safety nets. As the range of retirement benefits threaten the viability of financing systems, governments have revived their search for options that would either reduce the benefits or raise contributions. Improvements in medical technology, the growing resort to substitution of artificial limbs and life-saving surgeries, and the costs of medical services both in industrial and developing countries are revealing the full picture and implications of what was hitherto a less probed area, viz., medical cost inflation. The application of improved technology is an inevitable process and its progress is unlikely to be hindered by short-term measures of rationing of services. It is an inevitability that will have a steady influence on the growing costs of maintaining an aged population.

Second, there have also been major changes in other spheres of technology with concurrent implications for public expenditure. Maintenance of defence forces as well as the machinery to take care of domestic law and order, reveal a growing appetite for inevitably catching up with the latest trends in technology. As those engaged in terrorism or prolonged ethnic conflict become sophisticated in the deployment of latest weaponry, it becomes incumbent on governments, at the very minimum, to remain one step ahead. This process of updating and modernizing is a continuous one with no defined landmark where it can be considered, except in the extreme short term, to have reached its provisional goal. More significantly, the prices of the equipment needed are determined in a sellers' market and buyers, particularly in the developing world, have very few options except to buy on negotiated financing terms; what is negotiated generally is not the price but the terms of payment, which inevitably contribute to growing debt. For a policy maker, this often implies a Hobson's choice, and priority planning becomes an extremely complicated task with political implications that are often difficult to avoid.

Third, along with the inevitable compulsions for modernization of strategy, forces, and equipment, there are more compelling considerations on the development front which mandate higher and higher expenditures on poverty alleviation and provision of effective social services. Many developing countries in parts of Eastern Europe, Africa, and Southeast Asia (the island economies or land-locked countries are not exempted) have been through prolonged periods of civil strife, with an increase in the incidence of poverty. Improved governance, and the aim of establishing a civic society—a goal that is shared by governments as well as international development institutions—require greater efforts to alleviate poverty. In turn, this implies commitment to provide food and other basic services to the financially challenged sectors of the community. Moreover, short-term changes resulting from the movements in globalization may contribute to higher levels of unemployment for short periods, during which compensation may have to be paid by governments. Social services, too, are in need of upgrading and the IFIs insist that a specified share should be spent on these. Reaching these specified levels, which governments have to strive for in order to become eligible for international concessionary financing, involves a steady increase in the level of government expenditures.

Fourth, recent experience shows that many governments may have underestimated the total costs of mega projects undertaken by them, and the financial implications of rescuing of domestic financial institutions that have gone bankrupt owing to the enormous growth in non-performing assets. Estimates made in several countries reveal that the initial basis on which these policy decisions were made bear no resemblance to the eventual completed cost of these projects and programmes. The future expenditures of many governments are likely to involve substantial spillovers from these activities and related commitments. These, too, point to an inevitable growth in public expenditures.

Fifth, along with growing pressures for increased public outlays, governments are also compelled—as a result of increasing transparency in government transactions—to focus on the quality or changing composition of expenditures. In recent years, the rate of growth of current expenditure has been far higher than the rate of growth of outlays on capital formation, and increasingly, in a growing number of countries current resources are no longer adequate to finance current expenditures. In these circumstances, many governments have opted, with a view to reducing the overall fiscal deficit, for massive curtailment of investment and capital expenditures. This has, in turn, had an adverse impact on the overall rate of economic growth as the shortfall in government sector is not compensated by increased outlays from the private sector. This contributed to the view that fiscal sustainability was being achieved at the expense of much-needed growth in the economy. The civic society is not merely interested in a reduction of budget deficits but is keen to achieve a respectable growth in the economy, too. This remains to be achieved, while the pressures to curtail government spending, which dominated public thinking during the 1980s and 1990s, are yielding place to increased expenditure to meet the growing requirements.

SEEDS OF TRANSFORMATION

The experience of the last two decades of the previous millennium suggests that there were subtle changes in the role of the state, in the range of services to be provided by the state, and in the pattern of financing of services. This period also witnessed growing erosion in the credibility of governments in both industrial and developing countries. This erosion had its origins in structural factors as well as in systems of operation.

From a structural point, excessive resort to rhetoric and measures of financial populism contributed to a negative feedback in that a pervasive feeling has developed that each time a new government assumes power and makes promises, it is soon found to withdraw from its commitments. Similarly, the hope of establishing a civic society that was at once liberating and moderating, holding the heterogeneous elements of society in some sort of stable harmonious arrangement, while remaining autonomous of various entrenched vested interests and at the same time creating a more equitable order, came to be buffeted by economic cross–currents and was jeopardized. Meanwhile, the very classes of society that were sought to be brought into the realm of inclusion, remained outside and had very little role in the formulation of policies that continued to be dominated by the entrenched interests. Regardless of the efforts being made to dislodge them, or at a minimum, to reduce their massive influence, it appeared that the organized groups were a step ahead in the game and knew how to safeguard their role and influence. This aspect raised the more important issue of the limits of democratic governments, as many sections of society discovered the growing limitations on transforming some of their ideas into workable realities. While some discernible progress was made during this period in terms of participation in public policy making, it was confined mostly to the level of local governments, while major issues of fiscal policy were determined by the central or national governments, which continued to play a dominant role.

A representative government does not necessarily mean that all the people participate in making decisions in all matters all the time. In general, however, the citizen finds himself in a difficult situation, full of dilemmas that cannot be recognized at an individual level, and therefore at an aggregate level of society. At an individual level, he finds himself demanding more and more services from government to be provided at a subsidized rate or free. There is a basic reluctance to pay and it is expected that the government would be in a position to pay for the basic services. At the same time, the craving for fiscal sustainability, which every individual has as a participant in a market society, makes him desire a lean and efficient system that would also devise an adequate system of financing. This dilemma is further reinforced by the inability of the individual, either by himself or as part of a group, to achieve the goals of a civil society through the functioning of a representative government. From a worm's eye view, he finds that the legislatures, intended to be the primary means of a representative democracy, have become ineffective, as economic and financial decision making has effectively moved into the orbit of the executive wing of governments, and more policies are being determined through executive decrees rather than through legislation. The call for greater transparency and improved accountability has been met by greater effort at circumvention of the existing legislation and operational systems. Effective democracies need good leadership, and more importantly, many active and conscientious citizens. However, both these classes find themselves stymied in their efforts, by the invisible and visible working of vested interests, and large bureaucracies that know only too well how to protect their interests. As a consequence, efforts are directed at marginal changes addressed towards short-term requirements rather than medium-term structural changes. Their effect in the circumstances is limited and the major issues continue unabated. The re-emergence of major pressures for increased expenditures may in part be ascribed to this phenomenon. The most significant aspect of this experience is the fact that during this period major changes have been made in the ideas, operational systems, and institutional frameworks that play a role in the broad process of government financial management. If this is the case after a prolonged and continuing battle to moderate the growth of expenditures, it may well be imagined as to what situation would prevail in the absence of reforms in public financial management.

From the perception of the public, the continuing reality of waste, with a differing incidence from one country to another, is a sad reflection on the existing state of affairs. The appearance of corruption has only exacerbated the problem. To the public, there are too many layers of government—local, regional, national, and in some cases supranational—with competing claims and overlapping jurisdictions, suggesting a case of avoidable waste. The bureaucracy is often viewed as self-serving and as being primarily interested in the process than in the needs of the client. Indeed, it is suggested that the client is the last to get any explicit recognition. It is further suggested that while there has been a much-needed improvement in the payment systems of government, thanks to the introduction of electronic technology, many areas continue as they were, and the full benefits of computerization remain to be reaped. Organizationally, the changes in the bureaucratic structures of government have contributed to the strong emergence of NGOs as the focal points for the delivery of services. The belief that the latter are more effective than conventional government agencies still awaits empirical proof. Indeed, it is alleged that the 'red tape' involved here is not significantly different from that in government agencies, with the added disadvantage that most NGOs do not have a well-structured financial control system (internal or external) in place; balance sheets are not regularly published, and more often than not, external audit arrangements leave a good deal to be desired. Meanwhile, the need for elimination of waste, a goal that is never disputed, including by those who work in government, has itself become an election issue in at least one industrial country (United Kingdom). For example, the Labour Party contends that it would bring about changes and endeavour to secure an annual saving of £15 billion; the opposition Conservative Party vouches to secure an annual savings of £35 billion (for an interesting discussion of these claims and counter claims, see *Financial Times*, 17 February 2004). These competing claims, while being useful illustrations of the range of current and potential waste in government services, also reveal the relative failure of the expenditure management system in public bodies.

Yet another feature of the recent experience has emerged as a matter of concern, particularly for those concerned with organizational matters. The experience of many governments shows that contrary to the intent, the centralization of authority in central governments, and specifically in the ministries of finance, leads to the spending agencies, including the NGOs, becoming more dependent than ever on the central authority. This centralization, which was specific and transparent in a few cases, and brought about by stealth in others, has shifted the onus of financial management from the spending agencies to central agencies—a shift that has not worked well and is unlikely to be effective. Governments have grown so large that their interests are unlikely to be effectively served by a single monolithic agency. In many cases, the finance ministries are themselves in need of a major overhaul. Meanwhile, as a part of this centralization effort, redundant payment controls on a centralized basis, which would have been considered barbarous relics from the past, have been put in place at considerable additional cost, but with little functional value added to the process. These tactical shifts in management have effectively worked against the strategy of expenditure management and generated the view, that in several cases, the remedy may be worse than the malady.

The general growing disappointment with the reforms introduced during recent years is in part based on other general and philosophical considerations. Many observers recognize the rise of public policy research and the crucial role it has played in focusing attention on major issues and on the ways in which they may be addressed. There is a growing feeling that the inquiry initiated by public policy research has not been free from bias and that 'information' in public policy has rarely been objective. Rather, it appears that the think tanks and other policy research organizations have been guided by the interests of their own political advocacy, in the pursuit of which, false fears were generated through planting of misguided beliefs and distortion of policy effects. The activist research agenda of some organizations indeed influenced the course and content of expenditure management reform to some extent (for an excellent discussion on the approaches of many social and public policy inquiries, and the uneasy relation between truth and power, see Anderson 2003). This, in turn, led to the perception that reforms in financial management, even when needed, were introduced mostly at the behest of the elitist approaches supported by international lending agencies and may not have always reflected the politics and needs of the aid-receiving countries. The themes of the reforms were viewed as too broad to yield immediate results for the developing countries. In fact, it is suggested that there was very little ground support for the proposed reforms in the developing world. Financial management and related reforms in these countries were not matters of general interest that engaged the attention of the public. Rather, it was a debate, if at all, between visiting experts sent by the IFIs and the local officials of the aid-receiving governments. In this context, there was little public debate about the goals of reform and how they would address local problems, which in most cases were country- and situation-specific. The awareness of the reforms was limited to those who financed the reforms and those who implemented them in the countries.

A related aspect of the experience, however, gained importance in view of the negative perceptions it generated. There is a widely shared perception that too many goals were specified to be achieved during the short term, resulting in goal congestion. Moreover, there was no trade-off among the goals and all of them were to be achieved at the same time. Thus, expenditures were to contribute to: (i) economic stability through a reduction in the size of the deficit, (ii) improved delivery of services through appropriate revision of the administrative structure or through contracting-out, and (iii) additionally, yield sizeable economies through adequate improvements aimed at securing higher technical efficiency, contribute to improved quality of expenditures, and achieve a higher degree of transparency and accountability while devising a system of incentives that would lead to improved utilization of benefits of expenditure programmes. These goals, while always desirable, do not lend themselves to quick implementation. In the circumstances, the approaches of implementation become highly selective, and emphasis is laid on what is immediately needed, for example, financial stability, which may be achieved not through any major revamping of the management system but through a system of arbitrary cuts in allocations, and thus, in the services provided by the government. However, these highly short-term oriented measures leave an enduring imprint in terms of greater centralization—an unintended effect that is the very antithesis of some of the reform goals. The inevitable conclusion is that reforms were carried out in a manner that yielded contrary results.

Government institutions and their operational systems are never conceived, contrary to the way they may be depicted in some of the textbooks on public administration, as static. By their very nature, they tend to be and have no option but to be dynamic, responding to the changing patterns of power and, more important, changing demands and needs. Institutions have a deep and abiding obligation to respond to and to follow the agendas of society. But when these agendas are not properly interpreted, and the responses of the instruments of governance are not adequately and properly structured, the initiatives may contribute to and generate issues about the value, legitimacy, and relevance of institutions. When these issues are not answered properly, the value of the institutions is likely to decline, and this may very soon be followed by a growing vacuum which may get filled up, not by greater enthusiasm for more reforms, but by political turbulence and possibly even moral decline. Many studies conducted by political theorists and organizational experts tend to provide uncomfortable supporting evidence for this view.

In sum, the present setting, in so far as expenditure management systems are concerned, is one where despite a large infusion of ideas and systemic and institutional innovations, and a good deal of money (some of it in the form of repayable loans), the credibility of the system is largely eroded. As discussed earlier, the system is likely to face greater turbulence in the coming years in the form of more pressing demands for additional expenditures. When these demands are supplemented by the manipulative efforts of the wealthy and the politically powerful, the impact is likely to be even stronger and thus needs to be addressed. The paradox of the situation is that even as the credibility of governments is being eroded more demands are being made on the same systems to do even more than what has ever been done before. In turn, this implies that for those engaged in the reform of the expenditure management system there is no respite, and more significantly, ceaseless efforts are needed to restore the credibility of the system and to strengthen its institutional base so that both traditional demands and new pressures can be addressed. There is also an urgency which indicates immediate further effort. Any delays would only contribute to greater erosion in the credibility levels, endangering the tasks of rehabilitation and reconstruction. In addressing these twin tasks, the basic questions remain the same—how best to allocate resources? How can it be ensured that resources are best utilized with utmost technical efficiency and with constant attention to the needs of society? In what ways can the provision of information on the fiscal operations of governments be improved? And most important, how to have a viable system that guarantees the public the existence and smooth functioning of a machinery aimed at safeguarding their interests? The answers tend to be different, however, from those previously provided as there are new conglomerations of issues. In seeking answers and in attempting to provide a contemporary perspective on the issues, it is necessary to cover the developments that have taken place over the years, and in the light of the analysis focus on the path that one may take from here. To determine where one has to go, it is only appropriate that the paths previously taken be considered first.

EVOLUTION: A STYLIZED VIEW

It is difficult to provide a consistent and accurate history of government financial management over the last two millennia. The difficulty arises with the content and scope of financial or expenditure management as well as the absence of documentation of information on the role of government institutions. Inevitably, therefore, there is a good deal of ignorance about the working of earlier institutions and authorities in this sphere. Out of this general ignorance, an attempt is made here to provide a consistent narrative that is largely in accord with the trends in history and the facts that emerge from it.[1] Available evidence suggests that society itself has changed in numerous obvious ways and, in turn, the nature of the state and the form of governance have also changed, in that the state which started with a rudimentary form has become immensely complex as the tasks intended or advocated to be taken up

---

[1.] There are several factors which influence the approaches of a historian. For an early and interesting discussion of the cross currents faced by historians, see Carr 1961. For a more recent discussion, see Thapar 2002.

by governments are added, the focus and range of governance promises to change even more than can be imagined at the current stage. The application of electronic technology has shown that there are no real limits to the accumulation, storage, and retrieval of data. But at each stage of history, the notion of governance and the form of administration were inextricably linked, each one reinforcing the other. Despite the importance of governance, the study of institutions and government policies did not receive the due importance. Rather, the efforts of historians were devoted more to a survey of dynasties, the campaigns they led, and the territories annexed, and wealth amassed. In part, the lack of attention to the study of institutions and the changes therein may be ascribed to the belief in some circles that the institutions did not undergo much change. Recent studies, however, indicate that this was not the case, and that there were changes in the role played by these institutions (for a recent study of the role of debt in the management of public finances, see Macdonald 2003). In examining the development of the changing role of forms of administration, a clear distinction has to be made between myths and facts. A hitherto held belief was that a monarchy was generally associated with highly centralized fiscal, administrative, and military systems. However, recent evidence suggests that this was not always the case, and that some of these aspects may have been localized through the functioning of tribes (which traditionally enjoyed a degree of autonomy) and caste groups.

In an imagined state, it can be surmised that there is an official or groups of officials who exercise total control over the nation's finances (control being viewed as a process where an individual or groups of individuals are entrusted with the task of safeguarding the monarch's or nation's money, are responsible for the maintenance of records of transactions or the use of that money, and are empowered to regulate payments, including the authority to reject some claims). The reality as it evolved over the years is somewhat different. Although it started as a simple operation, expenditure management has become complex, and has come to play a crucial role in the management of a country's affairs, financial and others.

SERVING ROYALTY

The starting point of the system was the recording of revenue payments to the monarch. Kautilya's *Arthasastra*, written in the pre-Christian era, is one of the documents (along with those found in China and Egypt) that provide detailed accounts of the beginning of a system devoted entirely to the management of finances. Three stages became common features of work in all the civilizations. These dealt with the recording and safeguarding of the money received, verification of the money received, and payment of the money due (these three stages continue to be the main pillars of what is narrowly considered 'financial' or 'treasury' control. The contemporary terms, commitment, verification, and liquidation are mere refinements of these concepts. Kautilya described, in great detail, the processes of work at each stage and the tasks to be performed. The officialdom created for the purpose included an accountant (whose task was to register lands and deeds) and a tax collector (whose task was to oversee the revenue system). There was as yet no controller of expenditure, as the salary scales of different layers of civil and military officials (the distinction came much later) were specified in detail by law, and all salary commitments and expenditure on public works were limited to one-quarter of the revenues collected. This kind of ceiling specified in law, induced compliance from officials and, presumably, was helpful in containing expenditure growth. The expenditures of the kingdom, as evidence suggests, comprised outlays on military and related administration, gifts to those who participated in military campaigns, conferring of benefits and patronage to specific groups of people (based on either income or the extent of the support to the royalty), sharing of the spoils of campaigns (most soldiers were given rewards depending on the bounty received from the defeated kingdom), and loans to groups of people. In the absence of financial intermediation in the economy, the royalty acted as the intermediary and provided and received loans. The expenses of the royal court, which obviously was the big item (more like the President's offices in modern African countries which had and continue to incur sizeable expenditures in view of the large range, often disparate, of functions undertaken by those offices) were controlled separately by the chamberlains attached to the court. For the rest of the kingdom, the fiscal administration comprising tax collection and expenditures was, contrary to the general impression, more decentralized, reflecting in turn, the administration of the territories. At the apex level was the king and his court, followed by regions administered by military commanders (very often princes were appointed as apprentices for future assignments and royal responsibilities), with the local governments forming the third tier. A major part of the taxes collected—land revenue being the major tax—

was retained at the local level and a percentage given to the nation's capital for the upkeep (and retention) of the king. Given the diversity of people, local affairs were left to be managed by tribal chiefs, who also had the requisite autonomy. The three most important elements of fiscal administration were the tax collector, the accountant, and the auditor who verified the accounts. The role of the auditor was considered to be the most significant, and as appropriate, he was given extended powers to look into records, and to have daily access to the royalty who were briefed, according to the detailed account by Kautilya, on the fiscal status of the kingdom.

The central role in these operations was held by the treasury, which physically held vast quantities of precious metals, jewels, other physical movable assets that had value in the market, as well as collaterals provided by those who took loans from the ruler. The treasury was to be in a position both to defray ongoing expenses and to build up adequate balances that would enhance the wealth of the ruler, and more important, to deal with emergencies which, apart from natural calamities, largely consisted of wars either initiated by the ruler or by one of the contiguous states. A major activity of the rulers, until well into the Middle Ages and before the emergence of colonial empires that came to dominate the world map, was to engage in a series of invasions, and seek to expand the boundaries of the empire. Since Alexander's invasion through Central Asia, many rulers had one constant goal and activity, engagement in war, an enterprise that also influenced the approach of the common man who looked forward to participation in wars, and to return home with bounty, when the campaigns were successful. In this environment, the treasury became a regular barometer in that it enabled war campaigns to be taken up; it was drained during the campaigns, and replenished at the end of the campaigns, with the possibility of substantial additions. In a way, it also took care of the intertemporal aspects, in that while the royalty and the ruling dynasties changed, the treasury remained the same, carefully nurtured and strengthened (or weakened when the territories became a part of another empire) through the ages. The concern for fiscal sustainability expressed in current debates has its roots in these arrangements.

The maintenance of the treasury involved the maintenance of an accounting system that addressed the issue of payments into and by the treasury. From this emanated the concept of a core fund (that became by the nineteenth century the consolidated fund of the government), and the development of an accounting system in terms of simple formats that aided in the regular maintenance of records and, in turn, could be subjected to periodic inspection. It also became the focal point for the exercise of financial control, which primarily consisted in ensuring that there was no pilferage or leakage from the treasury in terms of officials retaining or taking away sums of money or packages of precious metals. Such total control was facilitated by the maintenance of accounting records, while the normal proclivity for stealing the monarch's assets was addressed through severe punishments for those found guilty. At the local level, the accounting system was enlarged in scope to show the status of public works undertaken and the expenditure incurred on them. The system, therefore, enjoyed a degree of solidity that was extremely helpful in the smooth fiscal operation of the kingdom.

A perusal of Western history offers similar approaches and some differences. Some of the arrangements were specified in the Bible, according to which the division of the spoils was to be carried out in such a way that God received 0.1 per cent of the total. In addition, as in the Asian empires during the pre-Christian era, the Israelites too established, as a part of the emerging State, a treasury that had control of the unproductive assets (the productive assets—livestock and virgins—were left in the hands of the people). The reverence to God and the obligatory contributions to the treasury enabled the people to tide over critical periods. Many studies of the contemporary situation reveal the working of similar financial arrangements in other regions and countries too. The striking feature is the establishment of a system that was intended to safeguard the finances of the society or the monarchy, as the case might be, and in each case, the endeavours and controls were the same. Many kingdoms engaged in a series of invasions and acquisition of territories and personal riches, that either added to the wealth or depleted it depending on the success or failure achieved in the battlefield. In these phases, the treasury acted as a buffer in meeting emergency military expenditure and providing food (from its stocks) to the community during periods of critical shortages.

GROWTH OF LEGISLATIVE TRADITIONS

In the subsequent periods, history reveals that societies were alternated between invasion and plunder and peaceful functioning. From the point of the public financial system, it alternated between situations where the fiscal core had a primitive form in that soldiers became tax collectors and were allowed to keep the proceeds in lieu of wages and the prolonged periods of peace and normality, when there was an effort to develop an orderly system of taxation and expenditure. Despite the chequered history and the emergence of several discontinuities, there has been overall development in the formation of a State, revolving round a monarchy or an elected council, that also required the assiduous development of a financial system, aimed at meeting the growing needs. Some milestones in this long process of evolution from a primitive or barbarian stage to a more civilized form require specific recognition.

In England, there was a gradual growth in the power of the legislature in that it acquired the power to levy taxation. The initial effort of the legislation was to shift the power of levying taxes from the Crown to representative bodies. But there was no similar effort on gaining power in the control of expenditures of the realm. This process took a longer time and achieved most of the goals, in terms of acquiring complete power on the determination of the destination and content of a parliamentary grant, only during the nineteenth century. A second feature, associated mostly with the European experience during the Middle Ages, was the development of a school of accounting, called Cameralist, that was primarily intended for the protection, safeguarding, and use of royal proceeds. Third, towards the end of the sixteenth and the beginning of the seventeenth century, there were developments in the management of finances that left an enduring imprint on the systems that have been in operation since. These related to the emergence of debt as a major source of financing and its consequence for the financial management system. Debt in the Hanoverian rule of England came to be contributed by a new class, the financial class or the wealthy land-based aristocrats, who also played a major part in the political life of the country, and became the largest investors in the public debt promoted by the royalty. As holders of debt, they came to play a prominent role in the legislative legitimization of public finances. They found that the records of public debt were woefully inadequate and that there was no systemic effort by the Crown and its treasury to maintain records that would bear public scrutiny. As a result, they exerted pressure to create a class of accountants in the treasury to maintain public debt records. This process came to be known as a kind of colonization of the treasury by the wealthy creditors and is, in a way, comparable to the pressure exerted by the international community of creditors on highly indebted countries towards the end of the twentieth century. The exertions of the wealthy class went beyond the compilation of debt data, in that it also forced the government to submit its annual accounts to the legislature, which were in turn scrutinized by a Parliamentary Commission, the forerunner of the Public Accounts Committee (PAC) now found in many parts of the globe. These steps paved the way for the full delineation of a system of democratic control of the country's finances in the form of the Exchequer and Audit Act of 1866, introduced and ably piloted by Gladstone, then Prime Minister of England. Fourth, another contemporary development had altered the course of financial markets, as they came to be known. As the demands of war finance increased, the range of contributors went beyond the conventional wealthy classes, and began to include the common person. To enable their increased participation, financial markets began to emerge, and London, Paris, and Antwerp, among others, became major financial centres with significant influence on the management of finances in many European kingdoms and other countries. As their importance and influence spread, the role of the democratically elected legislatures came to be less dominant and the influence of the financial centres became more decisive.

Fifth, there was, as a result of the preceding developments, a final effort (and in a way the beginning of more systematic efforts) consisting of the formulation and passage of the Exchequer and Audit Act of 1866 in England. It was the first piece of major legislation to codify the functions of the executive with regard to financial matters, and to define the functions of the legislature and audit. It may be recalled in this context that approximately a century before the enactment of this important legislation, there was an extensive discussion on the nature and contours of a financial management system at the time of the establishment of the United States of America. In envisaging the new constitution for America, there were two distinct and contrasting schools of thought. The first was led by Hamilton, who was substantially impressed by European practices, and in particular the central role played by the treasury in the formulation and management of the budget. In his view, it was imperative to have a strong central point that would guide the activities of the rest of the government while retaining a keen eye on the fiscal health. This was seen as the bastion of the traditional conservative fiscal values and a deterrent to the promotion of debt. The other school, led by Jefferson, was strongly in favour of a division of powers among the executive, legislature, and the judiciary, and accordingly was against the establishment of another centre of power within the executive. Rather, the President was the only power within the executive wing and the fiscal responsibility was shared with the legislature. These factors were once again considered in the context of the determination of the philosophical underpinning of the 1866 Act, and the opportunity was taken to reiterate the strong role hitherto assigned to the treasury. The Act also reiterated that the pursuit of 'economy' was a government-wide effort and every agency was expected to play a role in this pursuit. Ironically, however, the concept of economy itself was not given any precise or operational framework in the Act. It was not clarified whether economy consisted in a reduction of the aggregate or managing details in a way that would lead to all-round savings. The Act emphasized the need for economy and regularity without defining either term, and left the operational part to the executive. It was implicitly expected, however, that the enquiries of the audit department, which was now given proper legislative recognition, would pursue this aspect and promote operational savings. It was not recognized that individual agencies had little incentive to secure savings. From their point of view, whatever was allocated was to be spent fully; underspending meant that the parliamentary grant was not fully utilized, and this reflected poorly on the management of the agency. It took another century (and a little more) before a structure of incentives was put in place in Australia and the United Kingdom (during the 1970s), when the agencies were permitted to retain half of the savings procured for other activities.

Yet another feature of the Act merits recognition as the starting point of the accounting responsibilities of the agencies. Although there is no reliable evidence, it is quite likely that in making this firmly a responsibility of the agencies, the government was influenced by the debate sparked off by the Duke of Wellington a few decades earlier. At the height of the Napoleonic wars, he was reported to have written a letter to the treasury seeking direction as to whether he should spend his time reconciling the accounts of his regiment (and there was a minor discrepancy on which he and his subordinates spent their time unsuccessfully) or whether he should engage his energies in the pursuit of the French Army. The 1866 Act reiterated that, regardless of the context, it remained the responsibility of the agency to be accountable for all the moneys appropriated for that agency.

Sixth, during this period of a continuing journey for refinement, the functioning of the treasury system received further attention. The three main tasks of recording of transactions, their verification, and eventual liquidation of claims were recognized and the treasury came to be organized as a central system of payment with its tentacles spread to all the wings of government. Although the agencies were made responsible for the accounts of their operations, the payments and the maintenance of central liquidity were centralized as a part of the tasks to be undertaken by the treasury. Thus each commitment came to be recorded, and the subsequent verification and payments were also made after ascertaining the fulfilment of the specified legal condition. In due course, these features of the treasury system were replicated across major parts of Europe and Central Asia, primarily through Napoleonic invasions. Even where his invasions were unsuccessful, as in the case of Russia, these features came to be applied to the Tsarist system of finance. This feature is still in operation in most of Europe except that it is operated on a decentralized basis in Sweden and in the United Kingdom.

The specification of the role of the treasury, which came to be known later universally as the ministry of finance, and the roles of the spending agencies also contributed to the beginning of contentious relationships between the two. The process of providing initial bids, and being submitted to extensive cross-examination by the treasury, left many agencies with uneasy feelings that took years to crystallize, and eventually contributed to a greater decentralization of powers. The formal specification of powers did not always work in the way intended. Informal practices contributed to the development of two domains that tended to be somewhat independent and became exceptions to the general rule—defence and debt management. In view of the traditional importance of defence and reliance on it over an extended period as the primary means of an empire-building foreign policy, it enjoyed closer proximity to the centres of power and, as a result, commanded different treatment. Its budget making was far more autonomous, and in view of the extensive support from the legislatures, it received a kind of arm's-length treatment both from the treasury and the representative institutions. Debt too began to enjoy a similar status. In many cases, its day-to-day management was entrusted to the central banks as the fiscal agents of government, and in the United States, the repayment of debt came to enjoy an exceptional status, in that repayments that were legal obligations could be made without specific legislative appropriation.

WARS, DEBT, DEPRESSION, AND MANAGEMENT OF THE ECONOMY

The next phase in the evolution of expenditure management was heavily influenced by the events relating to the two world wars fought during the first half of the twentieth century. The wars saw the participation of many countries on both sides (Allied and Axis powers), and involved waging the wars in Europe, Africa, and Asia. Support groups came from other countries as well although there were no battlefields. The war involved a massive increase in expenditures, an extensive involvement in the control of the use of all financial and economic resources, and substantial use of contracting as the primary means of procuring the much-needed supplies. Contracting, which was also utilized during the previous wars (particularly in England during the American War of Independence, when all major supplies were provided by contractors), became more extensive, and greater and greater shares of expenditure came to be incurred on this. This meant that the role of the budget was limited to providing funding, while the organizational support was extended by the corporate sector. In turn, this contributed to the emergence of the corporate sector as a partner of the government, and the former began to play an active role in the development and promotion of new weapons of warfare. More important, the era saw the substantial beginning of a new issue—the determination and management of corporations for the services provided by the corporate sector—an issue that till date has not been fully resolved.

If the wars brought about a major change in the way expenditures were incurred, the Great Depression that occurred during the inter-war years had a far-reaching effect on the role of the budget. Hitherto, the role of the budget was viewed as one of compiling the needs of the government and as an instrument for financing the services provided. It was expanded to include the management of the national economy. The budget was expected to play a role in preventing, to the extent possible, major fluctuations in the economy, and to maintain a stable economic order that would allow economic agents to fulfill their roles. While it is true that historically, governments had played a significant role in promoting public works programmes (history is replete with examples), this now became a formal and legal responsibility of governments. There was a search for new expenditure management tools, and this search resulted in two features that continue to play a role in contemporary public management. The first was the introduction of a capital budget. Until then, borrowing was undertaken somewhat indiscriminately, and there was little or no creation of assets with productive capacity. As a part of the new apparatus, it was insisted that the proceeds of the borrowing be invested in the establishment of productive assets that would also help in the repayment of the loan (the golden principle). The intent was to make borrowing politically and economically more acceptable to the market forces. The issue of whether the newly introduced capital budget should contain depreciation provisions was also hotly debated, and some Nordic countries made efforts to calculate the depreciation provisions, although the methodology left a good deal to be refined. The second feature related to the introduction of extended grants. This enabled the governments to have an extended period, usually three years, to spend the amounts without lapsing them at the end of the fiscal year, as was usually the case. This facilitated the planning and implementation of public works undertaken as a part of counter-cyclical policy.

The experience with the wars also demonstrated, in some countries, the need for formal institutions to regulate the budgetary and accounting systems in government. Thus, at the end of the First World War, the United States established a Bureau of the Budget in the executive wing, and a General Accounting Office to undertake the audit of government activities and to regulate the accounting systems of various agencies. During the 1930s, and in the light of the new experience gained in the United States, formal accounting and auditing offices were established in many Latin American countries, although with a difference from the continental practices. In a few cases, the auditing and accounting function was integrated in a single office. It has been the general belief that these two functions should preferably be organized on a separate basis as one cannot audit one's own accounts.

In the United Kingdom, the experience revealed the problems associated with excessive concentration of power in the hands of the treasury, in that there had been a growing dependency of the spending agencies on the treasury. An inevitable consequence of this built-in concentration was the absence of a financial conscience in the agencies. In the late 1930s, this system was changed and the heads of agencies were made chief accounting officers directly answerable and accountable to the legislature. This was the beginning of a process of decentralization of financial powers to the agencies.

Meanwhile a fundamental change was taking place in the Soviet bloc of countries as a part of their intention to introduce centralized economic planning for development. The range of these plans was coterminous with the whole economy, and the language of the plans emphasized physical relationships and the formulation of priorities. Financial planning, particularly the arrangement of financial resources, was considered to be of secondary importance as all resources were owned by the government. Investment planning and the associated implementation that gained prominence during this period exercised enormous influence on the patterns of expenditure management thereafter. In particular, the idea of planning beyond the normal financial year, which had until then dominated the fiscal scene, began to gain support. The multi-year estimates that have become a common feature in most industrial and developing countries find their roots in this experience.

RECONSTRUCTION, DEVELOPMENT, AND THE WELFARE STATE

During the post-war phase, several developments took place, which changed the course of expenditure management. First, contrary to the general opinion that was held then, there was no general major compression in the size of public expenditures, as the post-war rehabilitation and reconstruction efforts were taken up immediately. In a way, this sustained the pace of activity and consolidated the extended role of governments. This effort received additional stimulus with the determination of many war-ravaged economies to introduce welfare-oriented measures, thus once for all transforming the nature of the state and the extent of its involvement in the daily lives of its citizens. Major extensions were made in the range of services provided: some were directly funded and provided by governments and some were funded by governments but provided by the private corporate sector. More important, the range of benefits to be enjoyed by the community were specified in the form of laws, conferring entitlements to the eligible categories. Specifications in the law meant that benefits were to be provided by the government regardless of its financial condition. This feature also contributed to a decline in legislative and executive controls. The legislatures were keen to reduce the growing executive power and to restore primacy of the legislature. Members of the legislatures felt that during the wars, there had been a massive shift in decision making from the legislature to the executive. In at least one country (the United States) wars were financed not from original appropriations from the budget but as supplementary appropriation, as if war was an afterthought. This feature continued in the United States through the Korean War, the Vietnam War, and the two invasions of Iraq. The legislatures were not happy to endorse decisions that had already been made. Instead, they wanted to enact laws that would restore the weakening control over the nation's purse. The new welfare legislation, and the emergence of entitlements, contributed to new categories of expenditure that were not subject to traditional controls. The estimation of these benefits was difficult as they were demand determined, and hence subject to wide fluctuations: they were not a part of the estimates of cash management; the day-to-day management of these benefits shifted to autonomous agencies and, in some cases, to private insurance companies. As these represented a new pattern of expenditures, different methods of control had to be introduced, and in many governments this took considerable time.

There were other groups of expenditure which came to be taken up on a major scale and which posed new problems of control. Governments began to take an active role in the promotion of research and development in science and technology. Some of it was spent directly by government agencies, part was contracted out to the corporate sector, and universities began to emerge as new centres of research, thus promoting a new partnership. But the basis on which allocations were to be determined and were to be distributed to the partners remained hazy and opaque for a long time. Similarly, the involvement of government in the promotion of industrial investment, and in the provision of some basic goods to the community at subsidized rates, led to the opening of a new chapter in expenditure management. Investment activity contributed to the conversion of governments into lending institutions, while the provision of subsidized goods and services contributed to open-ended subsidies. The former involved, as a part of appraisal, the determination of the repayment capacity of the borrower. However, the outcome in most cases was different from the intent in that the loans were generously written off and thus became routine expenditures. Both aspects forced the recognition of emerging new facets of expenditure control. The tasks seemed obvious but the development of adequate tools to address the new categories of expenditure took more time.

As these tasks were gaining importance, governments came to be extensively influenced by the management philosophy that then had sway on the corporate world. Policy implementation in governments took a long time and the process was needlessly cumbersome, largely due to the lengthy processes and procedures, and also because managers did not have the requisite operational autonomy. The alternative was to let the managers manage. But as a safeguard against excessive executive enthusiasm, the delegation of powers and operational autonomy were to be tempered by enhanced accountability in terms of performance or results, to the representative institutions. Expenditure management emerged out of this experience with a new dimension, viz. performance; accountability both for the amounts spent and the results achieved. Here again the tasks were abundantly clear but clear answers were still being probed.

While the industrial world was engaged in this search for new instruments to manage expenditures both in times of war and peace [this aspect received further stimulus from the community, which expected a peace dividend only to find that expenditures were growing inexorably, and in some countries were claiming nearly half of the gross domestic product (GDP)]. A major change was also taking place in the approach of the 'underdeveloped' countries (the phrase then in use; later, the term went through some mutation and became 'less developed' countries, and still later, 'developing' countries). The changing terminology did not, however, conceal the underlying stark economic and administrative realities. Many of these countries were beginning to be liberated from long colonial rule, and the goals of economic development that were hitherto dormant began to take a life of their own. They came to be articulated in detail and with utmost specificity and began to dominate the realm of economic and financial decision making. Longer-term economic development plans came to be formulated, becoming, in turn, the blueprints for government action. From an expenditure management point of view, the experience with development planning left a four-fold imprint. First, there was an explicit recognition that the colonial legacy in the form of the inherited administrative system was not adequate to address the manifold tasks inherent in development planning. Second, expenditure management and associated budgetary tasks came to be subordinated to the development framework articulated in the plans. The primacy of financial management appeared to have been lost. Third, investment outlays began to claim higher shares in the budget, with a major part in the form of loans or share capital in the rapidly emerging sector of state-owned enterprises. A smaller part was claimed by direct investment (these shares varied across countries and over the years). And fourth, expenditure management came to be viewed in a longer-term framework, mostly in a five-year period, and the horizons of the budget which were till then limited to one year (annuality was a dominant feature of classical budget theory) came to be informally extended.

In retrospect, this was an important period in the shaping of fiscal policies and expenditure management approaches. The enormous growth in expenditure and the complex nature of many of the tasks involved began to exert a good deal of pressure on the management system. As a result, it came to be recognized that expenditure could no longer be considered a part of an autonomous regime but as a part of the national economy in view of the intimate mutually reinforcing bonds between the budget and the economy. The budget began to acquire a stabilization function, in addition to the traditional production and distribution (not to mention growth) functions which implied that the size of annual expenditures was determined not merely in terms of the resources to be raised, but in terms of what the economy could bear. While the reliance on debt financing was both necessary and inevitable, it was the determination of the annual limits that became the more important and pressing task. The size of the deficit and the pattern of its financing became important considerations. The tasks of expenditure control, strictly from the point of ensuring economic stabilization, were: to moderate the rate of growth of expenditures, to help determine the acceptable levels of deficit, and once the levels were determined, to ensure that that levels were adhered to throughout the fiscal year. Fiscal slippages would have major consequences for the achievement of economic stability. As such, expenditure management gained an extra dimension in that the specified levels were to be scrupulously followed.

The pattern of annual budgeting itself had undergone a change in both content and language. Since policies and the determination of annual aggregates were made with reference to the developments in the economy, the calculation and compilation of National Income Accounts became an important task, as the forecasts of National Accounts helped in the determination of the budgetary aggregates. Resources, expenditures, and debt began to be analysed as shares of GDP and the language used in budgeting moved, ever so swiftly and subtly, from that of an accountant's jargon to an economist's jargon. Whether necessary or not, this new language became the medium for the discussion of annual budgets and related expenditure management approaches.

POST-WELFARE STATE, CIVIC SOCIETY, AND IMPROVED GOVERNANCE

The growth of the welfare state and similar growth in development outlays in developing countries became problematic when external developments became adverse for major economies. The increase in the oil prices and the emergence of inflation and stagflation in the ensuing years, brought added attention to the growth of government expenditure. Further, the increased reliance on debt financing contributed to steady increases so much so that debt servicing became an important expenditure category. In some countries, it claimed nearly half of the current budget. The issue then was, and continues to be, one of reducing the size of the fiscal deficit. In the public debate that took place during this period, governments were depicted as hobbled giants. Unable to move, and too disabled to address their own handicaps, in the final analysis they began to be deemed to be as problems rather than as solution makers. Necessarily, the conclusion reached in the process was to reduce the size of the government, its work force, some of its entitlement programmes, and to divest many of its traditional functions to the corporate sector and NGOs. In addition, it came to be believed that the government as an organization was riddled with too many problems to be successful in the provision of services. Too frequently, the claimed success of the corporation (it took some time, that is, practically into the new century) was held as the new model or the yardstick with reference to which governments were to be evaluated. Governments were urged to let competition into the whole arena of procurement of goods and services and in the provision of services. This approach, called fiscal adjustment to achieve medium-term fiscal sustainability, became the new overriding goal of governments.

Tasks

In pursuit of the above goal, many governments formulated a severe, if much needed, programme of retrenchment. The Governments of Canada and the United States were among those that gave thousands of employees incentives to retire early, and removed many more from payrolls. Many services were terminated, and more were shifted from the federal governments to the local governments (in many cases, without corresponding revenue transfers) or to the corporate sector, or payment of user charges became the norm. In some cases, the salaries of government employees were frozen over prolonged periods (leading to a real decline in the salaries; in the process leading to a large drain of trained manpower from public bodies to the corporate and voluntary sectors). Similarly, benefits under different programmes were frozen, or the contributions of the beneficiaries were raised to match the new levels of financing.

Influences

These efforts needed to be supplemented by a whole slew of new measures during the course of the fiscal year when revenues tended to be lower than estimated. The previous practice of allowing the level of deficit to rise further was no longer viewed as a viable option. As a result, expenditure management had to contend with the twin tasks of arranging an annual financial plan on the one hand, and to come up with firefighting measures during the course of the year, in the context of unforeseen adverse economic developments. It also gained a third task, which though not unique, had not been resorted to on a frequent basis during the last century. The search for financial viability revealed that the continued operation of state-owned enterprises would contribute to a continuing drain on the national cash register. Hence, governments had to undertake a programme of divestment and sale of publicly owned assets. If the task of expenditure management during the middle and later part of the twentieth century was to engage in investment, the task now was not only to discontinue that effort but to engage in the sale of assets. Here the task was to ensure that the assets received a fair price, and that the community got its money back.

The reform programme, aimed at improving the expenditure management capacity of governments, introduced in many industrial and developing countries had several features that were unique, and they merit explicit recognition. The programme was larger in scope and more comprehensive, and tended to view expenditure management not as an isolated segment but as a part of an overall effort to improve the quality of governance in the country. In addition to reiterating the conventional themes of transparency and accountability, the new approaches, which in some instances came to be called as a new management philosophy, were pursued very vigorously by the IFIs not merely as a part of their technical assistance programmes but as a part of the conditionality and the lending operations of the financial institutions. It also saw the ascendancy of accounting as a major factor, as against the previous economists' approaches, and there was a major advocacy in favour of introducing accrual accounting in governments. This is not to suggest that the views of the economists did not have much influence. Introduction of competitive pressures, emphasis on contacting out (including some policy functions), and greater decentralization to task managers, which were also a part of the reform package, had their origins in writings in economics. Together, these aspects had, and continue to have, a significant influence on the operational approaches of reform. The effort had also another major goal—to reduce corruption and minimize the grabbing tendencies in society. But this issue, although vital, is not the central focus of the efforts aimed at the improvement of the expenditure management machinery to better perform the tasks inherent in the situation. Accordingly, corruption is not considered here.

The influences on the content of the reform packages came from several directions. The improvement and efforts leading to the establishment of a civic society had their origins in the famous study of American democracy carried out by de Tocqueville. The participation of the individual involves the determination of what he should get from the government and from other sources. Therefore, the inclusion and empowerment as well as participation of the individual achieved paramount importance. An essential part of this effort was to provide the individual with all fiscal information needed so that he/she could make his/her own independent judgement on the policies to be pursued. Thus transparency became a major theme. Inevitably, in that context, the bonds between the voter and the representative institution (legislature) were seen as a kind of an unwritten contract between the legislature and society, to provide services. This, in turn, contributed to a greater emphasis on accountability. Since this was a revival of an old theme, it should be viewed as a renewal of emphasis rather than a de novo approach.

Following the tenets of the Public Choice Theory, greater importance was attached to the rule of law. It was recognized that the self-interest of the bureaucracy, political class, and business interests would keep on contributing to a perennial growth of expenditures, and that the primary means of curbing this proclivity was to introduce new laws (preferably through constitutional amendments: in practice, the reform packages were generally content with new legislation as constitutional amendments came to be considered as complex and unduly long). The laws were expected to bring with them a capacity to curb the enthusiasm of the vested interests. Similarly, following the Transactions Theory, it was expected that many of the organizational shortcomings in government could be overcome through greater resort to the contracting process. Essentially, all relations were viewed as a part of the network between a buyer (who wants services or goods) and a seller (who can sell them), and these relations were sought to be placed on a contractual footing. To some extent, this changed the conventional belief that hierarchical institutions and administrative organizations were better suited to provide services. It now came be held that the buyer–seller nexus had a more positive impact than the hierarchical institutions.

Management schools and corporate practices too had immense influence on the content of reform, in particular on the approaches of the new management philosophy. (The larger implications of this title did not deter the spirits of the protagonists or their enthusiasm. Where humility and modesty were considered as virtues, bravado became the new hallmark.) The general belief was that the corporations were successful (the role of deceit, which was uncovered later, did not figure in the discussion at this stage) largely because they were task-oriented, had task-related autonomy, incentives to perform, and were accountable. In contrast, governments had a variety (if often conflicting), of goals that were also frequently ambiguous. (It may be recalled that the goal of the First World War was to protect civilization, a theme so broad that it cannot lend itself to any specificity.) There were also no incentives, and accountability was so diffuse that neither the good performers were rewarded nor poor performers penalized. There was greater emphasis on 'inputs', and not enough on 'outputs' or 'performance'. Accordingly, corporate practices were brought in despite widespread criticism about the relevance of corporate practices for governments. Thus task-oriented agencies were created, and hierarchy yielded place to agency creation with a narrower focus. In the process, the overall structure of government institutions became somewhat flatter rather than pyramidical.

Technological Underpinning

Independently, the transformation that was taking place in the application of electronic technology had provided considerable 'tail wind' that helped the boats to move much faster than had been expected. The application came at a time when the transactions of government were growing at a phenomenal pace and the compilation of accounts was increasingly taking more and more time, creating an all-round avoidable frustration. Moreover, the changing technology and the declining marginal costs involved in the purchase (or mostly on lease) of equipment facilitated the governments to be in general conformity with the fast moving trends. The overall usefulness of the technology to the common person became more and more apparent as corporate sector financial institutions invested heavy amounts to upgrade their technical base of operations and to offer a new range of services at a lower cost. These factors enabled the citizens to appreciate the contribution and convenience associated with electronic payments systems. As a result, by the end of the previous century, more than 80 per cent of financial transactions were conducted through electronic technology. In fact, the daily transactions of these systems far exceeded the GDP of a few industrial countries, and looking back, it is natural to ask the question as to how those transactions could have been carried without electronic technology.

However, the application of the technology has not entirely been a smooth process, particularly in African countries. While rapid progress was made in Asian, European, Latin American, and to a lesser extent in transition countries (former Soviet republics and East European countries), the progress in the sub-Saharan belt was below average, although the corporate sector in the same group of countries made rapid strides in the introduction of electronic payments. In some countries the effective introduction of a payroll system (which is one of the first steps in the application of the technology) was hindered by the quick termination of the manual system and loss of essential records. Elsewhere, the maintenance of the system became difficult as there was growing dependence on expatriate technicians. While these problems persist, in some countries, notably the Russian Federation, there has been rapid indigenization of the equipment and operations. All in all, the technological application moved so fast that most budget processes are now conducted through this medium, in addition to the conventional payment system both by and to the government. The process of policy making had come to be facilitated by the storage and quick retrieval facilities offered by the new system, and the availability of information both within and outside governments was no longer a contentious issue. The general availability of information also reduced the dependency factor that was hitherto much in evidence in the relationship between the central and spending agencies, which was an irritant. The ministries of finance no longer resorted to the conventional process of raising queries and waiting for what appeared to be interminably long periods, as much of what they needed was already available to them. In the early stages of the application of this technology, there had been, of necessity, greater centralization of transactions, in view of the reliance on mainframes. It was then thought that it was better to locate them in the ministries of finance, which were anyway playing a central role. Unwittingly, the mainframe became yet another factor that solidified and strengthened the pace of centralization. This was more than countered, and a fresh beginning was made on the reverse path of decentralization, with the introduction of personal computers that effectively ended the supremacy of mainframes. While the progress was considerable, and beneficial for the most part, there was an absence of efforts to abridge administrative processes in governments that could and should have taken place. In the conventional administrative systems, the passage of paper (or 'files' as they were known) took time as it made slow progress from the bottom to the top levels (or decision making levels) of hierarchy. The introduction of information technology (IT) and related 'e'-governance (which rightly receives major support from IFIs) should have contributed to this process of administrative abridgement. In reality, however, all that it contributed to was the electronic processing of paper, while retaining the personnel and the paper process. More progress remains, to take place. While it is reassuring to recognize the strides made and new facilities organized, it is also clear that the ethos of expenditure management is far bigger than the capacities and opportunities offered by the technological changes. Technology alone cannot offer adequate solutions to the problems experienced.

Content and Discontent

The reforms introduced cover many areas, and for this purpose, only those which have been advocated by the IFIs and, in several cases, by the national authorities, which in the event have been outside the orbit of direct influence by the financial institutions, are taken up for consideration. It needs to be recognized at the outset that what has become an agenda for the IFIs was influenced by the newly introduced practices of the industrial countries. In the process of gaining ownership or laying claims thereto for some of these ideas, the lineage of the ideas and the following systems and institutional change, as well as the problems in the introduction of the proposed reforms and the overall impact on expenditure management are considered. It is only appropriate to add that the viewpoint of evaluation is not based on the general rhetoric relating to the proposed reform but is exclusively embedded in expenditure management.

Rule of Law and Fiscal Rules[2]

One of the main tenets of the Public Choice Theory is that decisionmakers (bureaucrats singly or jointly with the members of the legislature) may frequently depart from normal rules to further their self-interest, and this would have the effect of contributing to regular increases in expenditures. Since the primary goal of the recently introduced reforms is to promote a civic society where the rule of law will have primacy, it was felt that the arrangement could be advanced into the realm of expenditure management by formulating rules that would effectively place curbs on the proclivity of bureaucrats and elected representatives. The preference of the Public Choice Theory from the early 1970s has been for constitutional amendments that enforce balanced budgets. In reality, however, the movement for constitutional changes received setbacks in the light of the practical difficulties in amending the constitution [which in several countries is a long drawn-out process that also involves the approval of sub-national governments (SNG)]. Constitutional scholars also expressed scepticism that the introduction of constitutional amendments could well end up as cases for adjudication by the judiciary, contributing to legal gridlock. They recognized that the application of the principles of jurisprudence requires, at the very minimum, the existence of protocols as a precondition. Most processes in government, in particular those relating to budgeting and expenditure management, are governed by administrative rules and regulations that may not measure up to be considered as protocols. Accordingly, the reform movement shifted gears from advocating constitutional amendments to the introduction of 'binding rules'. (Can there be any rules that are not binding? But this literary oxymoron has become a part of common usage, courtesy of the IFIs.) Such an advocacy fitted admirably with the gathering support for the establishment of a civic society and rule of law. What started

---

[2.] For a comprehensive discussion of the proposal and practices in this regard, see *Fiscal Rules* (Banca d'Italia 2001), a volume of papers brought out by the Italian Central Bank (Rome). The volume contain papers by international financial experts. Readers who do not wish to read the 800 odd pages, may concentrate on the introduction, which is also a summary.

primarily as an advocacy by donor countries very soon became the agenda of the IFIs.

Other factors also provided added impetus to this approach. It was generally recognized that reduction in spending was difficult to achieve during the short term, especially during the course of a fiscal year. Expenditures gain their own clientele groups; these groups would be reluctant to see their services abandoned or severely curtailed; they would engage in protests and other means to ensure the continuation of services or benefits. Electoral, and associated political interests would very soon dominate the scene, effectively preventing the governments from following appropriate fiscal policies. The argument, therefore, was that the establishment of formal rules would enable governments to withstand public pressures and procure the needed reduction. The argument itself is not new and many countries, including those of the Eastern bloc, have many rules, informal understandings, and approaches about the type of expenditures that needed to be incurred in all events and those that can either be abandoned or deferred. In fact, the budget implementation laws in many of the transition countries explicitly provide for categories that can be reduced. To that extent, the practice in many countries may have been ahead of the advocacy of overarching rules that would enable governments to withstand pressures.

It was suggested further that the need for rules is inherent in a situation where the credibility of governments has already been at a nadir. The investing class, from domestic and international sources, wants to be assured that there is adequate legislation governing the stewardship of the nation's financial resources. Therefore, fiscal rules aimed at restoring the credibility of governments over the medium term would be helpful. This approach received additional stimulus from the enactment of the Fiscal Responsibility Legislation in New Zealand in 1994, which was followed by similar legislation in Australia and the United Kingdom. Very soon some developing countries, notably Argentina, Brazil, and India, followed with legislation aimed at specifying the medium-term course of fiscal policies. In some of these countries, the legislation also sought to place curbs on the initiatives of sub-national governments and thus present a national commitment. In India, the state governments—only a few—enacted fiscal responsibility legislation on their own, thus complementing the efforts of the Central Government. While a part of this effort was genuinely inspired by the need to address the deteriorating situation, a part was also influenced by the perceived eligibility requirements for securing loans from the World Bank. There was a widely held belief that the passage of this type of legislation would smoothen the transition for obtaining a loan from the World Bank—a link that is, however, officially denied by the Bank. Members of the European Union (EU) already had the Maastricht Treaty under which firm limits were placed on the level of annual deficits, and the amount of outstanding public debt. In Canada, while there was no legislation of the type at the federal level, some provincial governments enacted responsibility legislation to serve a variety of purposes, including shoring up their creditworthiness.

Inevitably, therefore, the provisions of the legislation among the above-referred countries (and others like Peru, who have joined this as yet select league) differ widely. Some differ in coverage, in that while most governments refer to the central or federal levels, the legislation in Brazil includes the sub-national governments. The Brazilian legislation also seeks to place limits on initiatives that can promote new legislation by members of the legislature. Unlike other British Commonwealth countries, members of the legislature in some of these countries can initiate new policies that also have the potential of adding to public expenditure. The new legislation specifies that this can be done only after there is an assurance that financial resources would be available from the existing avenues. In Australia, New Zealand, as well as in the United Kingdom, members of the legislature cannot initiate policies that would add to the level of public expenditure. All new proposals that have financial implications (and there is rarely a proposal without any additional expenditure) can be introduced by the executive only. Some legislation specifies the levels of deficit for the medium term, while some offer 'prudent management' without indicating mandatory targets, which are provided as in the past, as a part of annual budget legislation. While the acts are expected to be complied within the spirit in which they were made, there are varying costs for non-compliance. Sometimes, non-compliance reflects poorly on the government and could adversely affect the levels of trust (to the extent there is), between the legislature and the government and between the government and the market. In other legislation, there are sanctions of a financial type and there is also a provision for judicial intervention when some mandatory targets are not fulfilled. More important, however, is the fear that violation of self-imposed limits would severely damage and strain the credibility of governments. Considering that the legislation was intended, in the first place, to shore up the declining credibility of governments, in some cases, the passage of this type of legislation, although welcomed as a first step, had to be supplemented by additional legislation, as in the case of Argentina, which in 2002 enacted a zero-deficit legislation. Even this proved inadequate, and the government was quickly caught up in a financial crisis, from which it could not be saved by any amount of legislation.

One of the major considerations behind the responsibility legislation is to reduce the uncertainty and ambiguity about the course of future policy. The legislation was expected to provide, either directly or through supplementary rules, a firm road map through which the government needed to be steered during the future years. To that extent, there is an implicit belief that the future is relatively stable, and to the extent that the government is able to resist pressures for increasing expenditures beyond specified levels, it is possible to maintain a stable economic environment. In reality, however, some of the economic changes are notoriously unpredictable. As a consequence, rules formulated as a part of the legislation have to envisage all types of situations—an expansion, a recession—and dwindling or increasing economic fortunes. A major problem with the Maastricht Treaty that governs the activities in the EU is that it did not provide for a higher level of deficit in the context of a deepening recession. In essence, the role of fiscal policy as a counter-cyclical measure was not given adequate recognition and total reliance was placed on monetary policy and the use of interest rates—'all eggs in a single basket' approach. However, reliance on these is like trusting one's ability to push a string. In the context of structural imbalances that cannot entirely be addressed by interest rate changes, inevitably the burden falls on fiscal policy. But this has been prevented as the rules lacked, in many cases, the requisite flexibility (for a discussion of the Latin American experience, see Petrei 1998). In other cases, the coverage of legislation itself was so weak that it promoted divergent and contrary approaches. In the case of Germany, for example, special funds were exempted from the application of 'the golden rule' under which funds could be borrowed only for productive investments. The rigidity of rules, many of which were narrowly conceived, on the one hand, and the prevalence of divergent approaches on the other, reduced the utility of the legislation and generated resort to circumventing mechanisms. Rules are an extension of the policies proposed to be pursued. If the intent of the policy is to reduce some proclivities, that purpose is expected to be reflected in the process leading to policy making. Where there is divergence between the process and the rule, the latter may not prove to be very efficacious, as has been the case in Argentina.

Experience shows that in many countries the process and the supporting infrastructure were not adequately developed to serve the mandate implicit in the legislation. It is quite likely that the same feature had also contributed to the failure of previous laws, which were also expected to reduce some proclivities and govern related decision making. There was, in some countries, legislation that mandated the presentation of balanced budgets. In the event, the term balanced budget was interpreted liberally so that the overall receipts (including the proceeds of borrowing) were equivalent to the expenditure, which by definition they are. In the circumstances, the legitimacy sought to be provided through legislation was lost. In a few countries, there were mandatory ceilings on the staff complements: in some cases, there was specific legislation about the permissible growth controlling the annual level of domestic or external borrowing. Experience shows that the impact of these perceived restrictions was extremely limited. Staff limitations were avoided through the hiring of consultants; new expenditure on the acquisition of machinery was avoided through the leasing of the equipment, and limits on borrowing were avoided through the creation of a new layer of autonomous organizations that were engaged in borrowing from the public with guarantees provided by governments.

Enforcement of hard budget constraints on several units that comprise the government, and receiving their unstinted compliance requires information symmetries between the principal and the agents. The former, in their anxiety to secure stability, may seek to impose hard constraints and hope for compliance. In reality, however, the agents, given the information asymmetries, try to evade the constraints imposed from above through a variety of devices, such as fungibility of funds and related shifts in the allocation of resources, and seek to build up safety margins through organizational slack, and tend to meet the problems of uncertainty in ways different from those intended by the principal. In the circumstances, what is centrally planned tends to be managed differently than intended. This could lead to major conflicts between the principal and the agents and the fragile balance that exists in their relationship may break down, imposing, in turn, new costs of compliance. The costs may turn out to be far greater than the benefits that are estimated to accrue.

The process of building up multi-year estimates with reference to a moving three-year cycle, which was expected to supplement the proposed legislation by treating the future year estimates as ceilings, did not always turn out to be so. In many cases, these were treated as projections that were to be revised each year. Further, some of them used real rates, leaving the annual adjustment for expected inflation to be undertaken as a part of the normal budget routine. The rule that was expected to substitute for the normal process was not successful in this attempt. The implicit reasoning in all these processes is that the fulfilment of the new rules required a different institutional framework, and a different process, that recognized the unique features of the principal–agent relationships in government. But where these are recognized and the process is adequately equipped to gain enhanced credibility, the need for rules becomes less apparent. Where rules are added without ensuring adequate institutional support, the success of the rule(s) is rendered moot.

In the final analysis, the need for additional rules and their success in achieving their goals depends on three factors: (i) legitimacy of legislation, (ii) credibility of the supporting institutional framework, and (iii) the respect that the government commands in the society and with the market. The legitimacy of the legislation is in turn dependent on the content, and on its feasibility as well as its appropriateness. The new rules gain legitimacy not because governments seek it but because of their inherent virtue. This suggests that measures must be credible and must be so viewed by all the participants. Equally important, these rules are unlikely to achieve much where the governments are viewed as 'fallen states' and political instability is too rampant to permit smooth functioning of the rules. The community looks for an answer to the basic question—do rules constrain fiscal spending and secure fiscal stability? The answer is that where the legislation is not too rigid, where there is supporting administrative structure, and where governments are credible, there is a distinct possibility that there could be short-term gains. If the last two features are present, it is clear as daylight that there may be no need for additional rules. Annual budgets are also laws, and the weight they carry would be adequate to restrain as well as facilitate government management.

Medium-term Fiscal Planning

It has been noted in the preceding discussion that the annuality of the budget, which has its origins in legislative convenience, and associated schedules, is one of the most important limitations of the conventional budget systems. Since it was difficult to change the annual basis of appropriations, it was deemed more appropriate to develop a supplementary system through which a rolling system of forecasting could be introduced (for a background discussion of these aspects, see Premchand 1983, Chapter on 'Financial Planning and Expenditure Forecasting'). During the initial period, the system was used largely for internal purposes, but with experience gained, there was growing recognition that fiscal policies require time in order to yield results and should, therefore, be seen from a medium-term perspective by all concerned—policy makers in the executive wing, members of the legislature, and the community itself. Subsequently, the system received extended practice in the developing world from the impetus provided by the World Bank, in that the investment budgets came to be considered on a medium-term basis and are now prepared in most countries on a three-year rolling basis.

The intent behind medium-term expenditure planning is: (i) to estimate the future financial requirements of the existing policies and (ii) through that means to establish firm links with the resources needed. It was expected that this process would provide a good deal of clarity about the future role of current policies and the adjustments that needed to be made in the light of changing economic trends and, more important, demand patterns. Once the estimates of current policies are made, they are found to be very useful in the determination of resources that would be available for allocation to new competing pressures. Moreover, the use of systematic forecasts beyond the fiscal year is expected to reveal the intrinsic pattern of spending involved in expenditure programmes, in that some of them could have lower initial outlays that tend to balloon up later. Such aspects are expected to be clarified through this process. Furthermore, the forecasts enable government agencies to have clear arrangements in view of any strategic changes to be made, and in the associated service delivery and procurement contracts. As greater reliance is placed on the provider–buyer nexus in the changed financial management arrangements, this is also expected to reduce transaction costs.

As further progress was made in the introduction of medium-term fiscal planning, the scope of the exercise also came to be extended. Initially limited to an estimate of future requirements of current policies, the planning exercise now includes the implications of changes in existing policies (such as the impact of changing demographics on new enrolments in elementary schools) as well as new policies. Thus, the future estimates prepared now reflect the complete future requirements of a programme or a function, and thus provide a fuller and more comprehensive picture. The period for which the forecasts are to be made, proved, in the initial stages, to be a contentious issue. It was felt that given the limitations of forecasting in a fast changing world, an extended period such as five years could prove to be too long, and it was eventually agreed that a rolling three-year system would be adequate for the purpose. Another issue related to the basis of prices. Although during the initial period constant prices were used, this has increasingly yielded place to current prices. In a context where the overall inflation rate has been rather subdued in most countries, the practice of using current prices has not seriously limited the usefulness of the exercise. In some countries where inflation is high, the size of the reserve is kept in such a way as to accommodate these changes.

This feature is now common to both industrial and developing countries. France, which was one of the few industrial countries that resisted the introduction of this feature, is now engaged in the preparation of multi-year estimates. This exercise of medium-term expenditure planning is undertaken as a part of medium-term fiscal plans. It has come to be recognized that the preparation of expenditure plans, while useful in clarifying the future course of expenditure, needs to be taken up as a part of the overall fiscal plan, in view of the extensive dependence of expenditure on the rest of the economy. In effect, thus, there is now a full scale of annual budgeting undertaken each year for the next two or three years on a rolling basis.

The above practice should not be taken, however, at face value alone or in terms of the capacity or potential of the system, as there are a few factors that tend to affect the usefulness of the system. The first factor relates to the very nature of the exercise: is what is indicated for the future a projection, an estimate, or a ceiling within which spending agencies have to adjust their spending intentions? In several cases projections are undertaken at an aggregate level, such as a function or a ministry. A projection implies a linear extension of current trends. To the extent that it is merely a projection, it implies that no adjustment has been made in policies. An estimate, on the other hand, implies a deliberate attempt to look into the underlying policies and make adjustments so that the policies conform with the medium-term framework. When the estimates are converted into ceilings, they force the agencies to make adjustments in their spending aspirations and related wish lists. In most developing countries—given the uncertainties attached to medium-term plans—the forecasts retain, essentially, the character of projections. Where the countries are dependent on foreign aid, as is the case with several African countries, the uncertainty is exacerbated by the approaches of the donors. In most cases, the amount of foreign aid forthcoming is not known until the beginning of the fiscal year of the donor (as the amounts have to be appropriated by the respective legislatures), with the consequence that the medium-term projections have little practical value as they all have to be readjusted in light of the final aid from the donors.

A second factor relates to the way in which the forecasts are made and their relationships to the annual budget. All budgets are cooperative exercises between the central and spending agencies and medium-term forecasts are no different. In some countries, however, for example, Australia, the forecasts are viewed essentially as top–down exercises in that these are made initially by the central agencies and are then subjected to a series of sensitivity tests during consultations with spending agencies. Elsewhere, however, the spending agencies too participate in the exercise, although the prerogative of the formulation of ceilings rests generally with the central agencies, the cabinet, and other higher policy echelons. Notwithstanding the extensive participation, however, many of the spending agencies view the forecasts as 'floors' rather than as ceilings, and as entitlements for future years that have to be respected by the central agencies. Such an approach, however, reduces the utility of the medium-term exercise, and the final budgetary outcome remains uncertain. Rarely do the agencies formulate contingency plans for reduced allocations; as the estimates, once made, acquire a legitimacy of their own. In industrial countries, the estimation of entitlement payments, which is difficult even when undertaken as an annual exercise, is even more difficult when viewed in the context of the medium term. Most entitlement payments are demand driven, and it is not possible to estimate with certainty the number of people who would claim benefits, for example, for sickness. To address this situation, the medium-term forecasts generally provide for a contingency reserve. The problem with the contingency reserve is that once the size of the reserve is known, the distribution of the reserve itself becomes a contentious issue. If the size is not revealed, governments would be accused of a lack of transparency, and a tendency to centralize discretionary powers in the finance ministries.

A final factor relates to the role of interest groups in the formulation of forecasts and determination of ceilings. It is recognized now that the range of interest groups has grown widely both inside the countries and outside. Traditional interest groups include those associated with the military-industrial complex, construction complex, social service complex, and programmes associated with poverty alleviation (in view of the immense political implications of the role of this group). To these traditional groups should be added the creditors' group and the IFIs. The creditors are interested in making sure that adequate provision has been made for the timely repayment of debt. In securing this, creditors have gone to the extent of insisting that the general services or specific revenues such as oil, or sale of power, be earmarked and maintained as escrow funds, independent of the management of consolidated funds. The recent experience of Cameroon and Laos, among others, points to the fragmentation of policy making as a result of the endeavours of creditor groups. Similarly, some IFIs, such as the World Bank and regional development banks, as well as some donors, insist on higher allocations for education, health, and other sectors that are of importance to them. This insistence takes the form of specifying a share of the budget or a share of national income to be allotted to the agencies concerned. Two consequences follow from this approach: (i) an inevitable fragmentation in policy making and erosion in the integrity of the medium-term exercise and (ii) absence of a full assessment of the spending capacities of the agencies and consequent delays, that tend to be very long indeed, in the utilization of loans extended by IFIs.

The above features tend to interfere in reaping the full benefits of the exercise and, therefore, need to be explicitly recognized so that the issues may be addressed. The medium-term exercise represents the second step in the overall attempt to improve policy making. The third and supplementary step relates to the annual review of the spending estimates.

Annual Review

In the traditional system of expenditure management, the process of annual budgeting and associated process of submission of bids and review of bids and the final determination of the aggregates had a unique importance. This importance has, however, been somewhat reduced with the introduction of medium-term fiscal planning and medium-term expenditure planning. But this loss is more apparent than real in that most important fiscal decisions continue to be made as a part of the annual budget-making process, for that alone has the essential legal backing.

Over the years, annual budget-making developed several shortcomings that have not been adequately compensated by medium-term expenditure plans. The preparation of the annual budget is essentially undertaken in most countries (the United States is a major exception in that the preparation of the budget starts more than sixteen months before it is expected to come into operation) within a period of about six months before the start of the fiscal year. As a result of this tight time squeeze, the attention of the reviewers is focused on new policies, major increases in expenditures, and other immediate issues. Because of lack of time, some estimates may be included in the budget with a token provision, and a more comprehensive examination may be undertaken after the start of the year. This approach of making 'token' provisions has the effect of making budgeting a year-round experience. In any event, the focus of reviews, for the most part, tends to be on the initiatives, and the continuing outlays tend to get scant attention. In some countries, the continuing expenditures are almost taken for granted and adjustments for inflation and other factors tend to be made automatically, in that the outlays are increased by applying the same rate of growth as is applied for the forecast of the next year's national income. This approach is also accepted by some of the legislatures, which similarly concentrate on the new proposals. In some cases, where a fiscal crisis is looming large on the horizon, arbitrary 'cuts' may be made on the fringes of estimates. If the position worsens during the fiscal year, across-the-board cuts in terms of percentage reduction in all estimates of spending may take place. In either event, it needs to be recognized that the focus is on the periphery and not on the gravitas of most estimates. In the process, continuing expenditures acquire a legitimacy of their own and the mere fact that they have been continuing, with annual blessings bestowed on them in the budget process, make them immune to scrutiny and contribute to a steady inertial growth in expenditures. The fiscal situation in most countries, however, is so problematic or fragile, that it cannot be addressed through attention or adjustment to estimates on the margin. The need was felt for a device that would provide additional strength to review the estimates in substantial detail, in order to address the core issues.

The original device addressed to this need was in the form of zero-based budgeting (ZBB) that was introduced in 1961 and later in 1974 in the United States Government. The intent of this approach was to undertake a fundamental review of all programmes to determine whether they needed to be continued in the future. The implicit belief was that some programmes might have outlived their useful contribution and therefore were best abandoned. Although it was a radical departure from the previous practice, neither the original version nor the modified version (1974) became permanent features of expenditure management approaches. In the ensuing years, Canada introduced a variant of this approach, called 'envelope budgeting' (that was extensively applied in Australia during the 1980s), under which ceilings were determined for various functional envelopes so that the agencies could themselves undertake substantive reviews to remain within the envelopes. The difference between the two approaches was that unlike ZBB, the onus of review and substantial revision was conferred on the spending agencies. These approaches did not receive widespread acceptance, notwithstanding the fact that some developing countries made attempts to introduce variants of ZBB, but in each case, rhetoric had the better of intent, and actual progress and benefits remained moot.

The issue continued to be one of designing a device that would address the gravitas. During the 1990s, two responses were provided, respectively by Sweden and the United Kingdom. Sweden introduced, in full consultation with, and participation of the legislature, a triennial review system under which one-third of the government would be reviewed once every three years, in detail, including the core issues relating to continuing programmes. The results of this review were later incorporated into the annual budget. The United Kingdom, after the Labour Party came to power, introduced an ad hoc system of fundamental review of each agency. Later, it enacted legislation to the effect that every agency should be subjected to a fundamental review once in every five years. These reviews have proved useful in addressing the substance of programmes and projects and determining what needed to be continued.

This purpose was carried out in some countries through the appointment of national expenditure commissions and through selective inquiry. But the results have been less encouraging than institutionalized inquiries from within the government. A major hurdle of the governments, which is both a political and a psychological one, is to admit that there have been programme and project failures. This reluctance to admit the reality becomes stronger in the case of programmes included in development plans. Hitherto viewed as panaceas, governments tend to loathe to admit that some of them have to be abandoned or reduced in scope because of underperformance. With increasing emphasis on transparency and greater availability of information, it is to be hoped that admission of failure and consequent abandonment of programmes would be easier.

Risk Management

Hitherto budgeting was, as is evident from the preceding discussion, a relatively simple affair in that it primarily involved an evaluation of competing demands for additional resources and determination of what was to be finally included in the budget, which would then become an imprint of proposed macroeconomic policy and a statement of the services to be provided. But as the range of services to be provided both by government and the markets expanded, the need for a risk management policy became increasingly apparent. Now typically, the risks associated with limited liability operations, functioning of money markets, application of bankruptcy laws, workers' insurance, social security, product liability law, security for all, not to mention catastrophic risks emanating from natural calamities, have come to receive a good deal of attention and major laws have been enacted in many industrial and developing countries. During more recent years, as more and more countries are increasingly integrated into the world economy, the significant growth in monetary instruments, and their ability to cross the border at short notice, have brought to light additional issues about the adequacy of the regulatory framework, and more important, the need to provide safety nets, to innocent victims of market vagaries. In this context, the role of governments has become two-fold: to strengthen monitoring and regulatory frameworks so as to inspire and maintain market confidence, and to evolve safety nets that would provide an assurance of smooth transition against possible or inherent risks. As a consequence, risk management policies have now become so extensive (and are tending to be so in developing countries too) that they are viewed as a part of regular governmental responsibilities. In turn, these responsibilities imply that the annual process of expenditure determination also takes into account the spillover effects of existing risk management policies for additional expenditures and the patterns of financing. It is only during the last few years that the issue has become so important that it is being considered a part of risk management associated with annual budgets. But the focus of both national and international authorities tends to be narrower than is inherent in the task, leaving a greater part of the work to be done hereafter. In order to have a more detailed idea of the tasks that lie ahead, it is important to investigate the nature of risks encountered by governments.

Most intentions, and thus policies, of government are subject to a good deal of uncertainty. Far too many factors, anticipated or otherwise, tend to affect the outcomes, and to the extent that there are several exogenous factors that have an immense impact on the budgetary outcome, these need to be taken into account. For this purpose, five types of risks may be identified. The first is the implications of existing legislation. As a part of building a welfare state many industrial and developing countries have enacted, over the years, legislation of three types—that aimed at securing a proper environment for the functioning of the market and business; that aimed at securing a stable environment for workers, and that aimed at securing a proper environment for all citizens (these distinctions are based on the approach of David A. Moss, see Moss 2002). The first group includes bankruptcy laws, deposit insurance, company and country bail-outs, and exchange rate variations. The second group includes unemployment insurance, pension regulations (and bail-outs), and occupational safety and health regulation; while the third group includes disaster relief, environmental liability, life support programmes, and insurance guarantee funds. Over and above these three groups is the common but overriding theme of securing macroeconomic stabilization, which also implies that, in the event of extreme economic and financial crisis, the responsibility for providing a safety net and for financing it may fall either entirely or for the most part on governments. The second type is that of catastrophic risks. These relate to natural calamities that tend to severely strain the capacity of private insurance companies. In such cases, further safety mechanisms may have to be provided by governments, or alternatively, the risks may be shared with the insurance companies. The third type is macroeconomic risks which, essentially, relate to the fundamental assumptions that underlie the annual budget, viz., rate of growth of the economy, exchange and interest rates, and the rate of inflation. Changes in these assumptions frequently warrant changes in budget estimates, and the budget outcome may be different from the intent. To that extent, it is important to keep a constant vigil on these factors. The fourth type of risk emanates from contingent liabilities. These relate to the guarantees provided by the government to other public or private bodies, and the extent to which they have to be redeemed by governments by providing additional money in the annual budget. The last are microeconomic risks, which essentially deal with issues encountered by programme managers in the delivery of services—changes in weather, changes in funding, shortage of key materials, unexpected price increases in materials, contractual failures, all of which may imply additional needs for funds or alternative administrative arrangements.

From the viewpoint of expenditure management, three factors are important: how to reduce the risks; how to share or distribute the burden of the risks; and how to determine the annual share of the financial burden emanating from the risks. Implicit in all these is the belief that risk management is an essential part of the function of the government, and the view that the government has an obligation to provide coverage for risks, so as to ensure economic and financial security for all. Even the ardent advocates of market-oriented policies now realize the inevitability of the government becoming the ultimate risk-bearer. Efforts aimed at securing a reduction in risks include safety laws, banking and financial standards, standards for corporate and government accounting, and standards of governance for corporate and government sectors. In this area, the differences between developing and industrial countries are acute. In the former group, where capital markets are still at a nascent stage, legislation is being enacted and standards are being formulated and implemented. Even where these are in place, the risks may neither be estimated nor prevented, and the entire burden, with a view to avoiding a major disruption in the functioning of the market, may be borne by the government. In India, when the government-owned Unit Trust of India (UTI) incurred losses of hundreds of millions of rupees, the burden of compensating the unit holders was quickly shifted to the national budget. Similarly, in the Asian economies that went through a major financial crisis, efforts were made to compensate, at least partly, the losses of the depositors. In industrial countries, where a good deal of legislation to reduce risks already exists, the problem has been one of updating it so that leakages and deficiencies may be remedied. Such was the case in the wake of the Savings and Loan debacle in the second half of the 1980s, and the more recent efforts to strengthen the functioning of the Security and Exchange Commission in the light of the Enron affair. These activities involve the determination of the range of financial risks involved, and the permissible compensation to be paid. In each case, it is important to ensure that there are adequate arrangements for monitoring risks and safeguards against moral hazards.

In many countries, particularly in the developing world, the burden of risks is borne mostly by the governments. For example, in India, where natural calamities in the form of hurricanes, floods, and other phenomena are an annual feature, the entire burden of rehabilitation is on the government, and a separate fund has been set up to address the needs of states and the Central Government. As such, normal outlays are met from this fund. Only in extraordinary circumstances, when the damage is more than that can be reckoned by the fund, the burden is shifted to the national budget. Elsewhere, the arrangements, to the extent there are any, are in no way comparable to the arrangements found in industrial countries. As a consequence, the risks are borne by the government through its budget.

One of the areas that has received more attention, particularly from the IFIs, relates to the provision of guarantees. In many countries, a whole series of a second layer of government, comprising numerous autonomous organizations, has been set up, partly with a view to reduce the magnitude of national budget deficits. As these autonomous organizations are far from self-sufficient in their finances, they are permitted to borrow from the market. In view of their non-existent creditworthiness, guarantees are liberally provided by governments, leading to ever increasing contingent liabilities (for a more comprehensive discussion on liability management, see Premchand 1995). The use of the phrase 'contingent liabilities' is in effect a cover up, as these organizations are not equipped to repay the loans. Consequently, the burden shifts to the guarantor, viz., the budget of the government. The shifts have become a regular feature threatening the fiscal stability of governments. More significant is the fact that many governments do not have adequate arrangements to screen the requests for guarantees, or to maintain information systems about the outstanding amounts or the potential risks of default. With a view to addressing the problem on a more comprehensive basis, and mostly on the impetus provided by the IFIs, several countries have enacted legislation on the guarantees. In some cases, annual limits are placed on the guarantees that can be provided, and in a few cases, fees are prescribed to cover part of the potential costs in the event of default. Already, the problems associated with efforts of this type are becoming apparent. The annual limits, admittedly, can be a distortion device in that a single big item may claim the whole amount, leaving many distributional issues unanswered. Further, the burden is not shared between the loan provider, loan receiver, and the guarantor. In Norway, for example, the risk is shared among all the three as in bankruptcy proceedings. Also, the fee is more notional rather than reflecting the market realities. A good deal more remains to be done if adequate arrangements are to be made to reallocate the risks involved.

Advance planning for macroeconomic risks tends to be a very difficult exercise, because even if the likely direction of change in major variables may be estimated, the precise estimation of the rate of change is an extremely difficult task. The answer to this problem has been provided largely in the form of having a separate reserve in the annually prepared medium-term plan, which in turn can address the likely changes. In principle, this has the potential of providing adequate cover. In practice, however, neither the process of medium-term planning nor the maintenance of a planning reserve can provide an adequate solution to this difficult task. Both these aspects proceed on the implicit assumption that the changes would be largely marginal and the consequent adjustments would be marginal too—an assumption that is not realistic at all. Preparation for risk involves the possibility of several scenarios, each one with different financial implications. It is, therefore, essential that medium-term fiscal planning and the related preparation of rolling expenditure estimates is supplemented by envisaging different scenarios with different ranges of resource prospects (including foreign aid).

Microeconomic risk adjustment offers a different kind of problem. Here the problem is often viewed as a marginal judgemental change by the programme manager in the light of changing economic conditions and clientele demands. The implicit assumption is that these changes are largely administrative, and given the endowment of flexible use of rules by the manager, the changes may be successfully addressed. It is believed that the rules are rigid, archaic and, therefore, obsolete, and to that extent are obstacles in the path of successful implementation of the tasks involved. Since the traditional system of routine administration did not permit any deviation from the rules, it is suggested, as a part of the new management philosophy, that managers be given the freedom to engage in the flexible use of resources. Here again, the principle appears to be a sound one and should therefore be welcomed as a major point of departure from practice. In practice, however, micro risk management would involve the identification of risks in each area, and changing the rules indicating the extent of deviation, the range of flexibility, that may be permitted.

Risk management involves, the adoption of different approaches and planning instruments, to address the fast changing economic environment. What has been done so far should be considered, at best, a major first step, with more to be done to make it an integral part of financial and expenditure management.

Performance Orientation

The need for judging expenditure management, not merely in terms of the amounts spent, as provided in the annual budget, but in terms of the results obtained and the progress made in the achievement of programme objectives, has long been recognized. Its transition to government, and the application of techniques of performance budgeting, has taken a long time, and even now is best viewed, as is the case with a few other administrative innovations, as 'work in progress'. Part of the difficulty has been the complexities associated with performance budgeting, and part may be due to the changing approaches of governments to these techniques. In its early phase, performance orientation was viewed as a feature that had primary applicability at the local level, where the relationship between provider and receiver of services is compact and close. Later, however, with the rising trends in public expenditures, governments at the higher level were obliged to provide performance as an additional dimension of expenditure management with a view to appease the increasingly critical public. During recent years, it received additional importance, as a part of the packages of administrative improvements and reforms insisted upon by the IFIs. Although all financial institutions share the view that the provision of performance orientation as an additional dimension to expenditure management is essential, there is a difference in the emphasis attached. The World Bank places far greater importance on providing effective services, ensuring the achievement of minimum performance standards, and the implementation of a framework of accountability between policymakers, providers, and service recipients. This is evident from most of its publications, including the 2004 World Development Report, *Making Services Work for Poor People* (World Bank 2004). The International Monetary Fund (IMF), however, does not place as much emphasis on performance and delivery of services as on macroeconomic stability. It recognizes the difficulties in the introduction and proper implementation of performance budgeting, and is cautious about the use of indicators and measurements aimed at reflecting the quality of services provided. In reality, however, people do not seem to have a structured differentiation between macroeconomic stability, on the one hand, and improved delivery of services, on the other. Both form a part of legitimate expectations of the public. As a consequence, performance itself has acquired a wider connotation and now includes economic performance, financial performance, and programme performance. The concern here is with the programme performance only; economic performance relates to the much wider phenomenon of the rate of growth of GDP and much of it may be beyond the direct control of governments, although the policies pursued tend to have an extensive impact on the economy. Financial performance seeks to measure the difference between budgetary intent and outcome; if fiscal slippages are extensive, the outcome may be far different from that intended and the prospect of achieving medium-term fiscal sustainability would be bleak. Financial performance provides a direct measure of the success or failure of fiscal responsibility legislation and medium-term fiscal and expenditure planning.

Increasingly, governments are offering programme performance and improvements in the delivery of public services as a basis for energizing the choice by the people at election time. This feature has become particularly prominent during the last decade of the Labour Party's rule in the United Kingdom, as a part of its 'third way' approach to economic management. Consequently, performance identification and measurement which was an informed exercise within the innards of governments, has become, rightly, a matter of public debate and electoral choice. More significantly, as a part of the implementation of a new management philosophy, performance measurement and related specification has morphed into an essential part of a public service contract in the United Kingdom, between the treasury and the spending agencies. As a contract, it becomes more binding and, therefore, inviolate. In turn, the contracts are expected to promote a better delivery of services.

Performance budgeting involves the specification of programme goals to be achieved by the end of the fiscal year, and the results that may be expected to be achieved for the moneys spent. In order to assess the efficiency of resource use (technical efficiency), the system proposes the formulation of a series of indicators or measures, depending on the nature of the programme. In formulating these it is recognized that not all activities of government are directed to the provision of public services. Indeed, there are several areas of activities where the public may not be involved at all as beneficiaries. For example, purchases by governments for internal use, or human resource development measures, are some of those where the market may not be involved.

Also, there may be areas of continuing activities, where the achievement during a fiscal year forms, at best, a slice of what is intended and much of the work may take place, depending on the design, in the penultimate period of construction. To that extent, annual indicators may not reveal the full picture. In other areas, agencies are expected to formulate annual goals (with utmost clarity and specificity) and the supporting financial and administrative programme. As part of the latter, indicators or measures, where feasible, are formulated that reflect on the efficiency of resource use, and finally measures are also formulated to provide a basis for the evaluation of results, and the effectiveness of those results (impact of programmes). The measures so formulated enable a shift of emphasis from inputs, the traditional basis of determination of expenditures, to outputs and their impact. In the process, there are two significant departures that merit attention. First, it establishes, depending on the agreement or contract between the provider and the buyer (even if they happen to be two different layers of the same agency), a firm relationship between the moneys appropriated and the work programme/results offered. The technique of performance budgeting, in the process, becomes something more than a routine management technique and morphs into a basis for allocation of resources. The resources that are to be allotted are driven by the work agenda and, therefore, tend to be supply driven. As an extension of this approach, ceilings may be determined by a bottom-up process, where the resources needed in the aggregate are determined by the work proposed to be done. This process is very different from the devolutionary, top–down process of determining ceilings implied in medium-term fiscal planning approaches. With any change in the availability of resources, such as revenue shortfalls, a frequent phenomenon, performance targets need to be renegotiated. Performance budgeting as an allocative mechanism has not, however, received the recognition due either in the literature or in the frequent recommendations of the IFIs. Rather a steady, secular trend of growth and resource availability are assumed. Second, it provides a basis for the legislators and the community to get involved in the formulation, monitoring, and evaluation of performance and, therefore, has immense potential in terms of creating closer relationships between those governing and the governed.

Government programmes often tend to provide benefits very quickly, while the problems in the provision of such benefits may take a long time to emerge. The annual review should ideally be considered as an opportunity to reconsider the ways in which the services are being delivered, and take a view on an improved way. The problem, however, is often considered in terms of the narrow choice between direct provision and contractual agreements. A more important issue that is often not raised relates to the utilization of expenditure benefits. Schools may be established but there may not be teachers; hospitals may be set up but there may neither be preventive nor prophylactic action, and the reason may not always be budgetary. In India, even at the primary school stage, students are moving away in hordes from the government-provided free education system to privately provided education for which payments have to be made. In the event, it is a choice that is being exercised by the consumer against the government. Similar cases abound in different spheres in other countries. This process of non-utilization of benefits goes beyond the financial aspects, into the fundamental design of the programmes. In a few cases, it is found that the proposed outlays do not always reach the intended beneficiary. The expenditure-tracking system showed that in a number of countries, the intended money transfers to local levels have not taken place. These aspects, which go against the very intent of benefits, need to be examined in depth, and the annual review offers an excellent opportunity to learn from experience.

Given these advantages of the system, and the growing preference of the community to receive services in an effective way, it would be concluded that the application of performance appraisal to government operations would be met with all-round acceptance and that, over the years, steady progress has been made and that the expected gains have accrued. Experience shows that this conclusion is somewhat premature. Evidence shows that many countries took policy decisions in the late 1960s and early 1970s to introduce variants of performance budgeting. For a variety of reasons, that are discussed further, the experiments were abandoned and quick reversals were made to the traditional line-item budget. The advocacy of the system was revived in the early 1990s partly on the basis of the experience of the antipodal countries and partly at the insistence of IFIs. In the United States, legislation relating to growth and performance made it mandatory for federal agencies to produce performance-based annual reports for review by internal and external auditors and by the community at large. Notwithstanding these features, practical experience shows that a good deal more needs to be done. In New Zealand, performance measures and related budget classifications are being constantly improved, as they should be. In Australia, notwithstanding two decades of steady efforts, more remains to be done at the sub-national government (SNG) level (see Allan 2003, pp. 144–54). In the European democracies (West), major progress remains to be made except in the United Kingdom, where it has become an integral feature of day-to-day management. In the United States too, the approach is used more as an adjunct to comply with legislative requirements and has not replaced the administrative culture. In developing countries, efforts are being made ceaselessly by the IFIs and their brigades of evangelical consultants. But there has been a major change in their approach. If in the 1960s their role was a soft one limited to the provision of information on the new systems and their prospective benefits, it is now a part of 'hard' conditionality. A soft approach implies that the efforts, apart from being educational, were aimed more at moral suasion, while now it is an approach that relies on obligatory compliance, and refusal to release funds in the event of non-compliance. This approach is not without its amusing consequences. In India, at the insistence of the World Bank as a part of its structural adjustment loans, performance indicators were developed and the people were told about the improvements that could be expected. The community has its own way of assessing these improvements, and when it was seen that offices continued to start work only after 11 a.m. (an hour after the scheduled opening) as in the past, they drew the inference that no material change had taken place in the approach of the government. But these experiences, which are more instructive of the problems in implementation that have often been overlooked, deliberately or unwittingly, should not detract from the inherent merits of the system and its natural strengths over the traditional system.

It is, therefore, important that some other features of the system that have stood in the way of further progress are considered. A major issue that is often raised is that the system creates far more paperwork—even in an electronic age—that is costly and disproportionate to the benefits. To some extent this is true particularly in the transition stage, when budgets may have to be prepared both in the conventional and performance lines. Some argue, as the current debate in the United Kingdom suggests, that this paperwork would be minimized where the work is contracted out. However, this view is not supported by evidence. In both cases, the formulation and specification of performance measures involves extensive paperwork. The main issue with performance indicators and measures is that they reflect mostly on the quantity and not quality, tend to be diffuse, are often different from one agency to another and are mostly self-serving. The introduction of the system also has several administrative and political implications. From an administrative angle, it tends to solidify the distinction between policy making and policy implementation in that as per the service agreements, the provision of funding and the formulation of policies are the responsibilities of higher echelons, while the implementation and delivery of services become the task of the lower levels. In the process, a whole new class of administrators emerges with a compulsive preoccupation with monitoring, while the agencies, particularly at the street-level bureaucracy, would be anxious to achieve goals by any means, including some that are far from ethical. From a political angle, the policy makers are induced to recognize that the financial and performance goals have an impact on the way in which the institutions work, just as institutional constraints have limitations on policy effectiveness. More important, the specification of performance may also make the distinction of those who benefit and those who do not benefit from the progress much clearer. In turn, these could sharpen the clash between the beneficiaries and non-beneficiaries. Some argue that governments should take advantage of the situation and illustrate the policy gains made (for a discussion see Glazer and Rothenberg 2001). This may lead to less political machination, and the politician may make efforts to realize the policy objectives rather than subvert them. While political opportunism is an unpredictable issue, the fact remains that every effort should made to strengthen policy making while strenuously avoiding a new monitoring class.

Performance measurement also raises an issue in the context of federal financial relationships. In these cases, most of the provision of services takes place at the sub-national level, while the role of the federal level is largely limited to the design of programmes and the provision of financial resources. This may create the misleading impression that the performance at the national level is lower than expected. In such cases, the complementarity of functioning needs to be stressed. While these issues are important and need to be addressed, the alternative is not to continue the old system as it provides very little information on what can be expected from the government's labours.

Accrual Budgeting

The limitations of cash budgeting have been well known for years among policy makers, in that the system does not reveal the true financial condition of government. Moreover, the system does not have the capacity to capture the contingent liabilities such as the risks associated with guarantees and other types of risks already described. Since cash budgets do not distinguish between ordinary (or current) and investment budgets, the additions to national assets are not known, and the impact of the use of borrowed resources (debt) is not clear. As an extension, the system also does not facilitate the computation of costs that shows the use of assets acquired and installed. These limitations are real and cannot be glossed over. At the same time, it needs to be recognized that with recent advances in the application of computer technology, a good deal of information is available on the guarantees given and their risks, and on the compilation of debt records.

To compensate for the shortcomings, accrual budgeting and accounting have been suggested as alternative systems that should be adopted by the governments (as distinct from the enterprises owned by them, which anyway, following the commercial and corporate approaches—a feature common to all systems, including the former centrally planned economies—have accrual systems). There are two main differences between cash and accrual systems. In the former, a transaction is recorded with reference to the cash flow, both in and out, regardless of the extent of the liability incurred. In accrual systems, the basis of recording is the liability incurred regardless of the actual cash payment. The coverage of the latter reflects the actual condition and to that extent is truthful, a feature that is lacking in the cash system. A second feature relates to the maintenance of capital charge provisions and depreciation accounts. In day-to-day life, governments like others make use of assets, physical and others, that would need to be replaced after a few years. Depreciation helps to determine of the effect of the annual use, and financial provision for the use helps in the replacement of the asset when it is due. In addition, capital charge for the facilities used, such as buildings and often plant and equipment, helps to compute the actual costs incurred. Another distinction between the two relates to the links with monetary policy and the preparation of national accounts. Monetary policy is rooted in the movement of cash balances, and to that extent, the cash system enables greater coordination with monetary policy, a feature that cannot be ascribed to the accrual system. The preparation of national accounts is based, mostly, on an accrual system, and to that extent, the application of accrual budgeting and accounting system facilitates the task.

Although the features and distinctions have been known for years, the application of accrual systems to governments was denied, primarily on the consideration that governments are very different from the corporate sector in their objectives and operations. Profit motive is distinguished from service motive, and on that basis, it was felt, what was good for the former might have little application to the latter. Recently, however, with the growth of public debt, and growing fragility of fiscal balances, the previous arguments against the accrual system were given up, and the corporate model, including its management philosophy, and application of accrual budgeting, came to acquire greater acceptance. This acceptance though, is far from universal; three countries in the British Commonwealth (Australia, New Zealand, and the United Kingdom) and Iceland have introduced accrual budgeting. In the United States, budgetary appropriations continue to be on an obligation basis but with the overall cash ceilings determined for the year, while accounts are maintained on an accrual basis. Meanwhile, some countries, such as Spain, have introduced a modified accrual system under which transactions are recorded on a liability basis but no depreciation account is maintained. The view here is that governments do not have profit motives and that, in any event, the activities are so diverse that the feasibility of maintaining different depreciation rates is rendered extremely difficult. Where the system has been introduced, detailed accounting standards have been specifically evolved for each country. As a consequence, there are differences in the approaches of countries despite their common allegiance to the general principles of accounting practice. In New Zealand, the application of depreciation extends even to the defence equipment (which is at complete variance with the National Income Accounts approach, which treats it as current expenditure) and the rates of depreciation follow, for the most part, practices of the private sector. Further, all assets including land, with the exception of heritage assets, are valued at commercial rates, with the result that the assets situation is considerably inflated. In the United States, while the values of plant, machinery, and equipment are given, the land is not valued, and only the size of holdings is given.

In view of the limited application of accrual budgeting and accounting systems, several issues arise as to why the idea has not as yet gained greater importance. What are the relative advantages? And is the switchover or the complete replacement of the cash system necessary? These aspects need to be examined in depth. The primary advantage of an accrual system is that it permits an explicit recognition of the full extent of the liability and the relationship of the annual budget provision to the full liability. Once the complete liability is recognized, full annual funding becomes both necessary and automatic. To that extent, the annual reviews and associated uncertainties can be minimized. As an extension, underfunding can be avoided, and the macroeconomic risks, discussed earlier, can be identified with greater precision. These practices present complete departures from the existing cash-based system, which mostly masks the risks and the extent of liabilities. Further, the accrual system is expected to have a restrictive influence on the spending proclivities of the community and the government, because when spending is not matched by a corresponding increase in assets, the balance sheet—an obligatory feature of the system—would reveal the ugly truth and as a result the creditworthiness of the government would suffer. It should be noted, on the other hand, that considerable progress has been made in most countries in maintaining data on short- and medium-term liabilities and to that extent, the information needs of policymakers are met to a very large extent. In terms of estimating the outlays, the accrual system assumes a rather stable world in which necessary financial resources would be available to meet the growing needs. If requisite financial resources are not available, there is little alternative for the government except to reduce liabilities (for example, pensions and healthcare contributions) through major policy changes. The experience of the last three decades conclusively demonstrates that governments have indeed been making efforts to reduce the untenable liabilities. It also shows that the so-called shortage of complete information on the liabilities has not proved to be a serious deterrent in the pursuit of prudent fiscal policies. Similarly, the argument about the full revelation of asset use by government agencies and related capital charge is also met with some scepticism. While government agencies may not recover the capital charge, they have a notional understanding of the cost involved. Be that as it may, the fact remains that the cost of services is increasingly becoming an anchor of expenditure control and the computation of cost, on a cash basis, is to engage in a shadow game that has no utility whatsoever. Cost computations require the maintenance of a depreciation account and this is facilitated only by the accrual system. As an extension, however, it should be pointed out that this objective can also be achieved through selective changes in the cash system through supplementary systems of accounting, rather than through total replacement.

A more fundamental limitation of the accrual system is that it does not reveal the use of the existing assets. Their valuation shows their place in the market. Even this feature is only selectively fulfilled in that in some countries, as in the United States, information on the landholdings of the government is given in hectares, which illuminates no part of the use of the asset. From an economist's point of view, a system of accounting should enable an understanding of the way in which an asset is used, so that to the extent that an asset is underutilized or utilized in an improper direction, more profitable or remunerative uses can be explored. There are other limitations as well. The recent experience of the corporate world, in particular that of Enron and others, shows that the accrual accounting system can be extensively misused or abused. Given this potential, it is not a foolproof method with distinct advantages over the existing system. Moreover, the approach of accrual accounting is pegged to an 'entity', which is deemed to be the basic accounting or administrative unit in a government. For this purpose, the bureau, or a subdivision of a department has been considered as an entity, in turn implying that each entity would have a balance sheet of its own. In that context, there is no aggregate balance sheet for the department as a whole, that would enable a determination of the total performance of the department.

Available evidence does not suggest that policymakers in government or the investing class (who invest in government bills) are heavily influenced by balance sheet considerations. Ex ante, the application of the golden rule ensures that borrowing is undertaken only to finance productive investments. Even where debt is used to finance current expenditures, policymakers are guided by the hope that, with structural adjustments in the economy, there would be a revival that would enable them to repay the loans. Similarly, the investing class looks at the fundamentals of the economy, such as the direction of macroeconomic policy, measures taken to contain the growth of expenditures and deficits, and risk containment measures, rather than the total asset value of the country, for a major part of the assets may not be of a disposable type. If, on the other hand, debt is to be repaid through the sale of assets (other than through the divestiture of state-owned enterprises), then it is most likely that the financial credibility of the government is already so eroded that investors would be demanding a high premium. For these and associated reasons, greater emphasis is placed on the soundness of the macroeconomic policies rather than on the asset and liability position. That said, it should be recognized that the half-yearly statements furnished by governments as a part of the accrual system, which include the balance sheet, income and expenditure statements, sources and uses of funds, outstanding domestic and external debt, are far simpler and comprehensible than traditional appropriation accounts.

Given the relative advantages and potential and current limitations, the question arises whether the existing system should be totally replaced. Since the spread of the system is limited to less than a handful of countries, it is obvious that the replacement approach has been far from a resounding success. The reason for this lukewarm or even cold reception is to be found, apart from the traditional inertia in embracing new approaches, in the fact that much of the information that is sought to be provided by the accrual system is in fact built into the off-the-shelf computer accounting software. It enables the maintenance of information in terms of budgetary appropriation, initial and firm commitments, vendor lists, lags in the supply of equipment or services, submission of payment vouchers, and eventual payment or liquidation of claims. It, thus, provides data in terms of multiple bases, without additional cost. Similarly, data systems are available for the recording and maintenance of inventories and movable and immovable assets. Given the growing database, it is up to the user to devise an information system that meets the requirement of the cash-based as well as accrual accounting systems. Once the basic infrastructure is in place, it is expected that there would be changes in the way in which information is compiled, consolidated, and analysed, reflecting the large range of users (for a detailed discussion see Premchand 1995).

Contracting Out

Efforts aimed at improving expenditure management systems go far beyond the annual process of budgeting and related requirements of legislative approval to the very core of the administrative systems through which services are provided. It is contended that government organizations tend to be monolithic, wedded more to the compliance of complex procedures than to reaping benefits from competitive tendering for the delivery of services. In support of this view it is argued that traditionally government agencies received their supplies from other government agencies or through central purchase organizations. To the extent that it is the former approach, it is viewed as an inside transaction (known as book adjustment, in government accounting), that is little affected by the competitive forces prevalent in the market. If government agencies are permitted freedom to find their own best source of supply they would explore the competitive bidding processes to the fullest extent and avail of the advantage of big bulk buyers.

More important is the application of the principle to the provision of services, particularly those with most direct link to human development, such as education, health, water, sanitation and electricity, through contractual agreements rather than being provided directly, as was the case hitherto, by the governments. This approach leads to new arrangements between the buyers and the service providers, and also contributes to a separation of funding from the provision. These contracted arrangements, which have received the support of the World Bank and other regional organizations, are based on a set of beliefs that are both implicit and explicit and that are also highly debatable. The emphasis on government funding and private provision of services is based, in part, on the belief that government organizations have grown too big and unwieldy, and that their service provision is no longer economical. It is suggested, as a part of this approach, that bureaucracy has grown considerably but that this growth has not been accompanied by a corresponding growth in efficiency or the quality of services or in the attention to the consumer. In fact, the belief is that governments have become rigid and insensitive to the changing demand patterns of the consumers. As a result, consumers are leaving the public arrangements and are seeking services from the market, by paying for them. In such a context, contractual arrangements could contribute to a reduction in the size of the government and, more important, may provide the requisite flexibility to stay in the competitive field, while ensuring in the process that the original intent of service provision is fulfilled. Moreover, it is also held that to the extent that the contracts are awarded to NGOs, they would have an opportunity to be more active in their respective fields, and be more effective in the provision of services. In support of this view, the growing role played by the NGOs and the strengthened voices they acquired during recent years in areas such as environment and poverty reduction are cited as evidence. In addition, there is the implicit belief that contractual arrangements would contribute to closer relationships between the provider and the client, and to that extent provide opportunities to the clients to monitor the activities of contractors and make improvements even as the services are being provided.

The service delivery system seen across industrial and developing countries reflects the following structure: (i) services funded and provided by the central government; (ii) services funded by the central government but provided through contractual agreements; (iii) services funded and provided by local government; (iv) services funded by local government but provided by contractors; and, (v) service arrangements through clients and related groups who may, in providing services, imitate the market or resort to community controls or may engage in self-management or may, like the funding agencies, award contracts while retaining direct controls on the day-to-day management. The first four arrangements have been common features and a part of the traditional approach. Management by client groups is considered to be more appropriate when government policies seek the provision of vouchers to the poorer sections of the community. Experience shows that when vouchers are given for education, water supply, or sanitation arrangements, a greater opportunity is afforded to the client to exercise oversight on the quality of the services and to vary the quality, where needed, to reflect the diversity of the consumer. However, it is observed that client groups lend themselves to easy capture by vested interests and corrupt politicians, not to mention the bureaucracy, and may require a regulatory framework as an essential prerequisite.

The intent in seeking these arrangements is two-fold; to ensure greater improvement in the efficiency of public spending, and to ensure greater participation by the clientele groups in the determination of the parameters governing the services provided, and imparting a degree of certainty in the delivery of the service. The issue for consideration here is whether these purposes are being fulfilled, and to the extent that there are shortcomings, what can be done to improve the system. Available evidence, which is mostly anecdotal, suggests that in contractual arrangements there may have been a few successes, and many major failures. To the extent that it is mostly the latter, the needed improvement in public finances has not taken place, and the improvements in service delivery, while remarkable in a few cases, have also been spotty and too short-term oriented, and could not be sustained over a long period. The reasons for this emerging failure are to be found in the very principles and practices of contracting. This raises a more fundamental question. Greater resort to contracting out was suggested as an alternative to a state and public policy failure. If the new approaches have led to a contractual failure, what are the alternatives available and how they may be pursued? The answers to these issues are explored later. It is necessary to first consider the factors contributing to likely or actual contractual failure.

Social philosophers tend to think that every paradigm also carries with it the seeds of its own failure, thus paving the way for replacement by another paradigm. This is more or less applicable to government contracting too, in that there are several problem areas that need to be recognized and comprehensively addressed. It is evident from the above description that governments, at any level, may award contracts or may engage in the direct provision of services to client groups through the award of coupons and empowering them through introduction of self-management or through community control of vouchers. It is recognized, however, that client groups are often amorphous and lack a legal personality. While they can raise and spend their own resources, the transfer of money (and coupons represent liquid cash in a different form) or the management of vouchers to client groups suggests infinite possibilities of corrupt practices, politicization of the service to an extent, and possible subversion of the objectives. The client groups may not have a well-structured system of accounting, information generation, and monitoring, as well as arrangements for accountability. In other words, the system may develop a major leakage that is very difficult to plug and seal.

In theory, contracts appear to be advantageous to major organizations and bulk buyers such as governments, as they promote full play for the competitive forces. Experience also shows that where large amounts of money are involved, the bidding parties collude among themselves to thwart competitive forces and to pursue sharing arrangements. This effort is not diminished by the adoption of the Dutch or Swiss action systems, under which all bidders are given the opportunity to share the contract. The community of contractors is a forward looking one, always looking beyond the next opportunity to the series of opportunities that open up or down the stream in the following years and, therefore, are constantly on the lookout for possibilities of collusion.

The award of a contact implies that all the details of the work to be undertaken, including the design of equipment or proposed construction, are fully worked out and that there can be only marginal changes during the period of implementation. In practice, however, there are areas, such as defence, where the award of a contract starts with an idea that is still embryonic and that develops with time, as progress is made. In such cases, the conditions of the contract are usually stacked in favour of the contractors, and major revisions in the design end up contributing to major variations in costs, all to be borne by those awarding the contracts. The basis of cost determination for remunerating the contractors is also inherently flawed. To the extent that the contractor is remunerated on a cost-plus basis, contractors have little or no basis to seek economies. The United States Government has gone through a variety of approaches in the determination of the basis of remuneration and finally concluded that a 'moral' approach is to be preferred. Accordingly, defence contractors are required to certify that the costs incurred have been truthfully incurred, and should untruthful claims occur, they can be prosecuted under the Perjury Act. This takes the issue from practical accounting to self-regulated ethical behaviour.

Award of contracts in the realm of social services carries other types of risks that may not be present in, for example, construction contracts. In social services, particularly in the areas of services to children and the poor, a breakdown in service due to a contractual failure could have calamitous effects. Delays in construction may, at best, mean prolonged inconvenience to select groups of users, but in social services and related structured services, a breakdown causes serious dislocation in work and discomfort to many. In these cases, governments should be ready with alternative arrangements to permit continuity in the provision of services. This, in turn, implies the existence and the smooth operation of an infrastructure of monitoring and regulation of service standards where services are provided outside the funding arrangements by governments. Such an infrastructure implies the need for incurring transaction costs that tend to grow in proportion to the range of services and expenditures.

The use of NGOs for the delivery of services is another aspect that raises more questions than can be answered here. Available evidence does not lend full support to the argument that the use of these organizations is either economical or efficient. These organizations are also agenda driven, and often lack basic arrangements for acceptable accounting and accountability. Some of their transaction costs are very high, and too frequently, their operations are opaque. This is not to minimize the enduring contributions made by some NGOs all over the world. But the assumption that all of them are alike is one that needs empirical evidence.

Government organizations seek contractual arrangements as an alternative to their own inefficient ways of working. But contractual arrangements are not always a panacea, particularly from the point of expenditure management. The two relevant issues are whether these contracts lead to a reduction in expenditure and whether they promote greater efficiency and a better value for money. The available evidence, spotty, anecdotal, and varying from one field to another, is far from conclusive. An excessive reliance on contracts could lead to the emergence of a contractual state, where operational controls of expenditure would shift from governments to contractors; the issue then would be the adequacy of internal controls in the contractor's organization. Any long-term tendency to depend on contractual arrangements as an exclusive basis for the delivery of services is fraught with consequences that tend to be beyond the control of governments. These are aspects that merit more detailed enquiries and judicious conclusions, in particular, about the ability of contractors to reconcile the expenditure management objectives with service delivery, and with their own profit expectations.

Empowerment

The emphasis on establishing a civic society rests on the argument that in a democracy the will of the people should be reflected in all activities. The inspiration to this approach was provided by the writings of Tocqueville, published more than one and a half centuries ago. As he explained, 'I am speaking here of a government that follows the real will of the people, and not of a government that limits itself to commanding in the name of the people' (see Tocqueville 2002, p. 212). But the formulation of a government and the establishment of a responsive bureaucracy, which has been a relentless effort ever since the establishment of government, has not been easy. There has been a movement from monolithic central governments to federal systems in which the sub-national governments, viz., regions, provinces, states, and local government, have been given extended tasks and powers to mobilize requisite revenue resources. However, this forward step did not meet the requirements fully as SNGs tended to be controlled through a variety of means by the national governments, and the voice of the people appeared to have been lost in the vast labyrinths of the legislatures and bureaucracy. As Tocqueville recognized, 'the federal system rests, whatever one does, on a complicated theory whose application requires of the governed a daily use of the enlightenment of their reason' (Tocqueville 2000, p. 212).

Despite the above admonition, what has developed in practice in most countries is a system in which there has been and there continues to be a large gap between the requirements and resources at the subnational level, and as a consequence, a highly complex web of financial relations developed between the central and SNGs. In most of these cases, the power of financial decision making rests with the higher level of governments, despite the cognate powers of the lower-level governments. Initiatives with regard to new activities are undertaken, for the most part, by the federal government which, in the name of a variety of causes and pursuit of economic policies, issues mandates, both funded and unfunded, to the lower level of governments. The transfer of funds usually takes place with the imposition of a number of conditions, and the recipient governments have little flexibility, even where the local situation demands a variance, in the use of resources. As a consequence, there has developed a virtual integrated functioning in which policies are formulated, directed, funded, and monitored by the federal governments, and the SNGs tend to become subordinate appendages. In other words, the community which was to have a voice and some executive power to determine what it should have, and how and when it should have in terms of commonly funded services, has either ceded the day-to-day decision making to the federal government or has been usurped by it. In the process, there were two inevitable effects: a greater distance between the governed and those engaged in governing; and an immense complexity in expenditure management with a high degree of centralization.

The revitalization of society required that efforts be made to decentralize financial power, and to engage in the reverse process of empowering both the people and the SNGs. Available evidence suggests that the process of empowerment took three forms: (i) a greater financial devolution to SNGs as well as transfer of local tasks to the lower levels; (ii) selective empowerment of local governments to borrow from domestic and external sources (the latter is mostly restricted to borrowing from the World Bank or regional financial institutions); and (iii) empowerment of citizen or consumer groups, or clientele groups through oversight on service providers.

Each one of these areas reflects ongoing progress, with some positive as well as negative features. There has been a greater delegation of power and greater empowerment, in India (through a constitutional amendment), Mexico, Russia, and Uganda, among others. In some of these cases, the empowerment was less of a reflection on the intention of the federal government to distribute tasks, as much as a way out of the fiscal squeeze experienced by central governments. This was the major factor in Russia, but it should also be noted that after the break-up of the Russian Union there have been at least three reform waves, giving more powers in most cases, and taking away some powers in a few cases, to and from the national governments. In Mexico, it was undertaken as a first step in the streamlining, long overdue, of the local–central government financial nexus. In Uganda, it was undertaken as a part of a new effort to build democracy from the grassroots, and to revive the traditions of local self-government. The delegation of tasks and financial powers was not always accompanied by a financial devolution. As a result, empowerment posed more dilemmas for the local governments than before, and compelled them, in most cases, to raise resources from various avenues. While in the short term this contributed to innovative methods of financing, it also meant, in some cases, that there was little coordination in the national tax policy. In a few cases, the efforts at the lower levels ran counter to the approach of the national government, in that taxes or short-term assessments were levied on goods transiting through local areas.

A second element of empowerment was to selectively endow the local governments to borrow from the markets. The approaches in this regard hitherto varied from total freedom to borrow from the market to a total denial of entry into the market. In the United States, state and local governments as well as autonomous bodies under their control have been engaged in the issue of taxable and tax-free bonds for a long time. In the United Kingdom, the borrowing requirements of the central and local governments were pooled together and raised by the central government for the country as a whole. Elsewhere, state governments, for example in India, needed prior approval from the Reserve Bank of India (the Central Bank), and local governments were barred from market borrowing. Similar procedures are observed in the British Commonwealth countries. In China, provincial and local governments were, in principle and in law, not expected to entertain budgetary deficits and, therefore, not expected to borrow from the markets. In practice, however, both types of governments have been engaged in the issue of IOUs, a kind of informal borrowing. In Latin American countries, state-level governments had power to borrow from the market, which they exercised freely. As a consequence, state debt had to be redeemed, at a later stage, by the national governments. The new view was that if the lower-level governments were to be permitted to borrow from the market, they would be subject to market discipline, which, it was contended was far better and more effective than the hierarchical and administrative controls exercised by the national levels. Closer attachment to the markets would induce the local governments to be more financially conscious and fiscally prudent. In the pursuit of this approach, local governments in India (selectively and with the approval of the central government), Indonesia, the Philippines, South Africa, and in some transition countries including the Russian Federation, were permitted to borrow from the market. In some cases the borrowing plans, particularly where World Bank loans were concerned, were guaranteed by the federal government. It could be argued that borrowing with a federal guarantee is unlikely to promote financial rectitude at the local level as, in the absence of any sanctions, the repayment burden shifts to the guarantors. Essentially, however, the delegation of borrowing power equipped the local levels with yet another powerful fiscal instrument which, used judiciously, had the potential of contributing to improved fiscal and service performance, and when abused, would bring financial problems to both local and national governments. This liberalization effort was not universal, however. There were other cases, particularly in Latin America, where fiscal instability was contributed, among others, by the reckless abandon in spending and in borrowing that had to be eventually redeemed by the higher level of government. In this context, the approach was one of de-liberalization or imposition of massive restrictions or introduction of a new regime of greater involvement and heightened day-to-day supervision of the central government. In a way, this was a development that was implicit in the situation, and the opportunity of enacting fiscal responsibility legislation, as in Brazil, was taken to curb the excessive enthusiasm of state and local governments to engage in borrowing beyond specified limits. The split in the approaches toward liberalization and de-liberalization implies that what works during periods of economic stability might not work in a period of fiscal stress, and that indeed, greater centralization of powers might be more appropriate in the latter periods. But the proposition itself has not been debated in this way before.

A third element of empowerment was to involve groups of citizens and clients in the process of budget formulation, and more significantly, with the process of budget implementation and provision of services. It had come to be realized that centrally designed and funded programmes might not be uniformly suitable and that appropriate variations should be permitted to reflect local conditions. As such, local inputs were to be organized so that the design could be adjusted and the allocation process strengthened. But the way in which citizens' groups were to be associated with the process was never comprehensively examined and a blueprint, even as a prototype, was never prepared. Rather, what is found in practice is a selective application of this desire and the way in which citizens' inputs were generated and utilized. In the United Kingdom, citizens' groups were associated in the determination of the use of resources allotted for the National Health Service. In Oregon state (United States), citizens' groups were associated with budget committees and contract committees at the county government level, and their inputs were solicited both in the award of service contracts and in monitoring the implementation. In India, as a part of building up democratic traditions at the village level, several users' associations were formed (such as for water—mostly irrigation, which even at the best of times was a contentious issue in view of the embedded conflict between upstream and downstream users). Broadly, thus, empowerment took three forms, association with the design of the service and allocation of resources, general participation in the award and monitoring of contracts, and determination of the use of benefits created through the expenditure programmes.

The actual implementation of the idea of empowerment has yet to make a good deal of progress both in the conceptual design and additional aggressive efforts to spread the idea across countries. In terms of design, those who are engaged in this effort reveal their biases. Thus, for example, public finance specialists largely concentrated on the shift of power from central to sub-national levels. Others, who were more interested in building up stakeholders' organizations and in making full arrangements for the exercise of choice with regard to 'exit, voice, and loyalty', were more concerned with participation, however ill-defined it might be, in the administrative process. So far, however, it has not been clarified whether those groups have to supplant the existing machinery or supplement it. As viewed on the ground, it is mostly the latter approach that is prevailing. There is already an established institutional and systemic framework, including citizen participation through their elected representatives at each level of government, and to that extent the democratic forces have full opportunities to exercise their muscle. Since the existing machinery continues to function, it is to be assumed that the new forms of association envisaged are essentially supplementary and primarily intended to serve the notion that there are avenues for ventilating their grievances. But a lack of definition of their role, and the absence of a legal framework that buttresses the role, make implementation of these idea difficult. As a consequence, the efforts, at a nascent stage, are best viewed as palliatives served to an agitating group(s). Admittedly, more remains to be done, to clarify the role of citizen participation, and the emerging executive–people relationship.

The limited experience also shows that decentralization and empowerment were seen and interpreted in a way as primarily affecting the central–state–local relationships. There are two other major aspects that have not been given the attention due. These relate to the relationships between the finance ministry and the spending agencies, and the relationships between policy making and operational levels within the spending agencies. From an expenditure management point of view these relationships are of crucial importance. It is alleged that powers—both in regard to policy formulation and implementation—have been excessively concentrated in the finance ministries, and as a consequence, spending agencies have been deprived of their voice and autonomy of action. This situation has been further exacerbated by the frequent resort to tactical decisions during the course of the fiscal year, that effectively change the course and content of fiscal policy. The determination of resource ceilings and the passage of fiscal responsibility legislation have burdened with the spending agencies additional responsibilities, without the requisite power. The continuing uncertainty in the release of funds has engendered an era of uncertainty, and in the process, the ability of governments to provide services without interruption has been seriously eroded. Similarly, the relationships between the policy making levels and implementation levels in the spending agencies have evolved heavily in support of the former. It is contended that the role of policy making levels has become so pervasive (intrusive from the viewpoint of the implementation levels) that the distinction between the two levels is more notional than real. To the extent that these structural aspects are not addressed, empowerment would remain a hollow concept, desirable but with little real impact.

Transparency and Accountability

The premises described above—a civic society, an active citizens' participation, a decentralized bureaucracy with well understood distinctions between policy formulation and implementation—require, at the very minimum, full transparency on existing policies and proposed policies and related intentions. Allow sunlight and there would be little problem with pests, which tend to grow mostly under cover of darkness. Similarly, allow illumination on government transactions and facilitate a regular dissemination of financial data, and governments would remain on guard, and to that extent many of the purposes of the civic society would be served. This is the underlying approach. Available history, shows that the demands for financial information from government had far narrower intentions and were intended primarily to reflect the requirements of the financial class.

In any event, fiscal transparency as a goal had been endorsed by the governing bodies of IFIs, in particular the IMF, and in pursuit of this goal, guidelines and manuals have been published (for a complete discussion on fiscal transparency, see Chapter 5 of this book), and efforts are made, through annual missions, to ensure that dissemination efforts continue. Moreover, international standards have been developed for the reporting of comparable public finance data for industrial and many developing countries. This effort is likely to gain greater strength in the future as more countries are covered. Meanwhile, manuals have been developed to report data on an accrual basis, although given the extremely limited number of countries that now have accrual accounting systems, the progress that remains to be made is far more significant than what has been achieved so far.

While the efforts will continue, primarily because the efforts are funded by the IFIs, which as yet have little shortage of them, or a reluctance to expand burgeoning bureaucracies, it is important that not too much faith is reposed on the magic or successful results of the publication of fiscal data. To a large extent, this is due to the design of the transparency system, and in part, due to the reliance of a society on the uses of fiscal data. Publication of annual fiscal data indicating the out-turn and intent had been a part of the administrative tradition of both colonies and independent democracies. Countries of the British Commonwealth adopted, largely through colonial instruction, the financial procedures of Whitehall, and the form and the content and the design of the oversight legislative committees have been replicated. Their actual day-to-day use is of course a different matter. It is only in the former centrally planned economics that there was very little dissemination of either budgetary or annual accounting data. In a few Middle Eastern countries, where a kind of monarchical system prevails, budgets continue to be treated as secrets and the public access is limited to select extracts of aggregate indicators. More recently, however, in both types of countries, more and more data are being provided in the annual *Statistical Abstracts* published by the countries. So far, the efforts to draw them out, a most desirable labour, have borne little fruit, although optimists (and the international bureaucracies are inveterate optimists) tend to believe that results may follow from repeated exertions, in the next decade.

The experience of dissemination of data shows that there still are major areas of darkness, and that governments often tend to be selective in the publication of data, concealing or manipulating data that do not put them in better light. Data on tax expenditures, and information on the extent of public ownership of commercial and financial institutions, continue to be very sketchy, as also the information on the fiscal activities of sub-national governments. Similarly, the coverage of contingent liabilities, despite the progress made, is yet to become comprehensive. More significantly, the information on expenditure implications of new policies or changes in existing policies continues to be simply and totally inadequate for the community's requirement to evaluate their desirability. In other words, the community has to take governments more on trust than on hard data. To the extent that the goal of publication of data is to enable members of the community to exercise their choice and voice, this has not yet been fulfilled. Indeed, the design of the system is too limited to permit this.

Most data, particularly of the detailed type, continue to be published on annual basis, and what is published on a more frequent basis may not permit viable conclusions, as in governments massive adjustments take place in the data in the last two months of the fiscal year. Furthermore, the requirements of the financial class, that is, those who invest in government paper, are such that they have an enormous thirst for more frequent data, more so in periods of crisis when the contagion effect may be taking place, and these requirements are not addressed in the design. Nor does the design address the needs of the common man who is interested in the services provided by governments, as there is little emphasis on these aspects. This is all the more surprising in view of the fact that the IFIs have always emphasized the delivery of services as one of the key objectives of expenditure policies.

Experience also shows that publication of data by itself may not address the purposes of legislators or the community, in the absence of oversight bodies. Traditionally, these were part of the tasks associated with legislative committees. In the proposals for reforms, nothing was devoted to the revival, strengthening or modification of legislative committees. Rather, it was assumed that the very process of illumination, and related emphasis on performance measurement, and citizen empowerment, would transform them into powerful instruments.

In addition to fiscal transparency, the objective of achieving improved governance also aid emphasis on accountability. Historically, the concept of accountability has expanded in scope and moved from strict and narrow financial accountability to programme accountability (the results achieved and the overall impact on society and the economy) and to fiscal accountability, that reflected on the aggregate stewardship of resources and the sustainability of performance. Though the concept had expanded, there was no corresponding increase specified in the tasks of the legislative or other committees. Rather, in the event, the concept of accountability was left without any specification or detailed exploration of the feasibility of designing an operational framework, presumably under the impression that the formulation of the goal, generally a shared one, was itself adequate. Some international agencies emphasized the due observance of the process, as if that by itself would render accountability.

As a consequence, there was no major advance in terms of developing new patterns of horizontal or vertical accountability. Some countries, particularly those in the transition group—which have, on their own and with the support received from IFIs, making assiduous efforts to strengthen their legislative operations with a view to getting the upper hand in the traditional control of purse—set up budget committees for the approval of the budgets, and supreme audit institutions on an independent basis, with provision for the placement of the audit findings before the legislatures. But very few of them have counterparts of the PAC whose tasks involved an explicit review of the accounts and audit findings and their submission to the overall legislature for approval. The legislation enacted in many countries envisages performance audit to be taken up by the supreme audit agencies. The progress in this regard has not been significant, as the primary requirement of performance budget is itself not in place. Where there is no budget system that is performance oriented, and where performance goals remain unspecified, it is difficult for audit agencies to undertake a performance audit. In most developing countries, as a part of improving overall accountability (as distinct from fiscal, programme, and financial accountability) and governance, anti-corruption bureaus were set up and selective legislation was introduced to bring the political class, such as ministers, into the legal fold of accountability. But these were a part of the cleansing effort aimed at reducing corruption and had a minimal effect on the the other forms of accountability.

There have been other developments which had a negative impact on the accountability movement. The new management philosophy, which placed a good deal of emphasis on transparency, autonomy, and accountability could, unwittingly, contribute to forms of unaccountable governments, and more significantly, to a discernible decline in legislative control. The management philosophy emphasized, following the traditional adage, let managers manage, that with a view to providing an effective management, task-oriented agencies should be established and that their managers should be held accountable for the results achieved for the funds allotted to them. It was assumed, however, that the accountability would be rendered through the traditional channels of legislative oversight. In the event, however, once the agencies were created they were also taken away from the traditional ambit of government and a new layer created, with as yet unspecified accountability channels. In practice, this meant that the agencies were one step remote from legislative control, as their operations and annual accounts and performance results were outside the lines of immediate enquiry of legislatures. Their reports were made available to the legislatures, leaving them with no form of specified discussion or approval by the legislature. Rather, much depended on the individual initiative of the legislators to raise matters of interest. This had the impact of making accountability diffuse and lacking in purpose.

Meanwhile, the administrative class had been engaging themselves, as is their proclivity, in adding ambiguity to policy making that it is increasingly becoming difficult to pinpoint responsibility. The more important issue, however, is whether the efforts and approaches discussed here had the impact of strengthening expenditure management systems and whether, in turn, they had a beneficial impact on the maintenance of financial stability, provision of services, and procuring of economies in expenditures.

3. Advancing Structural Reforms
Themes and Issues

CHANGING IDEAS AND INSTITUTIONS

Change has, over the years, induced further change, depending on the external situation and internal content. The change may not always have been in the desired direction (from the viewpoint of later historians) or yielded the much-needed results. It is conceivable, in retrospect, that some changes had unintended consequences. Some changes were a part of a deliberate programme of mutation, while others were contextual. In the process, expenditure management in public bodies moved to a place of pre-eminence that could not have been foreseen even a few decades ago. It has moved from a process of routine accounting of the dull financial transactions of a major household (usually the monarch) to the preparation of an annual budget with immense importance for the country and the international community, and with a good deal of potential for changing the lives (for good or bad) of the members of the community. From being restricted to the next financial year, the expenditure plans are now routinely prepared on a rolling basis for the medium term, and some are advocating the preparation of expenditure plans for more extended periods of up to two decades. It has gained increased importance as it moved from the routine allocation of resources to financing major wars, and to the allocation of resources that would, inter alia, provide commonly desired goods and services, within specified time, cost, and quantity schedules, while ensuring macro stability; from autonomous stance, the movement to the establishment of fiscal stability gained for it a major place in the overall economic policy of a country. It also changed from being an exercise performed in the inner sanctums of bureaucracy, to a major exercise in the functioning of a democracy. While the content, form, and scope of democracies may differ from one country to another, the importance attached to expenditure management continues to be permanent.

Although the system (as it came to evolve) has been in a state of perennial transition, some features of the change need specific recognition if only for the reason that they provide numerous yardsticks or points of departure for the changes to be made hereafter. It is clear that as society progressed from one stage to another, it also placed on the system, regardless of its built-in capacity, many new demands and tasks. Although many of these came to be attached to the framework, often as single objectives; the consequence is that expenditure management today, has come to acquire, cumulatively, several objectives, not always internally consistent or in a coherent form where trade-offs can take place between one objective and another. It is further recognized that expenditure management cannot be analysed in a vacuum; it needs to be viewed not as an independent variable but as an integral part of the economic context and political environment. The achievement of economic stability is a loaded concept, as is the goal of the pursuit of a prudent, viable, and sustainable fiscal stance. In other words, the objectives of expenditure management are derived from the goals of economic policy itself. Similarly, the political context is important too, in that expenditure management forms part of the total arsenal available to public bodies and to the public to achieve their own self-determined goals. For these two reasons, it is clear that the design of expenditure management cannot be stable despite reliance on a few fundamental elements, but has to be flexible, and more important, versatile enough to achieve the growing tasks. Given this inherent need for flexibility, the long traditions of expenditure management may not provide firm guidelines for future action.

As a part of the evolution of the system, many ideas have come to influence the content of expenditure management. The idea of accountability, that continues to be as current and as controversial as it was more than two millennia ago when it formed an important part in the political debate about the development of Athenian democracy, came from the politically dominated legislature. The idea of fiscal stability came from the inter-war experience and the consequent change in the role of government, while planning for economic growth came from the experience of centrally planned economies. Pursuit of fiscal sustainability although inherent in any situation, has come to acquire a place of its own, largely reflecting the momentous changes that took place during recent years. Integrating these ideas into the day-to-day working of the expenditure management system took the form of investment appraisal, ex-post evaluation of completed programmes and projects, introduction of accrual accounting to estimate the costs reliably, application of management accounting and activity-based costing, as well as inter-governmental accounting. All these are a variety of tools that have enriched expenditure management by substituting substance, objective, and verifiable analysis to intuitive, heuristic, personality-influenced approaches.

The effort to improve and be effective also contributed to the emergence of new institutions and to a major change in the power equations between the government and the legislature and within the government itself. Thus, independent budget agencies were set up, some outside the traditional finance ministries: in a few cases, with a view to bolstering up the declining legislative control, congressional budget offices were set up. With a view to strengthening the system of internal controls in spending agencies, an Office of Inspector General (who also functioned as an internal auditor) was set up. Elsewhere, an Office of Comptroller General was established within the government to oversee the extensive financial control arrangements. Accounting organizations were shored up in some countries through a separation of audit and accounting functions. Elsewhere, the payment systems were strengthened, and in a few countries the function was contracted out and even serviced out of the country as maintenance of computer operations became cheaper in a few developing countries. In a curious and somewhat ironical twist, this not only reduced the technological divide but also contributed to a growing dependence of industrial countries on technological services provided by developing countries. In a major country, the scope of the audit carried out by the General Accounting Office was expanded and the office was charged with the duty of carrying out independent supplementary audit. In almost all transition countries, supreme independent institutions were set up: China, however, offered a variation on this approach with an audit office that functions within the executive wing of the government. In several developing countries, reflecting the initial enthusiasm for centralized planning, separate planning organizations came up and quickly superseded the traditional finance ministries, gaining greater power in the allocation of resources, particularly, the resources provided by external donors. As this contributed to an avoidable schism in financial approaches, planning organizations were later merged with the finance ministries. However, as this became too unwieldy, planning was separated, followed by a cyclical arrangement of integration, separation, and integration. As the role of internal and external debt in the financing of government budgets grew, some governments shifted the debt negotiation and management process from central banks to finance ministries, while in a few cases, independent public debt offices were organized. In some countries, legislative control was sought to be supplemented, more so at the local level, by a form of client or user group participation, so that services could be better organized.

The endeavour, although not always consistent, reflects a search for modernity, a keenness to re-engineer and a deep desire to adopt. Regardless of the consensus on the need or content of modernity, it is a fact of life that the systems in government are, and have been, undergoing change. Whether the change has been fully achieved or not, whether it has been a success or a failure, change itself has become far more pervasive than at any time in the past. In a constant search or drive for an idiom, there was a settled belief that with organizational improvement, introduction and application of proper theory, adequate emphasis on the collection and dissemination of hard and reliable numbers, and associated objectives, there would be a change in the mindsets, and there would be a change from routine administration that laid more stress on compliance and the observance of specified processes, to a management style and structures that stressed the importance of results and improved delivery of services (the perspectives of economists, organizational experts, and sociologists differ widely on the course and extent of change; for a stimulating sociological perspective, see Geertz 1995). It is likely that most developing countries were drawn by the experience of industrial countries as what was an issue for the latter today, became, too quickly, an issue for the former. It is no longer the levels of technology, but modernity, defined in one form or another, that sets off governments, economies, societies, and countries, from one another.

EVALUATION

Given the extensive change, it is now time to evaluate whether the changes have reinforced the organizations and made governments more effective in their response to the changing demands, or whether the effort needs to be enlarged in scope and made more consistent. In a similar way, it is also necessary to evaluate the design of reform proposed and frequently financed by the IFIs so that there can be informed discussion on the future course of expenditure management. The need for such evaluation arises less because the reform has been completed, which it is not, and in many cases, it is in progress, but because of the fact that new issues are emerging all the time, straining the imagination and inventive genius of governments. Are these issues inherent in the design of reform or the implicit content of what is believed to be modernization? Are they to do with the implementation process? Are they linked to the capacity to utilize the benefits? These are some of the many questions that are continually raised. It is facile to draw provisional conclusions but there can be no substitute for substantive analysis.

There are several problems in the evaluation of designs of institutional development. For one, the issue is one of determining the reforms that are sought to be evaluated. As has been noted several times before, institutional development has been a part of overall development for several decades. The objective may not always have been well specified and the design always well delineated, but implicitly it has always been there. Notwithstanding this inherent difficulty, some reforms can be differentiated from the previous ones, as has been the case with the package of reforms that came to be sponsored by the IFIs during the last decade, that is, the 1990s and later. Even here, there is an additional difficulty in that the financial institutions did not carry out a specific package except by implication. For example, the European Bank for Reconstruction and Development (EBRD), in its approach to the transition economies, did not even specifically refer to expenditure management, which was subsumed in the broad rubric of 'governance and enterprise reform' (see IMF, *World Economic Outlook*, 2000, p.101). The structural reform as enunciated by it dealt mainly with financial markets and institutions, competitive policy, banking reform and interest liberalization, financial law, privatization, trade, and the foreign exchange system. The IMF placed more emphasis on fiscal transparency and accountability (the two areas that have been entrusted to it by the Committee of Ministers), but was also engaged extensively in the improvement of the expenditure management system through its programme support (to those countries that had use of IMF resources agreements with it) and through technical assistance activities.[1] The

---

[1.] For programme support activities, see IMF 2003. The IMF also issued guidelines on fiscal transparency that were later made into a manual.

World Bank was far more explicit in that it identified public expenditure reform as a main component of its programme in view of its implication for policy making, service delivery, accountability, and important links with poverty reduction. While it did not specify the components of expenditure management, it explained its philosophy in terms of strategic changes for the future (from its previous practices). Two of these changes are important. First, it indicated that there was a need for joint efforts by the World Bank and its member countries 'to understand and address the broad range of incentives and pressures both inside and outside of government—that affect public sector performance' (World Bank 2000, p. xiii), and second, 'we need to start with a thorough understanding of what exists on the ground and emphasize "good fit" rather than a one-size-fits-all notion of "best practice". And we need to work with our clients and other partners to develop and apply analytic tools to do this efficively' (World Bank 2000, p. xv). Despite the lack of specificity, the role and activities of these and other regional financial institutions lend themselves to broad descriptions, and on the basis of available records and expenditure, the components of expenditure management reform are summarized in Table 3.1. As a preliminary setting for further evaluation, the table also comments on the progress made. It is more than likely, as is always the case, that some countries may have made more progress than others and, therefore, the 'remarks' in the table should be taken as broadly indicative, rather than as reflecting the actual position in a country.

Table 3.1
Transforming the Expenditure Management Process—Themes and Implementation

Themes	Remarks on progress made in implementation
Rule of law and responsibility legislation	Greater recognition of the need for rules that have the potential of curbing some of the proclivities of decision makers. Response to fiscal responsibility legislation has been limited in developing countries except for a few Latin American countries. There is a fear that excessive resort to law, and quantification of targets in the form of law may lead to avoidable rigidity. In the Maastricht Treaty countries, there is a new demand for a comprehensive review of the limits on budget deficits and outstanding public debt.

(Contd.)

(Table 3.1 Contd.)

Medium-term planning	The practice of formulating medium-term rolling expenditure estimates is fairly common in most industrial and many developing countries. The concept of preparing medium-term fiscal plans is also gaining increasing acceptance. The nature of forecasts tends to vary considerably and ranges from linear projections to carefully planned expenditure adjustment in the medium term.
Risk management	Expenditure forecasting continues to be a high-risk exercise with many limitations. Internalizing macro and micro risks is as yet an unclear concept in many countries. Recognition of liabilities is largely restricted to the contingent type.
Annual review	Given the poor identification and preparation for potential risks, annual budgets continue to be prepared on a putative basis, with frequent changes made during the financial year. Uncertainty continues to loom large and decisions tend to be tactical than strategic. Austerity management tends to be ad hoc and even arbitrary.
Accrual budgeting and accounting	Offered as a major alternative to the existing cash-based system, the application of the system has received very limited response. Meanwhile, however, the application of computer technology is enabling governments and their agencies to maintain data with reference to a variety of bases, including recording of transactions on a commitment basis: supplementary systems such as cash management are enabling them to estimate the lags between commitments and payments. As yet there is no acceptance of the need for maintaining depreciation provisions in government accounts.
Performance orientation	The need for recognizing the performance dimension of expenditure has gained greater acceptance. But the implementation of the idea, which formed a part of many programmes of budget innovations in the past, continues to be spotty even among industrial countries. Meanwhile, performance reporting is being developed as a separate but supplementary stream to the traditional accounts, in sectors such as health and education that have traditionally attracted the attention of donors.
Contracting out	The idea of promoting internal competition, and allowing agencies to contract out some of their services has gained greater acceptance. There is also the view that the gains are too short-term oriented and may not be sustained over the medium term. The separation of funding from service provision is also

(Contd.)

(Table 3.1 Contd.)

	contributing to several issues in expenditure management that are, as yet, not resolved.
Decentralization and empowerment	It is recognized that excessive centralization in the name of macroeconomic stability may contribute to several organizational problems that need to be addressed. Meanwhile, the progress towards empowering local governments, government agencies, and citizen or client groups, has been extremely limited. In most cases, the objectives of empowerment remain to be articulated.
Transparency and accountability	International efforts to promote greater transparency in fiscal reporting have started yielding results. Comparable data in conformity with international standards are being reported by many countries. The focus of the reporting countries seems to be the 'investing class' and, as yet, there is little emphasis on performance or delivery of services. The concept of accountability, although routinely emphasized in all public pronouncements, remains to be clarified in terms of its scope and content.
Technology application	The traditional divide between industrial and developing countries in this regard has practically vanished. Many countries have installed electronic systems for most of their operations, and as a consequence, payments and related reporting systems have become fast, less expensive, and more convenient.

The second consideration relates to the applicability of the corporate model of evaluating success to governments, in that they too are organizations and as such have several common features. But there are several limitations too, and some of them are so fundamental that it is difficult to contemplate the application of the corporate model to government institutions. The corporate model involves the identification of the distinctive capabilities of the company, matching markets to capabilities, sustaining and appropriating a competitive advantage, and adding value to the operation. The bottom line approach is to measure the value added in terms of current profits and shareholder return (for a discussion of this model, see Kay 1995). Admittedly, the operations of the government are very different, and there is no bottom line such as shareholder return or value added, although in some cases, the achievement of a current account surplus (primary surplus) in the government budget is viewed as a case of a government successfully emerging from an economic crisis. But that would not be a sufficient basis for the evaluation of government institutional development. Therefore, other criteria need to be applied. In the event, the criteria developed by Putnam (1993) have a good deal of relevance. With a view to ensuring that the assessment is neither whimsical nor impressionistic, he advocated that any assessment should have four features: (i) it should be comprehensive and reflect the diverse operations of governments; (ii) it should be internally consistent in that the evaluation must be alert for signs of 'multidimensionality'; (iii) it must be reliable and volatility should be extremely limited; and, (iv) it must relate to the objectives of the protagonists, and alien standards unrelated to the aspirations of the local community should be separated. These four principles too are not easy to apply, and in the case of expenditure management two major difficulties emerge. These relate to reliability and to the objectives of the constituents. In the former, the aim is to distinguish the temporary factors from the more enduring ones, as Chester Barnard called them, a long time ago.[2] But the separation of this factor and the assessment of its unique contribution to the eventual outcome in the performance of an organization is an extremely complex and a formidable task. In a similar fashion, ascertaining the views and judgements of the members of the community requires the conduct of opinion surveys. Expenditure management has thus far been a subject which remained largely arcane, and the understanding of the public of the processes and the administrative ethos of expenditure management is, at best, rudimentary. The community has a slightly better understanding of the economics of expenditures in terms of the sacrifice they entailed and the benefits conferred. This veil of ignorance has not been a matter of choice for the community. Rather, the main contributing reason is the reluctance of the bureaucracy to share it with the public, and to make it an issue of public debate. For these reasons, Putnam proposed that evaluation be undertaken in terms of (i) policy processes; (ii) policy pronouncements; and (iii) policy implementation. Information on all these aspects is available largely from financial institutions, and very little from the country authorities: to that extent we have very little option but to rely on the reports of the promoters and financiers, whose point of view may be different from those of the aid-receiving countries, with

---

[2] The term used by Barnard was 'endurance'. Barnard was more concerned with the forces that come into play when individuals make a collective effort through an organization. See Barnard, 1938, p. 28.

the distinct possibility of some reporting bias.

The reports of the IFIs are both of a general type and, in some cases, deal specifically with expenditure management. Reporting four years ago, the World Bank (2000, p. xv) stated that its performance in public sector management was weak and that weak governance, in general has contributed to misguided resource allocation and resource utilization. It also found, not for the first time, that World Bank interventions do not adequately address institutional concerns and that the mixed performance in institutional development promoted by it is to be found across 'virtually all sectors'. While admitting that its public sector management loans have traditionally been weak, it sought to redirect its own energies in more constructive ways. But the findings that only a low rate of satisfactory outcomes had been achieved, and that the programmes reveal in many cases 'a mixed record of quality', show that the progress achieved is far too little and that much remains to be done. The experience with respect to transition economies, where more concentrated and concerted efforts were made by the IFIs, was no better. Reporting in 2002, the World Bank noted that in several transition countries there had been a capture of the state by narrow vested interests, which modified policy to their advantage, often at a high social cost and that the discipline of hard budget constraint had not been effective. The main disconcerting feature of the experience was 'the diminished state capacity to provide public goods', and overall 'weak public sector management'. Specifically in regard to expenditure management, major progress remained to be made in the control of financial risks arising from contingent and other liabilities (see World Bank 2002, p. 12). In a similar vein, but in a more honest admission, the IMF noted that 'the importance of institutional reform was recognized at the beginning of the transition, but in practice it was given too little attention relative to macroeconomic developments by both policymakers and advisors alike, probably because the difficulties of these reforms had been underestimated and there was a lack of experienced personnel (IMF 2000, *World Economic Outlook*, p. 120) and went on to emphasize the need for continued fiscal reform, focusing on the key areas such as improving fiscal transparency and accountability, continuing expenditure policy reform and reforming fiscal federalism arrangements, or virtually the whole fabric of expenditure management. The situation appeared to be no better in those countries that had use of resources arrangements with the IMF. In a report published in 2003, the IMF noted that 'fiscal balances on average did not improve throughout the first two years of arrangement' and that 'excess expenditure as a share of GDP was the most frequent cause of the deficit'. It added, 'the evaluation results suggest that *slow progress in implementing structural and institutional reforms in the past puts limits on the quantity of fiscal adjustment* that can be achieved by a program in the short run' (emphasis added). As a consequence of this recognition comes the usual plea that 'a greater emphasis on structural reforms relative to the establishment of detailed quantitative targets will ultimately enhance the ability of fiscal system to achieve more durable adjustments and handle shocks in the future' (IMF 2003). In short, the evidence provided by the financial institutions shows that the reform in expenditure management did not have any discernible effect on the pursuit of macroeconomic policies, and may have unwittingly contributed to fiscal slippages, and stood in the way of enduring institutional development. This is not to say that there was no improvement in areas such as the protection of social expenditures, although evidence does not suggest that this protection has been accompanied by improved delivery of services.

FACTORS CONTRIBUTING TO STAGNATION OR FAILURE

Success, like spring crocuses, can hardly wait to emerge into the open. With the first burst of sunlight, it tries hard to emerge and stay in the open. Failure, on the other hand, can hardly be concealed. Even when there is considerable reluctance to reveal it, like a gas leak it will start nauseating people and they need no additional equipment to smell it. In much the same way where institutional reform is successful, it will soon start, with or without the assistance of financial institutions, getting replicated elsewhere. Where there is a failure, there will be few voluntary takers. The important question is why, with the substantial financial and technical help provided by the international institutions, the effort has not been as successful as it should have been. There are several reasons of which some have been identified by the institutions themselves, and it is appropriate that those are considered first.

First, the World Bank concedes that during the first decade of its history, development was primarily viewed as a technocratic change. Implicit in this view was the ieda that the world of institutional development was a stable one and all that was needed was to establish new institutions, such as audit in the transition economics, where they were lacking, introduce relatively new operational systems such as medium-term expenditure planning or evaluation after the completion of projects and programmes, and where necessary, introduce or update the technological infrastructure of the administrative system. In the process, the design of improvement became too simplistic, ignored the dynamic changes in institutional behaviour, and more important, reflected the rules of the game already embedded in the administrative process. In many cases the embedded rules have been there for too long and have become ingrained into the lives of those working there, and permanent fixtures of their approaches. Technology was a new tool of convenience but it did not materially alter the rules of the game or the policies. Even if, for the sake of argument, it is assumed that the countries welcomed the new package of improvement of expenditure management summarized in Table 3.1, and implemented it both in compliance of the spirit and the word of the agreement, the benefits were too short-term oriented (such as the reduction in the size of the government's work force, through re-engineering and introduction of compulsory or voluntary retirement schemes) and the core question of the continuing need to moderate the rate of growth of expenditure continued unabated. To some extent, the different elements of the package contributed to contrary pulls. Performance budgeting and changing social priorities such as education and preventive health maintenance came to be supply driven, and the overall expenditure pressures continued to grow without relief.[3]

Second, the World Bank relied, to a far greater extent than proved prudent and beneficial, on what it perceived to be models of 'best practice'. In expenditure management, the best practice, in the World Bank's parlance, referred to the experience of New Zealand, which in a radical departure from its previous practice of benign neglect of institutions, introduced a variety of reforms based on the precepts of public economics and corporate practice. Even as New Zealand was evolving its system and was engaged in continuous refinement, the IFIs created a bandwagon effect by proclaiming, much too early and without the usual consensual validation that was needed, the practices of New Zealand as the best ones that could be replicated in other developing countries. Not surprisingly, it turned out that the answers in terms of

[3]. This and the following discussion is based largely on the publication, World Bank 2000, p. 17–18.

the best practices were the best fits for local needs. The pullback from the best practice bandwagon took much time (and a good deal of consultant payments) before it realized that the 'perfect' is the enemy of the 'good', and that the search for a best fit was more appropriate. What is ignored in this process of self-discovery is the fact that the World Bank bestowed the title of 'best practice' without an assessment of the alternatives or an evaluation of ground requirements. It is possible that this experience also contributed to a serious erosion of the credibility of IFIs, which would have been greater had it not been compensated by the financial muscle of the institutions and the absence of any alternatives.

Third, there has been far too much reliance on interaction with small groups of interlocutors in aid-receiving countries, in designing the package of expenditure management reform. For the most part, it was discussion and agreement with central ministries such as finance and planning and a few spending agencies. In the process, it became a localized discussion between specialists from financial institutions and vested interests at the receiving end. Governments are not monolithic but reflect a conglomeration of different interests. Limiting the discussions with traditional whipping boys such as finance did not prove to be useful or right. Other major partners like the legislatures, the political class, and the clientele groups were ignored. This also happened to be the case with the reform of financial institutions promoted by the IMF. The reform was essentially viewed as an administrative exercise aimed at establishing or, alternatively, strengthening the existing regulatory mechanism, and hardly any role was envisaged for the legislative oversight bodies. As a consequence, no consultations were held with the representative institutions. An inevitable reaction in such a context is either total indifference to the reforms proposed or resort to subversion mechanisms. Both features figured prominently in the aftermath of the introduction of reforms.

The factors identified by the World Bank, more honest and forthcoming than some others, provide only a partial list. There are several other factors operating at the ground level that have also contributed, and continue to contribute, to a relatively poor implementation and even meagre results. To complete the perspective, these factors also need consideration. The package of reforms, which partly shared the characteristic of one-size-fits-all, was essentially seen as being externally prodded rather than being internally stimulated. In some case, the reforms were skyjacked by the local oligarchs or the traditional centres of power to consolidate their own power, rather than engage in decentralization. The reforms also contributed to the establishment of enclaves, and in developing countries, where an annual trip to Washington means a lot to one's career, the packages helped the advancement of a few careers, which were viewed with some concern, and in due course the unleashing of opposition forces, by the other groups. In a few cases, the authorities issued the necessary instructions in compliance with the conditionality agreed with the donors, but the changes at the ground level were minimal and without any profound or enduring impact on the system.

It also happened that many countries were expected to implement these reforms even as they were going through an economic crisis. In such a context, when too many steps were expected to be taken, governments concentrated their efforts on the major ones, and the areas that had no formal or informal lobbies other than the IFIs tended to be neglected. Further, the elements of the package (other than reduction in staff, which was a policy measure and only partially an institutional development measure) appeared to have no relevance to their immediate problem of reducing expenditures. The systemic measures aimed at providing clarity and improved division making processes. In the event, continued reliance was placed on traditional approaches to austerity management, which was at cross purposes with those proposed. It appeared at one time that with each step taken to advance the cause, the practical effect was that of a setback by two steps. What were the ground realities then and how they were being addressed remained questions awaiting more conclusive answers.

Finally, the issue was one of the design of improvement itself. It was at best incomplete, simplistic, and appropriate for a static rather than a dynamic environment. Its core emphasis was on the form rather than the substance of day-to-day financial management. Emphasis on law, or preparations of medium-term plans without addressing the root causes and many of the complexities, and a selective introduction of an archaic treasury system, were less than adequate to address the needs. These were tools that sought to enhance analytic approaches, while what was needed, or so it appeared, was 'interpretive thinking' that emphasized the 'larger frame around a situation, to understand it in its many contexts, to appreciate the deeper and often paradoxical causes and consequences' (Farson 1996, p. 43). But the 'collective think' that emerged more to reflect the Washington consensus did not explore, as will be demonstrated in the following discussion, these aspects. As a consequence, the efforts did not prove adequate, or did not yield results that were commensurate either with the intent or the general hope. Meanwhile, temporary distortions from partial implementation and partial technocratic formulations are already affecting the financial management systems in an adverse way, despite the fact that it was intended to foster new and creative approaches. The emphasis on hierarchical organizations led to a decline of legislative powers, and to a postponement of participatory approaches to decision making, and more importantly, to the way in which people are treated. An unfortunate paradox of the effort is that the ministries of finance and the spending agencies, which were to undergo most of the change, may have, at least for the present, changed the least.

The alternative is not to give up but to address the key problem of the design itself and make the remedy a viable and enduring force. Re-engineering the design requires an in-depth consideration of several factors, which are arranged here in convenient clusters to facilitate discussion. Initially the boarder themes are considered, followed by a discussion of the more technical themes.

Democracy and Expenditure Management

Experience conclusively proves that expenditure management has a unique place in functioning democracies, in that it enables the determination of the relative roles of the state and the public sector, the range of goods and services that the community desires to be provided by the state, the pattern of financing it envisages for the provision of the services, and the efficiency with which the services and goods are provided. This determination may take place through the representative institutions established for the purpose or through a direct revelation of voter preference in selected cases. Democratic functioning in an open society involves the recognition of all voices. Indeed, as Professor Karl Popper observed several years ago, there is a moral obligation to listen to arguments and to respond where actions by one individual or group affect another individual or a group. To facilitate this process of ascertaining voters' preferences and to institutionalizing arrangements where the arguments could be made and answered, democracies have established governments with separate wings for executive, legislative, and judicial affairs. Although the relative roles of each differ, conventionally, the issues relating to expenditure management were sought to be analysed and resolved through the specification of the respective functions and tasks of each wing of government. Following tradition, primacy in the process has been placed on the legislature, which is entrusted with the financial control of the purse. Hence, the approach that no money may be spent or raised except with the permission of the legislature. The pivotal role in this process is played by the annual budget, which has become the central expression of public policy and thus the basis of consideration, negotiation and bargaining, and approval by the legislature. But the roles and functions of legislatures and associated institutional arrangements differ from one country to another. In this context, and particularly in facing the question of reforming the public expenditure management system, two issues have arisen. Are the existing institutional arrangements relating to the exercise of power by the legislatures adequate? If not, what could be done to strengthen their role? The latter assumes implicitly that there has been a decline in legislature control and that more efforts are indicated for restoring the balance between the bureaucracy and legislature. Answers to these questions require a more detailed probe into the institutional arrangements available in democracies to permit and to organize public opinion into meaningful expenditure management approaches.

The most common form of government now, it is readily admitted, is democracy. The number of countries moving to the democratic form of government has increased and is growing by the day. But what is democracy is itself an open question in that, while all concede that it is a process where each individual has a right and an opportunity to express opinion, the forms of democracy and the associated institutional arrangements differ. For purposes of discussion, however, certain features of democratic functioning may be identified. First, the meaning of democracy as Bernard Crick has reiterated, is 'an essentially context concept'.[4] Second, despite the differences in the use of the term 'democracy' and the development of its content, it is best perceived as a congruent arrangement between democracy as a set of values and democracy as a set of institutional arrangements, particularly in regard to expenditure management. It should be admitted at this early stage of discussion that the achievement of this congruence has been most difficult, and continues to be a major and as yet not a fully resolved issue. Third, as an extension, it should be realized that democracy is a

[4.] See Crick 2002, p. 1. Parts of the following discussion are based on this eminently readable book.

doctrine, an institutional arrangement, and a type of behaviour. Each organization spawns its own set of values that in due course become the prominent characteristics of its culture and day-to-day behaviour. The tension in a democracy, another continuing feature (which frequently takes it to the point of continuing instability and frontiers of fiscal anarchy), arises, to a large extent, because of the fact that these three may not always go together. In particular, the obligation to participate, and the perception of duty that form a part of democratic behaviour may differ, and participation may not always be followed by the accompanying obligation of sacrifice and performance of duty. Fourth, because of these inherent features, good government has come to be variously defined. While initially, it was equated with representative government, justice, equality, liberty, and human rights, now a good government, from the point of view of expenditure management, is viewed as one that is fiscally prudent, stable, and sustainable, and where governments are transparent and fully accountable to the representative institutions, and where the rule of laws is the primary feature. Thus, the concept has been going through an enlargement, reflecting the changing modes of society.

The maintenance of democratic institutions and the pursuit of a democratic way of life could have other effects that are contrary to the intent. They may lead, in some cases, to the tyranny of the majority, and the rule by many may quickly translate into another form of functioning anarchy. The competing forces contribute to tensions and conflicts that were long ago recognized by Machiavelli, who believed that since the power of the people was great, it should be harnessed by being given a share in the balanced constitution. The theme since then has been one of maintaining balance through a creation of proper consensus of values, and the need for more effort in a democracy to manage the tensions. J.S. Mill and de Tocqueville took particular care to examine the problem of running a government in a democratic framework. Mill recognized the 'characteristic infirmities' of the system, and the effects of selfish mismanagement by a jobbing ... local oligarchy', and argued for a balance between individual liberty and the working of a democratic government. De Tocqueville, who saw the problem in absolutes rather than in relative terms, recognized the emergence of a State that is 'absolute, minute, regular, provident and mild', more like the authority or patronage of a parent. It was up to the State, in the exercise of its power, to be highly centralized and entrenched, but nevertheless the main arbiter of happiness of the community. De Tocqueville also saw the benefits of diversity, and in his framework assigned great importance to the formation of voluntary associations and build up, what is known in contemporary discussion as the social capital, the lubricant that would maintain a balance and become a countervailing power by, among other activities, defending their rights against the periodic encroachments and incursions into the common liberties of the community.

The important feature of a democracy then is the regular interplay between groups, vested interests, the state, and individual rights. The issue for consideration is how is decision making performed in a democracy, particularly in a context of entrenched interests, and how power is shared and exercised among the executive and legislative wings. These aspects have been analysed, over the years, by many economists and others, and several schools of thought have been advanced for consideration. There is, however, a fundamental distinction in these theories, which needs to be noted at the outset. Economists devoted their attention to the identification of the welfare function, the difficulties in that identification and the institutional arrangements appropriate for the implementation of the welfare function. The other group, largely reflecting the views of political scientists, dealt with the practical working of the legislatures and how the working of party discipline and caucuses tend to affect the approaches of the legislatures. That stated, it is appropriate to briefly consider the views advanced by both school of thought. While none of them are conclusively deterministic, they are helpful in illuminating, even if partly, this somewhat dark area.

The first step was the recognition, common to both approaches, that market functioning would not by itself provide welfare to the community. To compensate for this market failure, the government intervenes and seeks to increase the overall level of satisfaction. Such a process requires the collection and aggregation of individual preferences, which are several and range from simplistic personal demands to grand designs for the community, and which are inherently incapable of being attained simultaneously. As the difficulty is deep rooted, it is suggested that the solution be imposed after being determined either by an oligarchy or by an enlightened soul of the type envisaged by Plato. The oligarchy substitutes its judgement for that of the political market, and this function has come to be vested in the finance ministries and associated agencies who have been entrusted the responsibility of formulating and 'imposing' solutions on the community. Since in a democracy there can be no imposition, the proposed solutions are then processed through the legislatures, after appropriate compromises, and reconciliation of conflicting interests, and the necessary legislation enacted then becomes obligatory for all to comply. Can a public entity behave differently from the individuals or associations that manage it? It is here that another school—Public Choice Theory—has gained attention during the last three decades, particularly in the light of endorsement by the neo-conservative movement. According to this theory, voters constitute the market, which is then cultivated by the political leaders by making promises and pursuing financial populism. In the process, the interests of the bureaucracy (which mainly seeks advantage in enlarging the size of each agency's budget), the requirements of the political class who wish to garner more budgetary allocations aimed at pleasing the electorate, and the business class, who stand to benefit substantially from the institutionalized propensity, keep emphasizing the need for higher expenditure, as each expenditure increment is equated as an increase in people's welfare. To control this proclivity, market forces would be far from adequate and, therefore, reliance should be placed on constitutional and legal mechanisms. If the welfare school's advocacy contributed to a strengthened bureaucracy, the Public Choice Theory contributed to the provision of a reinforced legal underpinning in the form of fiscal responsibility legislation, but in the final analysis, to the strengthening of the bureaucracy and the central agencies. In the case of the latter, it was an unintended consequence of the reforms introduced after the 1990s: even in the United Kingdom, where a good deal of emphasis was placed on citizens' rights, the creation of the task-oriented agencies as a part of the next steps programme, the deposition of the responsibilities of a type of devolutionary budgeting in the treasury, and the introduction of what was called a 'permanent revolution' of targets, audits, and proxy markets has, it is argued, contributed to the decline of public realm and to a highly centralized new bastion of major power in the form of the treasury.[5] However, there is no gainsaying the fact that the Public Choice Theory offered an alternative that stressed the importance of citizens' preferences, and their flexibility to adjust their platforms, and also placed reliance on legal enactments to ensure that governments do not deviate from the

---

[5.] For a polemical discussion of these aspects, see Marquand 2004 and Sampson 2004. Sampson argues that the provision of public services has moved into the hands of anonymous and unaccountable financial institutions.

mandates they received from the community. In practice, however, citizens may not be fully aware of the ramifications of their preferences, may not be fully informed about macroeconomic implications, and more significantly, may not be able to unbundle programmes and abandon them in preference to emerging needs. It is necessary to recognize that most budget systems do not as yet offer the information needed by the common citizen to a decision on what programmes should be considered for additional allocation of resources. The guidelines on fiscal transparency place greater emphasis on the aggregate fiscal picture than on the relative merits of different and competing programmes. In reality, decision making may be hijacked by the organized vested interests, and as a consequence, public interest may suffer, as it is often different from what the public, particularly the organized segments, may be interested in. In the process of negotiation and compromise, policy stances and programmes may emerge that may be contrary to the principles of economic analysis and even the broader interests of the community. The Public Choice Theory has helped in creating greater awareness of the role of public institutions, on the interaction between citizens and institutions, and both of them in relation to what is deemed to be the democratic way of life, as well as the importance and limitations of the administrative instruments, for example the budget, selected for serving the needs of the community.

Two other theories selectively shed some light on the way in which the public reacts in the determination and provision of public goods. The game theorists hold the view that since a public good can be enjoyed by everyone regardless of his or her contribution there is also very little incentive for anyone to contribute to the provision of a public good. As a consequence, too little may be produced and the overall welfare may decline. Similarly, where collective action is involved, everyone may stand to benefit if all go on a strike at the same time, but those who raise the strike banner first may risk betrayal, as everyone waits to benefit from someone else's foolhardiness. These aspects illustrate how rational institutions and individuals can produce outcomes that are, in certain situations, far from rational, and to that extent have an impact on the way in which problems are resolved by them. In general, they also emphasize the role of the third party—a major coercive force such as the State—to enforce comity among the various groups. In the approaches of the Game Theory, however, the third-party enforcement cannot contribute to a stable equilibrium in which no one has an incentive to alter his behaviour. But even the protagonists of this approach recognize that the non-cooperative behaviour is less frequent than would be the case, as non-cooperation cannot be sustained when players are engaged in repeated games. On the other hand, the theory is helpful in enabling recognition of the forces on the other side and how they stand in the way of the achievement of common good. Also, it needs to be stated that political schools of thought have, from the beginning, partly in recognition of this problem, stressed the importance of the association of the community with decision making that affects its life, and to the development of trust. From an expenditure management point of view, Game Theory is helpful in recognizing that there would be agreement on services to be provided for common use from someone else's budget, while each agency would play games to protect its own share of resources.

The Theory of Transaction Costs, which like the Public Choice Theory has gained importance during recent years, is based on the idea that people act in their own interest and that a broad range of contractual relationships between the buyer and the provider can be arranged with mutual agreement. The approach is likely to be helpful in recognizing the separation of the services that are best provided by the state and its organizations and the services that can be provided by the market through contractual arrangements. The implicit idea is that organizations have a variety of problems that tend to limit their usefulness and that contractual relationships can be a useful alternative. Working backwards, it offers a basis, in part, for the allocation of resources and for the determination of services that can be directly provided by the state and those that can be arranged through market contractual agreements.

There have been other theories that deal less with the allocation of resources and more with the type of institutional arrangements that may be needed in a democratic society. Two of these may be briefly recapitulated here. The first relates to the Agency Theory, which is primarily drawn from the experience of the corporate world and is based on the idea that the relationships between individuals are in the nature of exchange relationships that take the form of implicit or explicit contracts through which one of the parties performs some tasks for payment by the other party. The former, who provides the services, is known as the agent and the latter is known as the principal, and hence the epithet, Principal–Agent Theory. It is suggested that in government there are a series of levels in which the buyer–provider relationships operate. The legislature buys services from the cabinet or the government for which moneys are appropriated by the former. This relationship is generally based on an undertaking and explicit understanding of each other's tasks and responsibilities, both of which are in turn drawn from a constitution, which a society formulates for itself to regulate its own conduct. In a parliamentary system, the ministers in government may not receive any sanctions even when there has been a contractual failure, for their conditions of service are drawn from other conventions. Even in congressional systems, where the members of the cabinet are appointed by the President, little action can be taken by the legislature. In New Zealand, when the financial management reforms were introduced in 1989, the Principal–Agent Theory was invoked to explain the buyer–provider relationship between the legislature and ministries. In reality, however, apart from the metaphorical application, there was little or no change in institutional arrangements, and no penalties were either envisaged or set out for performance failure. In fact, the only committee, the PAC of the legislature, which has always been charged with the task of reviewing and approving the fiscal accounts of the government, continued its work as before. There are two other levels of agency relationship that arise in a government structure; the first is between the central, state, and local governments where a task which is legally within the ambit of the central government and is performed by the lower level of government is funded and reimbursed by the former. This, in fact, has been known all along, long before the application of the Principal–Agent Theory, as an agency function, but has been carried out without an explicit legal contract. Governments enter into legal contracts only with non-government entities, and not with government agencies as all of them draw their powers of operation from the same chief executive. The other level of operation is between the policy making level, for example, a ministry or a department, and an agency responsible for policy implementation. As has been repeatedly pointed out before, the distinction between these two formal levels is not always sustainable. A problem of what is perceived to be at the implementation levels, quickly becomes a policy issue, and engulfs not merely the principal department but the whole government. These relationships tend to be dominated by uncertainty that cannot always be captured and contained in the form of a legal contract, and if contained, may be valid only for a short term. It is presumably for this reason that public service contracts, more a form of improved accountability, have become an annual feature in the United Kingdom. It is a form of performance budgeting that works in two ways: as a basis for the allocation of resources and as a statement of intended performance. However, the form of contract is a rather general one, more of a political document, than a legal one. It can be argued that the introduction of performance budgeting is easier, as it proceeds on the existing conventions of trust and mutual responsibility, rather than an extended legal contract system whose legality is severely suspect. The more important question is whether this strengthens the legislative control and exercise of its oversight function. The answer is that it may not add to the power of the legislature, particularly when there is no institutional change in its working. Rather, there is an impression that it has gained a new weapon of control. In reality, this is a very soft instrument and is far from being one that can enhance the legislative function.

Another approach, which is somewhat rooted in the experience of Latin American countries, has come to be advanced during recent years. This recognizes that fiscal outcomes are strongly influenced by the nature of budgetary procedures in operation (a tautological interpretation), and since the approaches of the legislature (which, it is believed, always wants more expenditures) and its activism tend to yield dysfunctional results, it may be far more appropriate to strengthen the hierarchical rather than the legislative organizations in governments. The approach, even in its nebulous form, is based on ideas that are highly provocative and debatable. It believes that the ministries and the civil servants, as distinct from the groups of legislators, would be far more prudent and conscious of fiscal discipline. The distinction is itself questionable as, according to the Public Choice Theory, the bureaucrats, ministers, and the business community constitute an iron triangle to promote their collective interests. To that extent, there are possibilities that their interests are common and all three groups stand to benefit collectively from the actions of government. Further, it ceases to be a democratic way of life when the legitimate functions of the legislature are transferred to the executive wing, and a basis for fiscal despotism is established in the form of a strong, centralized, monolithic, leviathan finance ministry. The experience of other countries shows that the initiatives for expanded policies and increasing expenditures have come from the executive wing. In the Westminster style of democracies, as noted previously, no initiative can be taken by the legislature in money matters.

The theories, singly or collectively, do not offer a viable framework for the functioning of a legislature in a democratic polity. Inevitably, in that context, the practice of the legislature in regard to public policy and, more specifically in regard to public expenditure, came to be developed largely through a historical process. The rights of legislatures vary in that the initiative rests with the executive in the Westminster type of democracy, while in a congressional system the powers are divided, through a process of checks and balances, between the executive and the legislature. There are several countries, particularly in the Middle East, where legislatures have a very limited role, largely limited to a debate, and members of the legislature may not have the right to vote. In countries that have a one-party system, as in China, the People's Congress, particularly at the national level, is more in the nature of an approving body rather than a deliberative one, where the requirements of departments are voted upon by the members of the Congress. At the provincial and county level the Congress takes a more detailed look into the proposed expenditures, depending on the situation, but a considerable degree of allocative power is exercised by the General Secretary of the party at each level.

Broadly, the powers of the legislature in regard to expenditure management can be analysed in terms of macro and micro approaches, and pure local interests of the members of the legislature. These approaches tend to differ from the pre-budget stage to the actual implementation of the budget, and the post-budget stage. In all these phases, the intent is to enable the legislatures, within the powers allotted to them, to exercise an oversight on government operations. These powers are enumerated in Table 3.2. In addition to these, there is a practice in a few countries, as yet limited to Ecuador, India, and the Philippines, where each member of the legislature is appropriated an amount (in India, it is Rs 200,0000 per year per member) to be spent, subject to the usual financial process controls in government, on programmes and projects of local interest, at the discretion of the legislator. While the amount is not significant, it provides a notional facility to members to involve themselves in local matters.[6]

In both types of arrangements, proposals on new services and policies require the approval of the legislature. In the Westminster system a good deal of ground work takes place before a proposal is submitted to the legislature and it is understood all along that legislative approval for the

---

6. It may be parenthetically noted that nearly one-third of the amount provided remains, according to the audit reports in India, unspent at the end of the fiscal year and is lapsed.

Table 3.2
Legislative Control of Expenditures

Category	Westminster type of system	Congressional system	Other types
Macro level			
Medium-term goals Level of annual deficit Level of outstanding debt	Initiative for legislation lies with the executive wing. Legislature cannot take initiative in money matters. These goals have come to be approved as a part of fiscal responsibility legislation in some countries.	Proposals may be initiated by the executive or the legislature. In either event, there are checks and balances such as the presidential veto. In most cases, agreement may be reached. In some countries there are overarching pieces of legislation that govern these aspects and thus impose limits on the executive.	The role of the legislature may be limited to approval without dissent. In some cases they may be merely informed and no legislation may be necessary.
Micro level (Annual)			
Permanent legislation	In most cases, annual approval of the legislature is needed. But some categories, such as social security payments and some subsidies may be left open-ended or uncapped.	Congress may enact entitlements on permanent basis. To that extent there are no annual controls. In some cases, trigger clauses may be provided that spur a review of the revenue position.	Very little role.
Sunset legislation	The duration of the validity of the legislation may be specified, thus triggering a periodic review of the need for continuing the progress.	This has become a common feature of the congressional system. It is a power that congress grants to itself to review expenditure progress periodically.	
Extra-budgetary funds	Unless specified as a part of original legislation these are exempt from legislative review.	Depending on the initial legislation, Congress may or may not provide for annual financial review.	
Government autonomous agencies	Although their primary source of revenue may be dependent on government grants, their	This layer of government is generally beyond the scope of congressional purview.	

(Contd.)

(Table 3.2 Contd.)

	budgets are not subject to the approval of the legislature. The annual grants are subject, in principle, to legislative approval.		
Exempt categories of expenditure	Some categories such as debt, pay of the chief executive, and judiciary are charged but not voted.	The annual appropriations for debt repayment are not specifically subjected to legislative approval.	
Borrowing and repayment	In general, there are no limits that the legislature imposes in this regard except for the obligations stemming from international obligations, for example, the Maastricht Treaty. In this sphere, the power of the executive wing is virtually unlimited.	While repayment is not generally subject to approval, some countries (Peru, Philippines) placed limits on the annual payments made to external creditors during periods of financial emergencies. Borrowing is subject to annual limits approved by the legislature but this has not proved to be a serious impediment so far.	
Agency appropriations	These are mostly within the realm of the executive as a vote against the proposed appropriations is considered as a vote against government and a defeat may lead to a change in government. Legislature cannot increase the proposed outlays but can reduce them. Powers of reapproprition are limited and may require legislative approval.	This forms the main part of the annual legislation and the work programme of the Congress. It has the power to increase, reduce, or change the direction of the proposed grant. Where expenditures are increased, Congress is responsible for specifying the sources of financing.	No power.
Staff levels	This is a subject that is totally within the control of the executive.	Legislature may specify the staff and grade levels through legislation.	
Salary revisions	These require the approval of the legislature.	Require the approval of the legislature.	
Intra-fiscal year money flows	These are determined by the executive.	Depending on the agencies the Congress may specify the amount of annual appropriation to be spent during each question.	

(Contd.)

(Table 3.2 Contd.)

Protected categories of expenditure	In the event of a financial crisis, ad hoc cuts may be imposed by the executive and no legislative approval is needed. What the legislature approves is eligibility for spending but funding is not obligatory.	The legislation provides priorities and the sequence of sequestration. Austerity management is a joint responsibility of the executive and the legislature.
Outsourcing	Agencies are subject to rules formulated within delegated power.	Legislation may (and indeed has) place(d) limitations on the activities funded by the budget and on the extent of outsourcing. Similarly, priorities in the award of contracts (as a part of overall affirmative action) may also be specified.
Guarantees	Subject to limitations proposed by the executive.	Subject to limits enacted by the legislature.
Redemption of contingent liabilities	Subject of decision making within the executive.	Subject to approval by the Congress which may on its own initiative place limits on such redemption.

Post-Budget activities

Annual Accounts	Annual accounts required to be approved by the legislative committees and on their recommendations by the legislature.	Submitted to the Congress. Their consideration either by the committees or by the houses is not obligatory.
Annual performance	A recent practice: these are submitted for the information of the legislature and require no action by it.	Are submitted for the information of the committees and the houses.
Special investigations	During the course of the year the legislature may, through its committee, undertake or cause to be undertaken, special investigations into specified activities.	The committees may take up direct investigation or may ask the audit or independent evaluation agencies to take up special investigations into some transactions.

most part is a formality. The issue is debated, opinions are expressed freely but mostly on party lines, and in the end, the proposal is approved in the submitted form. In the Congressional Forum, the proposal may come from either branch, but is deliberated by both Houses, and emerges in a form that is acceptable to all. In the Westminster style, the legislative function is formal, and functionally may not be of much consequence, as each issue becomes one of confidence in the government, with the potential of a change of power looming large on the horizon, if the vote goes against the government. In the Congressional system, the fear is that the individual legislator may bring initiatives that contribute to higher expenditures, which while providing a service to the community, may also prove to be highly destabilizing. The enthusiasm to do public good, therefore, needs to be held in check or tempered by a recognition of the potential impact of those proposals on the fiscal health of the community. For this reason, in some countries, notably the United States and others like Italy (which have switched over to the practice of the United States), the legislative wing functions under an omnibus ceiling on total outlays that is believed to be in conformity with the available resources. There are other differences as well between these two types in regard to borrowing as well as post-budget operations. There are also significant differences between the two approaches in the budget execution phase and post-budget execution phase. In the Congressional system, the legislature can, in a broad way, impose conditions that ring-fence the operations, and the Congress has powers to undertake special investigations into policy questions whenever it is deemed necessary. In the Westminster style, such powers are restricted but they have the obligation to approve the annual accounts. At the end of the year, it often morphs into an annual ritual conducted more in a perfunctory way. In the congressional system, such action is more discretionary than obligatory.

In the light of the extensive experience of both systems, it is appropriate that the main issues are considered at this stage. To what extent is the legislative control effective under both systems? To what extent have recent reforms, particularly the new management philosophy, strengthened legislative controls? And what is the role of the people's voice in the functioning of the legislatures in the area of expenditure management? The evidence available suggests that whether under the adversarial style of functioning or under the legislative inquisitorial approach of the congressional system, control has not been particularly effective. In the former as well as in the latter, power is really in the hands of the mandarins of the bureaucracy. In the former, it is more open in that all the initiatives rest with the government; in the latter, it is more subtle and nuanced. In both cases, there are powers to undertake expenditures, without legislative approval, either on an emergency basis, which are then regularized ex-post-facto by the legislature or through the creation of extra-budgetary funds that may be totally outside the domain of the legislature. More significantly, the power of the executive in the Westminster style to create long-term liabilities and contingent liabilities is practically unlimited, in that borrowing does not require the consideration or the approval of the legislature. This partly explains the reason why governments in developing countries place more reliance on borrowing from IFIs. In reality, a middle-level executive in the government of a developing country can initiate and conclude an agreement with a development funding agency without involving the legislature at any point of the usually lengthy negotiation process. The IFIs have now a greater role in public policy management in many developing countries than members of the legislature. The executive wing also has more powers during the stage of budget execution as, in the Westminster style, the finance ministries engage in massive underfunding of approved programmes and to that extent, may pursue an agenda of their own different from the intent of the legislature. To appease the latter, new items of expenditure may be included in the budget, but they may also be starved of funds, on a regular bias. To that extent, austerity management has become, more often than not, a bureaucratic exercise. Even in Congressional systems, the President has powers to rescind programmes and projects, which may then be rejected by the Congress on its own initiative. If they are not explicitly rejected, the recessions become, on a lapse-of-time basis, legislatively approved and thus appropriately legitimized. If in the Westminster style, executive wings have to deal with a sterilized legislative system, in the Congressional system the sterilization process has taken place largely through its own actions. With a view to reducing the role of the bureaucracy, the legislatures in the Congressional system have enacted permanent, or nearly permanent (such as 99–year leases) legislation for major programmes. As a consequence, the programmes requiring annual approval by the legislature have been reduced. In an era of increasing expenditures, the paradox is that the Congress reduced its own role through permanent legislation and establishment of entitlement programmes. This has taken place despite the oft-repeated plea that legislatures need to be strengthened and the bureaucracies need to be restrained. There is, as yet, no effective restraint on the actions of the bureaucrats, and as yet, no adequate accountability framework that renders them fully accountable. Legislative functioning has become, whether deliberately or otherwise, a sideshow, an innocent annual folk-rite, contrary to their own wishes and contrary to the wishes of those who are keen to see the effective functioning of democratic institutions, and the establishment of a democratic way of life.[7]

The new management philosophy is intended more to strengthen the role of the managerial class and it is more as an afterthought that the emphasis on increased accountability has been added. The so-called new approaches have contributed to the creation of numerous task-oriented agencies, most of them at an arm's length from the legislature. In the process, governments have expanded in layers, while the legislative oversight provisions have been substantially whittled down. In their impact, the approaches have been regressive and have contributed to a widening gap between the legislature and the executive wing (for a discussion of these and related aspects, see Foster and Plowden 1996). On the other hand, there is also the view that legislators engage in voting that reflects the interests of lobbies. This view is, however, not always sustainable in that the legislators in the United States claim that with vested interests arrayed on both sides of the issue, they feel relatively free to cast their own votes as they think best (Bok 2001, p.7).

The experience of the legislature with expenditure management is clearly an important aspect that warrants a careful look into the suggestions made from time to time to strengthen their working and to enrol citizen participation in the whole process. Suggestions vary from country to country, and from those offered from time to time by the IFIs, and they range from the procedural to the constitutional aspects. In the former group there are those which are somewhat ahead of their time and some that have greater relevance at a more practical level. The first major suggestion relates, in this group, not to a further strengthening of the legislatures but to a substantial weakening. It is suggested, for example, mostly on the basis of the experience of Latin American countries and the Asian financial crisis in the late 1990s, that a separate national fiscal council may be organized to monitor the levels of debt and budgetary deficits. The implementation of this argument is rooted in the belief that, just as an independent central bank is considered an ideal arrangement, a similar non-political arrangement for fiscal policy would also be useful. There are, however, substantial

---

7. Some of the congressional procedures have been adopted, with some success, in the former Soviet bloc. For a discussion of the Russian experience, see Remington, 2001.

differences between a central bank and the requirements of fiscal policy formulation. The former is, among others, a regulatory agency and its role is far more limited than fiscal policy. In a democratic setting, the people should have the choice to make their own policies either directly or through their representative institutions, and that task cannot be ceded to an independent body: a movement of policy responsibility to a technical body robs the very essence of a democratic way of life. It is quite likely, as George Stigler pointed out a long time ago, that bodies which are created to avoid political interference and management may run the risk of being captured by other interests, including the industries they regulate. What is needed, on the other hand, is a series of efforts that aim at revitalizing the role of the legislatures, the voice of the people, and to evolve a new system of checks and balances, that restores the credibility of legislative institutions. Suggestions advanced toward this end are both of procedural type and in some cases may need changes in the Constitution, a difficult task even at the best of times, and supplementary reforms in the bureaucratic system.

Among the procedural ones, there are two suggestions that merit recognition. One relates to the establishment of consultative legislative committees that enable the members to probe in greater detail into the current policies and programmes of administrative departments and agencies. In the current mode of the Westminster approaches, there are very few opportunities, other than the limited period offered during the annual budget debate, for their inputs. To avoid this, parliamentary consultative committees were established in the United Kingdom to look into expenditure plans of the spending agencies. In principle, this offers a constructive avenue to legislators to have their influence felt, and provides a less formal opportunity than the appropriation committees in the United States to scrutinize the proposed appropriations. In India, where this approach was tried, the consultative committees' proceedings were not made public except in a summary fashion, and to that extent their impact was not clear. Some contend that the opportunity of consulting is often used as yet another avenue to advance the pet themes and programmes of the legislators. Another suggestion relates to the omnibus resolutions that are usually presented with a view to avoiding legislative gridlock. Specific legislation is preferred to omnibus legislation and enables the legislators to come to grips with the specific issues of appropriation. Yet another suggestion relates to the provision of information on the proposed policies before taking final decisions on them. This approach is different from the fiscal transparency approaches proposed by the IMF, which emphasizes the provision of information, such as closed accounts of the fiscal year, after the event. Advance provision of information has the inherent advantage of making the community think about the proposals. But the implementation is not without its share of issues. Quite frequently, there is bureaucratic reluctance to provide full information, and in the case of revealing budgetary information there may be issues relating to parliamentary privileges which prevent it and, therefore, secrecy is required to be maintained. Also, experience shows that public opinion offers little help in specific policy issues, in that they may use the opportunity to demand higher expenditures without recognition of the full implications for fiscal policy. Furthermore, the process of eliciting the views of the public may be used by the business interests concerned to engage in heavy promotion of their causes through organized advertising aimed at persuading the public. To that extent, the issue may be shifted from the legislatures to the public arena, and in the final analysis, it may be difficult for the legislators to vote their own way and against the public opinion (for a highly stimulating study of how public opinion can be swayed by organized advertising by industry groups, see Beder, 2003).

The suggestions relating to the change in the constitutional provisions, where applicable, are also varied and include the following—change of the budget cycle to a biennial basis; change in the terms of legislators to restricted periods, such as two terms; introduction of ballot initiates before they are brought to the legislatures; formulation of citizen panels; and greater transfer of tasks to local levels. The change in the budget cycle was advocated by the Gore Commission on Reinvention of Government nearly a decade ago, and was extensively considered before it was abandoned. The idea behind it was that a lot of time and effort could be saved by making the term of the budget coterminous with the term of a congressman, viz., two years. In some state governments in the Unites States, the procedure of a biennial budget is in vogue, and it was hoped that a similar arrangement would be appropriate for the federal level. But what has been ignored is the fundamental role of a federal government, which has a major responsibility of maintaining stability in the economy, relative to the minor role of a state government. A few years ago, Malaysia moved to a biennial budget, and the experience has shown no great advantages in terms of saving time and effort; as a consequence, the change was being reconsidered. In a context where economic uncertainty continues to be a dominant feature affecting the budgets, and in a context where several adjustments are considered necessary during the fiscal year, the biennial budget may actually be a problem rather than a solution.

Similarly, the suggestion for two fixed terms for legislators did not make much progress, except in a few state governments in the United States. Apart from being viewed as a restriction on fundamental rights and therefore tending to be unconstitutional, the advantages were never apparent or convincing. The possibility that experienced legislators become entrenched and may, therefore, continue to work in support of their favourite causes has to be tempered by a recognition that experience is often an institutional asset rather than a liability. That asset would be lost if a limitation on terms were to be introduced.

The suggestions about ballot initiatives and citizens' panels too have their own quota of issues. In the current system governing the working of both types of legislatures, the issues are addressed through a resort to command and control procedures. Legislation aimed at addressing the issue is enacted and the procedures for compliance as well as penalties for non-compliance are indicated. In all these phases, the contact with the citizen is minimal in the Westminster system, while in Congressional system, notionally, public hearings may be organized. On the other hand, there is the general view that participation in public policy management may make people better citizens. This is countered by the lessons learnt from experience. In general, the public may not be fully conversant with the complexities of macroeconomic management and may not have the expertise needed to make an informed choice. Public behaviour has often shown that they tend to underestimate the financial implications of their choices and, in any event, public opinion has offered little help in the determination of aggregate expenditures or in the allocation among competing functions. Also, the conduct of ballots may be costly and may involve delays that can be ill afforded. Establishment of citizens' panels has limited advantages at the central level, while offering a psychological reward at the local levels, in terms of being associated with projects that may be of direct interest to them as beneficiaries. So far they have not been entrusted with any major legislative functions, which remain within the exclusive preserve of the legislature. Addition of a fifth wheel does not make the coach run either smoothly or efficiently.

Transfer of functions to the local levels, particularly when such a transfer is not matched by a corresponding transfer of resources, could be more problematic and the remedy may be worse than the malady. The issue of coordination among the various layers of government would then become more important, and indeed pivotal. Experience shows that there is often a tendency at the local levels to engage in fiscal perversity in that the local governments may be pro-cyclical when the federal government is anti-cyclical, and vice versa. Pursuit of macroeconomic stability in such a context requires stronger coordination devices that are not yet found in federal financial arrangements which, too often, consist of many soft and very few hard constraints. The alternative is not greater centralization. But the eagerness to decentralize should be matched by attention to the building up of adequate safeguards that contribute to smooth functioning at all levels.

The landscape of public policy management in a democratic society is thus full of problem areas stemming from the domination of vested interests on the one hand and growing voter apathy on the other. There is also the problem of bureaucracy and its built-in reluctance to share basic information with the citizens, while seemingly exploiting every opportunity, in the name of public service, to add additional burdens and sacrifices on the people. But it has also to be recognized that public opinion may not always offer clear and specific guidance on what the government agencies should do; this feature is observed even where the public has been co-opted, in the form of user councils, to monitor the effectiveness of policies. In turn, this shows that putting more power in the hands of the people may not always be a panacea and indeed may contribute to a different set of problems. The alternatives considered offer a wider agenda that is based more on hope and optimism than on practical feasibility. From the technical point of view of expenditure management the proposals considered above do not offer any viable and enduring results.

It is, therefore, appropriate to consider the ways in which the cause of expenditure management may be advanced independently from the wider agenda of electoral and bureaucratic reform. In considering the specific directions of improvement, the important question that needs to be answered at the very outset relates to the willingness of the people to rise to the tasks and their eagerness to participate. Here much can be said, and indeed has been said, on both sides. Such philosophical enquiries, while always necessary, may not always lead to definitive and acceptable solutions. Rather, it has to be ensured that a horse taken to the pond will eventually start drinking water, primarily for the reason that it is thirsty, and secondarily for the reason of availability of water. From an expenditure management viewpoint, two types of improvements in public policy formulation and implementation may be envisaged: (i) general availability of information ahead of making final decisions; and (ii) specific improvements needed in the light of the medium-term fiscal outlook.

On a general level, most proposed policies have enormous potential implications for future expenditure growth. In such cases three steps would seem appropriate. First, governments should give wide publicity to the proposals, their implications for expenditure growth, methods of financing, and the displacement of any existing expenditure programmes, if needed, to finance the proposed policies. Such provision of information, which should also be made available to the legislatures, should be considered as a kind of pre-budget legislative activity. Second, in tandem, the consultation process of the legislature may be expanded, not merely to deal with the agencies concerned but also with the public. As an integral part of this effort, donor financial policies and programmes should be subjected to similar processes so as to enhance the sense of ownership. Third, the opportunity of dissemination of information should be utilized to determine the role of the public in the utilization of the benefits that are to flow from the proposals. These three steps do not supplant the legislative process or their timetables but seek to provide a more firm basis for consultation and approval.

The second aspect seeks to throw greater light on expenditure management and the efforts of the government to improve it. For the medium term, the fiscal outlook is one of greater caution, given the highly fragile base, and even stress. New expenditure proposals may not be accommodated except when sources of financing are available or, alternatively, when some existing expenditure programmes are abandoned. In all cases, governments should provide an annual report on expenditure management, containing the efforts that are being made to secure more economies, higher recovery of costs, and where the fiscal outcomes are different from the intent, the efforts that are planned to minimize them. Such an annual report should be subjected to audit review and consideration either by the legislature or one of its committees. This approach supplements the legislative review of the financial accounts and enables them to focus on expenditure management, while forcing governments to look more closely and regularly into expenditure management efforts. More significantly, this step leads to the building up of a financial democracy along with political democracy.

Despite the inherent imperative for ensuring citizen participation in some form or the other, there may be severe difficulties in ensuring this in fallen or failed states. During recent years there has been, in some

Asian and African countries, a quick slide from democratic rule to chaos, with changing borders of the country, perennial internal strife, steadily escalating ethnic tensions, leading to armed conflict among organized groups (for two recent excellent case studies of this transformation, see Maier 2000 and Friend 2003). As a result of these factors, governments in those countries tend to become engulfed in contradictory themes—not as agencies for development but as agents of impoverishment, not to provide services but to selectively grab money from the people, not to provide drinking water but to pollute it. As a result they sit in the uncomfortable position of lacking validation, having lost the trust and confidence of the people. From an expenditure point of view, three features become quickly discernible in these types of countries. First, there is a continuous fight for the control of financial resources. Second, they seem to follow the dictum, 'when in distress, centralize all decision making': the role of the local authorities is reorganized and all important policy making functions move to the small group that runs the state administration. Third, some domains of the government, particularly defence and police, tend to get the bulk of financial resources, so as to prevent future crises from emerging from these organized forces. In all these matters, where governments seem to operate not to serve but to prey, the role of the citizen ceases to be inclusive but becomes marginalized—with no voice, no participation, and no choice in any matter affecting civic life.[8]

The issue then arises as to the type of expenditure control framework that is required in these situations. Is there a basic, minimum framework that is appropriate for these governments? The answer, in practical terms, is in the affirmative. It is not that one wishes to have a basic framework but it is a matter of settling down with a framework that, while being minimal, offers the prospect of implementation. It also provides an alternative to organized chaos. In organizing this minimal framework it is important that the following building principles are recognized. The framework cannot envisage the participation of the citizen in view of the restrictions imposed on him. Rather, what is aimed at is to inform him/her about the state of finances, and the prospects or limitations of burden sharing. During periods of internal power

---

[8.] For a background on these aspects, see International Monetary Fund, *World Economic Outlook*, April 2003: Growth and Inspections, and World Bank, *Building Institutions for Markets: World Development Report, 2002*, both published in Washington.

struggle, certain domains would continue to dominate all policy making, to the extent that hardly any decisions are taken. Conceivably, all powers would be centralized in those domains for the duration of the strife. While not seeking to change the role of those domains, it is important to ensure that their role is institutionalized and is known to all. In the period leading to more peaceful times, that is after the end of the political crisis, there is a normal inclination, as experience has conclusively shown, to engage in quick fixes. Most of the quick fixes do not work and, if any, tend to create additional problems that thwart further progress. More important, it is necessary to separate technical infrastructure from the policy-making apparatus of the government. During periods of crisis, governments are weakened, not merely in terms of political legitimacy but in the steady flight of experienced personnel from government payrolls. In such a situation, the maintenance of the technical infrastructure can even be contracted out and carried out by the corporate sector.

The minimal expenditure control framework envisaged for such a situation should have the following elements. The first element is an annual budget. It is clear that even in the difficult times described above, every country (with shrinking borders in some cases) still manages to present a budget, for it is considered to be a minimum step to ensure its standing as a member of the international economic community. The budget will continue to be the major instrument for securing macroeconomic stability, but the achievement of other objectives, such as links to service delivery and securing economies in expenditures, is postponed to more stable times. The budget, reflecting the political structure, will continue to show the unequal division of resources, but it would serve the important function of indicating the destinations of public money. Second, following the budget, governments would also be expected to maintain a set of accounts. While recognizing that they may be severely doctored, it has to be recognized that it is better to aim at some form of institutionalized collection of data on the money received and spent. Third and last, the technical infrastructure relating to payments, both to and by the governments, could most profitably be privatized and maintained by the corporate banking sector. This sector, which is always regulated by the central bank, offers a better opportunity, given the circumstances, to provide more reliable and less corrupt service. These elements, while not advancing the cause of the citizens in terms of a greater voice, seek to provide a basic framework that prevents further deterioration, while protecting, to the minimal extent, the interests of the community.

Institutional Development and Expenditure Management

Until a decade ago, the approaches of the macroeconomists centred around important policy variables such as exchange rate, interest rate, and the size of the budget deficit, and very little attention was devoted to the role of institutions in general, and the expenditure management system in particular. In part, this indifference or even benign neglect may be attributed to the way in which macroeconomics is taught in universities, which seldom makes any reference to the role of institutions except to assume that an independent institution free from political interference has a better chance to pursue effective policies. In part, this may also be attributed to the belief that the implementation of policies is a matter for the operational levels of governments and the role of the macroeconomic policy adviser is limited to the advocacy and formulation of viable policies. As an extension of this view, it was also believed, implicitly, that once the right policies are formulated, they get implemented on their own momentum. The contribution of the good or adequate institutional underpinning was not a subject of primary importance. Rather, in the hierarchy of subjects, implementation was always the one that was assumed away and that was to be addressed by the masters of the routine in the bureaucracy. To a further extent, this may have consolidated itself and become a part of the accepted wisdom and offered no specific reason to be recognized as an independent major factor, primarily because of lack of links between economic growth and institutional performance. Although research studies conducted during recent years offer no conclusive evidence about the link between economic growth and institutional performance[9] there is a growing recognition of the role of institutions.

This welcome change in attitude can be ascribed to two reasons. First, the recent emphasis on markets as the primary instrument for spurring economic growth also recognizes that most of the institutions that support markets are provided by the state. The ability of the state to provide them and to run them efficiently, referred to as governance, is now viewed as fundamental to the functioning of markets. Good

---

[9]. The report of the IMF (2003, p. 190) states, 'Other policy measures—including those reflecting monetary *and fiscal policies* as well as trade openers and schooling—*do not appear* to have a statistically significant impact on growth or on volatility when institutional differences are allowed for' (emphasis added).

governance includes the provision of sound macroeconomic policies that aim at creating stable markets and these, in turn, affect overall performance by fostering better policy choices. Thus, it is expected that good governance may play a major role in determining a country's ability to attract foreign investment, and given the mobility of international capital, countries that are known for established practices for the protection of property rights, for the promotion of the rule of law, and for efficient systems and procedures within governments, may have an edge over those that do not have similar arrangements. (In practice, the immediate economic advantages, such as low wage rates, may prove to be a decisive factor in attracting foreign investment even where the governmental systems are archaic and opaque.) Both these factors have contributed to a more detailed look into the way in which governments and their institutions work. The approach follows the dictum of James Madison (1788), 'You must first enable the government to control the governed; and in the next place oblige it to control itself'. In short, it is a case of *omnia mutantur, nos et mutamur in illis* (all things change, and we change with them)[10].

As a part of good governance, considerable importance is attached to the need for fiscal discipline, as the absence thereof could contribute to severe instability in the government and in the economy[10]. In the promotion of this fiscal discipline, five propositions emerge from the advocacy of the IFIs. First, while properly functioning government institutions may not themselves contribute to economic growth, the apparent stability stemming from smooth functioning contributes to the reduction of uncertainty in government agencies and, therefore, there is a need to ensure that the agencies are equipped with proper operational systems. In this regard, it is to be recognized that most agencies that function as a part of the rubric of expenditure management are task oriented, and have been a part of colonial legacy in most countries, rather than being newly established. Thus, every country that became independent found itself with a budget agency, an accounting agency, and an audit agency, and an established system of internal regulations that governed internal work within government departments. The issue, however, in the day-to-day working at a practical level is how they supplement each other and contribute to a coherent strategy regulating expenditure movement. It is not therefore the

---

[10]. See *Building Institutions for Markets, World Development Report 2002*. World Bank, Washington 2002, p. 12.

existence of the institutions, but their coordination and ability to forge a coherent expenditure management process that need to be considered. Second, towards this end, the IFIs, in particular the World Bank, suggest strong finance ministries with 'agenda setting powers relative to the legislature or spending ministries' as it becomes easier for central agencies to enforce fiscal discipline. While 'strong' is an ambiguous term, experience shows that fiscal slippages are no less when matters are controlled by monolithic finance ministries; most slippages occur in the area of public debt which is a part of the exclusive domain of finance ministries. More significantly, a shift of power from the legislature to the executive wing would make the system, as pointed out earlier, less appropriate for a democratic framework. The advocacy of empowerment and decentralization cannot be reconciled with strong finance ministries. The problems of expenditure management are no less in British Commonwealth countries, where there is an established tradition of strong finance ministries. Third, there is a strong preference for the promotion of legislation aimed at securing balanced budgets, or at a minimum lower budget deficits over the medium term. The World Bank's study points out that the evidence, particularly in Latin American countries, points to better or improved fiscal outcomes in countries where such legislation has been enacted. In retrospect, it appears that this facile conclusion has been reached on the basis of very limited evidence. As pointed out in the extensive discussion on the subject in the preceding pages, the law enacted in Latin American countries lacked the flexibility to address counter-cyclical needs. Further, the legislation by itself offers little protective cover when the fundamentals of the economy, are there to be seen by the public, legislators, and the investing public alike. In Argentina, in 2002, additional legislation in the form of a no-deficit rule was enacted to supplement the previous budget responsibility legislation. Under the new legislation, daily payments by the government were linked to the revenues flowing in. This legislation demonstrated to the world that in fact there was no government fiscal policy, and as a result, the crisis worsened. Once again, it demonstrated that what was more important was the policy, and the adequacy of the administrative technical infrastructure that would sustain it. In their perceived absence, the legislation by itself was incapable of inducing the much-needed change. Rules can and indeed are effective up to a point, but beyond that, tend to contribute to the accumulation of payment arrears. Fourth, the World Bank further avers that the possibility of successful fiscal adjustment tends to be high in the context of a majority government than where governments are managed by political coalitions. This is based on the belief that coalition governments inevitably involve greater horse-trading among the coalition parties, and inevitably, political compromises in such a context could lead to compromises on the approaches to fiscal adjustment. Although the World Bank conclusions are in part based on the experience of Organization for Economic Cooperation and Development (OECD) countries, the experience of the Netherlands and Italy shows otherwise. These countries had coalition governments since the end of the Second World War but pursued successful fiscal adjustment policies. While coalition politics do present formidable difficulties in the day-to-day management of the country, the possibility of crisis seems to induce greater policy coherence among the partners. To the extent that such cooperation is not found, it might even be induced by external constraints, as was the case with Italy in the mid-1970s, when it had a series of stand-by agreements with the IMF for the use of its resources. Around the same period, in the United Kingdom, which had a strong majority government led by the Labour Party, the internal dissensions within the party proved to be more difficult. As a consequence, a few years later the party lost power and it took more than a decade and a major change in its approaches to economic management (the adoption of the 'third way') to regain political power. In New Zealand, the party that introduced major changes in its fiscal administration in the late 1980s lost power to a coalition as it tried, according to the perception, to do too much in a short period. History offers plenty of evidence for both sides of the argument; but, in the event, it was selectively used by the World Bank to buttress its argument and advocacy. In some circles, this is called doctoring of evidence. Finally, there is an implicit difference, or lack of unanimity, in the approaches of the World Bank and the IMF in regard to the institutional reform to be undertaken by their member countries in the developing world. Both started with an advocacy of the best practices found in various countries, to be adopted by the countries. The World Bank has, as noted earlier, changed its emphasis from 'best practices' to 'best fits', as the former stressed technocratic exercises initiated from Washington that had questionable relevance to the specific needs of other countries. The design for improvement was to be relevant to local needs. Best practices soon degenerated into a one-size-fits-all approach, and the costs far outweighed the benefits. Apart from this, even conceptually there is no agreement on what is the best practice. Several European countries have highly centralized treasury and payment systems while a few have equally decentralized payment systems, administered with equal effectiveness. What is best for one country may be less than an 'ideal fit' for another country. In the initiatives taken through New Partnership for African Development (NEPAD), and the African Peer Review Mechanism (APRM), the IMF continued to concentrate on 'best practices' as a way to improve economic and fiscal governance (see IMF *World Economic Outlook*: Growth and Institutions, 2003, pp. 114–15). These continued differences between the two major IFIs may provide an opportunity for the countries to either make up their own minds or to enter into clever bargaining with each of them separately.

Do the above approaches offer a viable design for institutional development in the expenditure management area? The answer is in the negative. It is clear that these generalities often pose a problem rather than provide a solution to the specific problems experienced in the expenditure management area. The needs in this area may be examined in terms of the following four questions. Is there a need for new institutions in this area or is it mostly a case of revitalizing the existing institutions? If it is the latter, to what extent can the underachievement of the existing institutions be attributed to the process factors? To what extent are the technology factors contributing to the problems experienced? And finally, to what extent are the human factors contributing to policy management problems?

As has already been noted, a major part of expenditure management is task oriented, and it is for this reason that there is considerable commonality in the institutional arrangements. In every country, the centre stage is held by the finance ministries, both by tradition and explicit need, which are responsible for expenditure management. In some countries, the power and the management responsibilities may be shared with the president's office, with the planning boards or commissions, or independent bodies such as public debt offices that are responsible for specific segments of expenditure management. In most countries, the responsibility for the collection and consolidation of accounting information is located in the office of an accountant general, or similar organizations such as a comptroller or controller, who either work as a part of finance ministries or as an independent office. In the transition countries, arrangements were of a different type, in that major responsibility for this task was delegated to the spending agencies and one of the divisions of the finance ministry usually undertook the consolidation of government-wide accounts. In all governments, specific responsibilities are assigned to the spending agencies, which, together with the finance and planning agencies, constitute the essential pillars of expenditure management. In centralized management systems, spending agencies have a minimal role while in decentralized systems, they may have a major role, more so during the budget implementation stage. In addition to these traditional arrangements within the executive, in most countries there is an independent audit office to undertake an annual audit of government finances. The independence of the office and the range of functions undertaken by this office vary among different systems. Most transition countries did not have an independent audit office before, but this gap has been quickly filled up and almost all of them claim to have an audit office, some located in the prime minister's office and some outside the government endowed with a major degree of functional autonomy. Thus, all the essentials are provided, although the effectiveness of these institutions varies considerably, owing largely to the way in which the institutions function. Clearly then, the task is not one of establishing new institutions either to supplement or supplant those that are already in place.

The process factors refer to the way in which the tasks and responsibilities of the various pillars of expenditure management are delineated to promote a coherent functioning system. Does the process promote certainty through a specification of goals and allocation of resources for the purpose? Is there adequate coordination among the different pillars of management? Is there adequate communication and consultation among the agencies? Are there adequate arrangements for crisis management? Some of these issues were examined, albeit briefly, in the preceding pages and may be recapitulated here, mainly to point out that these are the areas where many of the problems lie, impeding or corroding the work of agencies. In many cases, it is the experience that multiple goals are sought to be addressed by the central agencies. The spending agencies, being at the receiving end, look for guidance on the goals to be pursued at any time and the trade-off to be undertaken among different goals. Experience shows that the central agencies often lack a coherent strategy and move in a tactical manner, from one short-term issue to another. Policy goals are changed frequently. When specified, requisite resources are not provided, and underfunding is widely resorted to in the name of stabilization. What they lack in policy coherence and consistency, the central agencies try to compensate through an excessive resort to process controls, in terms of holding up the release of funds or placing other obstacles. The result is greater uncertainty that tends to permeate through the whole process. There is confusion about the choice of the anchor of expenditure control, and each major domain in government seems to have its own covenants governing expenditure management. The result is fragmentation and uncoordinated working. The process is often outmoded and does not encourage the managers to manage. Rather, the emphasis is on compliance with archaic rules; the consequence is a 'triumph of process over purpose'.

Similarly, in the area of application of technology, the issue of what more could have been done was examined in narrow terms. Computerization has contributed to an overall enhancement of the levels at which the payment and accounting systems were operating in government. Recording, storage and retrieval of information became more convenient than was ever imagined. The current stage of technological development is such that more advanced facilities are available in many cases with the banking institutions, and successful attempts have been made, in a few countries, to contract out payment responsibilities to the corporate sector. This practice, which deserves to be extended on a more generous scale, remains at a nascent stage. In this context, the question of institutional development may also conveniently explore the areas that could be contracted out on a permanent basis.

Human factors relate not merely to the availability of trained talent but to the systemic factors that contribute to improved decision making. If decisions are not made in time or if there is too much paper pushing, up and down the bureaucratic levels, and if there is extended delay in the processing of even ordinary matters, then the issue is far more about the mental set or the administrative culture of the country. Both these are heavily influenced by process factors as well as human factors. In some countries, there is an abundance of talent, and invariably the best are drawn into the civil services, after a careful screening process. Even so, the process of decision making is no better. There are several reasons, but the approach of the administration is an important one. Incentives introduced to permit quick decision making are often abused, and the previous situation is restored. In that context, what type of personnel arrangements would be appropriate? What should be the relative emphasis on generalists and technocrats? And what areas remain to be kept within governments and what areas may be contracted out? These are the questions that need to be explored more but have not so far received the attention due. Rather, there has been too much emphasis on personnel retrenchment, an important issue from any point of view, but this has not been tempered by a recognition of the more important issues relating to the dislocation in work, and the post-retrenchment situation. These aspects would have a greater impact on institutional development and on expenditure management.

Fiscal Policy and Expenditure Management

The growing role of expenditure management in the pursuit of fiscal policies aimed at securing stability and fiscal sustainability has been broadly discussed in the previous sections. The conclusion that emerges is that expenditure management is firmly rooted in the fiscal context in which it is working, and without that context, it would be limited to the exercise of process controls to ensure accountability, regulatory controls to establish a smooth administrative system, and efficiency controls aimed at securing improved delivery of services and the efficiency associated with them. Although policy controls are important, they acquire greater importance in the context of pursuit of fiscal policy, which in turn provides guidance in the determination of criteria for the allocation of resources to various programmes and in the determination of aggregate levels of expenditure. To a lesser extent, the content of fiscal policy also guides the actual choice of expenditure instruments among direct expenditures, provision of guarantees and related efforts to stimulate economic activity, expanding loan portfolios, or a greater emphasis on tax expenditures. The impact of the final choice on the aggregate level of expenditure depends on the choice made. There is, however, a major difference between the policy discretion available to industrial and developing countries, particularly in the context of the determination of the role and precise content of the counter-cyclical policy aimed at reducing the impact of short-term recessions.

Industrial countries have, traditionally, a range of automatic stabilizers, such as social security payments and unemployment benefits, that protect individuals from short-term shortfalls in their incomes. The range of benefits differs from one country to another, depending on the nature and coverage of the social assistance and social insurance programmes. In addition, there may be other conjectural programmes aimed at providing short-term relief through quasi-public works programmes. In developing countries, the absence of well-established social security programmes makes it obligatory for governments to pursue more active fiscal policies through the provision of social safety nets, and through greater outlays on poverty alleviation programmes. The experience in this regard is rather small, as many of the developing countries are still engaged in refining these programmes. The pursuit of these benefit-oriented approaches has an immediate and enduring effect in terms of changing the composition of public expenditures, in that social outlays tend to garner increasingly higher shares in the total. In the longer term, this may change as there is a growth in cumulative needs of other sectors.

In principle, in both industrial and developing countries, the impact of current and investment expenditures may be the same in terms of stimulating economic activity. Both types of outlays contribute to higher disposable incomes and thus to more effective demand that in turn would promote greater economic activity. In developing countries, there is a greater preference for capital spending largely in the hope that it would lead to the creation of enduring self-financing assets. Such a preference is also justified given that a major part, if not the entire amount, of the capital outlay is financed by borrowing from the public. In the context of a general decline in economic activity, revenues experience a short-term decline and a loss of buoyancy, and since additional mobilization of resources through taxation or even cost recovery makes little economic sense, a higher level of reliance is placed on borrowing. This is also in conformity with the golden principle.

Generally, from the point of view of expenditure management, there are four aspects which merit specific consideration. The first relates to the choice of the instrument. To the extent that the issue is sought to be addressed through direct outlay, the responsibility of implementation falls squarely on public agencies. Provision of a loan to other corporate bodies or autonomous agencies shifts the responsibility to another level and the responsibility of the government becomes less. Further, the role of expenditure management shifts to monitoring the progress made by another party, on which it may have little or no control, and on ensuring that there is no delinquency in repayment. Provision of loans also has the short-term impact of improving the balance sheet of the government as the increase in liabilities incurred through public borrowing is likely to be matched by an increase in financial assets. In reality, as experience has shown, this may contribute only to false satisfaction, as more often than not, the loans so extended tend to end up as non-recoverable assets and the overall burden of debt on the government remains the same. Meanwhile, the choice of loans, or tax expenditures, or even guarantees would have the short-term effect of removing the issue from the purview of expenditure management. A second aspect relates to what the Japanese call the 'real water content' of the proposed outlays. During recent years, it has been found that several policy packages were introduced in Japan, in view of the relative weak automatic stabilizers that had greater 'headline' spending figures, although the 'real water content' (new measures that directly stimulate economic activity) was often significantly lower. This dimension is often obscured in the calculus leading to the determination of the total stimulation package, but is an important dimension that needs to be addressed. Third, the management system is also required to address the issue of investment lags and the periods during which results are likely to be obtained. The demands of counter-cyclical policy are such that the results are required to be reaped during the period of the cycle, so that its impact can be minimized. There have been several cases, however, common to industrial and developing countries, where the results surfaced long after the cycle was over, thus defeating the very goal of the policy. As a supporting mechanism, the management system should orient itself to the achievement of the specified policy goals. In turn, this demands that the system should have the capacity to assess the lags between the investment and the expected stream of benefits. Finally, counter-cyclical policies have an inevitable ratchet effect on the level of expenditures. Because of the planned investments and the adoption of stimulation policy packages, the aggregate level of expenditures ratchets upwards. The general hope is that once the cycle is over, the increase would gradually disappear and the expenditure pattern would return to normal. This, however, has rarely happened, and expenditure growth takes place from the ratcheted levels. This experience reveals that expenditure management, like policy management in other spheres, rarely has an 'exit' strategy. Much is dependent on the content of the stimulation package: if more loans are provided to stimulate activity, there is a likelihood, at least in principle, of a general softening of the ratchet effect. In the case of direct expenditures incurred by governments, the ratchet effect is unlikely to disappear, particularly where the duration of the cycle (as was the case in Japan) during recent years is prolonged. Although some tend to consider Japan as a fiscal outlier, its experience is unusual only in terms of the longevity of the trade cycle. Continuation of the ratchet effect has been and continues to be a common experience in many countries, and is a major problem area that has not been conclusively addressed by expenditure management systems.

The recent experience of industrial and developing countries, especially during the decades of the 1980s and 1990s, reveals a different and important dimension of expenditure management. The major effort during these years was largely one of achieving restraint in the growth of expenditures rather than a pursuit of counter-cyclical policies. Confronted by growing budget deficits, governments concentrated their efforts on mobilizing additional resources through higher taxation and privatization efforts, and through systematic pruning of government expenditures. The aim was to secure fiscal sustainability over the medium term, and the expenditure management system was practically retooled to achieve moderation in the rate of growth of expenditures. Accustomed as they were to planned increases in expenditures, year after year, and to the provision of expenditure benefits, the systems had to change gears, and concentrate on reducing expenditures. Toward this end, a variety of policy and systemic measures were taken.[11] These are summarized in Table 3.3.

Table 3.3

Measures Taken to Restrain the Growth of Public Expenditures

Category	Remarks
Policy measures	
Wage bill reduction	In several industrial countries, the total number of employees was reduced in a short period through several measures ranging from reduction in work force to the provision of incentives for voluntary retirement. Although the resort to the latter contributed to an increase in the expenditure levels during the immediate short term, the overall effect was beneficial.
Wage freeze	Despite threats of industrial action, some countries, notably Canada, managed to freeze the wage levels in government.
Reduction in pension benefits	In most industrial countries, the higher rate of expenditure growth was attributable to the entitlements, many of which had automatic cost-of-living adjustments.

(Contd.)

---

[11]. For a comprehensive country-wise discussion of the industrial world, see the collection of papers included in Banca d' Italia 2001. A less comprehensive but a broad review is presented in IMF, *World Economic Outlook*, May 2001.

(Table 3.3 Contd.)

	To moderate the impact from this aspect, eligibility requirements, level of contributions were changed, and in some countries, pension systems were also privatized or organized independently from governments.
Expenditure reduction in specific areas—defence, public debt charges, and public investment	In both industrial and developing countries, defence outlays were reduced. In developing countries, this was more than compensated by increases in social spending, particularly social safety nets, a new activity taken up by governments. Further, as greater efforts were made to raise revenues, there was a short-term moderation in the rate of growth of public debt service payments that was also aided by receding interest rates. Finally, governments reduced public investment and the levels of capital formation declined in the public sector.
Systemic measures	
Promotion of legislation about the size of deficits and other aspects	Restrictive legislation such as the Maastricht Treaty, fiscal responsibility legislation, budget honesty legislation, were enacted during the 1990s. Prior to that, there were pieces of ad hoc legislation such as the Gramm-Rudman-Hollings in the United States, aimed at reducing the sectoral allocation. There were also attempts to introduce sunset reviews. Having failed in the enactment of constitutional amendments (notably in the United States), efforts concentrated on the more modest goal of passing separate legislation with similar effect. The Budget Enforcement Act in the United States also provided for a trigger clause that sought an immediate policy review when the fiscal trends were moving toward a crisis.
Improved techniques	
• Medium-term expenditure planning	It has been recognized that policy goals could be achieved only over the medium term, and as a supporting systemic measure, medium-term expenditure planning was introduced and is now a part of the regular approaches to budget-making.
• Introduction of fundamental reviews and strengthened	The emphasis on the scrutiny of new expenditure proposals is now matched by an equal concern on the review of the essentiality of continuing programmes. Evaluation machinery was strengthened to weed out the

(Contd.)

(Table 3.3 Contd.)

evaluation measures	ineffective existing programmes, and in the case of the United Kingdom, fundamental reviews were made obligatory every five years.
• Firm budget ceilings	As a part of the annual budget, spending agencies were given firm ceilings on outlays, and they were to ensure that unexpected increases and cost overruns were accommodated within the ceilings indicated.
• Supporting institutional changes	In some European countries, the idea of responsibility centres, which was always a part of the conceptual framework of management accounting, was revived, and spending agencies were required to become responsible centres. In the United States, attempts were made to install chief financial officers responsible for all financial management matters in spending agencies, and finally some improvements were made.

Admittedly, some of the measures taken, such as reduction in the working force and wage freeze were fairly conventional and were implemented several times during the period. No sooner was there an improvement in the situation that growth was allowed to resume and the experience of recent years was no different. The remarkable feature of the efforts was to evolve a continuing institutional response aimed at moderating the growth rate of expenditure. Three factors require specific recognition here. First, the enactment of new legislation brought new compulsions that had a restrictive impact on the aspirations and ideas of the political and administrative class. Like all legislation in the past, such as the balanced budget, the new legislation may also contribute to the emergence of escape mechanisms but the short-term effect of novelty cannot be totally ignored. Second, there is now firm recognition that efforts aimed at reducing the rate of growth of expenditure should include both new and continuing outlays. Hitherto, the emphasis was on new outlays, in particular, subsidies and capital expenditures, which tended to be the pet aversions of policy makers during periods of crisis. But the techniques chosen, such as the fundamental review, or the triennial review (initiated in Sweden), were not very different from some of the new budgetary techniques such as zero-based budgeting (ZBB) that first appeared on the fiscal scene during the 1960s. The difference was in the phasing, and the way in which it was implemented. Learning the lessons of experience, the reviews in the 1990s were jointly undertaken by the finance ministries and the spending agencies, rather than being left to the spending agencies—an approach that was analogous to a person going on a diet also being given the key to the storeroom and to the refrigerator. Moreover, the fundamental reviews were undertaken as an independent exercise from the preparation of the annual budget. Third, there was an added importance given to institutional development and to infrastructure development along with the introduction of new policy approaches. It was recognized that the two streams of approaches should supplement each other rather than each one being taken up independently. This mutual reinforcing helped strengthen the overall policy environment and brought in explicit recognition of the need for austerity in all phases of government life.

While the strengths described above offer points of radical departure from the past, there were also several drawbacks that contributed to the beneficial impact of the efforts being too short-term oriented rather than enduring over an extended period of time. Notwithstanding all the emphasis and support extended to the improvement of the expenditure management system, it did not develop the capacity to anticipate crises and engage in preventive action. Even when the crisis was known to be imminent, a combination of political reluctance to take strong measures, and the usual bureaucratic inertia made the system less strategic in outlook and more tactical, responding to situations as they arose. Getting rid of the conventional cobwebs took a good deal of time, and in several cases needed a change in political parties to run the governments. Also, the choice of policy instruments was fairly conventional and to that extent outmoded. And when some new instruments were selected, such as performance orientation and public service agreements, as well as the introduction of contractual services, they were found to be not facilitating but impeding the efforts to reduce the rate of growth of expenditures. Where performance levels were specified, commensurate resources had to be provided, in turn contributing to the growth in expenditures. The conflict between the two approaches became clear much later, as the new management philosophy which was brought in did not recognize the contrary pulls among the different components of the packages, and no efforts were made to resolve them. Achievement of fiscal stability could, and often does, involve adjustment in the range and quality of services offered. The trade-off was to be explicit. But in the event, it became an issue between the finance ministry and the spending agencies. This continues to be an issue that needs to be addressed.

In retrospect, it appears that there was a considerable dissonance between the malady and the remedy prescribed, in that the factors contributing to expenditure growth were not sought to be explicitly and directly addressed. Experience shows that five factors have a major contribution in the rapid growth of expenditure. First, the basis for the determination of personnel positions and related staff growth is entirely supply driven. New posts are created in governments on the basis of prescribed yardsticks, and where work grows, the number of staff positions also grow. It is assumed that work is growing in response to growing demand, which may indeed be the case where the agencies are involved in the provision of street-level services. But the proposed increases in the staff positions are not always related either to the needs or to the available resources. The supply-driven forces are such that there is little option but to allocate resources. Second, the supply-driven forces also contribute to grade inflation in that there may be more posts and manpower than may be actually needed. Further, compulsions of career stream contribute to steady increases in the higher levels of the service, and the top becomes increasingly flat rather than pyramidical. To some extent, this problem was sought to be addressed through fundamental reviews; since the reviews are infrequent, the grade inflation continues for a period until addressed as a part of the review. Third, because of technological changes, the equipment, more so in the case of defence and health sectors, tends to become costly. Historian Ferguson (2001, p. 32) points out that fighter aircraft now cost two hundred times as much as they did during the Second World War, and aircraft carriers are twenty times as expensive. While comparable data for the medical sector remain to be compiled, it is accepted that the rate of cost increases has always been higher than the inflation rate. To some extent, this may reflect the numerous changes made in the technical design, and partly, the limitations on patents which make it obligatory for the firms to recover costs and claim profits during the twelve-year period for which the patents are valid. The alternatives available to policymakers and expenditure controllers in this context are extremely limited. Indeed, there may be no alternative where defence equipment is concerned. Fourth, as economist Baumol pointed out a few years ago, there is a natural tendency for costs to go up in government operations. Annual pay increases (increments or steps in individual pay scales) given as an incentive to stimulate active work, together with the accumulation of costly equipment and grade inflation contribute to this phenomenon. While obviously, some factors have greater impact than others, the overall increase is a steady inertial growth in expenditure. And the problem is further compounded by the way in which budgetary allocations are made in several countries for 'running costs' of various programmes. This catch-all technical phrase involves personal emoluments, as well as other expenses, such as on travel and utilities that are an inevitable feature of any organization. Annual budget provision for this category is made, in most countries, at the same rate at which the GDP is estimated to grow for the next year. Alarm bells are rung, and as a result greater scrutiny is made only when the bids submitted by spending agencies exceed the budget guidelines which usually seek to limit the increases to the projected rate of growth of GDP. This approach allows, indeed routinely sanctions, the steady growth in expenditures except in times of fiscal crisis. The approach implies benign neglect of an important factor contributing to growth. Finally, the pattern of financing of budget deficits has also had an impact on cost increases. As explained further on, greater reliance has been placed, during recent years, on debt as a source of financing. There are multiple effects emanating from debt financing: it contributes to an immediate increase in expenditures reflecting debt servicing; it also leads to an increase in programme costs that are totally beyond the control of the programme managers. In addition, as debt increases, the debt holders tend to acquire a dominating voice on the management of state finances and, very soon, key decision making shifts from governments to groups of creditors. To the extent that these are the main factors contributing to expenditure increases, conventional reliance on short-term limitations on recruitment, and deferral of important projects is unlikely to yield any enduring results. A consequence is the periodic occurrence of crises. It also implies that crisis is being addressed by outmoded weapons that become inadequate with the flux in time. Equally, experience shows that there is little coherence and consistency in the policies followed. On the one hand, efforts are initiated to control expenditures. On the other hand governments continue to rely on approaches that contribute to steady increases in expenditure. This internal contradiction in expenditure has never been squarely addressed.

Experience also reveals a few other problem areas that need to be recognized if further progress is to be made in strengthening expenditure management in public bodies. As a result of a general lack of anticipation, and consequent lack of preparation, governments in most developing countries failed to prepare the community to accept a cut in services. In several cases, across-the-board cuts were imposed with a view to ensuring that the short-term budget deficits would not be too high. But this approach implies that all expenditures are equal, which they are not. Some are more essential than others, and it requires that governments make up their own minds, and prepare the community to make up its mind, on the choice of areas where expenditures are to be reduced. Policy choices were not properly addressed, as is abundantly clear from the fact that capital and development expenditures were severely limited to contain the budget. Thus the very contribution of government to economic growth was adversely affected as was its capacity to attract foreign investment. The latter requires an adequate infrastructure, and when additional needs and maintenance requirements are adversely affected by budget cuts, then investment from other sources would not be forthcoming to the extent required. The limitations on developmental outlays, apart from their impact on economic development imply that governments attach far more importance, either by intent or by default, to current outlays, which are mainly devoted to wages and salaries of employees than to the developmental needs of the community

It is also clear that the central agencies had not lived up to expectations in performing their own functions. They are legitimately expected to be equipped to anticipate fiscal crisis, and to be prepared to deal with it. In practice, however, their anticipation was limited or non-existent, and to that extent where firm guidance would have served the government and the community well, they ended up generating greater uncertainty, and their reliance on ill-equipped machinery proved to be costly and contrary to the wishes of the community. This is the situation observed in many countries as they emerge from years of continuing efforts aimed at fiscal consolidation. What does this experience reveal about the capacities of governments and their expenditure management systems to deal with future challenges of fiscal management?

A cursory examination shows that there are already a number of factors that are likely to create additional pressures for increasing expenditures. First, years of efforts to restrain expenditures have left governments in a state where their equipment is obsolete, and is in need of replacement. Rehabilitation of the economic infrastructure alone is a major challenge. In addition, development expenditures cannot continue to stagnate or decline in real terms. Changing political and economic compulsions require an immediate increase in development outlays. Second, the recent benefits that governments enjoyed through lower interest rates, and hence lower public debt charges than would have been the case, cannot be expected to continue and hence would contribute, as was the case before, to expenditure growth. Third, the restraint on public debt that was witnessed during the 1980s has already given way to sharp increases in public debt in selected industrial countries, and more so in the emergent economies. In the industrial countries, the war and counter-cyclical pressures have contributed to increased expenditures, higher deficits, and to higher levels of debt. Recent data show that debt has already started to grow in emergent economies, in part reflecting the role assumed by the state to take over many contingent liabilities from the banking field and in the restructuring of the banking system. The rate of growth in public debt has already started raising the concerns of the IFIs (for a recent review of these developments, see IMF, *World Economic Outlook*: Public Sector in Emerging Markets, 2003). Fourth, the effect of ageing populations on pensions, health, and related life support programmes undertaken by governments would continue, in part reflecting the changing picture of the net liabilities of the pension systems. It is now expected that all pension systems face net liabilities in the decade ahead, even after taking into account asset positions, and projected contributions from current and future workers. Fifth, with increasing technological sophistication, the equipment used in defence and internal order areas would maintain its high growth trajectory, leaving the governments with no option except to acquire the equipment at any cost.

In short, many of the old problems would continue, and there would be many more that await resolution in the near future and over the medium term. Inevitably, the changing contours of fiscal policy have implications for expenditure management. It is clear that the revitalizing process of expenditure management should envisage a four-fold improvement of the system. First, serious efforts would be needed on a continuing basis to secure economies in expenditure from existing policies and programmes. New demands for additional resources, which would be many, can be met only to a limited extent from additional taxation, and similar sacrifices would be needed on the expenditure front. The annual budget-making would, therefore, have no option but to emphasize the abandonment of programmes that have ceased to be useful. But many of these programmes would have, by the sheer force of history, developed their own clientele groups and entrenched interests. Their exclusion from the budget would be a difficult political exercise requiring strong political determination. The necessary atmosphere for dampening future expectations could be created through rolling medium-term expenditure plans. To serve the underlying purpose, these rolling plans should endeavour to depict the changing expenditure implications of continuing current policies and their implications for the future, and should indicate, through a specification of policy priorities, the programmes that could be considered for elimination so as to pave the way for new programmes. Following the rolling plans, advance indications should be given about the size and the content of expenditure adjustment. This would require a major departure from the existing approaches that mostly concentrate on new expenditures. To identify the programmes that need to be severely pruned or eliminated, detailed fundamental reviews and reviews of cost implications would be needed. The management system should therefore develop a capacity to undertake this review on an objective basis.

Second, it is important that the expenditure management strategy is proactive and forward looking, so that the vulnerabilities can be monitored, and efforts initiated to address the issues. The system should, therefore, develop a capacity to anticipate major macroeconomic risks. In this respect, it is a matter of record, and some consolation, that in most countries, indices have been developed, either by governments or central banks, or jointly, to collect data on aggregate demand and supply factors (consumption, investment, balance of trade, output, wage growth, productivity, expectation surveys about developments in each of these areas, and public sector budgetary performance), financial sector indicators (monetary aggregates, market interest rates, exchange rate, monetary conditions, interest rate and exchange rate expectation surveys), inflation expectations (indexed debt, inflation expectations, market forecasts of inflation), price indices (consumer price indices, wholesale indices, import–export prices, property prices, financial asset prices including those of derivatives), and the demand patterns for government services. This major storage of data and regular monitoring are helpful in anticipating major economic risks. The expenditure management machinery has an obligation to internalize the economic developments in the above spheres, and to determine the timing and extent of changes needed in the size and content of expenditures.

Third, changes in the financial conditions would require changes in the performance agreements concluded either with government agencies or with corporate sector bodies, and others, who have been entrusted with the delivery of services, while funding is provided by the government budget. Performance cannot be considered, simply because of the supporting legal agreements, to be an unchangeable goal. Rather, it is subject to the same vicissitudes that the general economy is subject to. In turn, this implies that the management system should be capable of undertaking revisions in performance agreements whenever so required by the changing economic situation. Programme managers, like the clientele groups, wish to be assured about the certainty of funding and contributing in service provision. Both these aspects would have to be subjected to organized change, rather than abrupt and incoherent responses.

Finally, continuing reliance on public debt as a major instrument for financing government expenditures raises a series of concerns, particularly in the case of countries that have had to face financial crisis. The interlinkages between debt and expenditure management have become so extensive and vast that expenditure policies can no longer be considered in isolation of debt management. As an integral of this recognition, expenditure management is expected to pay attention to the changing profiles of debt, and their implications for the fiscal aggregates and for expenditure programmes. Failure to renegotiate debt in time could have a serious impact on the aggregate size of expenditures and their components.[12]

In sum, the managing machinery is in need of considerable strengthening if it is to serve the changing objectives of fiscal policy.

ALLOCATIVE MECHANISMS AND RIGIDITY

At the heart of expenditure management is the issue of the considerations and processes relating to the allocation of financial resources for competing and even expanding demands. To a large extent, this major question was treated as being determined, in a generic way, by ideological considerations, and in an incremental way in which all existing activities are allotted some increased level of funding to deal with growing needs, and the way in which the budget is finally approved by the legislature or other similar bodies through a series of political

---

[12.] For a review of the experience of the Latin American countries, see Charles Collyns and G. Russell Kincaid, *Managing Fiscal Crisis*, 2003.

compromises or agreements among the various power centres within and outside the government. Such a treatment, apart from being narrow and incomplete, is far from realistic and does not illuminate the area to facilitate an identification of the problems and a consideration of the alternatives available. Conceptually, the allocation of resources takes place through a series of interactions among five levels. At the highest level, the allocation of resources is between the government and the community it represents and the resources that the latter places at the disposal of the former to be utilized to meet societal needs. Second is the issue of allocation of resources among competing levels of governments. For the purpose, government cannot be considered as a single level; the more representative term is the 'public sector'. Government, in turn, comprises three levels—central; state, regional, and provincial; and local or municipal. Each of these levels represents a different set of tasks and responsibilities. While, in practice, much of the decision making may be taking place at the central or federal level, the other levels also have their own operations; the distribution of resources among these levels reflects on the efficiency of allocative mechanisms. Third, once the size of resources to be managed by governments is determined, the allocation of resources takes place in terms of competing functions, and their programmes and projects. To a very large extent, the budget of any country for any year comprises continuing policies and projects, and the slate is much written on than being clean. The amount of additional spending may be very small, and usually the attention, during the annual budget-making, may be limited to the programmes and projects that have to be included in the budget. Fourth, as a part of the annual decision making, attention also has to be paid to the relative shares of resources to be allocated for the purchase of services (or objectives of expenditure) needed to run the government (payments for manpower), purchase of plant and equipment (the technological infrastructure of government operations), and the transfers to be made to individuals, enterprises, and other levels of government. Finally, the allocation of resources requires, as an integral part of the above exercise and in some ways preceding the process, a determination of the choice of expenditure instrument to achieve the proposed policy. This, in turn, requires the determination of whether the proposed policy is to be implemented directly by the government or is to be transferred to another level on an agency basis (where the funding would be provided by the higher agency and commensurate work would be performed by the lower level government), whether the purpose could be served through the provision of a loan (in which a financial asset is created with the possibility of recovery in the future), or a guarantee to another entity which is seeking to raise resources through credit arrangements, through a tax-expenditure of a tax incentive, which implies foregoing legitimate revenues, or through a public–private partnership envisaged either as a part of the budget or outside the normal budgetary process. The choices made at each level have an impact on other levels of decision making and the final choices made at multiple levels form the heart of expenditure management, and thus the annual fiscal policy embodied in the budget.

The determination of the relative roles of the government and society or the market is a part of the constitutional framework within which the government operates. But it is preceded by the more philosophical issue of whether governments are necessary and whether the functions cannot be carried out by the markets themselves. For all the claims made about the virtues of market, including as a social coordinator (for a recent discussion, see Lindblom, 2001), the fact remains that it cannot be self-regulating (to a level considered acceptable by society); it cannot offer economic stability or assure full employment. For these reasons alone, governments are necessary and it is this recognition that has contributed to the assignment of an important and dominating role for them in the constitutions of countries. The role of the government, and the type of interventions that it can make, each one with its impact on the economy, have been subjects of long controversies. For the past two decades, there has been a greater recognition of the contribution of free markets to economic growth. This view holds that a greater liberalization of the markets and allowing the markets to get the prices right (which also ensures the right allocation of resources in the market systems), would lead to higher economic growth in the markets. This is followed by an advocacy for smaller governments, and also less interference by them in the day-to-day functioning of the market system. There are, however, many cases where government intervention has been of a positive type, and where it has contributed to steady and higher rates of economic growth, while at the same time promoting vigorously functioning markets that also ensure an appropriate allocation of resources. The proper role of the government, in terms of this approach, comprises six tenets (for a discussion of these tenets, see Wade, 1990). The first tenet is to secure economic stability. This function continues to be the primary responsibility of governments when destabilizing forces emanate from government actions as well as from the activities of the corporate sector, as was the case during the Asian financial crisis during the mid and late 1990s. The second tenet is to provide physical infrastructure that involves enormous investments and provides major external benefits, in turn stimulating private investment in other sectors. Although these activities have traditionally been the forte of governments, a major change has been taking place in the way in which investment infrastructure is taking place. Compelled by fiscal stress, governments had to compress their capital expansion expenditures and seek collaboration agreements with the private sector. As a consequence, public–private partnerships of a wide variety have come about with varying agreements regarding the sharing of risks, duration of agreements, and the return of original rights to governments. The third tenet is to supply basic goods, including defence, national security, institutions needed for the maintenance of the political, economic, and legal system, and related aspects that would normally not be undertaken by governments. The implication of this is that the government has a monopoly in providing these services. In practice, however, there have been changes in the financing of these services, and the methods of provision to these to the community. Defence and security are funded entirely by governments, but in several cases, the activities are managed in a fashion that tends to blur the traditional functions between public and private sectors. In many industrial countries, defence research and production of defence equipment may be undertaken by commercial corporations, whose policies may be specified by governments and whose entire output may be bought by governments or the sale of equipment both within and outside the country may be regulated by governments. In addition, the funding is provided by governments. In fact, much of the investment in these activities in the corporate sector takes place under the control or guidance by governments. In the provision of social services, for example, education and health, governments compete with corporate organizations and NGOs. Even in this field, as is true of investment in technical infrastructure, funding may be provided by governments while the actual provision of the service, for example, education, may be contracted out. As for health, the services may be governed by third-party agreements under which the service provider, a doctor, would be reimbursed for the services provided either fully or partly. Where the arrangement specifies a part payment, the recipient of the services may also be called upon to pay. The fourth tenet is to contribute to the development and ensure the smooth functioning of labour, financial intermediation and other related areas through the establishment of independent regulatory authorities and the enactment of supporting legislation. The fifth is to minimize price distortions that arise in cases of market failure and the sixth tenet is to provide life support programmes that aim to give relief to the poorer sections through social safety nets and other insurance and assistance arrangements.

The allocation of resources between governments and the rest of society is far from simple and straightforward and has been in a state of flux. As a consequence, public expenditures, as traditionally defined, may in fact understate current and future outlays, as for example, when activities that are usually undertaken by the government are ceded either for a specified period or on an indefinite basis to the corporate sector under arrangements where the risk and financing may be shared. Where financing is jointly undertaken, the share of government would be reflected in the budget, but where the risk is shared, the impact may be felt only on future outlays. Furthermore, there are several other areas of operations that have an impact on the allocation of resources. The state is often the biggest buyer and the biggest employer too (for details of these and related aspects, see Premchand, 2000). In its capacity as a buyer, its policies affect current and future investment in the economy. Subsidies provided by governments may be intended to stimulate activity as much as to protect selective groups of clientele. As a supplier, its activities may promote further investment or may hinder the activity, as is the case with government outlays on education, heath, and housing. Enormous investments envisaged by governments in these sectors may, at least in the immediate short run, dissuade commercial firms from stepping up their activities in these fields. Governments are often engaged, both directly and through regulatory activity, in promoting investment through active management of credit and banking facilities. In a few countries, subsidized credit, with costs borne entirely by governments, is provided. Finally, governments tend to be the biggest borrowers, that shift money from private individuals to government management. All these activities involve many transactions that have an offsetting nature. It also means that the budget is only one, but by far the biggest, instrument that seeks a balance in the allocation of resources between governments and societies, and any effort to understand the complicated relationship must be tempered by the recognition that there are several other areas where the division of resources is affected by the prevailing economic and political philosophy and by the mutual goodwill or the lack of it between the two sides.

The second level of allocation of resources takes place among the various levels of governments, viz., between the central or federal government and the sub-national governments. Essentially, the basis of allocation is a political agreement among the contenders that also aims for fiscal equalization. In general, there are three ways in which the resources may be allocated. The division may be specified in the constitution, and as such resources may be apportioned every year on the basis of the legal provisions. In some cases, there may be separate legislation that has the same effect. In a few countries, the claims of the sub-national governments may be reviewed periodically, usually once in five years, by quasi-judicial commissions whose recommendations are generally considered to be binding on both sides. This second method has been popular in British Commonwealth countries, notably in Australia and India. This approach implies a desire to move the issue from a political minefield to a more stable and independent judicial environment. The third approach comprises assistance released by the central government to the sub-national levels for specified development purposes or for providing public services. Supporting this arrangement, borrowing by the sub-national governments may be either severely limited or undertaken on their behalf by the central government, or the determination of the magnitude and timing of borrowing may take place in consultation with the central government. Thus, the implicit view is to ensure that sub-national governments are fiscally responsible.

While the above arrangements appear reasonable and even adequate, several problems are observed in day-to-day life that tend to have a serious impact on expenditure management. First, the legal provisions in the constitution or other legislation imply a degree of rigidity in the allocation, and most efforts are concentrated by both levels on the discretionary levels of transfers from the central to the sub-national governments. The realm of decision making on discretionary transfers is located, in its entirety, in the central government. In its desire to be consistent and apolitical, the central government often relies on quantitative and objective methods to determine the transfers. This may often lead to the imposition of a degree of uniformity, and the sub-national governments could feel that money is being provided where the need is not great, while there is no money for what they consider essential needs. Second, the transfers are usually fenced with many conditions that govern the use of the money at the receiving end. In reality, however, the central government has no means of ensuring that the transfers are spent for the purposes indicated, other than through inspection. No sanctions can be imposed for non-compliance, except that the proposed transfers may be stopped. At the receiving end, however, many problems are experienced. The discretionary transfers as well as the legally provided transfers, may not be fully funded when a revenue shortfall is experienced at the federal level. This sudden and frequent resort to underfunding leaves the lower level of governments to function amidst growing uncertainty. In several cases, the release of funds may take place towards the end of the fiscal year, which may leave the lower levels with little time to actually use the funds. Meanwhile, they may be induced to resort to informal borrowing in the form of accumulation of unpaid bills. Further, in several cases, the annual accounts of the lower levels are not audited by independent authorities, and may not, in a few cases (as with provinces in the Russian Federation) may not be audited at all. Two major issues with reference to the adequacy of expenditure management system can be evaluated, these relate to the hard and soft constraints in the management of the budget, and the progress achieved in fiscal equalization. As noted above, the considerable degree of centralization of fiscal decision making in the central government may also empower it to enforce a hard budget constraint that would make the sub-national governments comply with the specified expenditure levels. In practice, however, the fabric of controls is so porous that any number of escape mechanisms may be resorted to. The practice of issuing quasi-official bonds or other forms of indebtedness attests to the leakages in the system. The idea that centralization would also ensure fiscal equalization is, also in need of empirical evaluation. Far from achieving equalization, the allocation of resources, despite the constitutional provisions and quasi-judicial commissions, is such that disparities are far from minimized. Both these aspects suggest that the instruments of expenditure management in this area do not fully measure up to intentions and expectations. In a deeper way, they also reflect on the growing gap between funding, on the one hand, and delivery of services and the achievement of fiscal stability, on the other.

The third level of allocation of resources takes place within governments, among various institutions, agencies, departments, and bureaus. In an ideal setting, where politics and administrative processes do not interfere, the allocation is undertaken on the basis of bids submitted by the agencies for funds to cover their operations and for any proposed extensions during the next year. Since all the available resources flow into a general pool, the departments make claims to the general pool. In a perfect world, as Keynes remarked at one stage, there may be no need for a finance ministry to undertake a review of the competing claims and make draft proposals for the approval of the cabinet regarding resource distribution. The imperfect world we live in requires a central agency which is fully aware of all the resource inflows, and is cognizant of the resource limitation, to undertake an objective review of the allocation principles and criteria. In practice, the operating field is not a level one. The claims to the general pool are already made, even before the annual budgetary process starts through an invitation for bids, by the continuing activities that are also presumed to continue for another year. The general pool may be adequate for financing current activities, and if new activities are to be financed, additional mobilization of resources would be necessary. Current or continuing expenditures reflect a priority plan that continues to cast its long shadow over the next year.

There are several other factors that tend to affect the distribution from the general pool. In several cases, the revenues that flow into the pool may be earmarked for specific purposes: for example, levy on motor vehicles to be spent on the maintenance of highways; revenues from taxes on cigarettes and tobacco may be allotted to provision of health benefits to those suffering from lung diseases. Such earmarking may be minimal or extensive. In several Central and Latin American countries, the levels of earmarking are very high. Indeed in the case of Costa Rica, more than 80 per cent of revenues are earmarked for specific categories of expenditure. In such cases, the annual allocation of resources becomes a routine exercise of allotting revenues to areas that are specified in law. At one stage, earmarking was undertaken by the legislatures in a very active manner, primarily to restrict the freedom of the bureaucracy and to ensure that their wishes incorporated in laws are respected. Consequently, the allocation process became rigid and far from a level playing field.

The allocation of resources is also affected by the methods deployed for project financing. It is more than likely that in developing countries, where aid inflows are sometimes more than a quarter of the proposed budget, the financing of projects and selected programmes is arranged through loans from international institutions and donors. The financing of projects and programmes by others also involves compliance with several conditions that form part of the agreements of financing and the resources provided are not fungible. Even in the context of a mid-year financial crisis, when priorities change, the projects that are financed through assured funding continue to receive their allocation, as these funds form a separate and protected segment of the pool. As such, it is common experience that such projects continue to be implemented even when expenditure policies change because of mid-year financial exigencies. Yet another factor of a similar nature also affects the patterns of allocation of resources. In some countries (including the United States, Russian Federation, and other countries in the former Eastern bloc) there is legislation which specifies 'protected categories of expenditure', that need to be financed regardless of the changing fortunes of the governments (revenues). These categories include wages and salaries of defence personnel, wages and salaries of government employees, provisions and entitlements benefits, and public debt servicing. In such cases, the allocations made for other services are severely curtailed and only the protected categories are left untouched. In a few other cases, the legislation may leave the implementation of public policy to the 'chance availability of resources'. In some countries, there is legislation to the effect that payments would be made by governments with reference to the daily inflow of revenues. Those claims which are awaiting payment would be paid until the daily revenues are exhausted, and the payment process is so organized as not to respect any priorities, or the basis of original allocation of resources proposed in the annual budget. If in the past, budget allocations were made to those agencies that thumped the table harder, now allocations would be made with reference to the order of the line awaiting payments. This is a procedure which is intended to bring some sense of order to the liquid position of governments, however, it also negates the very fiscal policy proposed to be followed, as the actual patterns of payment may be far different from those proposed.

Recent experience conclusively demonstrates that the allocation of resources is also heavily influenced, and indeed guided by external considerations including pressures (undoubtedly well-intended) from IFIs. As a part of the overall development policy to be pursued by member countries, the IFIs suggest certain norms to be followed in the allocation of resources to education, health, and the development of the general infrastructure of the economy. Since the developing countries tend to take the view that non-compliance of these notional standards could jeopardize their chances of getting loans from the institutions, they feel obligated to implement these even when there is a lack of resources. In the process, informal guidance becomes formal, rigid, and entrenched. As a result of these multiple factors, the general pool ceases to be general, while the protected or earmarked categories tend to develop an 'enclave' mentality that is inimical to the pursuit of macroeconomic stability and to the establishment of a level playing field, wherein all bids have the same credentials. Some are far more advanced, and far more essential than some others, and unwittingly, the laws and the administrative approaches contribute to enhanced levels of rigidity in the allocation of resources.

In addition, the above approaches also contribute to 'resort to escape mechanisms' that tend to distort the allocation of resources. There are always intense political and economic pressures on the central agencies, seeking higher allocations or even public provisioning for new programmes and projects. Since funds are not available, the central agencies, conceding the essentiality of claims, make token provisions in the budget, that tend to grow with time, and with more demands for money. Meanwhile, such provisions tend to obscure the reality and may even provide a misleading picture.

The fourth level of allocation of resources takes place in terms of objects of expenditure or budgetary inputs, viz., manpower, machinery, and money transfer. The last category, which usually deals with transfer of money from one level of government to another in the form of grants-in-aid, is usually specified by law. Other transfers, to state-owned enterprises or to corporations, which partake the nature of subsidies, reflect the existing policies and have, in theory, a greater discretionary element. Payments made under entitlement programmes also form a part of this category. Since these are established by law, the flexibility for annual changes is very limited and, in most cases, non-existent. For the other categories there is, in principle, greater flexibility, which has tended to grow during recent years despite the intentions to the contrary. Generally, the manpower component of a programme is determined in terms of standards and yardsticks that are, as previously noted, supply driven. In some cases, as in the United States, the staff complements of selected agencies and programmes may be prescribed as a part of the annual appropriation law. In the past, both the legislation and the yardsticks were considered inviolate. But the practice of contracting out work, and the hiring of consultants to perform the same work that government employees do, has more than compensated the stringent staff cuts imposed by many governments to secure fiscal sustainability. The experience in many industrial countries reveals that the hiring of consultants, often at very high prices, has nullified the intent of reducing the government staff. Also, the restrictions on staff were compensated by the extensive application of computer technology, a choice that was not hitherto available to decision makers. In effect, therefore, the management of this category has become far more flexible than might appear at first sight.

Finally, the allocation takes place in terms of expenditure instruments, such as direct expenditures (which enable governments to secure the goods and services needed to perform their functions), loans to other parties, guarantees to both public and private sector firms that are in need of additional creditworthiness, or tax expenditure under which tax incentives are provided to stimulate selected activities. The level of direct expenditures is determined as a result of the interplay of forces during the preceding four stages, and as such there is little wiggle room in the penultimate stage of budget-making. The provision of loans is determined, in addition to need, by two other factors. In many cases, these may be funds received from donors that are re-lent to other levels of government or to autonomous agencies. The role of the central government in this case is limited to being a conduit. In other cases, the higher level of government may borrow funds from the market to meet the needs of other levels or autonomous agencies. In these cases, the loans extended broadly reflect the terms on which the higher level of government has borrowed from the market. In addition, a risk premium may be added to cover for any delays in payments or even defaults. The important consideration in determining the level of loans is the potential impact on financial markets and on rates charged. Where the demand is large and persistent, very soon higher interest rates may have to be paid. In much the same way, guarantees may also be provided by the higher-level government to provide additional security and to reduce the risk premium that would have been otherwise paid by the borrower. Provision of guarantees does not have any immediate impact on the level of government expenditures. It is only in the event of default that government expenditures tend to rise. With a view to forestalling such a situation, some governments have introduced, through legislation, limits on the extent of guarantees that can be provided. Such limits can provide misleading assurances, as what affects the expenditure levels is the risk factor inherent in the business that is guaranteed than the overall level of guarantees. Also, a good deal is dependent on the arrangements for risk sharing, and in the event of default, the whole burden may not fall on government expenditures. Tax expenditure, on the other hand, is an opaque area, where the relationship between the incentive provided and the actual benefit procured is less than clear.

Many governments do not have complete data on the incentives provided and their effect on the revenues, and the achievement of policies. But this lack of data has never hindered governments from engaging in tax expenditures. The recent guidelines on fiscal transparency require the full disclosure of the amount of revenue forgone as a result of tax expenditures. However, this is a guideline that remains to be fulfilled.

The five levels discussed above often take place in independent spheres but they converge, as a part of the annual budgetary process, into a definitive policy framework. The implementation of the budget during the fiscal year, however, puts to test many of the underlying tenets of resource allocation. The estimates may overshoot or undershoot and the actual results may vary considerably. Further, new areas may surface requiring new allocation of resources. In such cases, supplementary budgets may be prepared as and when necessary. The full gamut of forces traversed in the preparation of the budget may not be covered in the allocation of supplementary resources and policy making may be limited to the new claims on resources. Where, however, the variations between the intent and the actual purposes are considerable, and too frequent, and where the distortions emanating from the initial decisions are persistent, budget-making may cease to be an annual activity and may become a regular day-to-day exercise in government.

The preceding analysis shows that expenditure allocations have tended to become rigid for a variety of factors, and that this rigidity may have contributed to a situation where the allocative process is less than optimal or adequate. It is important, if the fiscal objectives are to be achieved, that there is a level playing field and that all claims are given a uniform assessment. This is not to say that there should be no priorities. Indeed, any government worth its name and legitimacy would have priorities determined in the light of political, economic, and social considerations. But what is debatable is whether such priorities should morph into legally specified earmarking that would also have the effect of taking them out, in effect, from the annual budget process. The need of the day is a broader expenditure evaluation framework, while what is available, in most cases, is a body of settled policies and firmly allocated resources, that excludes large areas from decision making.

More important, the budget emerging from the above considerations does not demonstrate the explicit nexus between annual policies, budgetary allocations, and the expected results. Restoration of credibility of governments and their allocation of resources requires that this nexus be made amply clear and explicit in the budget. At the minimum, it is expected that each agency specify three major objectives proposed to be pursued, the allocations made for the purpose, and the results estimated. Fig. 3.1 provides a brief illustration.

Agency

Objective 1	→	Allocations	→	Estimated results
Objective 2	→	Allocations	→	Estimated results
Objective 3	→	Allocations	→	Estimated results

Figure 3.1: Objective–Allocation Nexus

A statement of the above type shows at the outset the purposes of the detailed annual appropriations and provides an implicit basis for a notional contract with the public, while also clarifying the mission of the agency and its own programme to achieve it.

Anchor of Control: Portfolio Management and Institutional Hurdles

Traditionally, expenditure controls relied, both for reasons of convenience and shortage of time, on one or two of the allocation bases described earlier. To a very large extent, the anchor chosen by most governments, both in industrial and developing worlds, and common to most levels of government within a country, has been the control of manpower. Such an anchor was justified on the consideration that the single biggest block of expenditure in the budget is the one devoted to wages and salaries, and pensions of the administrative class when organized as a deferred wage, rather than on a contributory basis. The implicit logic was that this category was also the one prone to high annual rates of growth, reflecting in turn the annual adjustments for inflation, and the increase in staff needed to meet increasing demand for services. Hence, it became a pivotal category or anchor of expenditure control. To dampen expectations, annual guidance given as a part of budget-making lays special emphasis on the need for exceptional prudence in seeking additional positions. Given that this is a contentious area between those seeking increases and those seeking to deny them, the determination of the actual increases is sought to be done in an objective and apolitical manner by entrusting the task to neutral bodies, such as public service commissions or manpower regulatory agencies in governments. These agencies have often based their judgements on norms and yardsticks but not on the available resources, a choice that is made only by the finance ministries. The norms are, as noted previously, supply driven and have invariably resulted in annual additions to the staff. The control exercised by the finance ministries was mostly on the fringes and, in the event, a lower figure for staff increase is accepted by all, and accordingly, appropriate funding is provided. In some cases, the views of the finance ministries may not prevail, as the assessments of neutral manpower agencies are believed to be relatively scientific. This major reliance on staff increments as the anchor of expenditure management continued for several decades, and is still continuing in a few countries. But experience has shown that primary reliance on this anchor alone is not adequate. Also, introduction of organized central planning and expansion of government work in several areas brought forth a massive increase, that illustrated the futility of according expenditure management on staff complements. In fact, as fiscal crisis became a more common and a regular phenomenon, policies increasingly began to focus on the need for retrenchment from existing levels rather than the determination of the size of annual additional staff. This purpose was sought to be achieved in two ways: first, a reduction in staff levels through enforcement of compulsory and voluntary retirement programmes, and second, avoiding future increases through tight budget constraints such as reduced ceiling on resources given to agencies. The former approach was limited in its application to a few years; the latter became a standard budgetary technique that was believed to be in conformity with the new management philosophy, in that the determination of the new manpower levels (including work to be done by consultants, and through greater deployment of technology that would reduce manpower requirements), would be left to the agencies. In the process, the determination of staff ceased to be an anchor of expenditure management. In a few countries, for example, Australia and New Zealand, the agencies were expected to be guided in these efforts by the public service commissions or manpower agencies.

The gradual decline in the reliance placed on staff controls was sought to be compensated by a greater focus on the development of objective criteria for project appraisal, and their final inclusion in the budget. Such a shift was only appropriate in a context when much of the development effort came from the budget in the form of stepped up investment in the infrastructure of the economy, and in the establishment of a variety of state-owned enterprises—all of which were dependent on government capital. In the process, expenditure management gained an additional anchor, and many governments continued to rely on staff and project controls as a means of moderating expenditure growth. Until this period, the running expenses of programmes received less emphasis, as they were considered to be a part of necessary, concomitant expenditure. But having seen that staff controls and project selection did not prevent the massive growth in public expenditure (in fact, a major part of the growth was contributed by the latter group), there was a search for new avenues to control expenditures. In developing countries, where foreign exchange became a pivotal scarcity, efforts were concentrated on quantitative foreign exchange restrictions. The industrial countries sought greater control over running expenses. The major ingredient in this approach was the examination of major programmes and the determination of wages and other expenditure associated with it. Initially, the focus was on the examination of major programmes and the determination of the resource or funding levels needed for their implementation. But this was recognized to be a difficult exercise, as not all agencies had a programme structure that could serve the purpose. Also, once the resource complements were determined, the new levels became legitimate floors from which increases could be claimed, particularly in a context of high inflation, where adjustment became practically automatic and not discretionary. As an easier way out of the difficult situation, many countries were content to provide the annual increases in running expenses at the same rate at which the GDP was estimated to grow for the year. In fact, this contributed to a relaxation, rather than tightening, of control. What was more, there was little clarity on what the anchor was and what its effect would be.

Meanwhile, the worsening fiscal situation forced many countries to envisage more drastic approaches such as fundamental periodic review of agency work. The experience during the period reveal's that governments were straddling two different, and generally opposite, paths. On the one hand, influenced by the new management philosophy, there was a keenness to shift the burden of expenditure management from itemized review to a broader base, which while meeting the broad policy requirements was also endowing a degree of functional autonomy to the managerial class. At the same time, forced by economic and fiscal realities, there was a resort to detailed reviews and across-the-board cuts. Admittedly, this straddling cannot be a way of life. There are changes in the underlying situation that need to be recognized and adjustments made accordingly. The task of expenditure management is to engage in an identification of those factors and formulate an anchor (or anchors) that addresses them.

Looking into the future, with the knowledge gained from experience, it is understood that an anchor of expenditure management should be clear (with no built-in ambiguity), consistent (over a period of years: constant change cannot produce a solid anchor), and viable (capable of yielding results over a specified period). From these points of view, the only anchor, available in theory but not yet extensively used in practice, is the cost of a programme or a project. Such a cost can be computed even from the existing information and does not require, as a prerequisite, the introduction of accrual accounting with depreciation provisions and capital charges. First of all, it has to be recognized that cost computation need not be undertaken for all programmes. Such uniform application would be a waste of resources. Rather, it should be applied to areas and programmes where annual increases tend to be the order of the day. In these situations, the application of activity-based costing would yield information on the factors contributing to cost increases. The difference between cost on an ex-ante and ex-post basis is the test of the success of expenditure management. As more and more tasks funded by governments are undertaken by NGOs, the only effective anchor is cost control. Much, however, remains to be done in this direction.

The system of expenditure management in governments is also influenced, to a very large extent, by their expenditure portfolios. Increasingly, central and federal budgets of many countries have become centres of large transfers to other levels of government, to corporate bodies, and to NGOs and individuals. Transfers to individuals are largely based on entitlement and poverty alleviation programmes under which direct transfers of money are made during periods of unemployment, or to provide medical assistance. Transfers to corporate bodies and to NGOs are intended to finance activities undertaken by them on a contractual basis for governments. These transfers, which were relatively minor in the preceding decades, are now a major feature of many government portfolios in industrial countries, and increasingly in developing countries as well. For example, in the United States, the share of expenditures on directly provided services is less than 10 per cent of the total. Clearly, an expenditure management system that was oriented to staff controls or to the containment of running expenses would not be appropriate in a situation where much of the work is performed by non-governmental bodies.

The expenditure management system in this changed setting should, ideally, have three major points of focus. First, the administrative overheads in terms of policy management should be small. Where contracting out is undertaken regularly, there is a clear, identifiable, and measurable distinction between policy formulation and implementation. Those who are seeking contractors are the ones who are engaged in policy formulation, while those who have been awarded the contracts are responsible for implementation. In such cases, the share of expenditures on monitoring of implementation should, in no case, exceed 5 per cent of the programme outlay, particularly in a context where computerized information systems are in operation. Second, the cost basis of contracts should be clear, firm, and specific. Where costs are vague, or are estimated in an ad hoc way, cost revision follows as a regular feature, mostly to the advantage of the contractors. The difference between estimated cost and the actual bid is often equivalent to the gains of competition, or the rigging of contractual procedures. Third, the accounting and financial management infrastructure of the recipient organization should conform to certain specified standards. In the present situation, this is largely an unregulated area, particularly in the case of NGOs. Most of them are not subject to the observance of any standards and may not be subjected to annual independent audit either by government audit organizations or others. If NGOs are deemed to be essential complementary tools for government affairs, then it is only appropriate that the technical infrastructure of these bodies is subjected to standards and inspections.

The effectiveness of the expenditure management system is either impeded or facilitated by the institutional relationships between those agencies that are responsible for the formulation of fiscal policy goals, that is, intent, and those that are responsible in a collective endeavour to produce an outcome that is in conformity with the intent. It is usual in governments that the former task is carried out mostly by finance ministries, and depending on the degree of integration or fragmentation, by others such as planning agencies, while the latter task is away from the authority stemming from goal determination and its pursuit, to the more mundane, if practical, issue of 'who directs whom?' and the determination of the command–compliance relationship. In expenditure management, the controlling agenda, and the authority (generally) to prevail over contrary preferences of others, as well as power that can make a significant difference in the proposed goals and the outcomes, are located in the finance ministries, and it is this power, or at any rate the perception of excessive centralization that has come to be questioned.

Much is dependent, however, on the influence, rectitude, and respect commanded by the finance ministries, not by virtue of centralization of power but by the way in which it is exercised. It is in these three respects that finance ministries are found wanting. It is frequently suggested that the decision making is secretive, that the communication of economic realities is seldom effective, therefore, the influence that it would have commanded is vitiated by its own lack of objectivity and the frequent resort to arbitrary decision making. Its approaches to allocation of resources and to crisis management are viewed, mostly, as ad hoc reactions rather than as properly organized, coherent policies. In terms of rectitude, and as an exemplar, it is common experience that finance ministries have little to show that distinguishes them from the rest of the government. It is in this context that there is a demand for empowerment, and for a more cooperative and communicative system.

Expenditure management is a common endeavour of all agencies and should be reflected in the approaches to policy formulation and implementation. While it is recognized that the pursuit of stability in the economy endows greater leadership function to the finance ministries, there has also been growing fragmentation of controls: development projects, and coordination of foreign aid came to be handled in several cases by planning agencies, similarly, the personnel management function, the task of tendering and contracting, and the task of evaluation came to be entrusted to independent agencies and, as a result, the power that was hitherto wielded by finance ministries came to be shared by other agencies. But these arrangements did not last too long, and the hegemony of finance ministries returned during the last few decades with reinforced vigour. Fiscal crisis and the pursuit of austerity management brought the finance ministry once again to the forefront and all shared power arrangements were brought within the fold of overriding powers of finance ministries.

Power, to philosopher Bertrand Russell, was an instrument to achieve the production of intended effects, and to that extent it was a quantitative aspect.[13] In reality, it was quantitative in terms of

---

13. For a comprehensive discussion of power in a historical context, see de

determining the aggregate level of expenditures, and the ceilings on allocation for various ministries and agencies, but more qualitative in day-to-day arrangements as it reflected the institutionalization of authority and binding obligations of the collective agents. As the finance ministries see it, expenditure management acquires legitimacy not in terms of those exercising it but by the values inherent in the system, where the authority is based on the need for the attainment of goals, and as such, both the endowment and exercise of authority are legitimate. Indeed, there cannot be any other interpretation of authority, is the argument generally advanced by finance ministries. On the other hand, it is equally recognized that power is an important part of the responsibilities of the administrative or spending agencies. In the historical evolution of governmental organizations, finance ministries or their predecessors, the royal treasuries, came first, reflecting the primary concerns of the monarchical system. The extensive power that was built into the system was formalized in later years, with the rule that no action involving expenditures or any claims on government money could be carried out without the explicit permission of the treasury or the later-day ministries of finance. This inevitable centralization, both in theory and in practice, contributed to two highly debatable views, that had an extensive influence on the approaches and behaviour of government agencies. One view, often held by the ministries of finance was that there was no financial consciousness in spending agencies, and that it was to be found only in the ministry of finance. The other view was that there could be no financial consciousness in the spending agencies in view of the fact that all aspects of expenditure management, starting from policy formulation to the actual payments and liquidation of claims on government, were either under the direct day-to-day control of finance ministries, or under their direct supervision. This centralization of tasks and responsibilities continued in most countries well into the 1930s, when it was recognized that governments had become so big that the growing operations could no longer be controlled by the treasuries; and if financial consciousness was to be developed, there was a need for greater decentralization, and devolution of selected areas to the spending agencies. Resources could be saved or more effectively utilized only when the spending agencies had a stake in their management. But the process of decentralization was not universal, and

---

Jouvenel, (1993). A discussion of the concepts of power, in its various settings, is provided in Lukes, (1986 and 1992).

many governments, especially in developing countries, tend to have pervasive finance ministries. The relationships between those that issue commands and those that comply with them need to be seen in terms of three zones: green, yellow, and red. The red zone which comprises tasks relating to the pursuit of macroeconomic stability, and the determination of the aggregate level of expenditures, and functional level allocations, is to be within the fold of the responsibilities of the finance ministries. The other zones refer essentially to budget implementation tasks, where given the current state of financial information systems, more responsibilities can be entrusted to the spending agencies. In all these areas, many an irritant experienced can be avoided by the finance ministries, which should concentrate more on equipping themselves with the capacity to anticipate situations and to manage risks.

In sum, there is a good deal that remains to be done. In public bodies, the effort aimed at adaptation and improvement is a relentless one. Machiavelli wrote a long time ago, 'Physicians say of consumption, that in the early stages of this disease it is easy to cure but difficult to diagnose; whereas later on, if it has not been recognized and treated at the beginning, it becomes easy to diagnose and difficult to cure. The same thing in affairs of state'. This should serve as a note of caution to all those engaged in public institutional improvement.

4. Ethical Dimensions of Expenditure Management

'It is clear that ethics cannot be put into words. Ethics is transcendental.'

Wittgenstein, *Tractatus*

'The fault, dear Brutus, is not in our stars, but in ourselves.'

Shakespeare, *Julius Caesar*

The ethical dimensions of public expenditure management (PEM), which essentially deal with the expected patterns of behaviour or professional conduct in regard to what we value the most—an objective and reasonable assessment of policy proposals and their alternatives, as well as the appropriate implementation of policies—have never received the attention due, notwithstanding the growing recognition of the crucial place of PEM in the functional approaches and work of public bodies. Rather, far too much attention has been paid to corruption, particularly since that issue has come to take an important place in the conditionality and associated lending approaches of IFIs. The focus on corruption, important though it is, may have deflected attention from the equally important and much-needed exploration of the ethnical dimensions of PEM. The lack of attention may be ascribed to several obvious factors. The processes of PEM are largely related to the internal flow of information and its processing through various layers of governmental hierarchy, and the multiple dimensions of these processes remain, for the most part, outside the record of public debate. Rather, this has remained a subject that is often discussed within the cloistered confines of government ministries. In part, it is also due to the lack of coherence on the part of those who are at the receiving end of government actions. The beneficiaries of government policies, along with those who claim to be victims, come from different groups of the political spectrum, income levels, economic and social backgrounds, and have rarely been united. The various interests occasionally come together and even form temporary alliances to achieve common ends, but the divergence in their interests does not permit a continuing unified front. Yet another factor may have been the narrow focus of some of the academic disciplines in examining the conduct of governments in the formulation and implementation of public policies. For example, political scientists have addressed the issues relating to the participation of citizens in policy making, and how policy making in general could be improved, as well as the provision of public services along more efficient lines. The macroeconomists, on the other hand, were more concerned with the impact of budgets on economic stability, and whether some of the normal proclivities associated with governments could be controlled through constitutional amendments, legislation, and binding rules.[1] Inevitably, in the process, some of the more important issues came to be left out.

Meanwhile, the lack of coherent logical, and rational processes has contributed to a higher incidence of human depravity with growing costs to the community. There are several compelling reasons to consider these issues in some detail. First, there is the paradoxical situation in which, for reasons of fiscal stability and sustainability, governments in industrial and developing countries have been pursuing, some more vigorously than others, policies aimed at reducing the role of the state and readjusting its boundaries. This cause has also been supported by the IFIs, who have become the most vocal supporters and funding agencies for the re-engineering of governments. Even as these developments are taking place, there is also a growing emphasis on improving 'life satisfaction' and promoting more options for democratic involvement, as well as ensuring a more positive appraisal of public expenditure (see, for example, Donovan and Halpern, 2002). If this initiative were to gain more support in the future, it is a certainty that there will be more expenditure programmes aimed at raising the level

---

[1] In the early 1980s there was a doubt, even among responsible policymakers, whether there was in fact a proper budget policy. David Stockman, then the Director of Office of Management and Budget in the US government, said that his response about budget policy was to recall the words of Mahatma Gandhi, when he was asked what he thought of western civilization. 'It would be a good idea' replied he. See Feldstein (ed.) 1994, p 270.

of life satisfaction, and at improved governance. Second, a similar paradox is found in the growing emphasis on the promotion of standards of public life. Ever since the Nolan Commission in the United Kingdom (1994) reiterated the need for selflessness, integrity, objectivity, accountability, openness, honesty, and leadership (seven principles that were also openly endorsed and continued by the Blair Government) there has been a growing perception that many of these qualities are absent in day-to-day governmental management. Each time these or similar principles are enunciated at various fora, the public seems to be more assured that there is something crooked in the timber of the governments. Third, there is another paradox in that when the governments are claiming success in controlling expenditures and in improved delivery of services, as well as in enhanced user participation in public policy making, there is a growing deep-seated distrust with the government. It is pointed out that while substantial advances have been made in establishing forms of welfare states, and in making obvious improvements in the technological infrastructure, there has also been a steady increase, (according to this perception), in the dominance of vested interests in policy making, in the rules and regulations governing the delivery of services to an extent leading to a tyranny of rules, and despite safeguards, there has also been a good deal of wasteful spending. Surveys carried out in various industrial countries reveal that this basic distrust is receiving, from time to time, additional adherents. In part, this reflects the changing landscape of the role of the visual media, which brings the horrors of the effects of governmental decision making to the citizens everyday. Citizens want improvements, and as yet they are not confident that the economic reforms and related financial adjustments are working in their favour. It is the pervasive perception that governments engage in prevarication of facts, that they are more economical with the truth and that, in short, there has been a perceptive decline in the ethical standards of government. These factors make it imperative to consider these issues.

If future progress is to be made, it is important to stem the erosion that has taken place in the credibility of governments. A weak government, hobbled by its own internal systemic vulnerabilities and a growing lack of trust on the part of the public, can hardly be considered as adequately equipped to deal with the multiple growing expectations on the one hand and the stark realities of life, on the other. Samuelson wrote more than five decades ago, in a private memo to the then President-elect Kennedy, 'Even an ostrich cannot avoid the economic realities of life'. It cannot avoid the declining abilities of governments to perform too, and immediate efforts are indicated, first of all, to restore the credibility of governments. Such a restoration requires concerted efforts on the part of the community, national authorities, and the IFIs. A much-needed preliminary step in this direction is the consideration of the ethical dimensions of PEM.

The analytical framework in this chapter is divided into two parts. In the first part, 'Public Policy Making', the ethical dimensions of PEM and, more important, those that are constantly abused or misused by governments and how those deviations contribute to distorted policy making and related implementation, are considered. The second part, 'Alternative Proposals', is devoted to a consideration of the alternatives pursued by the national authorities and the IFIs and it is argued that many of the initiatives would hardly make a dent in the present situation even if they are fully implemented, and would hardly have the desired impact on improving PEM. Rather, it is important to begin thinking of developing ethical codes, and countervailing powers so that a responsive and responsible, and most important, a credible government is restored.

PUBLIC POLICY MAKING

It is generally accepted that all public policy making, regardless of the final shape it takes either in the form of a separate statement or as a part of the annual budget, or a presidential speech, or the birthday occasion of the monarch or the prime minister, or as a separate piece of legislation, is the result of an interplay of facts, values, and interests. In theory, each of these groups is separate, and to a large extent objective too. In particular, facts refer to those phenomena that are empirical and verifiable, while values and interests are largely the products of thinking and are relative to every human being; and as Kant pointed out a long time ago, such values are unlikely to be objective. But this distinction between 'objectivity' and 'relativism' of values may not be sustainable in the form of a clear boundary. In fact, many 'factual' statements may also be value statements, and to that extent, there may not be a fundamental political divide between the two (for a general discussion of these distinctions, see Hundert 1995). The values are often relative to the subject of cultural groups, and it is important to recognize that the government does not represent a single culture. Governments are huge organizations comprising several domains that are distinct, and that have separate value systems. Policy analysts have often divided the government, with a view to identifying the role of private interests in national policy making, in terms of four sectors—agriculture, energy, health, and labour (see for example, Heinz et al. 1993). Admittedly, this is too inadequate and hardly representative of the several other important areas such as defence, social services, and economic infrastructure. Each of these domains tends to develop, like every human being, a set of its own values through which it evaluates the policies of governments. These values tend to be very general and stable over a period. Both the general nature and enduring stability form the hard core of beliefs and begin to dominate the thinking of every official entering into the distinctive domains of government. The terms 'defence mentality' and 'finance mentality', frequently used in governments, reflect the respective subcultures and their dominant value systems. These values become so ingrained over a period of time that they tend to affect the objectivity of the decision made or policies formulated.

In democratic societies, the initiatives in regard to public policies may come from a variety of sources including the executive, judicial pronouncements (particularly in countries where the judiciary plays an active role), findings and recommendations of independent commissions of inquiry, the legislatures, active public groups, and during more recent years, the advice of IFIs. It is noteworthy that in countries that are heavily indebted to external creditors, the latter play an important role in the promotion of economic policies and related regulation. When the initiatives are taken from outside the executive wing, several factors may be at play, including the vested interests that have a specific policy outcome in view. When, however, the policy advice comes from independent commissions of inquiry or from judicial sources, the normal impression is that the recommendations are objective and have not been contaminated by political considerations. Regardless of the origin of the proposed policies, all policies that have financial implications require the explicit support of the executive before they can become operational. Under the British type of parliamentary systems, no money bills can be proposed for legislative approval except at the initiative of the government. Since all policies have some financial implications—minor or heavy, recurring or irregular—they have to be considered and endorsed by the executive wing of the government if they have to become laws and moneys are to be appropriated by the legislature.

Once the initiatives are brought within the reach of the executive, there are specified and unspecified ways of processing them. In each domain, the systems and the individual groups are different and they may not fit into preconceived neat logical categories. Frequently, the real world may never function according to normally held beliefs and there are blends, coalitions, incongruities, and irrationalities that are not easy to explain. Bismarck is reported to have remarked that watching a legislature (or executive) make laws (policies) is like watching a butcher make sausages—unpleasant, routine, and dull. The executive is basically concerned with the internalization of the four basic roles of policy—a political role of meeting a part of the ideological framework of the party in power, a problem solving role, in that it is addressed to a problem or a group of homogeneous problems, a judicial role, in that the benefits of the proposed policy do not accrue unfairly to certain groups of people and that the distributional effects are in accord with the expectations of the community in terms of what is perceived to be fair,[2] and a specified role for the community which is expected to make financial sacrifices in support of the proposed policies or engage in other forms of contribution. In turn, they assure the community implicitly that the proposed policies would be cost-effective and that they reflect the intent and design and aspirations of the community.

Notwithstanding differences among various governments and their operational systems, there are some common features associated with policy making. The administrative systems are large and elaborate, and have their own internal control processes. Most of them reveal, in day-to-day practice, the existence of an oligarchy of institutions and an oligarchy of individuals that are responsible for government-wide policies, as distinct from specific sectoral policies, that have far-reaching effects. These institutions and individuals ensure that the centres of powers, influence, and responsibility are regularly in the picture through established formal procedures or through informal networks. Thus, the political interest groups, civil service interest groups, influential legislatures, go-betweens from the government and the corporate sector,

---

[2.] In several cases, these aspirations and expectations may be embodied in the form of constitutional provisions. See, for example, Part IV of the Indian Constitution, containing the Directive Principles of State Policy, which being not enforceable in a court of law are '*nevertheless fundamental in the governance of the country*' (emphasis added). The Constitution and the laws do not, however, specify the organizational forms, institutions, and operational systems through which the goals are to be achieved. It is for the executive wing to develop the requisite tools that would, it is hoped, convert the goal into reality.

external creditors, and the IFIs are regularly consulted. Experience shows that the large range of government products and services has spawned several powerful organized interests such as the military-industrial complex, construction complex, social service complex, and poverty complex, each with its own clientele groups and distinct forms of support. Public policy making as a system is neither white magic nor black, neither a formula for easy salvation nor a sanctimonious fraud. Its tools and operational systems are to be judged by the results separating ideas from fact, intent from outcome and viewed as a self-contained system. As a system, it can be sharp, timely, judicious, and effective. It can also produce policies that are poor in design that contribute to results that are expensive, and far different from those anticipated. The strategies and decisions may, at times, reflecting the numerous factors at work, be excessively value laden or have short-term political ends in view and therefore have the potential of becoming more controversial with the distinct possibility that the remedy may be worse than the malady. Each public policy also involves an explicit choice and selection from among the various instruments that form the arsenal of PEM.

Conceptually, governments can achieve their policy objectives through direct expenditures, or provision of loans, or provision of fiscal incentives by forgoing the taxes due, or through public–private partnerships, or provision of guarantees, or through quasi-fiscal accounts maintained at the central banks and usually financed from their reserve funds. These instruments are not perfectly substitutable with each other, and thus the final choice may reveal an eclectic combination of these instruments rather than an exclusive reliance on any one of them. It is best to view them as comprising a portfolio, where each instrument may be deployed to its potential. Each instrument brings with it a discipline of its own as distinct from others. To that extent, there is no single generic phrase generally used to describe the total phenomenon. Each instrument has its own implications for ethics, as well as for the most important relationship with the legislature, which in theory has the final control of the purse in an operational democracy. Many of the instruments involve a departure from this principle of legislative control. The instruments may not be available to all levels of governments; for example, quasi-fiscal accounts are not available to sub-national governments but are at the exclusive disposal of central governments.

In the academic approaches to this subject, a distinction is made between policy formulation and policy implementation. This has its origins in the contributions made by President Wilson in the United

States nearly eight decades ago. According to his views, the world of government is neatly divided into spheres of policy formulation and policy implementation—the former being the exclusive territory of departments at the apex of the administration hierarchy, and the latter being the responsibility of the field or executive agencies. It is now generally held that this distinction is somewhat outmoded in that policies are made as they are implemented. Several changes may take place in the actual course of implementation, and what comes to be viewed as the policy is the one that is implemented. In the world of expenditure management, the transition from policy formulation to policy implementation involves a shift of emphasis from allocative efficiency to technical efficiency, from funding to service provision, and the formulation of a more precise relationship between purchaser and provider of services. The ethical conduct of officials concerned with these aspects has a critical importance in the overall process.

Principles and Protocols

Expenditure policies of government are carried out, for the most part, through an annual budget. The considerations of allocative and technical efficiency, as well as those relating to the maintenance of macroeconomic stability are expected to be kept in view while formulating the expenditure estimates of the budget. The ethical dimensions of formulation of expenditure estimates have, however, been never formalized in the form of a law nor has a protocol been established, which if violated could be brought into the purview of the judiciary. Rather, they have been in the form of general principles expected to be followed by everybody concerned. The lack of legislation does not reduce their importance: on the other hand, they become a code of honour for those engaged in the formulation of expenditure estimates. These principles, which have grown over time, and which have always been implicit, may be reiterated in terms of three categories (for a more detailed discussion, see Chapter 5 of this book).

1. Stewardship of Resources: The estimates should facilitate an evaluation of the current state of finances and their future sustainability. Towards the end, the principles of unity or total comprehensiveness should pervade the preparation of estimates and should, therefore, cover the financial implications of ongoing as well as new policies, and current and long-term liabilities. Moreover, the estimates should be accurate

for they imply a bond with the legislature which approves them, and more important, with the community.

2. Operational adequacy: The estimates and related financial information should enable an appraisal of the adequacy of the PEM machinery to deal with the current and future tasks of the government. As an integral part of this effort, it is expected that the tasks and responsibilities of governmental agencies are made abundantly clear.

3. Decision making approaches: The estimates are expected to be clear in their intent, and in the specification of intended beneficiaries so that the community and its elected representatives can understand and deliberate on the contents of expenditure estimates. The estimates should form a public document and be available in the public realm.

These principles, which appear to be reasonable, should have been easy to comply with. Experience, however, shows that departures from these principles have been more common than adherence. It is in this process of applying the principles that 'original sins' (for a more detailed discussion of the theory of original sin or moral error, see Dunn, 2000, p. 19) or 'malcontents', as Herodotus described them a long time ago, arise.

Original Sins

The application of the above principles does not necessarily mean that one would reach, as did Bacon's crew of a sailing ship in his *New Atlantis*, and find a haven where the government is wise, generous, and incorruptible. Rather, the intent is to examine how various choices are made and how ethics are observed in the day-to-day working of governments. A cursory examination of the fiscal experience shows that many choices of fiscal instruments are made deliberately in the knowledge that they may imply a departure from the accepted world of morality. The experience in this regard is best examined in terms of the framework already described (for a discussion of this framework, see Premchand 2000), viz., resource allocation, resource utilization, and resource-use accounting.

Resource Allocation

Instrument Choice: The first choice relates to the instruments of fiscal policy. If it is pursued through direct expenditures, it implies unambiguously that the intent is to operate within the framework of traditional budget and its discipline. If the choice involves loans or guarantees, it could imply a short-term preference for the creation of a financial asset that may be more advantageous than direct expenditure, while a guarantee may take the matter totally outside the budget. To that extent, it could involve, in the absence of adequate legislation or similar safeguard, the emergence of the issue of moral hazard. Further, what is granted as a loan has every possibility of being converted into a grant or being written-off. Reliance, on quasi-fiscal accounts, on the other hand, may once and for all take decision making outside the realm of the annual budget and associated legislative control.

H.L.A. Hart wrote that 'men are neither angels nor devils: that makes morality both necessary and possible'. The experience with regard to the choice of instruments, particularly during the last three decades, in both industrial and developing countries shows that the behaviour, in the absence of formal legislation, has been far from angelic. In fact, many of them plumped for the creation of autonomous agencies that were financed either by loans from the government or by guarantees given by it. In reality, many loans were non-performing from the day they were given and the guarantees in several cases meant redemption of a deferred liability. Similarly, with respect to public–private partnerships, the fiscal risk remained for the most part with the governments. In the absence of efforts to reduce or distribute the final risk, additional liabilities became a common feature of governments at all levels. A likewise expansion in tax expenditures reduced the tax base of governments, while the results of those incentives remained debatable. Many of the financial crises experienced by governments can be explained in terms of the wrong choices made at this stage.

Estimational Fraud: The annual decision making in regard to the determination of aggregate expenditures as well as sectoral allocations is expected to take place within a specified macroeconomic framework. The determination of the funding is made in terms of continuing policies and new programmes and projects. The eligibility of the latter category for funding is very much dependent on the availability of additional resources in the form of current account surpluses or external loans from IFIs. In both cases, it is common in the industrial and developing worlds that attempts are made, as indicated above, either to escape the scrutiny that normal budget discipline entails or to understate the financial implications everywhere. Most policy making seems to follow a predictable pattern. First a crisis is created; second, pressure is brought on the government to find an immediate way out, as the alternative of inaction will result in major economic disaster; and third, governments are persuaded to begin making budgetary allocations to fund the proposed alternative (for a very interesting case study of this approach, see Greenberg 2001, the subtitle of the book is of particular interest). In this context, understatement of costs serves the vested interests, while providing an easy and smooth path for decision making. It is realized that once a project or a programme is included in the budget and an allocation, however small, has been made, it gains legitimacy and a momentum of its own that is difficult to stop. It raises expectations, leads to the establishment of formal or informal client groups that very soon become entrenched interests, and it becomes difficult to even contemplate an abandonment of these projects or programmes. Similar approaches govern the inclusion of mega projects. A recent analysis of fifteen mega projects undertaken in several countries shows that decisions were not made on the basis of 'honest numbers' and that 'project promoters often avoid and violate established practices of good governance, transparency, and participation, in political and administrative decision making either out of ignorance or because they see such practices as counter-productive to getting projects started' (for more detailed analysis, see Flyvbjerg et al. 2003, p. 5). The result of this myopic decision making is that 'cost overruns and lower-than-predicted revenues frequently place project viability at risk and redefine projects that were initially promoted as effective vehicles to economic growth as possible obstacles to such growth' (Flyvbjerg et al. 2003, p. 3).

It is also observed that a bout of undue optimism takes over the budget decision makers in the process of making the annual budget. In an attempt often motivated by a desire to influence the market and the community, governments tend to manipulate estimates to achieve a desired level of deficit. In turn, this could imply inflation of revenue estimates and a downward estimate of expenditure. Since the Reagan years, these two approaches have come to be embodied in the budgetary lexicon as 'rosy scenarios' and 'magic asterisks' (expenditure reductions will be announced later, the footnotes explain). But as the year progresses, recognition of the reality dawns on policy makers, and the rest of the fiscal year is spent in making adjustments—in some countries even on a daily basis. The annual budget presented, approved, and enacted into law by the legislature, then becomes a putative budget, and budgetary decision making ceasing to be an annual rite, becomes a daily scramble for resources. Instead of certainty, it engenders on a regular basis, uncertainty in the availability of resources. More significantly, the adjustment process becomes a power play in which those who are protected in terms of special categories such as wages, pensions, or military, or those who thump the table harder, or those with political clout, end up getting more funds. What was expected to be an objective, and a relatively technical exercise, becomes loaded with political sideshows and decision making that may be anything other than ethical.

The understatement of outlays (the phrase 'costs' is deliberately avoided here, as in most cases of programmes costs are rarely computed in governments; costs of projects are computed, however, even if on a tentative basis, as they are often submitted to donors and IFIs for financing) has other major implications for allocation of resources. Those who get a toehold in the budget begin after a stage to claim more resources than originally estimated, and gradually crowd out other deserving projects. Furthermore, since the initial estimates are understated, there is no strong desire or effort to secure savings at the design stage. A more serious matter of concern is that the understatement of costs as well as other aspects may end with the government playing the role of a toady to the corporate sector, particularly in the area of medical research and associated development of drugs. A recent study on science and politics in the United States reported that 'mercenary motives were sometimes involved in these episodes of fabrication, falsification and plagiarism—the formally proscribed categories of scientific sins'.[3] Such motives are common to several other areas where estimates are routinely manipulated for a specified remuneration.

[3.] See Greenberg 2001, p. 349. Greenberg cites several cases of drug development where government-sponsored academic research ended up supporting the case of drug manufacturers through fabricated data. One way of avoiding this is to develop a code of ethics in research, but those involved with these matters testify that the process will be time-consuming and 'even pointless if they (the scientific community) are not prepared to *enforce* whatever codes they adopt' (p. 352, emphasis added). Those who are engaged in the discussion of the philosophical implications of these approaches point out the major difficulties in establishing the truth, which to them is a myth. While truth may have a liberating influence, the discovery of truth may also diminish human happiness. In an imperfect world, it is difficult to pursue truth for its own sake, as theologians have done it. The alternative, Kitcher (2001, p. 197) argues, is to work in ways that 'approximate the requirements of well ordered science, and

Those engaged in the management of government finances may offer two explanations in support of this approach, which has become almost second nature to them and has come to be firmly ingrained in their psyche. First is the state of knowledge regarding the project or programme under consideration. In this regard, a case was made a long time ago by Aristotle, who wrote in *The Nicomachean Ethics* that 'it is the mark of a trained mind never to expect more precision in the treatment of any subject than the nature of that subject permits'. The inadequate knowledge and related database can often be major factors in sharply limiting the capacity of the policymaker in carefully examining all aspects, including the possible changes in economic parameters such as exchange and interest rates. Preparation of estimates is based on the knowledge available when those estimates are prepared. While changes can be factored in, it is difficult to be too precise about the possible changes throughout the life cycle of a programme or a project. Although the theoretical base of the argument cannot be denied, the more important issue is whether this factor alone explains the major difference between intent and outcome. It is here that the second factor assumes importance. It is the tradition of estimate making that governments wishing to advocate a policy always underestimate the costs and overestimate the benefits. Spending agencies routinely underestimate costs, and to acquire legitimacy they even commission studies by external consultants who deploy their scientific tools to cover up the truth. There would appear to be radical differences in the approaches between a medical doctor, a historian, and a government analyst. A doctor concedes that his diagnosis is fallible given the mystery of the disease and the uncertainty of its mutation. A historian may admit possibilities of different interpretations as more light is thrown by subsequent researchers. A government analyst, however, rarely entertains doubts about his own approaches or his estimates. If doubts were entertained, then nobody would trust the government. An analyst in government therefore starts, more often than not, with a goal that has

---

where this is impossible, because of impotence and institutional entanglement, to do what they can to bring the practice of science closer to well ordered science'. He adds, 'these obligations are especially clear at a time when scientific research is increasingly co-opted by entrepreneurs whose interest in profits is likely to have little to do with the tutored collective preferences of other citizens'. That well-ordered science remains, however, a normative goal and the end is not yet cited or even specified.

already been defined, and analysis is just a way to get it through the various stages of consideration. In reality, these stages may not add to value, as what is done in each successive stage is to ratify what was approved in the previous stage. To gain that first-stage approval, the analyst may be economical with the truth and may believe what he/she wants to believe. In the process, truth may change colours depending on the need to be served. Since people expect error-proof statements from governments, repeated assertions are made in public about the thoroughness of the enquiry and about the sanctity of the findings. In essence, it becomes a sideshow, gathering its own momentum depending on what is proposed. Meanwhile, the start made with a wrong premise subverts the expenditure management process.

Secrecy: The process of decision making in governments reveals several features that tend to solidify the prevailing degree of centralization and associated veil of secrecy. In several countries, the determination of expenditure programmes and their allocations continues to be carried out in utmost secrecy, which is a direct violation of one of the principles listed earlier. Further, there are some protected or reserved categories, such as defence where even the aggregate expenditures, let alone the programmes and activities, may not be revealed to the public. Similarly, negotiations about the projects and programmes to be funded by external donors are often carried out in outmost secrecy, and information is selectively released to the community only after the deals have been concluded. This implies that the public voice may not be heard until after the final decisions have been made. To that extent, the process reveals an absence of a constructive and open manner for consultation with the public. In some cases where arrangements are made to consult the public, the discussions may be dominated by organized vested interests, while the poor and less educated sections of society remain politically unorganized and therefore weak.

To avoid this, a few countries such as the United Kingdom have taken to issuing green papers containing proposals on which the reactions of the public are solicited. In one state in India (Andhra Pradesh, in 2003) a radical departure from the previous tradition was made and a draft budget was placed in the public realm to solicit reactions of the citizens. While the step was progressive, the discussion was dominated in the event by organized political interests both inside and outside the legislature. It is not clear whether the feedback resulted in any major reversals or modifications in policies.

Resource Utilization

Shortage-Induced Behaviour: Many of the above problems continue to affect fiscal management during the budget implementation phase. Since many of the estimates tend to be based on optimistic forecasts, it soon becomes necessary for the decision makers to scale down their expectations and to adjust to the changing realities. In most cases, this takes the form of underfunding, in that the final release of funds to the spending agencies may be substantially less than that indicated in the approved budget estimates. This, in turn, calls for a kind of reverse budgeting in the agencies, which many find difficult to do in a meaningful manner in the context of heavy backlog of commitments. Their annual vision is mostly regulated by the provision in the budget, and when that provision gets reduced through informal means, the agencies find it more convenient to accumulate arrears in payments. The arrears so piled up reflect involuntary lending on the part of the creditor at zero rates of interest. Because the government flexes its muscles as the single biggest buyer in the economy, the creditors accommodate it but at a price, in that their original quotation for supply would also include the risk premium for non-payment in time. This also has an impact on the creditworthiness of the government in that it may have to pay a higher interest rate when resorting to borrowing from the public. To that extent, the transactions become more expensive at the very juncture where technical efficiency is sought to be achieved through marginal adjustments in the implementation of programmes. The original sins contribute to continued distortions in decision making. Underfunding also leads to major changes in the way services are provided to the public. Here again, some categories of expenditures escape the proposed adjustment, even if they are less urgent than some others, by virtue of exclusive funding arrangements, such as with donors. These programmes get implemented as proposed, while locally financed projects and programmes are subjected to severe reductions.

Year-end evasions: It is common experience that substantial segments of the annual budget get spent during the last quarter and the last month of the fiscal year. Since the allocation for the next year may be partly based on the rate of spending during the current year, agencies struggle hard to utilize the full (or reduced) allocations by the end of the fiscal year. This pattern of behaviour has not changed much even in countries such as Malaysia, which has recently adopted a form of biennial budgeting. In such cases, where the amounts are shown as spent, they may not in reality be spent but may be transferred to other accounts, frequently called deposit or personal ledger accounts, to be spent in the following years. This practice, which is common in the Indian subcontinent and in some British Commonwealth countries, involves problematic features. It starts with a falsehood in that the amounts are claimed to have been spent whereas they are notionally transferred to another account. It also leads to the creation of a parallel budget that is outside the purview of the legislature and, in many cases, of the audit too. In effect, it becomes a clandestine operation that is regulated by the finance department and the agency concerned.

Contracting out: Contracts have an important role in the process of budget implementation; the supplies of materials for internal consumption by the government are routinely arranged through procurement contracts. Since the early 1990s, and as a part of the introduction of the new public management philosophy advocated by the IFIs, the scope of contracts has been considerably expanded, and includes contracts for personnel services, contracts in regard to public–private partnerships, and contracts with regulatory agencies. In fact, contracting out has become a core technique of today's government. Its legality, however, has not been examined in any detail. It now transpires that this technique has doubtful legal standing. Anne Davies points out, in a very detailed analysis, that contracting out reflects a failure of the constitutional law as well as administrative law. The study reveals that the legislature has little involvement in a discussion of contracts either as a policy instrument or in specific instances. Her conclusion is that 'the failure of constitutional law to control government by contract means that it lacks democratic legitimacy' (Davies 2001, p. 11). Similarly, in the case of internal contracts such as between the provider and purchaser, when both parties belong to the government, she finds that (they) 'are not subject to any law at all, administrative or private' (Davies 2001). Where services are provided by corporate firms, the details of contracts may be claimed to be commercially confidential, and the judicial system may not permit the audit office full access into the records, as happened in Canada.[4] It emerges from this exhaustive legal

---

[4.] Nearly a decade ago the Auditor General of Canada filed a case in the Supreme Court against the Government of Canada seeking full details of a contract. The Supreme Court's judgement was in favour of the government, which claimed that revelation had the potential of injuring the competitive commercial interests of the contractors.

analysis that in their eagerness to promote market pressures, the proponents of government by contract may have taken up an area which, in addition to potentially reducing public accountability, raises a legal hornet's nest and the more important, and as yet unanswered, issue, of whether contracts should be used to enforce social goals. These issues can be answered only when there is a well-designed contracting policy supported by an accepted legal framework. Meanwhile this aspect, which is not considered legal, cannot be deemed ethical.

Implicit Contract with the Community: The annual budget implies a profound agreement with the community about the benefits that are sought to be provided to it. In the process of utilizing allocated resources, governmental actions tend to be affected, depending on the area of operation, by a wide variety of forces; changes made by force of circumstances, political or economic, ought therefore to be conveyed to the community at an early stage so that as economic agents, the members of the community may make necessary changes in their own behaviour. But this has been rendered difficult due to the absence of a detailed agreement in the first place, and second, due to the fact that changes, such as underfunding, may be made at executive discretion, and may not be known to the public until after the fiscal year is closed. This creates another choice between the ethical obligation to periodically report on the discretionary action taken by the government, and the need of the government to be selectively secretive about its operations. Hitherto many governments have opted for the latter, with the inevitable consequence that the ethical obligation has been be neglected or ignored.

Resource-use Accounting

Governments are expected to provide information on the ways in which the allocated resources have been used. Traditionally, this was sought to be served through the submission of audited annual accounts to the legislature either for information, or where legally required, for its approval. More recently, several countries have also accepted the obligation of intra-year reporting, mostly on a monthly basis, in accordance with internationally accepted standards. It should be noted, however, that this information is totally financial in nature and does not throw any light on the service benefits accruing to the community. As will be discussed further, the design of this monthly reporting was intended to meet the need of the investing class, and not of the broader community. Moreover, monthly reports on government tend to be misleading for a major part of the fiscal year, as the more dominant developments with significant effects on the annual budgetary outcome tend to take place in the last month of the fiscal year.

The interest of the community in seeking resource-use reports is to ascertain how its heterogeneous demands have been met, how the conflicts in implementation have been resolved, how they have been affected by the political, social, and economic events, and, finally, whether the operational systems have been adequate to meet the diverse requirements of managing the economy and the provision of resources. From these points of view, government accounts have proved to be a total failure of intent. The accounts, in several cases, are too brief or too elaborate, incomplete in many cases and provided in a format that is certainly not intended for the common person who is supposed to be the main client. Even if it is intended for a legislator, it has to be recognized that his understanding is not very different from that of the common person. In the process, accounts are prepared by one set of specialists, for another set of specialists who then comment on them, to be taken up pro forma by one of the legislative committees later. This ritual, although well intended, has since lost sight of its main client, and many of the issues raised here remain to be answered.

The preceding discussion shows that PEM has come to be excessively manipulated by the executive to an extent that some of the original intents have been subverted. The skewed decision making, with its origins in unfounded optimism, contributes to year-long adjustment efforts, and to frequent failures in the provision of services. There has been, as a result, an extensive shift in the day-to-day management of power into the hands of the executive. Its machinery is found wanting in several respects to achieve the purposes for which it was originally designed. Government's ability and capacity to break the law is only matched by its capacity to make laws. Its actions, in the name of secrecy and technical expediency, leave a good deal to be desired. Complacency at this stage would only accelerate the journey that is already headed downhill. It is in this context that the alternatives proposed need to be considered.

ALTERNATIVE PROPOSALS

During the last decade, several proposals have been, and are continuing to be, set out, aimed at the improvement, in a general fashion, of PEM systems in various countries. The impetus for this came from the larger effort aimed at improved governance, and therefore improved institutions, operational systems, and related techniques. In analysing the alternative proposals for improvement, two features need to be noted at the very outset. First, the problems described have not been identified in this specific manner any time before. When the 'Washington consensus' was forged, there was a general recognition that many of the PEM systems had not been effective in serving fiscal policy purposes and were, therefore, in need of improvement along with a systemic improvement in tax administration, and in the policy approaches toward state-owned enterprises. Within this framework, the IFIs developed their own areas of expertise and professional specialization. The diagnosis of these institutions differs from the original sins described earlier. That said, there are many ingredients in the framework of IFIs that have an impact in avoiding some of the above problems. Second, in addition to the IFIs, there have been some independent proposals too, which together constitute the total set of alternatives available for consideration by those engaged in institutional improvement.

For analytical convenience, however, the alternative proposals may be examined in terms of four broad groups, viz., (i) rules and fiscal responsibility legislation; (ii) identification of risks; (iii) transparency and accountability, and (iv) infrastructure development.

Rules and Fiscal Responsibility Legislation

The establishment of a civic society and its continued smooth functioning require, at a minimum, the rule of law. The general contention is that the existing laws have not been effective in checking the egregious errors of PEM, which is seen as having been largely manipulated by powerful political interests, guided primarily by short-term goals. To check this, appropriate rules have to be established. Rules in government have been largely devised for a variety of purposes. First, from the point of view of the Public Choice Theory, it is the monopoly power of the government which has contributed to a form of tyranny, and if that is to be avoided, rules have to be established to check the proclivities of governments. The rules aim at limiting the power of coercion of the government (for a more detailed examination of this approach, see Hayek 1960, particularly Chapter 15, pp. 220–33). Second, rules seek a fair allocation of power among the various agencies of the executive wing of governance. Third, rules seek to establish a kind of uniformity in approaches, in a context where there is a multiplicity of policymakers and decisionmakers. Fourth, rules are distinct from principles in that they have an element of control on what an individual or group of officials can do. And finally, rules can prevent political intervention, paving the way for a smoother functioning of the bureaucracy. Rules may not be needed in all cases or countries, as the same purpose may be served by the common law system. Rules, inevitably, can have their own rigidity, as there are limits on their inventiveness, nor are they error proof. To that extent, the application of a rule could also mean the application of the Theory of the Second Best (an examination of some of these aspects is found in Schauer 1991). In recognition of the general virtues of rules, it has been suggested that the credibility of fiscal policy stands to be considerably enhanced, if the goals of government are specified in some detail in the form of a law, so that the possibility of discretionary intervention may be minimized. Although the annual budget, which embodies the policies of government, is itself enacted into a law, the suggestion was that broader supplementary legislation would add credibility to government actions.

It was for this purpose that fiscal responsibility legislation, containing the principles of prudent fiscal management, was enacted by New Zealand in 1994. Although there were precedents in the form of stability and growth acts in what was then West Germany in the 1960s, the initiative taken by New Zealand came to acquire unusual importance, and a belief has gained ground that the IFIs would prefer the New Zealand model to be adopted by other countries. As a result, several countries, ranging from Argentina to Peru, enacted fiscal responsibility legislation, and a few more, including India (as well as some state governments in India) are in the process of attempting variants of this approach. The content of legislation and the rules that follow differ from one country to another. In New Zealand, the formal legislation is nothing more than a reiteration of the need for the pursuit of prudent fiscal policies, and a major part of the operational framework is contained in the annual specification of medium-term fiscal policies. Elsewhere, there are formal limits to increases in the fiscal burden, and ad hoc ceilings on nominal rates, and ceilings on specific categories, as well as the general level of public expenditure.

Although the experience with this approach is rather limited, several questions arise that need to be answered at this stage. Does this legislation add to the credibility of government? The answer is, it depends on what is contained in the legislation and how adequate it is to address a specific situation in a country. For example, Argentina enacted a no-deficit legislation in furtherance of the fiscal responsibility principles in 2002, at the height of its economic crisis. Nevertheless, this action did not win any support from the market forces, which saw it more as a cover-up than as providing a viable solution to the fiscal problems. More recent analysis suggests that much is dependent on the actual content of the specific measures taken than on umbrella legislation. It also points that the 'rules may be helpful in achieving fiscal consolidation ... but they are not clearly necessary in all countries'.

A second issue is whether the enactment of rules would by itself bring about enforcement. Here again, experience is the best judge. Several countries had, in the past, many rules intended to influence budgetary decision-making. These included, for example, the golden rule under which borrowing would be undertaken only for viable investment projects; yet another rule was intended to achieve a balanced budget. Some countries, notably Japan and Indonesia among others, had this rule as part of their constitutions. Both rules were simple, and in a way beneficial, but both were increasingly disregarded in practice. Would the new legislation have some improved chances of implementation? In part, the answer to this question depends on the penalties for violation of the proposed rules. In some cases, judicial sanctions may be issued, while in many cases, there may be a loss of reputation, adversely affecting the chances of re-election of the party in power. In judicial sanctions, it is often difficult to determine the responsible individual, particularly where the budget outcome becomes the reference point for determination of the extent of violation. In fact, excessive emphasis on the budget outcome may make the government achieve that goal through illegal means, primarily through an accumulation of unpaid bills—another egregious ethical lapse referred to already.

Would legislation not make the whole process more rigid and inflexible? Recent evidence on the experience of Maastricht countries shows that the restrictive provisions on the national levels of deficit and outstanding debt, which were hailed as great achievements a decade ago, are now being described as too inflexible to permit the much-needed counter-cycled fiscal policies. At issue is whether these purposes could be achieved by institutional development, more specifically, through the strengthening of policy formulation. Fiscal rules of the type discussed so far do not minimize the built-in undue optimism or the introduction of expenditure proposals without full consideration of their financial implications. The task of improving policy formulation remains to be undertaken. Meanwhile, the responsibility legislation, which may have the educational effect of expanding the fiscal horizons of the community, would by itself not avoid the 'original sins'.

Risk Identification

The implementation of the fiscal policy as embodied in the budget requires an explicit recognition of many of the forces, domestic and external, that have a direct influence on that process. A change in the exchange and interest rates could contribute to expenditure increases which in the absence of revenue mobilization efforts could contribute to higher than intended budget deficits. It is therefore urged by the IFIs and others that these risks be identified at the outset, in the hope that such identification would be followed by formulation of strategies aimed at addressing them. While this is important, it has to be realized that risk is a far wider phenomenon in governmental operations than is commonly recognized (Banca d' Italia 2001, p.16).

Apart from the macroeconomic risks, there are risks associated with major projects in terms of potentially higher costs as well as lower benefits. Advocates of fiscal transparency drawn from the academic world emphasize the need for informing the public about these risks.[5] In addition, there are unintended consequences of government polices that tend to affect some sections of the community more than others. Furthermore, governments have the responsibility of creating a secure economic and financial environment for their citizens. This may include disaster relief, financial guarantees in the event of failure of financial institutions, environmental liabilities, and others. In many developing countries, these aspects are addressed as they arise, which in several cases may be too late. Given the growing scope of these risks, public risk management becomes simply unavoidable and becomes a necessary part of governmental efforts at regulation, and more importantly, at making suitable arrangements for the possible reduction or reallocation of risks (Moss 2002 provides an excellent account of the US experience in this regard). In all these areas, more remains to be done in making institutional arrangements for the recognition, measurement, and

---

[5.] For a recent advocacy of this sort, see Flyvbjerg, *et al.* 2003. This aspect is not touched upon by the IFIs despite the extensive involvement of the World Bank in the financing of projects.

possible reductions of risk, as well as a more precise identification of their impact on public expenditure.

Transparency and Accountability

The functioning of a democracy has been viewed historically in several ways. In one way, it was viewed as being oriented to the public good, and in doing so, public debate shapes the public policy in a consensual fashion, and every citizen recognizes his/her public obligation. In more practical terms, democracy has been viewed largely in economic terms as competition among diverse interests and in which the stronger group gets to make public policies, mostly intended to further its own interests. The concept of civic society, although not properly defined, is largely derived from the former approach. In either case, public policy requires the preparation and dissemination of large data that are expected to illuminate the issues and facilitate decision making by economic agents. Such information tends to be more objective in the first type of democracy, while in the second, the vested interests might be more inclined to manage the data that are supportive of their design. While information covers a large area, and is coterminous with the scope of public policy, the efforts of IFIs have been largely limited to the organization and provision of fiscal information. These institutions have not, however, been equally engaged in the development of accountability systems, presumably under the impression that the dissemination of information would by itself create pressures for the creation of proper channels of accountability and their effective functioning. In regard to fiscal transparency, a manual has been issued, while no similar effort has been made with regard to accountability.[6]

The manual on fiscal transparency attempts to delineate the roles and responsibilities of various levels of government, the nature and coverage of fiscal information (which should be complete, verifiable, and made available in a form that permits in-depth analysis), and the adequacy of the fiscal management machinery responsible for the fiscal conduct of the government. The attempt, while laudable, presents some general issues, as well as issues relating more specifically to PEM. In general, the effort is geared more towards that section of the public which is

---

[6.] See IMF, *Manual of Fiscal Transparency*, 2001. It makes several references to accountability in a general fashion but does not deal with the subject in any detail. Also see World Bank, 2000.

engaged in investment in government and debt instruments, that is, the financial class. The manual makes a feeble attempt to touch on the delivery of services and the need for performance orientation but does not go into the details of the subject. Its concerns remain limited to those of the financial class and not those of the general class. The manual proceeds in the belief that the provision of information would make governments more accountable, although the long history of governments conclusively illustrates that in the absence of oversight bodies, the usefulness of information would be severely limited. In addition, while it is concerned with greater transparency in regard to the relationship between the taxpayer and the tax administration, no effort has been made to examine the vast area of the implicit compact between the community and the government in regard to the nature, quantity, quality, cost, and timeliness in the provision of public services. This is a serious gap that remains to be filled, more so in the context where Transparency International is dredging up and publishing information on the payment of 'donations' for getting children admitted to schools or payments for getting admission into hospitals.

Similarly, accountability has been viewed in very narrow terms, dealing mostly with financial accountability, which was the conventional domain of audit and related legislative committees in the British type systems. The content of general and managerial accountability remains unexplored, as are the limitations of conventional tools, and the factors hindering conventional accountability (for a detailed account of these aspects, see Chapter 6 of this book). The overall issue is whether transparency by itself would have the potential impact of transforming the PEM and making it more honest. The experience of many industrial countries shows that the original sins referred to above do not have a lower incidence in the fiscally transparent democracies as compared to other countries. The attempts made by the IFIs constitute, at best, a beginning and certainly not the last word on these important areas.

Infrastructure Development

The suggestions for improvement and ongoing efforts may be considered in terms of three components: (i) computerization of PEM and related accounting systems; (ii) introduction of multi-year expenditure forecasts or medium-term expenditure frameworks (MTEF); and (iii) introduction of accrual systems for budgeting and accounts. Of these, the first requires no detailed explanation of the underlying approach or rationale. Rather it is the experience that reveals a mixed picture. In several African countries, the experience shows that in their eagerness to move to computerized systems, manual records were discarded leading to severe problems in their operation. In some cases, the system was far too elaborate for the local needs. While these teething troubles are inevitable, there is no gainsaying the need for the application of electronic technology to this area, as the experience of several other countries, including the former centrally planned economies in Eastern Europe and elsewhere, reveals the extensive beneficial results from this technology.

The MTEF, which is now usually insisted upon by the IFIs in all the borrowing countries, is essentially intended to promote improved policy formulation over the medium term. Toward this end, a rolling MTEF is expected to be prepared each year for the next three (or more) years, showing the future financial implications of current and new policies. In principle, this approach has the potential of clarifying the continuing draft of future resources from current policies and the margins available for expansion, or alternatively the range of reductions needed. In practice, however, its utility has been considerably reduced in view of the limited coverage of the system (contingent liabilities are not covered) and the technique used for forecasting (mostly simple projections without detailed policy planning). Moreover, MTEF would have only a limited role except in the context of a medium-term fiscal policy. Experience also shows that in both industrial and developing countries, there is frequently an attempt to manipulate even these estimates in that whenever reductions or savings in expenditure are to be made, they are shown in the latter years.

The limitations of the cash-based system for budgeting and accounting have been recognized for quite some time. Essentially, they do not reveal the complete financial picture, nor do they permit the computation of the cost of programmes and activities. But the introduction of accrual budgeting and accounting systems which record transactions at the time firm commitments are made, regardless of the fact when actual payments are made, are considered to be more useful, particularly when depreciation accounts are also maintained. Such an introduction has been facilitated by the computerization of accounts, which permits the maintenance of data in terms of a variety of bases. Some, however, contend that a full accrual accounting is not necessary in a non-profit organization such as the government and have, therefore, opted for a modified accrual system, that is, without depreciation accounts. While accrual budgeting and accounting systems have the potential of providing a broader picture of government finances in terms of assets, liabilities, and contingent liabilities, they are not totally immune to the excessive optimism shown in the formulation of estimates of either current policies or new initiatives. They also do not address the issue of the compact between the taxpayer (or the wider community) and the government on expenditure benefits.

TOWARDS IMPROVEMENT AND SUSTAINABILITY

The preceding analysis illustrates the fundamental gap between the available instruments and the desired ends of civic society. Even where instruments exist, they are subject to extensive subversion by the executive wing of governments. Clearly this situation cannot be allowed to continue for it could only mean an approval of the continued ethical violations witnessed in daily life. The issue is not merely one of instruments, but also one of the failure of oversight mechanisms that were specifically aimed at preventing extensive subversion. Over the years, however, there has been a steady decline in the legislative power, and the real decision making power has moved to the bureaucracy. It is no more a case of choice between accountable bureaucracies or a civic society with established channels for public participation: if the latter is to be achieved, there should first be clarity about the purposes. From this point of view, it is essential to restore the credibility of governmental systems by formulating a programme aimed at achieving improved PEM. Such a programme should necessarily include: (i) improved internal control systems; (ii) restoration of the balance between the executive and the legislature; (iii) supplementing legislative oversight with a layer of social audit; (iv) development of an ethical code for governments to follow; (v) establishment of effective channels for public participation; and, (vi) development of a public expenditure compact specifying the services to be provided between governments and society. This is an agenda that is far wider, and necessarily so, than the one sponsored and largely funded by the IFIs. The fiscal responsibility for seeking improvement rests with the people of a country. External stimulus has many limitations of its own.

The main or the critical question, as Bok (2001, p. 384) has mentioned, is 'how much effort citizens are prepared to make to help their government function effectively'. The paradox in this context is 'the wide and growing wide divergence between the meagre effort citizens devote to politics and public affairs and the pervasive influence that governmental policies have on their lives and that they in turn have on their government' (Bok 2001, p. 390). The only way in which the paradox can be eliminated is through the gradual recognition by the community that its role is too important to be neglected, and that continued neglect would exact a heavy price from the community. In due course, with a gradual demystification of the PEM process, the community will develop its own expectations, priorities and, more important, the development of channels through which informed public opinion would be felt.

5. Fiscal Transparency

HISTORY OF FISCAL TRANSPARENCY

The contours of fiscal transparency and its content were shaped over the years by two distinct trends, a desire to make public officials accountable for their actions, and the political arithmetic of the times reflecting the concerns of the financial class and their interest in investing money in instruments of indebtedness. The evolution of fiscal transparency to date can be analysed in terms of five stylized stages. During the first stage, the concerns of financial accountability of the monarchs and the concerns of an active society seeking a role in the utilization of public money—a feature associated with the Athenian state in the pre-Christian era—dominated the fiscal scene. The concern of the king was the preservation of the wealth of his own domain, and this required him to devise ways and penalties that would prevent, his officials from stealing. Writing more than 2000 years ago, a prime minister of a small North Indian kingdom cautioned his king to 'Look well to the treasury, for it is the key to all.' Variants of this approach were followed in China, and this subsequently became the main feature of the Cameralist school associated with European kingdoms during the Middle Ages. The emphasis in a monarchy was on transparency that was intended for only one person, viz., the king, and his audit agency. The concerns were the same in the development of the Athenian state, where there was explicit recognition, amongst others, by Aristotle, of the risks associated with the handling of large sums of money by officials and the need for systematic accounts that would illumine the whole area (see Chapter 6 of this book).

In the second stage, there emerged an investing class, and the political and financial arithmetic associated with their investments in government during seventeenth-century England had an impact on the content of fiscal transparency. A continuous engagement in wars depleted the British Treasury and made it dependent on private sources of financing, raised through borrowing. The investing class was keen to have detailed accounts of fiscal transactions of the government so that the financial health of the government could be ascertained. As these accounts were not forthcoming, the investors resorted to the appointment of their own staff to undertake independent compilation of accounts. In due course, however, this had the effect of the government appointing its staff, and this led to the emergence of accountants as a class in government. The overall development of a new nexus between governments and the investing public contributed to the colonization of the state by financial interests (Brewer 1989, Ferguson 2001). During this stage, the need for transparency received wider acceptance, although it was seen primarily as of interest to the investing class.

During the third stage, reflecting the gradual development of the legislative institutions and their powers to review the 'wisdom, faithfulness, and economy' with which parliamentary grants were spent, efforts were made to appoint a Commission of Accounts and a Commission on Audit (a predecessor of audit as practised now), culminating in the establishment of a permanent national audit agency to review the use of approved financial resources. This stage emphasized that transparency was not an end in itself but was a means for the legislature to ensure accountability of the government and its officials. What was, however, within the domain of the legislature, was also within the reach of the public. These British practices were, in due course, replicated in the British Commonwealth countries and variations of the approach were introduced in others. A result of these efforts was the explicit recognition of the need for fiscal transparency as a feature of a democratic government.

The fourth stage represents the more recent experience of governments, particularly since the 1950s. The growth of the welfare state, as well as the steady expansion in the size of governments and the range of activities undertaken by them, contributed to an inexorable growth in expenditures and, over the years, to growing fiscal deficits and crisis. The emergence of fiscal crisis contributed to the erosion of the public trust in government and to greater demands for the involvement of the public, along with its legislative institutions, in shaping their own fiscal destiny. It was suggested that improvements in governance required the empowerment of the community and its participation, whenever possible, in the formulation of policies. In turn, this implied that there should be greater fiscal transparency so that the community recognizes where it is and determines where it should go. The idea of improved governance came to be dependent on the reality of fiscal transparency.

The fifth stage reflects the series of financial crises in the 1990s that had a substantive impact on the emerging market countries. These countries, dependent on capital inflows, were highly vulnerable to sudden changes in market perceptions (that is, perceptions of the investing class) and their destabilizing effects. Preventive action, aimed at forestalling the crises, or at a minimum reducing the intensity, required the strengthening of the fiscal system, and enhancement of fiscal transparency. Such transparency was aimed at correcting information asymmetries and associated belief systems. Cumulatively, the result is that extensive fiscal transparency has become an essential feature of governments. The content of fiscal transparency has not, given the diverse developments, however, been articulated coherently, except to some extent by IFIs (IMF 1998, 2001).

OBJECTIVES

Reflecting the various influences in the mutation of fiscal transparency, the objectives sought to be achieved comprise three groups.

Stewardship of Resources

Governments should provide data on the state of finances, for the past, present, and the future so that the community can make its own assessment about the viability of the policy stance, including the preventive actions taken or contemplated to reduce or avoid financial market failures. This requires that the information be comprehensive, and include all activities, as well as contingent liabilities, on a consistent basis. The data must also comply with specified standards.

Adequacy of the Fiscal Machinery

Information is needed on the various aspects of tax administration, expenditure management, lending and borrowing operations, sales and purchase operations, and management of the financial portfolio. Efforts in this regard are aimed toward restoring the credibility of the public management systems as well as assuring the community of the continuing effective functioning of the fiscal machinery. As an integral part of this effort, attention paid to ensuring the due process, prevention of opportunities for corruption, and the smooth working of the accountability channels associated with legislative or other forms of social action is revealed to the public.

Decision-making Approaches

There should be a window of opportunity for the community to be informed about the decision-making approaches behind the fiscal policies sought to be pursued. The window should enable an understanding, even as decisions are made (and not after they have been made) on the main components of fiscal policy— the pursuit of macroeconomic stability, effective performance in the delivery of services, and pursuit of economy and efficiency.

These objectives aim at the complete fulfilment of fiscal transparency and, to that extent, go beyond the guidelines issued by international financial organizations. The guidelines issued by these organizations place more emphasis on the legal framework (intended more for international audiences), linkages with macroeconomic trends and policies, operational procedures, dissemination of fiscal data, and channels of accountability with legislatures. Correspondingly, there is lesser focus on the adequacy of the fiscal machinery and delivery of services, aspects that are of critical importance to the community.

CONTENT OF FISCAL INFORMATION

The fiscal information provided to the public and the arrangements for transparency have their roots in the government accounting system, which is a homogeneous source of supply. The users of the information are, however, varied and heterogeneous groups that include the community, legislatures, market analysts, investors, policymakers, external donors, and others. Information aimed at meeting these diverse requirements is provided through various channels. The features of the information supplied are shown in detail in Table 5.1.

USES AND LIMITATIONS

The demands for additional information on government fiscal

operations have grown during recent years. Along with these demands, the capacity of government to meet them has also increased several times. To a large extent, this has been facilitated by the application of computer technology to government transactions, transforming a long-drawn-out, slow, and often tedious process into a quick and often cost-effective way of using information for policy making. Notwithstanding the assiduous efforts to improve the coverage and content of fiscal transparency, from the user's point of view, several problem areas remain to be addressed.

In the current situation, approximately one-third of the world's population has little access to budget details and, thus, to the fiscal policies that have a profound and continuing impact on their lives. People living in centrally planned countries, such as China, Vietnam, or quasi-monarchies like the Gulf kingdoms, and similarly placed governments receive few budget details. This is in stark contrast to the former Soviet Republics, which have made a quantum jump, in a short period, to the establishment of fiscal transparency as in other democracies.

The transactions of government and the structure of their portfolios have changed during recent years. In several cases, central governments have become funding and policy agencies, while operations are conducted by the other levels of government, as well as by NGOs and the corporate sector. Information in regard to the latter tends to be brief where provided, and aggregative in nature. To the extent that these shadow governments are not fully covered, the usefulness of data on fiscal operations tends to be reduced.

Fiscal transparency does not yet take the community into confidence in the realm of public policy making. In taxation, concerns of secrecy, with regard to defence, and concerns of security, have contributed to a large degree of opaqueness (North American Treaty Organization, (NATO) countries have begun efforts to provide more information on defence costs). Similarly, little information is available about the effectiveness of the fiscal machinery (see Premchand 2000 for a discussion of the limitations of audit and legislative control).

The data provided are mostly intended to meet the requirements of the investing class and do not go far in illuminating the fiscal status for the common man. The language of data is generally complex and, without the aid of a professional interpreter, may not be clear to the general public. The community's preference is for analytical data, rather than voluminous raw data about operations.

Fiscal transparency, unaccompanied by channels of public

accountability, is not likely to be effective. In many cases, however, these channels are yet to become effective; thus, more remains to be achieved.

Table 5.1
Fiscal Transparency—Components, Instruments, and Features

Functional area	Instruments	Features
Structures and policy spheres		
Structures		
• Functions and fiscal responsibilities of central, state, and local governments	• These are, in general, specified in the constitution and associated legal framework.	• In federal types of countries, the financial relationships among these levels tend to be complex.
• Transfers from the central government to the state and local governments; where revenue collections are decentralized, states, regions, or provinces may make transfers to the central government	• These transfers may be specified in the Constitution. Annual transfers determined with reference to legal criteria may be shown in the budget documents; where budgets are not available to the public (see below), the quantum of these transfers and their utilization may not be known.	• The experience of federal types of countries shows that these transfers, including devolution of resources, are determined in a quasi-judicial process; the findings, as distinct from proceedings, are made public. • Experience of unitary governments is far more diverse; the details are contained in the budget documents (and are specifically shown as transfers), while in a few cases, they remain obscure.
• Autonomous bodies of the central governments • State-owned enterprises	• These bodies have, in general, their own budgets, and the extent of dependence on government is shown therein. • Enterprises are obligated, in most cases, to publish their annual balance sheets and accounts. Their budgets, where the activities tend to be commercial, are not made public. The main instruments of transparency are the accounts	• Access to these documents is problematic and dependent on the laws governing the autonomous bodies. • Their accountability to the legislatures differs very widely. • The accounts and associated reports may not specify the costs of non-commercial objectives that the enterprises follow at the behest of governments. Moreover,

(Contd.)

(Table 5.1 Contd.)

	and the periodic reports published by them. These reports may be more frequent where there is a high degree of dependence on the capital markets.	subsidies given by governments may not have the specific end use, given the fungibility of resources, indicated by governments.
• Relationship with central bank/ monetary authority and other public financial institutions	• These relationships are usually specified in the form of a law, inter alia, indicating the tasks and responsibilities of the institutions in the management of public debt. The financial institutions publish their annual accounts and other reports that are within the public domain.	• Although the accounts are available, the quasi-fiscal accounts or activities undertaken by them may not be fully shown. Standards in this regard are evolving, and it is likely that more detailed information will be available on the quasi-fiscal activities.
• Relationships with the corporate private sector	• In most cases, the patterns of government equity ownership and the responsibility of governments in regard to regulation are specified in law (example, Companies Act). In some cases, regulation may be enforced through autonomous agencies.	• Laws and associated guidelines are generally matters that can be enforced through judicial means. In some countries, however, the ownership patterns are both highly complex and opaque.
• Relationships with legislatures	• The patterns vary among countries. Broadly, there are three types of legislatures: (i) where legislatures have the dominant role, (ii) where the executive has the dominant role and (iii) where legislatures do not have any role in terms of annual management of finances, except that they are kept informed on all key aspects. In several countries, there is a framework of delegated legislation within which the executive wing of the government has powers to levy taxes, duties, fees, etc., and to spend the proceeds. • Legislatures are provided with medium-term fiscal strategy,	• The usefulness of the documents prepared by governments to determine the current fiscal status and its viability varies considerably among countries. In some countries, budgets are not available to the public; instead, summaries of the main features are presented.

(Contd.)

(Table 5.1 Contd.)

Primary fiscal instruments	development plans, medium-term budgets, annual budgets, and supplementary budgets. All these documents are in the public domain.
	• The range of fiscal instruments has expanded over the years. In addition to the annual budget intended for purposes of legislation, several documents seeking to provide background information are provided. These include multi-year rolling budgets and other documents referred to above. The most important instrument continues to be the budget. To serve the purposes of transparency, budgets are required to be:
	  a. Comprehensive, covering all transactions, including foreign aid, proceeds of taxation, gross spending, gross borrowing and lending, and gross buying and selling.
	
	  b. As an integral part of the above and reflecting the full status of finances, data on extra-budgetary accounts, quasi-fiscal activities, tax expenditure, guarantees provided, and consequent contingent liabilities are also needed.
		• Although all countries have budgets, their features vary considerably.
		
		• In many cases, large chunks of expenditures may be organized in the form of extra-budgetary activities or as quasi fiscal activities. This feature limits the usefulness of the main budget. More significantly, in the absence of data on guarantees and related contingent liabilities, the community may not have the data to assess critically the current status of government finances and their sustainability.

(Contd.)

(Table 5.1 Contd.)

	c. On a gross basis; to avoid misleading conclusions, expenditure offsets, etc. are to be avoided.	• In general, many budgets are organized on a gross basis, but a frequent resort to netting is also common.
	d. On an accounting basis, that reflects the cash position as well as liabilities.	• Most budgets are organized on a cash basis. During recent years, attempts have been initiated to introduce forms of accrual budgeting.
	e. A classification of government transactions into a functional programme, as well as economic types, to illustrate the broad purposes of expenditures.	• Patterns of classification vary considerably among countries. Different practices are in vogue for budgets and for international reporting. Categories such as defence remain, for the most part, opaque.
Fiscal management		
Objectives	• The range of instruments includes fiscal responsibility legislation, medium-term rolling framework, and development plans. These documents provide the essential context within which the annual budget serves as the most important fiscal instrument.	• During recent years, some countries such as Argentina and Brazil have, following the experience of Australia and New Zealand, enacted fiscal responsibility legislation indicating the broad goals of fiscal policy.
Consolidated budget	• The budget and its supplementary instruments seek to reflect the totality of government finances within a country. Because regional/state/provincial budgets have an important role, they need to be consolidated for the country as a whole.	• In unitary forms of government, budgets reflect the total picture. In federal types, however, the lower levels of government formulate their own budgets. In several countries, these are consolidated, usually after a lag, and made available to the public. Even here, the budgets of local governments (county and city governments), being too many, may not be included in the consolidation exercise.

(Contd.)

(Table 5.1 Contd.)

Macroeconomic framework	• The purposes of the annual budget reflect the times. To facilitate an understanding of this crucial element in fiscal policy, assumptions about the growth in the economy, exchange rate, inflation rate, aggregate demand factor, and estimated capital flows are indicated.	• The actual experience in this regard varies considerably. In most cases, the macroeconomic framework may not be explicit. In some cases, autonomous research organizations may publish them as a part of their studies. Objectives, where indicated, tend to be too general and may not constitute a strategy.
Annual policy making	• The annual budget, being the main vehicle, is expected to indicate the following:	• The approaches to annual budget vary among countries, depending on the role of the legislature.
	a. New policies to address the problems in the economy. As an integral part of this effort, new outlays are distinguished from continuing policies.	• Although new policies are highlighted, the expenses associated with them and their continuing financial implications may not be adequately analysed.
	b. Changes in revenue policies, including changes in tax expenditures. c. Changes in lending policies.	• Tax expenditures, guarantees, and changes in lending policies do not, in general, receive specific focus in the documents.
	d. Policies aimed at deficit containment, including austerity management.	• Deficit reduction has been a dominant theme during recent years. Austerity management, however, may not be specified in detail to prevent lobbying by interest groups.
	e. Changes in public debt patterns, including maturity.	• Although data on outstanding domestic and foreign debt are provided, their holders and maturity patterns—in particular, in the area of foreign debt—may not be indicated in detail
	f. Changes made in delivery of services and expenditure benefits.	• Expenditure benefits have not received adequate attention until recently.
	g. Identification of high-risk areas (example, foreign aid).	• Risk areas and associated efforts at risk management

(Contd.)

(Table 5.1 Contd.)

	• Some of these areas may be made public before the presentation of the annual budget, through public announcements, white papers, and sessional documents.	remain, where undertaken, at a nascent stage.
Detailed objectives of department and agencies	• The objectives to be achieved during a fiscal year are to be stated in detail in each agency budget.	• Objectives, where indicated, tend to be too general and may not constitute a strategy.
Performance orientation	• The agency budgets should also indicate the achievements, in terms of delivery of services, expected during the fiscal year. This constitutes an important vehicle for full accountability. As an integral part of this, data on cost-service-quality linkages are sought to be provided.	• Performance budgeting in government has had a chequered career. During recent years, there has been a revival of some aspects of this system. Many countries have yet to implement this.
Pursuit of efficiency and economy	• Agency budgets are also expected to indicate the specific efforts made to achieve economy and efficiency.	• To a large extent, this remains to be fulfilled.
Changes in supporting administrative infrastructure	• Governments announce, through annual budgets, changes made in the tax collection machinery, expenditure management, and debt management. In tax administration, the effort is to augment the legal specification of the tax basis, while reducing the administrative discretion in its application. In expenditure management, the intent is to facilitate internal financial operations of the spending agencies. In debt management, the instruments seek to provide more information on the currency of debt, separation of interest from principal, etc.	• In tax administration, the major area of darkness continues to be the use of discretionary powers by tax officials and related rent-seeking behaviour. In expenditure management, procurement and related contracting remain, as noted below, less transparent. Debt transactions also remain, in some cases, shrouded in secrecy.

(Contd.)

(Table 5.1 Contd.)

Implementation of budgets	Notwithstanding differences of degree, several stages of policy implementation are common to all countries. These include the following: a. Phased release of budgetary authority b. Organized cash management that facilitates a link-up with debt management c. Award of contracts, procedures for tendering and contracting d. Procedures to ensure budgetary outcome as intended e. Specification of performance measures	Several of the activities enumerated are usually considered as 'in-house' activities and, as such, may not be open to the public. The primary issue for the community is whether there is adequate machinery empowered to deal with these aspects and whether the machinery is working effectively. In practice, the most controversial area is the award of contracts. The range of contracts has widened considerably and now includes services such as day care centres. These contracts may not, in several cases, be in the public realm. Specification of performance is still at a nascent stage. The budgetary outcome may, in some cases, be technically managed through the accumulation of payment arrears.
Accounting and reporting	The accounting system is intended to ensure that the tasks inherent in the stewardship of money are being handled. It should therefore specify (i) the basis—cash, accrual, etc., (ii) the procedures for payment and budget monitoring, and (iii) the compilation of periodic and year-end accounts. Accounts provide the data for the past, whereas the budget contains the present and projected trends.	Emphasis on procedure varies. In general, however, accounting systems are designed to handle the tasks enumerated. During recent years, however, significant leakages have become common. These relate to the exclusion of off-budget accounts, guarantees, contingent liabilities, quasi-fiscal activities, and tax expenditures. Periodic reports on the status of government finances are now being released by several countries in conformity with the desire of IFIs to publish

(Contd.)

(Table 5.1 Contd.)

		standardized fiscal data. Intra-year trends may, however, be significantly different from the year-end outcome as developments in the last quarter have a unique pace.
Administrative reports	• Fiscal and other agencies are required to issue annual reports illustrating their activities. These agencies include the tax collection machinery.	• These documents, which vary enormously in content and coverage, are in the public domain in most countries.
Evaluation	• Government activities are evaluated by their own agencies to gain experience in the utilization of resources.	• Evaluation is limited in most governments and, where conducted, may not always be available to the public.
Audit	• There should be adequate arrangements for an independent audit agency to verify the appropriation accounts and carry out accountancy, financial, and performance audits.	• Although many countries have independent audit offices, their effective contribution is dimmed by their limited purview (policy matters are excluded) and lack of firm legislative arrangements for a review of the findings.
Independent standards	• Standards are specified for the maintenance of accounts and audit. Similar arrangements exist in some countries (for example, Sweden) to rate the overall financial management systems, including the tax collection machinery.	• Accounting standards for government are evolving and, as a result, more governments may have them in place in the future.
Legislative review	• Submission of the budget, consideration of new policies or changes in the existing ones, and annual accounts provide several opportunities to the legislature to exercise the traditional control of purse.	• In practice, the powers of the legislatures vary considerably. Even where endowed with requisite powers and instruments, they may not exercise them in view of the party discipline and related procedural limitations.

6. Public Financial Accountability

What is accountability? What is it that the community is interested in? Answers to these questions have never been easy. Not a great deal has been said about the components of accountability or the means through which it may be achieved, although routine incantation of the need for accountability has become a notable feature of national and international debate. In some quarters, it is being offered as an instant aspirin that helps minimize fiscal problems. There is, however, a need to go beyond slogans and discussions of general propositions into the details, and to delineate the contours, contents, and potential fault lines of accountability in general and, financial accountability in particular. In addition to the two important issues raised above, it is imperative that a variety of questions that arise in this context be answered. How did accountability evolve? Why is there a current emphasis on financial accountability? What are the features and instruments of financial accountability? Are the instruments adequate for the purpose? If they are underachieving, what are the contributory factors? What constructive agenda may be followed hereafter?

The need to provide answers to the above and a multitude of related questions has assumed greater importance in the context of the impact of four factors. First, two decades of fiscal turbulence have contributed to a substantial erosion of the credibility of governmental fiscal machinery, and to a growing distrust of governments. Second, the gradual spread of globalism has put policymakers in many countries in a reactive rather than a proactive mould; external developments that do not always lend themselves to precise identification would appear to have a greater role, indeed a dominating one, on fiscal policies. Information asymmetries have made the already formidable tasks of policymakers even more complex and intractable. In the absence of crucial information, the risks faced by the policymakers have increased significantly. Third, the change in the nature of government and its gradual withdrawal from production activities has made it take an active role in regulation, which adds to the complexity of financial accountability. Fourth, there has been a major change in the composition of expenditures of central and federal governments. Apart from the sizeable outlays on the servicing of public debt, expenditures at the central government level are increasingly devoted to transfers to the private sector, entitlement payments, and transfers to regional and local governments. This has contributed to a separation of funding from the actual provision of services and has affected the pattern of financial accountability.

This chapter is devoted to a consideration of the above issues. Such a consideration requires a comprehensive perspective on the evolution of accountability. Only in the light of that perspective can financial accountability be distinguished from general accountability. In order to provide a detailed background that would facilitate an appraisal of the current issues, the evolution and practice of the idea of accountability is discussed first. This is followed by a discussion of the anatomy of financial accountability and its inherent aspect of underachievement of goals. The chapter concludes by listing out a constructive agenda for the future.

It will be argued in this chapter that, notwithstanding the fact that the idea of accountability is inherent in the actions of an institution and its employees, the means of achieving it have varied over the years and have moved from a simple to complex, if frequently expensive, machinery. Despite the complexity, however, the capacity to achieve full accountability has been and continues to be inadequate, partly because of the design of accountability itself and partly because of the widening range of objectives and associated expectations attached to accountability. It is further argued that if accountability is to be achieved in full, including its constructive aspects, then it must be designed with care. The objectives of accountability, it is argued here, should go beyond the naming and shaming of officials, or the pursuit of sleaze, to a search for durable improvements in economic management to reduce the incidence of institutional recidivism. The future of accountability consists in covering the macro aspects of economic and financial sustainability, as well as the micro aspects of service delivery, including specific attention to public and/or private partnerships. It should envisage a three-tier structure of accountability: that of officials (both political and regular civil employees), that of intra-governmental relationships, and that between governments and their respective legislatures. Further, it is argued that the existence of numerous institutions and established procedures for financial accountability does not necessarily contribute to the realization of the goal of full accountability, and that the fulfilment of financial accountability does not necessarily mean improved fiscal status for a country. Improvements in the existing systems, which are undoubtedly needed, should be envisaged with due regard to cost-effectiveness and possible paradoxical results.

EVOLUTION AND PRACTICE OF THE IDEA OF ACCOUNTABILITY

Accountability has been viewed since times immemorial as a channel for ascertaining the use of power by an individual or an organization, entrusted with the task of performing prescribed tasks. The means through which accountability has been achieved, have varied over the years. The concerns of financial accountability, whether in a kingdom, which was the more common form of government, or that of a democracy in the pre-Christian era, were the same, viz., the preservation of the wealth of the king or the society. Writing nearly three hundred years before the beginning of the Christian era, Kautilya, in what is easily recognized as the first manual on bureaucracy, observed that human nature was disposed to acquire public money for private gain. He wrote: 'Just as it is impossible not to taste honey or poison that one may find at the tip of one's tongue, so it is impossible for one dealing with government funds not to taste, at least a little bit, of the king's wealth'. He added: 'Just as it is impossible to know when a fish moving in water is drinking it, so it is impossible to find out when government servants in charge of undertakings misappropriate money' (Kautilya, 1992, p. 281). In recognition of this human proclivity, Kautilya went on to formulate a series of checks and balances in the administrative system. He wrote that 'in all cases (where) an official has caused loss of revenue to the state ... his property shall be confiscated.[1] A similar set of practices was observed in contemporary China (see Premchand 1995 a).

[1.] Kautilya 1992, p. 294. This principle is now included in the financial rules and regulations of many countries. In practice, however, the application of this principle has been relatively rare.

In the Athenian state, the hallmark was 'its concern for the accountability of its officials'. For them, 'to have officials accountable was the key to responsible government, unaccountability meant lawlessness' (quoted in Day and Klein 1987, p. 6). To this end, officials were required to report on their conduct ten times a year to the Assembly of the Citizens. If the explanations did not meet with the Assembly's approval, officials were subjected to a trial, and indeed, where necessary, to impeachment. It was noted by historians that the prospect of being sentenced to death by the judicial system was often greater than the risk of dying in battle. Aristotle wrote: 'Some officials handle large sums of money: it is therefore necessary to have other officials receive and examine the accounts. These inspectors must administer no funds themselves. Different cities call them examiners, auditors, scrutinees and public advocates' (cited in Day and Klein 1987, p. 9). From that time, accountability went through six stylized stages (described in Box 6.1.) More important is the fact that during this period of evolution, attention turned from estate preservation and management to accountability for actions and results. Estate preservation, however, has not been neglected. In fact, the idea behind the introduction of accrual accounting in recent years is to ascertain the trends in the net worth of a country, a concept similar to that of estate management.

Box 6.1: Conventional and Enhanced Financial Accountability

Over the years, events and ideas have forged some conventions of financial accountability. While it is difficult to be precise in enumerating the historical phases of financial accountability, some stylized stages can be construed from the pages of world history. Broadly, six stages have contributed to the expansion of the scope of financial accountability and thus to changing conventions. First, there were the practices of treasury management associated with kings and royal rule. As Kautilya wrote more than two millennia ago, 'all state activities depend first on the treasury. Therefore a king shall devote best attention to it' (p. 253). All revenues and expenditures were to be recorded in prescribed forms; these were then subjected to audit (inspection). Kautilya added: 'Accounts officers shall present themselves for audit at the appointed time' (p. 275). The king, advised Kautilya, should devote the 'first 1½ hours after sunrise—to reports on defence, revenue and expenditure'. Similar practices

(Contd.)

(Box 6.1 Contd.)

later were found in contemporary China and Greece (the latter was not a monarchy). The endeavour in this phase was to devise machinery for the preservation and enhancement of royal wealth, or estate management. The above practices continued for more than a millennium and were enshrined in the principles of accounting devised by the royalty in England, and later in the approaches of Cameralists in Europe. The second stage refers to the developments in England during the seventeenth century when, in response to the steady and growing demands of members of parliament, committees were appointed to review the 'wisdom, faithfulness, and economy' with which parliamentary grants were spent. This stage represented the assertion of the rights of legislators and endeavours, as a part of the procedures of the control of purse, to ensure financial accountability. The continuation of these endeavours contributed to the appointment of a commission on accounts (a predecessor of audit as practised now) as well as a commissioner of accounts. During the third stage (nineteenth century), as a part of the Gladstonian reform of exchequer management and its oversight by legislative committees, an independent audit agency was set up to review the regularity and economy of expenditures. The annual audit report was to be reviewed by a committee of the legislature representing the final stamp of approval or qualified approval of the financial transactions of government. The fourth stage refers to the developments during the twentieth century, in particular after the Second World War. The emergence and the gradual consolidation of the welfare state enabled the diversion of both governments and people from economy in expenditure (although it continues to be an important principle) to greater participation by the people and to greater public scrutiny of public transactions, as well as to delivery of services. The latter, in turn, contributed to a greater emphasis on performance or outputs. The response to these developments was in the form of economic development plans that reflected the people's needs, and to performance budgeting in government, as well as performance contracts. Later developments contributed to refined systems of budgeting that emphasized economy (in the use of resources), efficiency (in achieving greater results within allotted resources), and effectiveness (in achieving programme objectives). In the process, the scope of financial accountability came to be expanded rapidly

(Contd.)

(Box 6.1 Contd.)

and significantly. During the fifth stage, in addition to the above dimensions, emphasis was laid on prudent macroeconomic management. Governments were expected to be prudent (in using resources and in considering what could be achieved at what cost) and to take into account explicitly the assessment of the linkages between the budget and the economy. As a result, a kind of three-dimensional financial accountability emerged. The three dimensions are: (i) expenditure choices (to ascertain the degree of prudence); (ii) programme management (propriety, economic management, adequate delivery systems); and (iii) regular dissemination of information (showing material matching, that is, a process by which outputs and income are related in a time frame to the cost of services). The sixth stage, which is yet to emerge in final form and is meanwhile groping for clarity and acceptance, envisages enhanced financial accountability. In addition to conventional financial accountability, now governments may be accountable for ensuring that there are adequate systems to secure and improve results and to maintain the financial condition of the state (economic sustainability, flexibility in the use of resources, and reduced financial vulnerability). Furthermore, governments are expected to demonstrate that the selected programmes are a part of the legitimate functions of a government and that the community can afford them. Financial accountability has thus expanded, reflecting changing tasks and expectations, and now people expect enhanced financial accountability to be fulfilled while complying with the requirements that constituted accountability in the preceding stages.

Meanwhile, however, the growing public administration and management sciences have explored in some detail the functions of a modern executive. Barnard has devoted a considerable part of his attention to these aspects. In his view, an individual's actions are guided by an informal code of ethics (drawn from his moral environment), and more explicit and formal codes of organizations. He noted that 'morals are personal forces or propensities of a general and stable character in individuals which tend to inhibit, control, or modify inconsistent immediate specific decisions, impulses, or interests and to intensify those which are consistent with such propensities' (Barnard 1938, p. 261). He added that the responsibility was that of the individual: 'The point is that responsibility is the property of an individual by which whatever morality exists in him becomes effective in conduct' (Barnard 1968, p. 267). This concept of individual responsibility is partly included in Simon's system of values that have a prominent part in decision making (see Simon 1997). These points of view indicate the distinctive beginning of managerialism as a school of thought, with its own impact on the concept of accountability.

Available history shows that the concept of accountability, which was always inherent in the tasks, responsibilities, and broad administrative behaviour of governments, has changed in terms of the clientele group to which it was addressed. From personal accountability to the king (a civil servant was expected to give his life for king and country when necessary) there was a shift towards a responsibility to the elected representatives of the people and now, in addition, to the people themselves. (The various stages in the evolution of the concept of accountability are shown in Figure 6.1). Accountability, now a multifaceted phenomenon, involves three distinct segments relating to general accountability, fiscal accountability, and managerial accountability (as shown in Figure 6.2). Financial management in most of these development stages remained rooted in the principle that no individual official was to be trusted. For this reason, in a greater part

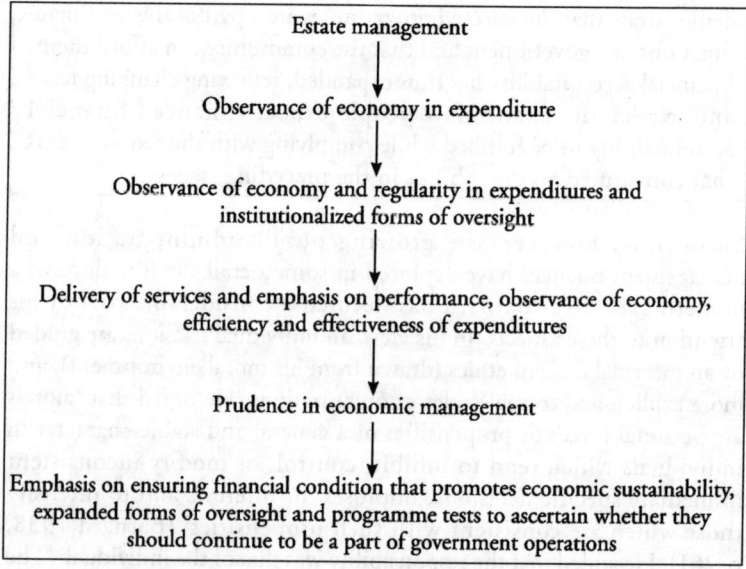

Figure 6.1: From Conventional to Enhanced Accountability

of financial management, time and process was devoted to the verification of payment claims and arrangements for the custody of money. The managerial approach, in contrast to the traditional belief, is based on the idea that an individual official, in order to be a creative and innovative manager, should be trusted and endowed with commensurate autonomy. But autonomy is not equivalent to independence. Rather, the official should be subjected to accountability for results. The orientation to results is a significant departure from the previous practice and is intended to be a vast improvement over process-oriented behaviour, and subjection to continuous second-guessing at various levels in the hierarchy.[2] It is in this context that the specific aspects of financial accountability need to be considered.

Accountability

General Accountability
- Answerability for action
- Sanctions where justification is not adequate
- Ability to revoke a mandate
- Public scrutiny of governmental actions
- Citizen participation in the design of programmes

Fiscal Accountability
- Approval of policies and actions having financial implications by a representative body
- Approval of an annual or a medium-term budget
- Framework to ensure that in the process of economic management no actions to impair the fiscal capacity of the community

Managerial Accountability
- Appropriate rules are observed and authority is not abused
- Risks are taken within delegated powers to achieve objectives
- Responsibility for service delivery within specified cost, quality, and time schedules
- Observance of economy and efficiency

Figure 6.2: Contents of Accountability

2. A civil society needs freedom to think and act and to function effectively. Such freedom implies a substantial degree of trust on the part of each individual regarding the actions of his fellow members of society. The question arises as to how one can get on with one's life in the absence of that basic trust. Financial management systems were designed without taking this factor into account. Management philosophy, however, embodies this principle in its operational approaches; indeed, it has made

FINANCIAL ACCOUNTABILITY

Financial accountability, too, has grown within the range of the parameters described. In the process, it has developed its own chain of operations and institutions. The broad financial accountability chain, common to many governments, is shown in Figure 6.3. In considering the relative roles of the institutions indicated in this figure, it has to be recognized that the role of donors, IFIs may be different from one country to another, as is the role of NGOs and others (this category includes a wide range of contractors and other providers of services funded by different levels of governments), and of legislatures and client groups. In the former centrally planned economies, client groups are represented, in principle, by party representatives. In other countries, clients may form significant pressure groups having pervasive, if frequently subtle, influences on policy-making and the allocation of resources.

The main instruments of financial accountability are government budgets, periodically published data on public finances, annual accounts,

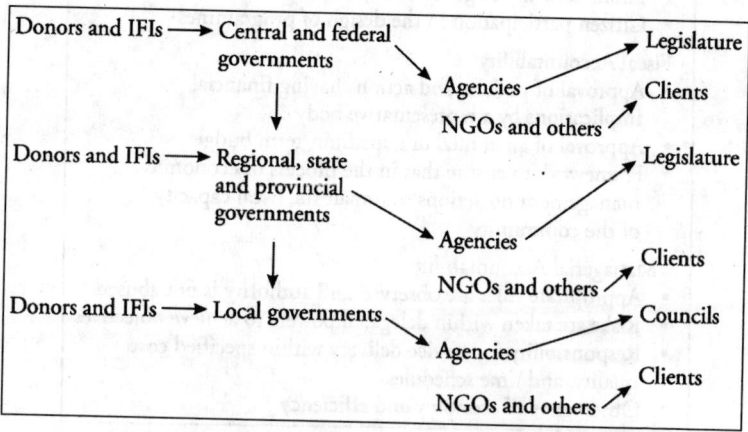

Figure 6.3: Financial Accountability Chain

---

it a cornerstone. Breach of the implicit trust is to be addressed as a part of the accountability framework. Government operations have grown so enormously that it is difficult to live without endowing every administrator with that degree of trust that every citizen shows to his fellow citizens. Continued dependence on misanthropy is likely to be counterproductive.

and the investigative and other general reports prepared by independent agencies. The main components of these groups of instruments, their features and limitations, and the way in which they contribute to the fulfilment of financial accountability are illustrated in Table 6.1.

Table 6.1

Instruments of Financial Accountability—Features and Limitations

Functional Area	Instruments	Features	Limitations
General fiscal status	Medium-term fiscal strategy	Shows the current status of the economy and the future directions	Often too broad to constitute a strategy
	Development plans	Lay out the plans for future investments, maintenance outlays, and financing patterns	These plans concentrate on investments and new programmes; quantitative aspects are specified
	Medium-term budgets	Show the future financial implications of current and future policies	These are mostly intended for purposes of information of the legislature and are generally not binding on governments
	Annual balance sheets	Show the changing picture of assets and liabilities as a result of government's fiscal operations Show the	These have yet to gain currency in many countries. Also, the preparation of balance sheets involves several technical issues that remain to be resolved

(Contd.)

(Table 6.1 Contd.)

	Inter-generational accounts	burdens on future generations arising from current operations and their patterns of financing	The methodology of these accounts, as well as their usefulness are subjects of intense debate. Developing countries have not as yet shown any appetite for this
Annual fiscal management	Annual budget	Contains revenues, expenditures, and debt estimates	Many countries have yet to endow legislatures with powers to approve or reject proposals. In some countries, these are viewed more as debating fora rather than as legislative bodies. Some countries have well-established legislatures patterned on the UK or US models In some countries, multi-year appropriations are in vogue for developmental projects. In a few countries, extra-budgetary accounts are substantial and may not require legislative approval
	Approval of policies underlying annual budgets	In some countries, medium-term strategies and policies are sought to be discussed with the legislature prior to the submission of annual budgets	In some countries, legislatures have established consultative committees to channel constructive and crucial policy inputs before final decisions are made. The contribution of these committees remains to be assessed
	Estimates of revenue and new tax proposals	Show the expected revenues from current policies and new policy initiatives	These estimates, often considered to be needlessly optimistic, are now being reviewed in some countries by the audit agency (for example, Britain). The added value of this review remains to be proven. Legislatures have their own means, where they are empowered, to assess the reasonability of estimates and to alter them. In British-type systems, legislatures can

(Contd.)

(Table 6.1 Contd.)

Estimates of expenditure	Show the outlays on programmes and projects and serve as the basis for legislative appropriations	reject government proposals only at the risk of resignation by the party in power. Legislatures, where empowered, authorize outlays on programmes and projects. These appropriations, which provide the legal authority for spending, may not always assure full funding. Funding may be subject to the discretion of the executive. In practice, there may be extensive underfunding, impairing the implementation of projects and programmes. In some cases, there may be legal earmarking and as such programmes may not require annual legislation and may not suffer underfunding Benefits from expenditure programmes may not be fully shown and in any event may not reflect binding contracts except in the context of performance contracts Some segments of expenditures, for example, public debt, may not require annual legislative approval in most cases
Public debt estimates	Show the servicing costs and the amounts of debt to be raised	In most cases, these estimates do not require legislative approval. New loans to be raised, including those raised externally, may not need legislative approval
Donors and foreign aid	Estimates, where provided, show the amounts likely to be received from donors and IFIs	In most countries, foreign aid budgeting and accounting continues to be weak Project loans and externally raised loans do not, in most countries, require legislative approval Agreements with IFIs may not be submitted in most cases to the legislature, as no legislative approval is required IFIs have a number of means to ensure full compliance and accountability through extensive ring fencing, regular monitoring, and imposition of sanctions in the event of non-compliance

(Contd.)

(Table 6.1 Contd.)

Overall objectives and policies	Described above		The non-achievement of objectives such as macroeconomic stability, income distribution, service provision, patterns of financing, may receive general attention in the legislatures and other bodies but entails no sanctions or penalties except through the ballot box. The leeway available to the executive is considerable, while accountability is limited. Further, the above instruments except for entitlements, are not justiciable in any court of law
Budget implementation	Release of funds to spending agencies	Plans for time-sliced releases of funds	In some countries that have a system of exchequer control, release of funds may require approval of the controller or auditor general, on behalf of the legislature. In a few others, legislation may specify the periodicity of releases from approved appropriations
	Cash management		This is a function of the executive. Experience shows that this could lead to patronage and to a form of crony capitalism
	Award of contracts	Specification of work to be done	Contracts are not required to receive legislative approval. Details of contracts are not required to be reported to the legislature At the level of local governments, however, committees entrusted with the award of contracts may include representatives of the community
	Carryover of funds	Funds may be allowed to be carried forward into the next fiscal year	With a view to avoiding year-end rush of expenditure, some governments are now allowing select carryovers of funds This procedure constitutes a violation of the contract between the legislature and the government. Despite this, these transactions are not reported to the legislature
	Outlays on transfers to other levels of government and on entitlements	Reveal the portfolio of government expenditures	Most transfers are determined, as are entitlements, by previous legislation and as such, do not require specific approval by the legislature

(Contd.)

(Table 6.1 Contd.)

	Personnel limits, reappropriations	These are areas on which limits may be imposed by the legislature	Governments have considerable leeway to work within limits. Frequently, limits may be circumvented, for example, temporary employees, leases rather than purchases, unbundling to escape limits, through legal means Reappropriation may be selectively undertaken by the executive within the framework of delegated powers
	Performance contracts and measures	These contracts are of relatively recent origin and provide a legal basis for services. Measures reflect quantitative aspects aimed to enhance the quality of accountability	Many governments rely on regular civil service and performance contracts, these have yet to gain extensive acceptance. These contracts do not require approval by the legislature, although they may be submitted for the information of the legislature Performance measures are mostly given for projects and selected programmes. These measures are devised by the executive and are neither binding nor required by the legislature. Any failure to achieve may entail, at best, a justification
	Supplementary budgets: Recessions	Addictions and restrictions on allotted funds	Supplementary budgets require legislative approval. Although there is a prescribed timetable, legislation may be enacted when needed. Selectively, expenditures may be undertaken in anticipation of legislative approval Rescissions or reductions in allotted funds may be undertaken by the executive and may not even be reported to the legislature
	Excess expenditures	Expenditures over specified limits	In British-type systems, excess expenditures are required to be approved on an ex-post basis. In the US-type systems, excess may be collected from the official responsible for that act Limits are often circumvented through hidden debt including arrears in payment which need not be reported to the legislature

(Contd.)

(Table 6.1 Contd.)

Accounts	Appropriation accounts	Show the disposition of the funds approved by the legislature and the extent to which the budgetary intent has been fulfilled	Audited accounts are required to be submitted to the legislature for its review and approval The structure of accounts varies among countries, but is mostly too aggregative in nature. Accessibility to the public is limited
	Periodic reports	Show the intra-year status of government finances	Until recently, these were neither submitted to legislatures nor published in the media. Now, however, in response to the demands of financial markets, governments are slowly engaging in the periodic publication of fiscal data In countries where the fiscal performance is subject to credit rating, financial data are now regularly published
Evaluation	Periodic reports	Show the results of programmes and the cost-effectiveness with which they have been carried out	Evaluation is primarily a technique used by the executive. The application of this approach is still limited. The reports, when published, may be made available to the public and the legislature In some countries, legislative committees may undertake evaluation with the assistance of the audit, or on their own In either case, there may be no sanctions for failure. Justification may be provided
Audit	Annual audit report	This shows the failures of the executive in the financial area	Audit reports are frequently delayed. Most of them concentrate on financial and regularity audit The purview of audit does not include policy aspects. It is dependent for its success on the legislative support it receives
	Periodic investigative reports	Show the misuse or fraud in selected areas	The application of this technique is still limited; when applied, however, it has the potential of resulting in sanctions
	Efficiency audit	Shows the efficiency in the process of resource utilization	As with investigative audit, the applicability of this technique has been limited largely for the reason that government budgets have, in several cases, not yet adopted performance approaches in operationally binding terms.

Some specific features that have a significant impact on the financial accountability debate may be noted here. First, although the instruments may be wide ranging, it needs to be recognized that not all of them are found in all countries. Some countries have minimal instruments such as an annual budget and a set of annual accounts. The other instruments have yet to find acceptance and practice in many countries. Second, it appears that in most countries where the instruments are basic and not very sophisticated there may still be an effective machinery in regard to the financial relationships with donors and IFIs. This is largely due to the extensive range of techniques used by the donors and others. Aid provided by donors also comes with stiff and far-reaching conditionalities. Donors and IFIs have regular and systematic approaches to monitoring actual progress in the field. In some cases, they may also supervise the projects and programmes they finance. Moreover, fear of losing financial support makes the recipient countries pay particular attention to foreign-aided projects and agreements with IFIs. Furthermore, the violation of agreements could have a significant and quick adverse impact on the credit ratings of a country. These aspects suggest that where oversight bodies are keen to be effective, there are improved chances for the fulfilment of financial accountability. The regrettable aspect of the financial transactions with donors and IFIs is that most of these may not require explicit approval by the legislature and information on them may not be available to the public, although this weakness is being addressed through the opening of web sites by IFIs. But in countries where access to cyber-technology is limited, such information may not be available to the public. The dissemination of information in this regard depends, to a very large extent, on the approaches of recipient governments. They may be less inclined to share information with the public if that information shows that government has pursued policies that have not been conducive to improved economic welfare and, on the other hand, have increased the burdens and further diminished the benefits to the community. This also illustrates how public scrutiny, an important component of accountability, is adversely affected.

Third, many of the dimensions of accountability still have to be fulfilled. In many countries, performance aspects of programmes and projects, and their linkages to financial resources, are not specified. A consequence is that while governments are generally responsible for providing a service, the community has very scant information for assessing the efficiency with which the service is being provided. In most cases, cost information is not available even to governmental agencies.

Thus, where no quantitative targets are available, there can be little accountability. Moreover, the services may be provided by NGOs with funding from governments; the accountability of such providers to the legislatures is somewhat distant and often weak. To that extent, it may not be easy to locate responsibility for failures in the provision of services, and even if it is located, sanctions may not be feasible. These aspects illustrate that the machinery for providing fiscal accountability has over the years lagged behind the pace of growing demands on accountability (as shown in Figure 6.3). Many financial management systems have yet to achieve the capability to secure economies in expenditure and efficiency in operations. The preponderance of soft constraints and perverse incentives (such as the rush to spend as a fiscal year draws to a close) effectively preclude economies. The same may be said about prudence in economic management and achievement of improved performance. Where quantitative targets are not available, the effective exercise of oversight becomes difficult.

FACTORS HINDERING FINANCIAL ACCOUNTABILITY

Experience shows that several factors have hindered the effectiveness of institutions that are responsible for ensuring financial accountability. These include the following:

(i) Certain expenditures are excluded from the purview of oversight bodies. Some expenditures are incurred outside the budget. These transactions may be carried out through extra-budgetary accounts or through executive decree. Further, defence expenditures continue to be shrouded in secrecy for reasons of national security.[3] Although it is generally difficult to evolve suitable measures of performance with respect in regard to defence operations, selective costing could be computed for some programmes. Several industrial countries have made considerable progress in computing the costs of selected operations. However, in most developing countries, progress in this area remains to be made. Similarly, public debt operations, which continue to

---

3. Defence opaqueness reflects a cruel irony. Outlays on protecting the common man are not fully revealed to the public with the result that an individual has no idea as to how he is protected or the full costs of protection, not to mention the effectiveness of that protection.

dominate government budgets, have received little scrutiny. Experience with privatization also shows that the realm of accountability has been relatively small in comparison to the totality of transactions.

(ii) Established systems of oversight such as audit and legislative control have many limitations. Specific factors contributing to this underachieving machinery are described in detail in Box 6.2.

Box 6.2: Financial Accountability—Factors Contributing to Underachievement

In many countries, institutions and procedures have been established to achieve financial accountability. The two most important institutions in this regard are independent audit and the legislature. Experience shows, both these have been less than effective in fulfilling their charters, let alone the expectations of the public. The underachievement is mostly due to the limitations that these institutions encounter in the process of fulfilling their mandate. These are described here.

Audit

In a number of countries, audit agencies still have to develop fully and become completely independent. Even in countries where audit has existed for several years, its contribution has not been effective in ensuring financial accountability. This is largely due to the following factors:

1. In most cases, audit is not empowered to review policy matters. Audit agencies do not have full authority as yet in most countries to follow the trail of the budget peso or rupee to the last stage where it is spent. Thus, local governments, non-governmental bodies, and private contractors who perform agency functions on behalf of the central or federal government are not within the orbit of primary audit. In most cases, the audit conducted by the audit agency is limited to financial compliance audit (regularity and compliance of laws), and efficiency audit remains to be fully developed.

2. In a large number of cases, audit agencies have yet to develop expertise in areas such as public debt (which represents a significant block of government outlays) and foreign exchange management.

3. Audit agencies in many cases follow the track of accountancy and

(Contd.)

(Box 6.2 Contd.)

appropriation audit and place very little emphasis on investigative audit into special areas. Even in countries where investigative audit is undertaken, a judicious combination of regular audit and investigative audit remains to be achieved.

4. The effectiveness of audit, even in its own chosen areas, is dependent on the support it receives from legislative institutions. These institutions may often be governed by party politics or by issues of the day, rather than by considerations of institutional development.

Legislative Institutions

The practices in this regard vary considerably from being forceful and decisive to being complaisant or without deliberative and legislative powers in regard to budgets. Moreover, the following limitations stand in the way of the realization of the full potential of financial accountability:

1. In several countries, particularly those that have practices modelled on Whitehall's legislatures can only reject government policies (which run the risk of a change of the party in government), but cannot modify them. In recent years, consultative committees have been set up in some countries to provide opportunities for legislative inputs into policy making. Experience in this regard is limited and does not justify optimism. Elsewhere, experience shows that legislators may be more interested, where party discipline permits, in pork barrel politics rather than on the major premises of macroeconomic policies.

2. In many cases, major portions of public outlays are covered by existing legislation, thus limiting the scope of legislative control. In some cases, for example, public debt, governmental operations may not require legislation. Until recently, agreements with IFIs were not submitted for legislative approval or information.

3. Legislatures rarely have opportunities to discuss macroeconomic policy issues. Also, the discussion is largely handicapped because of lack of expertise in this area.

The portfolio of expenditures of central governments, as noted already, has been changing in recent years. Central governments are increasingly becoming cash counters transferring funds to autonomous agencies, NGOs, and state and local governments. Services provided by the street-level bureaucracy are mostly within the realm of state and local governments, while funding responsibilities reside with the central government. In some cases, such as in the European Community, disbursing power has moved from national to supranational governments. This growing distance between funding and delivery of services has exacerbated the problem of financial accountability and, as yet, a satisfactory solution has to be evolved to reduce the gap between the two. In some cases, it is argued that state and local governments have their own audit agencies and legislatures and, therefore, the composite picture of accountability is complete. In practice, however, oversight bodies at the state and local levels differ in their approaches, and the expected complementarity among the various levels still has to be achieved. Financial relationships between governments and NGOs continue to be a black box. More often than not, NGOs lack the expertise; and an adequate regulatory framework for monitoring the activities of NGOs still has to evolve.

It is generally agreed that, as in corporate governance, public organizations, too, should endeavour to hold managers accountable for their actions. The implementation of this simple (at least in appearance) requirement in public organizations has become a complex and frequently intractable matter.

Two factors appear to have contributed to the complexity. First, most public organizations are hierarchical in nature. Even where tasks and responsibilities have been decentralized, in practice power may be concentrated in a few hands. Hierarchical organizations such as those in the civil services, defence management, and police administration contribute to a thick fog of diffused responsibility, making it extremely difficult to pinpoint the person or the authority responsible for poor performance. To tackle this problem, performance contracts with chief executives have been drawn up, and task-oriented agencies that are primarily concerned with policy implementation have been created. But the application of these approaches, it is argued, has been carried out in 'too crude and simplified a fashion' (Foster and Plowden 1996, p. x). In most cases, the agencies have yet to form a consensus on the type of accountability they should have. Experience shows that the local bodies or the policy-making departments (ministries) tend to view accountability as a form of control. Consequently, the paradoxical result has been that ministers and chief executives become more powerful through direction and arm-twisting. Performance contracts, too, cannot be all encompassing and there are grey areas where responsibility for actions is difficult to locate. Meanwhile, the monitoring of performance contracts and their enforcement has brought added costs, at the same time that the distinct cost advantages of chief executives over the traditional civil service remain to be proven.

1. The formulation of performance indicators through the establishment of direct and explicit relationships between the inputs of money and manpower and the tasks of an agency has been and continues to be a formidable task. Several problems are being encountered in this regard. First, a one-size-fits-all approach is apparently being taken such as through the formulation of workload data for categories like 'policy formulation'. Government departments tend to have a distinct personality of their own which is not always captured through these general, ambiguous, and frequently non-empirical categories. Second, the formulation of agency tasks tends to be broad and general, notwithstanding exhortations to the contrary. At one stage, the task of the Health Authorities in Britain was to 'carry out the priorities of the government of the day' (Day and Klein 1987, p. 84). This type of approach has the effect of redefining the problem rather than solving it. Third, the formulation of performance indicators has been and continues to be a unilateral exercise undertaken by the executive wing of governments, which is somewhat akin to the defendant in a legal dispute determining the parameters and course of the judicial process.

2. The overall framework of financial accountability gives access to the public by providing information on the actions of the executive. Such access may not, however, enable detailed scrutiny for several reasons. First, the annual accounts and related documents show the overall results of actions taken during a year but are less helpful in throwing light on the factors that contribute to a specific action. Second, in several cases there may be full compliance with the budget estimates, and all laws and regulations may be fully adhered to. But this compliance by itself does not mean that the objectives of budgetary policy have been achieved or that the services have been delivered properly. The audit, too, is concentrated in several cases on the financial control process rather than achieving value-for-money or efficiency audit. Third, the government, which has monopoly on the information needed for accountability, has not been above managing the information to its advantage. It is suggested that, being economical with the truth has become, an ingrained habit of the bureaucracy.

As a result of all the above factors, citizens often feel that their access to information does not necessarily translate into full-fledged scrutiny and accountability. The other means available to them (Box 6.3) may be expensive and incapable of yielding immediate results. The opportunity to use the ballot box as a means to revoke the policies is limited as it has its own schedule, and, therefore, may not be exercisable with the prospect of immediate results.

Box 6.3: Citizens and Financial Accountability

The overarching purpose of financial accountability is to keep the citizen informed of the progress made in the mobilization of financial resources and in their use to meet the needs of the community.

Citizens have a variety of instruments at their disposal to make financial accountability a reality. In principle, citizens have the power to revoke the decisions made by the executive and the legislature; they have the capacity to move the judiciary when they find policies and decisions to be discriminatory or having an adverse impact on the community; they can undertake public scrutiny of government policies through their access to the information available in the public domain. In some instances, they may participate in making financial decisions, in monitoring the progress made by various programmes, and in evaluating the results of policies. Selectively, public opinion may also play a significant role in the imposition of sanctions and penalties against delinquent officials.

In practice, however, in each of the above areas, the citizen remains somewhat distant from the focus of financial accountability. This aloofness stems from the nature of the instruments chosen for the purpose of financial accountability. In most countries, revoking the decisions made by governments tends to be difficult except in the tax area. In several countries, full budget documentation is not available to the public. Although progress has been made in recent years in publicizing the nature and magnitudes of fiscal deficits, the issue remains confusing to many in view of the existence of many extra-budgetary accounts and numerous transactions between these and the general account, and the constitutional imperatives of a balanced budget. There have been many instances, however, where tax proposals have been altered or withdrawn in the light of popular

(Contd.)

(Box 6.3 Contd.)

opposition and potential political consequences. Details of expenditure programmes are rarely provided, and where provided, are highly aggregated and sketchy. Thus, public scrutiny, which is the basis for financial accountability, is rarely fulfilled. An associated feature is that periodic financial data, which have been published selectively in recent years, are directed more to the financial markets than to ordinary citizens. Audit reports are primarily intended to serve the needs of legislatures and their committees and are not structured to address the concerns of citizens. The voice of citizens in regard to the delivery of services tends to be muted in view of the growing distance between those responsible for funding and those who deliver services.

Citizens can take recourse to the judiciary, but only in those cases where there are inequities in the existing legislation. Although general issues may be taken up in public-interest litigation, judicial intervention has been more in the tax area than in expenditure matters.

At the local levels, citizens in many western democracies have gained a voice in determining contract awards, in monitoring progress, and in evaluating completed programmes. But in most developing countries, the executive continues to have a dominant role and the options of citizens are limited to discussions within party caucuses, or organized protests to air their grievances. In these countries, citizens have little role in the imposition of penalties and sanctions.

Thus, the language and structure of financial documentation limits the scope of public debate and scrutiny. A good deal of progress still has to be made in bringing financial accountability closer to the public.

It is in this context of a sense of disenchantment with the existing systems of accountability and the lack of their effectiveness that there has been a growing demand for improved and more effective systems of financial accountability. The additional stimulus for achieving financial accountability (Box 6.4) is being addressed in different ways.

Box 6.4: New impetus for Financial Accountability

Although accountability has always been inherent in the responsibilities of an official or an institution, it has acquired a new impetus and many dimensions in recent years as efforts to strengthen fragile democracies and the links between the civil society and forms of government continue. The new impetus and the growing demands for stronger accountability in general and financial accountability in particular have their origins in the following factors:

1. In recent years, notwithstanding a steady increase in the size of the bureaucracy, there has been a perception of continuing sizeable waste in government operations. The socialization of inefficiency has contributed to distrust of governments. Opinion polls conducted in western democracies since the Second World War reveal that this distrust has been growing.

2. As an integral part of the above perception, there is also the generally shared view that bureaucracies tend to be self-serving with scant regard for their clients' needs. Moreover, it is also believed that bureaucracies lack accountability.

3. While in normal circumstances, legislatures would have been expected to perform a major role in ensuring financial accountability, they tended to be ineffective as bureaucracies acquired additional powers in day-to-day economic decision making. Legislatures may discuss the policies of governments and may approve or reject them. In reality, however, policies reach legislatures at too late a stage—in aerodynamics terms, when the plane is about to take off, aborting the plan could mean unpleasant consequences. Opportunities for crucial inputs into policy making are few, and major chunks of expenditures are either already committed or beyond the scope of legislative intervention. Year-end scrutiny tends to be spotty, with major attention devoted to issues of sleaze or those that damage the political prospects of the ruling party. There is also a perception that the machinery for accountability, where it already exists and operates, is often slow and parochial, contributing to a discord between the rapid pace in the advancement of expectations and the scope of response of the institutional machinery. Experience also shows, as in the case of the European Community, that where the institutional machinery has been designed during recent periods, insufficient

(Contd.)

(Box 6.4 Contd.)

attention has been paid to ensuring adequate financial accountability.

4. Recent efforts to install or strengthen management capabilities (prompted by the new public management philosophy) envisage greater roles for managers. They are expected, within the limits of financial resources and endowed autonomy, to deliver services at the specified cost and quality and within the given time frame. Such additional delegation of financial powers and autonomy as a part of the new public management approach may further weaken the accountability machinery with its already hollow core.

5. There is an overall gap between the intent and performance of governments. The reality, as perceived by the people, is that services are deteriorating even as the debt burden increases, and the community's suffering has increased even as governments traditionally considered strong and fiscally viable have become weak because of other internal and external developments.

These factors accentuate the need for appropriate financial accountability to stop the erosion of confidence in government and to restore credibility.

MOVING AHEAD: RECENT DEVELOPMENTS

In recent years, particularly in the early 1990s, there has been a growing recognition of some of these problem areas. As a result, there have been greater efforts to consolidate the progress made towards financial accountability. More specifically, these efforts have involved further strengthening of financial management in government agencies, imparting a set of moral values in public service, and, on the part of IFIs, formulating a fiscal transparency framework.

In the area of financial management, accounting systems are being organized on an accrual basis and corporate approaches are being applied. (A few advanced countries have already moved to accrual accounting; (for an account of these developments in Australia, New Zealand, United Kingdom, and the United States). As an integral part of this effort, accounting standards with specific applicability to government operations are being developed. In some cases, budgets, too, are being prepared on an accrual basis. Once these innovations are fully implemented, there is a distinct prospect that activity-based costing will emerge as the anchor for expenditure management and financial accountability. In a number of cases, performance contracts are being developed as concordats between agency heads and the government. Although many of the difficulties relating to performance measurement continue, the hope is that with more experience, improved indicators with the potential to enhance accountability can be developed. Moreover, it is likely that the shift of emphasis from inputs to performance and results will transform the culture of government organizations into a management-oriented one. Audit agencies, too, have been developing agendas combining traditional financial audit with investigative audit and oriented to ascertaining value for money (for example, in European countries). In the United States, since 1998, investigative audit has been combined with the financial audit of all the operations of the government, as required under law. While these instruments are not entirely new, the emphasis and, in some cases, the revival of some ideas merit recognition.

Moral values, as Barnard envisaged them, were essentially a part of the informal and, to some extent, private aspects of an official. In recent years, however, there has been a view (for example, in the United Kingdom) that in order to restore public confidence in the system of public administration, standards of public life are needed. Accordingly, there has been an emphasis on the need for selflessness, integrity, objectivity, accountability, openness, honesty, and leadership.[4] These qualities, which have always been essential, would undoubtedly increase public confidence in governments. At the same time, it must be noted that if at least six of these qualities were firmly entrenched in public administration, then accountability would be automatic and even self-enforcing. Experience suggests that mere exhortation of the need for these values would not have any major impact, particularly since the laws aimed at penalizing corruption in public life have had so little enduring effect.

Meanwhile, IFIs, which have seen their developmental policies

[4.] The exhortation for standards in public life may be inherent in human condition in view of what Montaigne called a long time ago, the 'ordinary vices' associated with human behaviour. Included in these vices were treachery, disloyalty, cruelty, and tyranny. Judith Skhlar suggested that 'dishonesty' be added to the list. Despite these periodic reminders, and admonitions from the religious establishments that some of these sins might invoke divine wrath, ordinary vices continue to dominate day-to-day economic life. Indeed, some of the public standards, for example, selflessness, may be contrary to the spirit of economic rationality that emphasizes the virtue of maximizing profit.

jeopardized by the levels of corruption and the consequent losses suffered by society, have also initiated efforts to strengthen institutional development. They have begun to formulate a framework to promote financial transparency and accountability. The framework proposed is more in the nature of a minimum agenda (Box 6.5). Many countries already have the features of the proposed framework. The problem, as noted earlier, is not the lack of institutions and instruments but the lag between the intent and the practice, and other factors contributing to under-achievement and, in a few cases, to failure of the prescribed machinery. It would appear by implication that the suggested framework is applicable more to formerly centrally planned economies that have yet to make the complete transformation to democratic forms of government. Even in these countries, there is a good deal of vertical accountability (within the hierarchical system of organization) and often quick and severe penalties for violations. In terms of horizontal accountability, the party congress, particularly at the provincial and local levels, plays a crucial role in the allocation of resources, their utilization, and accountability. What needs to be recognized is that these countries have their own form of accountability even though it may not be similar to that found in some democracies.

Box 6.5: Financial Accountability—Minimal Agenda Not Adequate

Recently, several IFIs have taken initiatives to issue guidelines on the ways in which financial (the term used by the international agencies is 'fiscal') transparency and accountability may be achieved by countries. Being international guidelines that seek universal applicability, they are concerned more with the general rather than the specific features of a particular country. The guidelines envisage (i) a medium-term fiscal strategy, (ii) a comprehensive annual budget, (iii) periodic data to be published on the status of government finances and annual accounts to be submitted to the legislature, and (iv) identification and publication of government liabilities, including contingent liabilities. The guidelines envisage the functioning of a legislature endowed with powers to review the budget and annual accounts.

Many of the features described above are found in most democracies, in one form or another. The role of the legislature as a deliberative body and engaged in the enactment of legislation is yet

(Contd.)

(Box 6.5 Contd.)

to be established in some of the former centrally planned economies (most such economies in Europe have already made this transition). Meanwhile, the party congresses have been taking an active role in the consideration of the annual report on the economy and the budget. They have also made a beginning in the establishment of an audit agency. Here again, the former centrally planned economies in Eastern Europe have made rapid progress (with the help of European Organization of Systems Audit Authorities and the audit agencies of some industrial countries) in the establishment of independent agencies endowed with powers to undertake financial and investigative audit.

The experience of many countries in regard to the features enumerated by IFIs shows that they provide, at best, a modest beginning in the process of achieving financial accountability, largely because the systems and operational techniques utilized by the relevant governmental institutions leave a good deal to be desired.

Several countries have medium-term fiscal strategies, either in the form of development plans or global visions, or in the strategies formulated in the wake of economic crisis experienced, during recent years, by some Asian countries. These strategies are too general and are more indicative of the likely goals to be reached and are scarce in the specification of the means (as required by a strategy) to achieve those goals. Moreover, insufficient attention is paid to uncertainty, high-risk areas, and associated vulnerabilities. The strategies also lack enforceability and the imposition of sanctions, in the event of failure, as needed by financial accountability.

The budget, even on a comprehensive basis—a goal that remains to be achieved by some Asian countries—is far from accessible to the general public. Budgets tend to have a unique language of their own, and some mysteries that defy probing by the public. Details on expenditure programmes and the likely benefits are scant and in many cases doctored.

The periodic reports, which are published by many countries, are too aggregative in nature and are intended for the benefit of domestic and external financial markets. Annual accounts, which in most countries are required to be audited, are not of recent origin. Indeed, they have been a part of the framework of legal accountability for a long time. These accounts are mere records of transactions and do

(Contd.)

(Box 6.5 Contd.)

not offer any benchmarks for performance assessment. They remain inaccessible to the general public.

The effort at revealing liabilities, particularly in a cash-based budget and accounting system, is a welcome one. The most significant part of liabilities is external and internal debt. Data on debt are regularly published by many countries although, on occasion, some countries have attempted to doctor them too. Several countries also publish data on contingent liabilities stemming from guarantees (although the coverage is far from uniform or comprehensive). No attempts are made to publish data on liabilities relating to arrears in wage payments, repayment of debt, and settlement of claims by contractors. Hidden or informal debt remains an area of darkness for the public.

Thus, the framework of accountability offers a hollow core rather than an effective one. Provision of information is equated with public scrutiny; the existence of an audit agency of a legislature is viewed in this oversimplified model of accountability as fulfilment of financial accountability. The important need is to look into the working of the institutions and ascertain as to why their potential is not being realized fully.

TOWARDS A CONSTRUCTIVE AGENDA

A paradoxical feature of the current situation is that the expectations and demands of the public are growing faster than the existing machinery for accountability can handle. The solution does not lie in reducing the scope of accountability but in producing more viable and responsive accountability machinery. In evolving such machinery, the following aspects merit specific attention.

1. Financial accountability is no longer limited to ensuring that the budgeted amounts have been spent and that the specified annual objectives of an organization have been met. While these elements will continue to be important, it appears essential that accountability be enlarged to include the success achieved in ensuring economic sustainability. The interest of the community is in satisfying itself that the policies pursued enhance the strengths of the economy and that the financial balance of the community is not jeopardized. This enhanced

accountability should be the cornerstone of every effort. Accountability for economic performance should go hand in hand with financial performance and the provision of services.

2. Accountability will not be achieved unless it becomes an integral part of service delivery, and of political agenda at the national level.[5] To achieve the former, it may be necessary to arrange for more formal participation of the client groups. At the national level, legislatures may not be very interested, depending on the political climate, in pursuing limited accountability. There is thus a need to strengthen the role of the legislature in the management of the economy through more opportunities to review and approve government policies. Categories of expenditure that are now exempt from legislative approval should be reviewed and reduced. In addition, society should have more opportunities to review policies and programme results and, where necessary, to impose sanctions.

3. The measurement of economic and programme performance should form an integral part of financial accountability. The formulation of performance measures should not be left to the executive but should form a part of tripartite deliberations comprising client groups, the executive, and the legislature. The formulation of performance measures is a complex task and the pursuit of a one-size-fits-all approach is bound to be counter-productive. Rather, the diversified nature of government transactions needs to be explicitly recognized. To this end, organizations may be divided, as a first step, into those that are: (i) production-oriented (where outputs and outcomes are observable), (ii) procedural in nature (where internal activity, but not the outcome, can be monitored), (iii) craft-oriented (those engaged in ensuring compliance of rules and regulations), and (iv) those that are responsible for coping with difficult situations (where outputs and outcomes may be uncertain) (this approach is adopted from Wilson 1989, pp. 160–71). The performance measures should facilitate risk taking and should be flexible.

4. Accountability should not be limited to the imposition of sanctions. If this were the primary objective, then there would be a good deal of defensive policy making and the bureaucracy may be inhibited from

---

[5] Accountability is not a mere technical process and, therefore, cannot be entirely apolitical, even when fully objective. A distinction needs to be made, however, between proper political use and abuse of the accountability process. The former seeks to enrich the level of political discourse so that the community's understanding may be illuminated; the latter is a tactical weapon in an adversarial process.

taking risks. Accountability should, therefore, aim at investing resources to secure lasting improvements in the administrative machinery that would also prevent or minimize institutional recidivism (Box 6.6).

5. The accountability framework should reflect, in the light of the preceding observations, vertical aspects within a hierarchy and among supranational, national, and sub-national governments, and horizontal aspects reflecting the relationships with the legislature, client groups, and the society itself.

Box 6.6: Beyond Financial Accountability

Financial accountability involves the identification of the losses suffered by the community. Inevitably, the identification contributes to the 'naming and shaming' of individuals, organizations, and institutions whose actions have contributed to such losses. This is frequently viewed as an integral part of the audit system. The identification of guilty individuals and organizations is expected to lead to the imposition of penalties and sanctions on them. This represents the concluding stage of accountability.

The 'naming and shaming' and the imposition of penalties can lead to tension, hostility, or adversarial relationships between those that are in governmental agencies and those outside. The continuation of such adversarial relationships could also harden obsession but not necessarily lead to improved systems. While human failures should be punished, it must also be recognized that many of the lapses may be systemic. Addressing individual crimes and misdemeanours without looking into the underlying contributory factors could lead, and indeed has led, to institutional recidivism.

Just as a judicial system looks beyond the incarceration of the criminal to the correction and reform of the individual to reduce potential crimes, so also governments and the community have the need, indeed the obligation, to reform the system of financial management, to strengthen it so that the hopes of the community can be fulfilled with minimum friction. The experience of many countries shows that, apart from greedy individuals who seek to exploit situations for personal gain (which translate in this zero-sum game into losses for the community), the financial management system that has structural and procedural flaws needs to be improved. This positive aspect of investing in improved financial management systems should form an integral part of a constructive agenda.

(Contd.)

(Box 6.6 Contd.)

> Recent developments in technology are such that their gradual deployment is likely to give a strong boost to participatory decision making. In the not too distant future, electronic technology may make possible a kind of town-hall meeting, where each individual in the comfort of his home may indicate his or her personal preferences in regard to a proposed action. Such participatory decision-making, which is a significant step towards linking the democratic tradition with a civic society, could lead to yet another phase in financial accountability. Financial accountability envisages the promotion of a management culture in public organizations so that performance may be specified and evaluated. The increasing provision of public services by the corporate world has widened the choice of benchmarks. Here again, an agenda that envisages a greater involvement of the community in the promotion of a management culture is likely to contribute to improved financial accountability. In sum, the emphasis on punishing the guilty should be tempered by an explicit recognition of the need for improved systems of financial management and the promotion of a management culture of accountability.

In evolving the above type of framework, care should be taken to avoid having too many laws, rules, and regulations, and too many layers of officialdom (craft organizations). Otherwise, accountability could become an oversight mechanism that is too invasive and that stifles initiative and imaginative handling of public affairs. The shift in concern from the process to results and performance would be difficult to achieve if management is not endowed with the needed freedom to act. Maintaining a balance between delegation of autonomy and direct oversight is indeed a difficult task but the success of accountability is dependent, in the final analysis, on the ingenuity shown in this respect.

CONCLUSIONS

It is important that the framework for financial accountability be formulated with care and caution, so as to inspire public confidence and restore the credibility of government. Accountability which is narrowly defined and which aims only at financial process controls is no longer adequate. The scope of accountability needs to be expanded to include overall economic management as well as delivery of services both by governmental and non-governmental agencies. The objectives should not be limited to the pursuit of sleaze, but should include a more constructive agenda aimed at strengthening operational systems of public administration. The dimensions of accountability have grown over the years, and access to information on government operations, while facilitating public understanding, does not by itself complete the process of public scrutiny. Many of the initiatives taken in recent years still have to be fully implemented or taken to their logical conclusion. A framework of financial accountability encompassing all these aspects remains to be formulated and that by itself constitutes a major agenda for the future. This need for enhanced accountability has to be tempered by recognition of the extensive preparatory work implied in this effort. Accountability can be fulfilled only when organizations are given specific goals and, more importantly, are endowed with additional capacity to achieve these goals. Countries have a good deal to do on both these fronts. Emphasis on one goal without corresponding effort devoted to the strengthening of administrative infrastructure could contribute to underachievement of goals and even further erosion of the credibility of governments.

7. Expenditure Management and Life Support Programmes

INTRODUCTION

Protection of the financially challenged classes of the community has always been, in differing degrees, a matter of concern for public policy. The need for such protection received formal support and recognition with the introduction of New Deal policies that specified the four freedoms—from fear, want, belief, and expression. In the decades that followed the New Deal, there has been extensive legislation aimed at providing a vast range of benefits, funded by government budgets, to protect the vulnerable sections of the community. The legislation enacted by several industrial countries created a category of entitlements that conferred legal rights on eligible citizens to claim benefits regardless of the financial condition of the government or the availability of funds at its disposal. The legislation and the associated claims for benefits have contributed to the growth of benefit-providing organizations both in the governmental and non-governmental sectors, and also to growing public expenditures. In several industrial countries, the share of expenditures devoted to the provision of welfare benefits ranges from 40 to 60 per cent. The strategies for the provision of benefits are multiple; the organizations engaged in the provision of these benefits are large and several, and the range of benefits is substantial.

In the earlier periods that witnessed an eagerness to expand benefits, there was relatively little recognition of the impact of these strategies on the overall financial condition of governments and on their ability to pursue appropriate policies aimed at securing macroeconomic stability. Experience during the last three decades of fiscal turbulence has shown that the enormous range of benefits conferred by legislation contributed to higher budget deficits and thus, crippled the government's ability to pursue stability. In turn, this ushered in an era that focused on the macroeconomic impact of the benefits and the need for changes in eligibility, in the range of benefits, and in the forms of financing the benefits.

Meanwhile, there was also a perception that many of the programmes were not effective in curbing the growth of poverty, that programmes were too diffuse and costly relative to the benefits, and that the bureaucracies tended to be more concerned with internal administrative processes than with the clientele groups or with the delivery of services. There was also the view, undoubtedly based on the experience of a few countries, that in the context of fiscal turbulence, government actions tended to be unpredictable, adversely affecting the delivery of the services. In addition, there was the view that fiscal turbulence has contributed to a growing concentration of power in governments, while organization experts felt that many governments were poorly organized to provide the benefits and that there was a fundamental mismatch between what was sought to be done and the organizational ability of governments to deliver them.

Meanwhile, as governments in the industrial world were grappling with the major issue of reconciling the range of benefits with the needs of macroeconomic stability there has emerged a growing demand for the provision of government-organized social safety nets in developing countries on the lines of the experience of industrial countries. This apparent paradox of conferring more tasks on governments which are already perceived to be organizationally weak can be ascribed to the growth of democratic governments, on the one hand, and to government organizations, on the other. The need, it is argued, is not to do away with government organizations but to make them more effective and responsive in the wider context of enhanced transparency and accountability.

It is in this context that government financial management needs to be evaluated. To what extent has it been helpful in the pursuit of macroeconomic stability while ensuring an economical provision of services? What are the problems experienced in this regard? Are there major differences in this respect between industrial and developing countries? What are the ways in which it can be strengthened? Answers to these and related questions require a more detailed probe into the nature of life support programmes and their linkages with financial management.

SCOPE OF LIFE SUPPORT PROGRAMMES

As a part of the efforts aimed at providing freedom from want, governments are now engaged in providing a vast range of services to the community. In analysing the range of services, it is appropriate to make a distinction between a broader and narrower interpretation. The former includes protection of life from external aggression and providing an atmosphere of domestic peace in which the community can perform its ordinary tasks and engage in productive activities. These services aim at securing freedom from fear and providing a civil identity to members of the community. This identity, with emotional and sentimental subtexts (that are generally considered as a part of the study of nationalism), provides a distinctive label that separates one community from another. The benefits of these programmes accrue to the whole community and, as such, are indivisible and non-exclusive. For this reason, outlays on these activities are considered as those incurred on the provision of pure public goods.

A narrower and more conventional approach, however, excludes these broader categories and is restricted to activities undertaken by governments aimed at providing income support, employment support, social service support, production support, consumption support, and infrastructure support. The general range of programmes covered under these support programmes is illustrated in Table 7.1. The income support activities are, for the most part, covered in many industrial countries through a variety of social security programmes. A precise definition of a social security system is generally difficult in view of the range of activities covered under it. Two considerations have been proposed for the determination of a social security system: (i) the objective of the system must be to grant medical care to maintain income in the event of loss of income, and (ii) the system must have been set up by legislation attributing the power of administration to a public body. Following these criteria, the system is considered to consist of compulsory social insurance, certain voluntary social insurance schemes, family allowance schemes, special schemes for public employees, public health services, and public assistance. Within this sphere, three major approaches are identified: social insurance, public service, and social assistance. The most common form of social security is the social insurance programme that is funded by contributions from employers and employees and is operated as a separate authority with benefits linked to contributions of coverage of the fund. More often than not, deficits in the fund, that is, the gap between contributions and benefits, are financed by transfers from the government budget. Public service primarily consists of the direct provision of a service or a cash payment from the government budget to specified categories of the community. The third approach of social assistance consists of payments that are also made from the budget to recipients whose financial status is subject to investigation in order to determine the need and the amount of assistance they receive. In addition, there are quasi-social security measures such as provident funds for government employees and public provident funds for self-employed professionals. These funds comprise contributions by employers and employees that are paid with interest in the event of a contingency such as old age, invalidism, or death. These three types as well as other related programmes covered under the broad rubric of income support are shown in Table 7.1.

Table 7.1

Life Support Programmes and Fiscal Instruments

Area	Instruments	Remarks
Civil identity support	Outlays on defence and maintenance of law and order	Benefits from these outlays aim at maintaining the civil identity of the members of the community. Basic security is available to all and as such, the benefits are indivisible
Income support	Automatic stabilizers in the form of temporary unemployment support, pensions for the elderly and other low income groups; child support; national calamity relief and related programmes; relief to compensate for buy-out programmes introduced as a part of public sector reorganization plans	Several countries have legislation governing the provision of these benefits. In some cases, automatic stabilizers may be funded by insurance programmes
Employment support	Public works programmes during periods of economic downturn; promotion of self-employed schemes; provision of training to people on economic schemes; provision of training to people on economic support programmes so that they may gain income generating	Outlays from government may be direct and unconditional. In some cases, they may take the form of soft loans, provided from the government budget or by financial institutions at the behest of governments with subsidies from the national budget

(Contd.)

(Table 7.1 Contd.)

	employment; provision of training to public sector employees to secure other employment after retirement from government	
Social service support	Provision of preventive and curative public health services; provision of educational services from primary to university levels	Benefits in these areas may be provided directly by government maintained organizations or may be funded by governments but provided by others. Here again, benefits may be provided by direct outlays or through loan. In addition, extensive tax incentives may be provided to NGOs working in these areas. Benefits may be general (for example, free education to all at the primary level) or targeted to specific income groups who may be given vouchers to claim benefits
Production support	Subsidies for subsistence sectors (for example, fertilizer supply to farmers); provision of cheap energy to small-scale and cottage industry sectors; provision of tax incentives for export promotion in some sectors; provision of support prices for selected agricultural activities	Governments may spend directly or may seek to achieve the objectives through the provision of loans at subsidized rates or may provide guarantees to those who face difficulty in getting credit from financial institutions. Some governments have set up quasi-financial institutions to promote production activities in the small-scale sectors
Consumption support	Provision of essential commodities with dual pricing; provision of food stamps	In many countries, governments engage in the provision of basic commodities such as rice, wheat, kerosene oil (cooking and heating), sugar, etc. In some, lower income groups are provided with vouchers or stamps to enable them to purchase essential commodities
Infrastructure support	Provision of subsidized water, electricity, and urban transport	Programmes in this regard may be targeted to specific income groups or age groups such as school children and the elderly, or those who are handicapped. Here again, services may be provided directly by governments or by others with funding from government budgets

Governments also provide employment support to sections of the community. It is generally contended that governments in less developed countries become employers of both first and last resorts in the absence of social security programmes. In some countries, graduates of universities are entitled to employment in governments, and the burgeoning growth of government employees is ascribed, in part, to this approach. During more recent years, governments that are engaged in the restructuring of public sector and social security systems have been, as a part of this activity, providing training in marketable skills.

Social service support and other forms of support shown in Table 7.1, should be deemed as illustrative and not exhaustive; nor should they be deemed to be applicable to all countries; rather they show the broad range of activities undertaken by governments.

DIFFERENCES BETWEEN INDUSTRIAL AND DEVELOPING COUNTRIES

Experience during the second half of the twentieth century shows that policies undertaken by industrial countries are soon followed by similar approaches in developing countries. Notwithstanding this pronounced tendency, there are significant differences in the provision of life support systems between industrial and developing countries. The first difference relates to the use of social security systems. In most industrial countries, social security systems have become a normal integral part of civic life. In several developing countries, social security systems are yet to be organized, and where organized, they are, for the most part, in their infancy. The extensive spread of the informal sector and the predominance of agricultural labour (underemployed, for the most part) would appear to inhibit the spread of social security systems. In the absence of these insurance types of programmes, life support in the developing world takes the form of public assistance, described earlier. As an extension of this feature, life support outlays become a significant factor in the determination of the size of automatic stabilizers, which are parts of the social security system, and which emerge in the event of need. Thus, short-term unemployment may be covered by independent social security organizations, while in developing countries, the planning and formulation of annual budgets have to explicitly take these into account and provide for relief or remedial action.

To that extent, what is automatic in industrial countries becomes a separate factor that needs to be identified, measured, and explicitly provided for in the budget in developing countries.

In industrial countries, some services, such as Medicaid (medical services for the poor), Medicare (services for the elderly), and others may be provided by the private sector while being funded from the government budget or autonomous funds established for the purpose. This reliance on the private sector has contributed to a separation between funding and provision of service. Services which are provided by the private sector and are compensated by the government have contributed to what are called 'third party payments', where neither the recipient nor the provider of the service are a part of the direct sphere of influence of governments. In industrial countries, there is extensive reliance on the network of NGOs, particularly in the area of education, child support, and training for unskilled persons, to provide the services. In developing countries, services are provided, for the most part, by organizations (schools, clinics, health centres) that are under the direct control of governments. In these cases, funding and provision of services form two sides of the same activity. Moreover, a string of public enterprises, owned and controlled by governments, is organized with the explicit purpose of pursuing non-commercial objectives. Thus, banking institutions owned by the government may provide subsidized credit, and public enterprises may be engaged in providing water, electricity, and transportation at cheaper rates. This implies that governments may pursue policies through state-owned enterprises rather than from their budgets. Moreover, the reliance on NGOs continues to be rather limited.

Another distinguishing feature relates to the use of electronic technology in the financial management processes of governments. In industrial countries, the management of third-party payments would have been impossible without the support of computer technology. The range of service providers and beneficiaries is too vast to be managed by a manual process. In developing countries, notwithstanding the recent progress in the application of electronic technology, for the most part, processes continue to be operated manually. In turn, this contributes to delays and higher costs of operation. It can be expected, however, that this gap would be increasingly reduced in the years to come.

FINANCIAL MANAGEMENT CYCLE

Financial management is an administrative process in governments intended to assure the community and taxpayers that there is an adequate system regulating the collection of public money (regardless of forms such as taxes, fees, and grants), its safe custody, allocation, and utilization. This process, in turn, comprises three major phases: resource allocation, resource utilization, and resource-use accounting. In these phases, it is expected that there would be a good deal of transparency and accountability, so that the community may exercise requisite oversight either through elected representatives or through other forms of monitoring and evaluation. For purposes of discussion, the focus here is on spending, rather than on collection of moneys.

The financial management processes in government have gone through a process of evolution, making the gradual transition from serving the needs of a monarchy to the larger role envisaged in a functioning democracy. Although the forms and processes of financial management tend to vary among countries, not in purpose but in the details of administrative means, it is possible to formulate a general conceptual framework applicable to a major part of the world. Table 7.2 shows the various aspects of the financial management cycle, the instruments utilized in different phases, the techniques of management, and the tasks performed.

Table 7.2

Financial Management Cycle

Area	Instruments	Techniques of Management	Tasks
Resource allocation	• Direct expenditures • Provision of credit • Provision of tax incentives • Provision of guarantees • Organization of quasi-fiscal activities	• Medium-term fiscal framework • Medium-term development plans • Target based expenditure plans • Annual budgets	• Consideration of new initiatives and existing policies with explicit consideration of their financial implications and impact on macroeconomic stability • Allocation of resources for each activity to pursue macroeconomic goals and programme objectives • Specification of organizational assignments and responsibilities • Assessment of risks associated

(Contd.)

(Table 7.2 Contd.)

Resource utilization	• Quarterly or monthly appointment of budgets to spending agencies • Cash management • Tendering and competitive contracting • Monitoring of financial commitments • Organization of payments	• Organization of networks for delivery of services within specified cost, quality, and output parameters • Operational management plans that specify contracting procedures, terms of lending, asset acquisition, etc. • Cost management • Performance management • Strategic revisions and flexible use of resources	with policies and formulation of contingent approaches • Securing the approval of the legislature and the community for the above tasks • Delivery of services for the intended recipients in time • Achievement of programme goals for which resources have been assigned • Ensuring that the utilization process is efficient and that wastage is minimal
Resource accounting	• Cash accounting • Accrual accounting	• Preparation of monthly and annual accounts showing financial status • Approaches to liability and asset management • Activity cost management	• Monitoring progress in the implementation of the budget and dissemination of information to the public • Identification of programme and fiscal slippages and learning lessons of experience • Specification of accounting standards
Transparency and accountability	• Budget documents • Periodic and annual accounts • Audit and evaluation reports	• Specification of standards for transparency • Establishment of oversight bodies that reflect legislative concerns • Social audit • Participation of citizen groups in selected activities	• To ensure that the resources have been effectively utilized and that the overall goal of macroeconomic stability has been achieved while also fulfilling the more specific goals of programmes and activities • To ensure that the objectives of social oversight have been achieved

Financial management in governments is dominated and regulated by the annual budget. The annual budget is a general financial and work plan that reflects the policies of government that are proposed to be pursued during a year and the funds needed to achieve the goals implicit in the policies. The preparation of the annual budget involves the analysis of programmes and policies with reference to their financial implications, and how the aggregate outlays would impact the economy. The analysis is not undertaken in an isolated fashion. Rather, the outlook for the national economy is reviewed and in that light, the administrative agencies are guided so that they may formulate draft estimates for spending. Budgeting, in most governments, has now become a continuous activity, and in general, annual budgets are conceived as integral parts of a medium-term fiscal framework. During the resource allocation phase, agencies analyse the continuing requirements of existing policies as well as the implications of new initiatives. These are then processed internally within governments and a document in the form of an annual budget is presented, depending on the constitutional and legal framework to the legislature. The roles of legislatures vary from discussion to approval to a radical reorganization of the executive budget proposed.

Budget preparation for life support programmes, (shown in Table 7.1), tends to be different from the preparatory work relating to other programmes. For the most part, outlays on life support programmes tend to be demand driven. Thus, the outlays on automatic stabilizers may depend on the extent and duration of unemployment, while outlays on medical benefits may depend on the incidence of diseases. Expenditures on production and consumption support depend on agricultural cycles, as well as on the domestic and international prices of commodities that are subsidized. In normal activities, most agencies prepare their budgets in terms of what they propose to do; in life support programmes, the focus shifts from what the agencies can do to what the client or what the claimant for services needs. Agencies prepare their normal budgets with a major concern for the relationship between inputs and outputs or eventual performance. In life support programmes, inputs and outputs tend to be identical in that what changes is money which moves from governments to claimants or service providers. Where, however, the basic facilities, such as hospitals and educational institutions are maintained by government agencies, the traditional approaches to budgeting are applicable. Outlays on life support programmes are also different in other ways. In most cases, these outlays may be funded by dedicated revenues and to that extent, the nature of resource constraint tends to be different from those outlays dependent on general revenues. Moreover, the benefits envisaged may be governed by permanent legislation, such as entitlements in industrial countries, which have to be funded regardless of availability of funds. In that context, the annual budget and the annual fiscal year represent arbitrary points of time in a continuum. In traditional areas, however, the annuality of the budget is an important limitation in that funds cannot be carried over into the following year.

The resource allocation phase is followed by the utilization process. Here again, the procedures relating to life support programmes tend to be different. In traditional areas, the central agencies such as ministries of finance, engage in a time-sliced release of budgeted funds so that there is the maximum possible congruence between resource inflows and overflows. Life support programmes, however, given their demand-driven nature, are exempt from this limitation. Concerns relating to the management of costs and the provision of services are, however, common to all activities of governments.

Moneys spent need to be accounted for so that the community may be assured about the efforts made to avoid abuses such as defalcation and fraud. In the process, it needs to be ensured that assets and liabilities are properly managed and the risks of hidden debt are minimized. The annual financial management cycle reaches its concluding phase with the rendition of annual accounts, their audit, and their review by the appropriate oversight body. This phase, which is expected to be fully transparent, shows not merely how the budget was utilized and how services were provided, but more importantly, the financial condition of the government and the country.

ISSUES IN PRACTICE

The functioning of the financial management system, however, reveals several weaknesses. The evaluation of the practical utility of the system requires a specified framework of criterion. The existing literature on government financial management is more descriptive than evaluatory and where the latter is attempted, it is more anecdotal than empirical. Notwithstanding this gap, three criteria may be specified in terms of the requirements of fiscal policymakers, the needs and tasks of financial managers, and finally needs of the community receiving benefits. From these considerations, three criteria emerge: (i) to what extent is the system of financial management enabling a successful pursuit of macroeconomic stability; (ii) to what extent is the system providing an economical (using fewer resources than estimated), efficient (obtaining more results than expected), and effective (achieving programme objectives) utilization of resources; and (iii) to what extent is the system enabling proper delivery of services to the eligible sections of the community? Given the wide range of programmes and services provided, it is likely that the analysis here may not be uniformly applicable to all of them, and some conclusions may be more applicable to a few categories than to others.

Policy Management

The role of financial management is dependent on the role assigned to it in the initial stages of policy formulation and implementation. Policy formulation, in turn, involves the choice of appropriate design of the programmes, and the proper design of the fiscal instruments. Experience of industrial and developing countries during recent years reveals the existence of a powerful social service complex lobby, comparable to the military-industrial complex and construction complex, that has a major role in the formulation of policies. Annual policies are determined, to very large extent, by the likely developments in political and economic markets. Policymakers may be concerned with the demons and angels in the legislature, or with the specifications indicated by IFIs (which play a major role in the financing of proposed programmes and keep a vigilant eye on how the proposed policies or changes in existing policies would be received by these groups). Although, in principle, it is expected that these would represent the interests of the needy, in practice, they have their own compulsions that may be, and are, frequently different from those of the clients. In this process, what is done is neither the ideal nor the necessity. It is what is acceptable, contributing to the inevitable process of sub-optimization and sub-optimal solutions. It is to avoid these annual pressures and aberrations that recourse has been taken to permanent or continuing legislation. Many countries in the Western Hemisphere have permanent legislation governing the provision of benefits. In some countries, provisions of the constitution specify the percentage of resources to be allocated to services such as education. While permanent legislation provides an escape from annual politics, it has also contributed to three types of major problems. First, the legislation was undertaken without taking into account the resource constraints. Resources of governments are not unlimited and each attempt to raise more revenues to meet the growing needs of existing benefits may have, through higher budget deficits, an adverse impact on the market, in that they may contribute to higher rates of interest and growing burden of debt servicing. Permanent legislation, therefore, has the impact of restricting the options and manoeuvrability of policymakers. To meet these situations, some countries have attempted to introduce trigger mechanisms that would usher in changes in the financing of benefits. But these changes have been few and far between. Second, as a result of recourse to legislation, programmes have become, in several cases, uniform, while the actual requirement may be for a greater degree of diversity to meet the changing needs of the local community. The incidence of poverty is uneven in terms of space and time. In federal types of countries, this approach of federal mandating and funding has contributed to avoidable problems for the lower levels of governments. And third, many programmes which are designed to help the poor may unwittingly lead to situations where substantial segments of the poor may not be covered. These aspects of programme design tend to reduce the potential benefits.

From the fiscal point of view, policy makers have, in theory, a wide choice, viz., direct expenditures through government budgets, loans to prospective beneficiaries, tax incentives to service providers, provision of guarantees to organizations for raising more resources that are, in turn, intended to cover the benefits, and organizing quasi-fiscal activities outside the budget for the purpose of providing benefits. These instruments are not perfect substitutes for each other and are, therefore, selectively deployed. During periods of financial crisis, there may be a greater tendency to provide loans, as they are, technically, deemed to be repayable and to that extent, constitute financial assets for the government. However, experience shows that the loan becomes a grant when the recovery proves difficult. To that extent, the initial description may mask the underlying reality. Similarly, provision of guarantees may mean that in the event of default, the burden of repayment falls on the government budget. In all these cases, the unspecified intent is to not reveal the complete financial implications, as the recognition of these implications could lead to the rejection of the proposed policy. These practices imply that, in general, there is sub-optimization in terms of defining the contours of the policy and in the choice of fiscal instrument, and that the expedients may be preferred notwithstanding their medium-term implications. This process is also aided by the structural feature of the budget, which being for a period of one year, limits the scope of consideration to the immediate short term. Further, its cash basis reveals only the flows of money and not the underlying use of real resources.

Segmented and Integrated Approaches

The experience in several countries reveals that in the anxiety to address the concerns of the poor, a series of programmes are launched by federal, central, state, and local governments. And within each level, there are several programmes and projects administered by agencies. These programmes imply the adoption of multiple strategies rather than an integrated, single-window approach. An inevitable consequence of multiple strategies is the proliferation of programmes with a significant overlap among programmes and higher costs of administration. Where programmes are expected to be economical in the use of resources, the multiplicity and overlap have the potential of contributing to higher operational costs from the very inception of programmes such that even the best financial control systems cannot reduce them.

Intent and Outcome

It has been noted earlier that most of these programmes tend to be demand driven, and to that extent, there are formidable difficulties in precise estimation of outlays in this regard for a budget year. This problem is further exacerbated by the fact that in some cases budgets are required to be formulated and submitted to the legislatures almost one year ahead of time. The longer this advance time, the greater is the difficulty in being precise. Although a variety of advanced econometric techniques are used for making budget estimates, the actual outcome at the end of the fiscal year tends to be different, usually higher than the initial estimates. A recognition of this possibility and the need to avoid higher budget deficits forces policymakers to take action. This implies that the initial view at the time of budget formulation of these outlays being uncontrollable, is revised and actions are taken to reconcile, in theory, fiscal responsibility with a balanced provision of services. In practice, however, services are usually underfunded (this is particularly true in developing countries) in the hope that such a process would contribute to reduced demand. Experience, however, shows that underfunding is usually a false choice but is resorted to largely because there are no other techniques in the arsenal of governments to address this problem. A consequence of this band-aid approach is the injection of a large dose of uncertainty about the continuing availability of funds for the agencies responsible, and discontent among those receiving the services. More significantly, underfunded day care centres, schools, health centres, and hospitals contribute to serious erosion of the trust of the public in the management capacity of governments.

Anchor of Expenditure Management

The major issue for financial management relates to the choice of the anchor for the control of expenditures, and the timing of the exercise of the technique selected for this purpose. Traditionally, the device for control was to examine the personnel requirements in the belief that most of the social services were labour-intensive and, therefore, checks and caps imposed on personnel growth would contribute to a moderation of growth in expenditure. This view yielded place in industrial countries to the formulation of caps on running costs, including personnel, of programmes. Towards this end, ex-ante estimates of specified procedures in the area of medical services (such as costs for screening and in-patient care) are prepared on a comprehensive basis and these estimates are then used to make budget allocations and to monitor the actual use of resources during the course of the year. As greater progress is made in medical technology, governments are compelled to be alert to incorporate the changes in cost estimates. In developing countries, however, the tradition of personnel and payment controls continues to be dominant. Experience shows that control of the former represents an incomplete exercise (as it excludes running costs), and the latter is misplaced. Payment controls essentially involve the compliance of laws in that they have to ensure that a payment is made to the correct persons after ensuring that the services have been received. This predominant emphasis, however, does not address the range of key factors contributing to expenditure increases. To that extent, there is a mismatch between intent and instrument.

Delivery of Services

The provision of services has, over the years, contributed to two distinct features. First, in a number of cases, the growth has been such that bureaucracies tended to be more concerned with their own interests, and with the administration of relevant laws, than with the provision of services. The perception is that bureaucracies have become inflexible, rigid, and lacking in clientele orientation. This appears to be the case particularly in areas such as provision of medical care, where the judgements of professionals are subject to approval by financial controllers. Second, in a number of cases, there has been a separation between funding and the actual provision of services. In several countries, in both the industrial and developing worlds, central or federal governments have become cash disbursing centres to lower levels of governments which provide the services. In a few cases, services paid for by governments are provided by NGOs, and in the area of medical care by private practitioners. The controls exercised by central governments do not go beyond payment controls, and any failure in the delivery of services becomes an issue between the provider and the receiver. The nexus between funding and providing agencies is so nebulous that the former has very little power to enforce its wishes. In the case of medical care provided by private parties, the consumer has some choice, while in other cases, he or she is held captive by the governmental agency. In the process, the very intent of providing services is jeopardized.

Fraud and Waste

Many programmes appear to have built-in features that facilitate fraudulent claims and payments, thus reflecting a collusion of interests between service providers and receivers. Several tests are conducted in the area of medical assistance, which often prove to be unnecessary, but are expensive to governments. Enforcement of rules is often not possible for there are loopholes that permit these procedures. As a consequence, it is said that more than 10 per cent of the payments made in the United States represent those with doubtful validity. In developing countries, experience shows that purchase of medicines and maintenance of stores reflect a landscape that is littered with too many financial scandals to be enumerated here. Besides, the experience with NGOs reveals that many of them do not have the basic or minimum accounting and financial management systems. Moreover, there are no regulatory bodies entrusted with the task of providing guidelines for the financial conduct of these organizations. In the absence of the involvement of the local community, and measures aimed at their regulation, NGOs are perceived as results of top–down elitist approaches. In the end, the very categories of people that are expected to benefit from these programmes may turn out to be double losers, in that they not only do not get the intended benefits, but contrary to the intent of policy, service providers end up getting the financial benefits contributing, in the process, to a further widening of income disparities.

Neglected Fault Lines—Transparency and Accountability

It is expected, at least in theory, that the types of problems described above can be addressed by the people or their elected representatives, if there is adequate transparency about the transactions and how decisions are made, as well as a framework of accountability. In both these areas, experience shows several neglected fault lines.

Transparency involves the complete provision of information so that the community may review the policies if it chooses to. But this process is adversely affected in several countries, by the built-in features of their financial management systems. In many countries, particularly in the former central planned economies, as well as in some kingdoms in the Middle East, budgets are not published in their full form. Instead, summary tables are published and these are inadequate for providing any meaningful illumination about the intent of governments, range of expenditure programmes, and their benefits. Even where budget and related annual accounts are published, they are prepared in an arcane language that opens up vistas only to a few, particularly to groups engaged in market trading. For others they are impenetrable, with the result that the interactive role expected from the community does not materialize except in regard to new revenue impositions. In some countries, arrangements are being made to place the relevant documents on web sites. This remains a device that is waiting to be used by a larger section of the community.

Similar problems afflict the process of accountability. The scope of reports prepared by independent audit agencies is severely limited in most cases. They are not permitted to review 'policy matters' nor do they have the requisite legal authority to audit the records of NGOs or contractors engaged in the provision of services funded by government budgets. These features reduce the functional utility of audit reports. Furthermore, their usefulness depends on their covering all the aspects of delivery of services fully. In practice, however, only the financial aspects are included. Even in this area, the effectiveness of the contribution depends on the legislative use of the reports. In this regard, experience reveals that the eagerness shown in launching programmes is not matched by an anxiety to ascertain whether the intended benefits have been received. In several countries, annual accounts are submitted with a lag, and when they are submitted, the vagaries of legislative schedules may not permit their discussion in the appropriate chambers. More significantly, these features reveal that a proper framework of accountability—that goes beyond the technical propriety of financial regulations, and throws light on the use of resources and on the effectiveness of programmes—remains to be evolved. The language and currency of accountability remain to be formulated.

TASKS AHEAD

In addressing the problems of poverty, not much attention was paid to the need for an adequate system of financial management. Rather the existing system was adapted, mostly as an afterthought, with minimal changes. The result has been a mismatch between intent and the choice of instrument, and problematic consequences from the pursuit of segmented approaches. The many objectives of financial management, viz., macroeconomic stability, proper delivery of services, and pursuit of economy, efficiency, and effectiveness, have in the process not been achieved, implying a collective failure of systems. If Shakespeare were to write *Julius Caesar* today, he might make Cassius say, 'The fault, dear Brutus, is not in our stars, but in our systems'. It is for this reason that governments cease to be masters of fates, reminding us of the words in *Hamlet*, 'Our wills and fates do so contrary run, that our devices still are overthrown; our thoughts are ours, their ends none of our own'.

The primary task now is to move away from rhetoric and to focus attention on the design of the financial management system, on its ability to serve life support programmes, and on the accountability it provides to the community. In all these respects, there is no respite for those engaged in institutional reforms.

8. Public Expenditure Management in Sub-national Governments
Status and Issues

> A central power, however enlightened, however learned one imagines it, cannot gather to itself alone all of the details of life of a great people. It cannot do it because such a work exceeds human strength. When it wants by its care alone to create so many diverse springs and make them function it contents itself with a very incomplete result and exhausts itself in useless efforts.
> — Alexis de Tocqueville, 1835

Public expenditure management (PEM) has been an essential component of governments, both at the central and sub-national government (SNG) levels, from the very inception of governments. The design and the content of the system are dependent on the changing policy goals that are both strategic and contextual. In a federal set-up, the design of the system and the success with which the instruments and techniques of management are deployed are influenced in the day-to-day administrative life, by an explicit recognition of the coordinate and independent roles of the SNGs. The large network of administrative, consultative, and coordinating devices inherent in a federal set-up adds a distinguishing feature to the working of the PEM system in the SNGs. The overall process, while being within the constitutional and legal framework of a federation, is expected to provide an effective machinery that enables the federal government to achieve national policy goals, while retaining the complementary roles assigned to SNGs. In a unitary government, the role of the SNGs is more subordinate to the central government and policies pursued by the centre are followed at the SNGs, as they are deemed to be integral parts of the unitary set-up. The relationships between the central government and SNGs cover several areas, usually specified in the constitution. This chapter is concerned with a discussion of the current status of PEM systems in SNGs in both types of systems, how effective they are in the achievement of fiscal policy goals, and how their working is influenced by the design of the system and the tripartite participation of central governments, SNGs, and the public.

Two interrelated factors contribute additional urgency to the detailed consideration of this subject. First, there is evidence in many countries, of a deterioration in the fiscal health of the SNGs. Problems are experienced in the day-to-day fiscal management of these levels, reflecting the structural constraints of solvency and liquidity. A state government in India has, for example, noted in issuing a white paper on its finances that 'the presentation of this (white) paper has been necessitated by the realization that government is unable to fulfil its sovereign commitments to the people. It is unable to pay cash on cheques issued or make payments on items already included in the budget document. The embarrassing question before the government is that items, which find a place in the budget and are not even afterthoughts or additional authorizations, cannot be honoured today. This has created a tremendous problem of credibility of government assertions' (see Government of Kerala 2001, p. 3). This experience is not by any means a solitary one (the Governments of Andhra Pradesh, Karnataka, Maharashtra, Orissa, and Punjab have issued white papers with similar themes). Several other state governments in India have issued similar white papers, all of which indicate a deteriorating fiscal situation and the emerging fiscal crises. Experience elsewhere also shows that SNGs are facing serious fiscal problems and that their severity tends to be exacerbated in the downward phase of the business cycle. This raises fundamental issues about the capacity of the PEM system in addressing the current and future concerns of the SNGs.

Second, the fiscal machinery, in general, and the PEM system, in particular, in the SNGs, represent in most cases, microcosms of the central or federal machinery. During the past several decades, improvements made in the PEM systems at the central level have found their way, in some cases very slowly, to the SNG level. In some cases, such as in the United Kingdom and the United States, expenditure management systems in local governments have shown considerable skills in the introduction of enduring budget innovations. In developing countries, there have been significant efforts, in many cases, to computerize fiscal information systems and to introduce innovative payment systems. In some cases, improvements have been made in fiscal transparency and related accountability arrangements. In a few cases, the traditional administrative controls, a prominent feature of PEM systems, have been supplemented by market evaluations of fiscal sustainability of SNGs. Notwithstanding these developments, there is a general perception that these developments have not been effective in serving the macroeconomic requirements, nor have they been successful in providing services in an economical manner. The deterioration in fiscal balances, and the growing erosion in the credibility of the expenditure system, are serious issues.

Following a consideration of some of the general features that have an impact on the PEM system, this chapter provides a perspective on the general instruments of management that are considered integral parts of federal financial relationships and discusses the various aspects of resource allocation arrangements, processes of resource utilization, and resource-use accounting. This is followed by a discussion of the ability of the expenditure management system to cope with the tasks of austerity management, and risk management, as well as the technical infrastructure relating to accounting, reporting and auditing, and the accountability framework. In all these areas, the major issues are enumerated first and then the directions of improvements attempted as a part of structural lending are considered.

PRELIMINARY CONSIDERATIONS

It is essential, however, that some preliminary features of the current situation are considered at the outset.

First, for purposes of discussion, three broad levels of government are recognized. These are: the federal or the central government, the regional, state, or provincial governments, and the municipal and county governments. These terms are used in an interchangeable manner. The discussion here focuses mostly on the state and provincial governments, and the consideration of the local government is less exhaustive. In several countries of a federal type, for example, India, greater efforts are being made to empower the local governments and extensive legal arrangements have been made for the assignment of tasks to be performed and for the necessary financial devolution arrangements to support them. While these aspects are mentioned wherever necessary, the primary focus here is on the second tier of government.

Second, regardless of the form of government—unitary or federal or of the type where provinces (or the second tier) contribute to central government financing—the financial arrangements involve some common elements. These include the fiscal assignments (which level collects, and retains or distributes what resources, and the arrangements for their division), determination of the formulae for division of resources where there is a greater degree of centralization of fiscal resources, and negotiated settlements between the various levels. In addition, there are several transfers ranging from subventions (constitutionally assured devolution of resources in the form of a grant to be utilized in any form determined by the second or the third tier of government), grants-in-aid that may be in the form of bulk grants or may be specific or conditional, or may be based on matching principle. These transfers have become a significant factor in the financial relationships between the three tiers of government, and more significantly, on the approaches to resource allocation and utilization in the recipient governments. In effect, these transfers determine the financing patterns of the expenditures at the lower levels of government.

Third, the above arrangements have contributed three features that need to be recognized. To a very large extent, the arrangements may reflect a growing dependence on the central government. For example, in the United Kingdom, 75 per cent of the local finances are transfers from the central government. In India, states' own resources, as a ratio to aggregate expenditure, have declined during the decade of the 1990s, from 43.5 to 41.5 per cent (RBI 2000, p. 25). These developments reflect (i) a separation of funding agency from the one responsible for providing services; (ii) reduced flexibility in the end use of resources; and (iii) the emergence of a structural constraint in the PEM systems in SNGs. Separation of funding implies a long physical and administrative distance between those that are responsible for funding the services and the SNGs entrusted with the task of providing services. Funding implies a capacity to call the 'tune' of the piper, and to regulate the financial activity of the SNGs. Detailed specification of the conditions of their use empowers the grantors with extensive supervisory and inspection authority, while the latter may become regular supplicants for resources. The growing dependency and the associated conditionality reduces management flexibility in the SNGs. The procedures of resource allocation in the SNGs have to reckon with these transfers and the uncertainty inherent in the situation. In essence, the overwhelming and constant shadow of the central government in the management of expenditures at the SNG level needs to be recognized.

Fourth, the evaluation of the expenditure management machinery at any level poses several challenges in terms of choices, such as the intent and outcome, or the adoption of a counterfactual approach. For the purposes here, the system is examined from three interrelated points. The first is the ability of the system to serve macroeconomic policy purposes. In this regard, the role of the expenditure management machinery is to assist in the determination of the size of the deficit/surplus, to ensure that the size, once determined, is firmly adhered to throughout the fiscal year, unless otherwise warranted as a part of a changing business cycle strategy; and to ensure that the fiscal outcome is congruent with the intent. As an integral part of this, the enforcement of the golden principle, where applicable, will also be examined. Second, the machinery should facilitate the delivery of services in a timely manner, and be consistent with the underlying cost and quality premises. Third, a basic purpose of the expenditure management machinery is to be on the lookout for possible economies in outlays and for enhancing efficiency in the delivery of services. Effective utilization of public money requires regular efforts in this regard so that the future and somewhat inevitable increases in outlays may be moderated to the extent possible. Abandonment of unproductive and wasteful programmes and similar efforts aimed at evaluation form a part of these endeavours. The systems will also be assessed in terms of fiscal transparency and adequacy of accountability of arrangements.

INSTRUMENTS OF MANAGEMENT

The instruments of expenditure management have grown substantially in terms of number and impact during recent years. Some of these instruments are common to several countries. But there are many countries that are yet to implement them in entirety, although gradual progress is being made. The progress in their application at the level of SNGs is more problematic and the experience varies considerably from one country to another. These instruments have an additional feature at the SNG level. For sovereign governments, the major non-tax revenue item relates to the foreign aid received by it. At the level of SNGs, as noted earlier, the transfers from the central government are sizeable. These transfers, in turn, are several and vary both in intent and impact on the expenditure management system.

These transfers, along with other instruments of PEM, are illustrated in Table 8.1, to indicate the state of the art. The instruments cover several themes and together provide a perspective on the administrative processes and the underlying technology. These instruments, and their application in the day-to-day administrative life may give rise to several issues. Their application is not a refined science, and much is dependent on the context in which they are applied, and the benefits sought to be gained. The absence of application may, on the other hand, show the progress that remains to be made.

Table 8.1

Instruments of Public Expenditure Management

Functional Category	Instruments	Remarks
Financial planning	• Development plans	• Many countries have medium-term development plans that inter alia indicate the finances of SNGs. Local governments, being more numerous, may not be covered in detail.
	• MTFF	• Some governments have taken up the preparation of rolling MTFFs that develop full scenarios on finances
	• MTEF	• Either as an integral part of the above, or as an independent exercise, several governments have taken up the preparation of rolling MTEFs. In some countries (example, United Kingdom), the local expenditures are also included in this exercise
	• Vision documents	• Some central governments and SNGs have also been engaged in the preparation of vision documents indicating future finances for extended periods
Determination of annual budget policy	• Policy statement/white papers	• A recent innovation, some governments have taken to the publication of annual fiscal strategies that govern their budgets
	• Legislated limits on size of deficit and borrowing	• A common feature in several countries is the legislated constraint on the level of deficit that can be incurred at the SNG level. States in the USA, in most cases, cannot incur deficits

(Contd.)

(Table 8.1 Contd.)

	• Fiscal responsibility legislation	in their current budgets. Borrowing may be similarly regulated • Following the example of New Zealand, some countries, including Argentina and Brazil, have enacted fiscal responsibility legislation. The legislation includes, in some cases, the SNGs too. In Canada, some provinces have enacted this legislation but not the central government
	• Fundamental reviews/ZBB	• To moderate expenditure growth, many governments have introduced variants of these budgetary techniques. In India, these have been introduced at the state level, the scope and content of these techniques however, differ from one to another and also from what is internationally recognized
Receipt Planning	• Devolution	• Where revenues are centrally collected or prescribed, they are distributed to the participating states in terms of specified formulae. Similar devolution takes place from the states to the local governments
	• Devolution subventions	• In addition to the above statutory budget support, grants may also be given to the SNGs from the general pools
	• Foreign aid	• Until recently, foreign aid transited in most developing countries through the central budgets. In some cases this is being provided directly to the SNGs, including local governments
	• Block grants	• Federal governments may be engaged in the provision of grants for clusters of similar activities
	• Specific/ conditional grants	• Grants may also be conditional and to that extent, share the features of earmarking in that they cannot be used for other purpos.
	• Matching grants	• Grants are conditional on being matched by similar or specified shares of local expenditures
	• Loans	• In some federations, notably in India, the federal government makes extensive loans (including some relent funds) to the state governments

(Contd.)

(Table 8.1 Contd.)

Contingent/ hidden liabilities	• Own revenues	• Own resources of SNGs have a major role in the determination of the annual budget
	• Guarantees	• Subordinate agencies of SNGs may be engaged in public borrowing with guarantees provided by SNGs and counter guarantees in some cases by central governments. These have become problematic during recent years
	• Hidden debt	• This includes unpaid bills, IOUs, legislative commitments to be fulfilled in the future, and implementation of judicial verdicts. Introduction of accrual systems permits a better identification of these debts
Fiscal year	• Annual or biennial budgets	• Most SNGs have an annual limit on their budgets. In some countries, SNGs may have extended budgets, particularly for investment outlays
Budget coverage	• Role of extra-budgetary accounts	• Many SNGs have extra-budgetary accounts. Lack of consolidation makes comparisons very difficult
Budget structure and classification	• Classification on a functional programme and economic basis	• In some countries, there is uniform classification covering the federal government and SNGs (for example, India, Malaysia and Nigeria). Classification patterns, however, vary in several cases. To a large extent, they may not help in rendering fiscal transparency
Annual budget process	• Advance indication of priorities and portfolios of ceilings	• In several SNGs where multi-year fiscal planning has taken roots, these may be indicated. In other cases, there may be an aggregative type of budgeting
	• Investment priorities	• SNGs also have separate budgets for capital/investment/development and priorities may be developed in each area
	• Risk identification	• Governments have been engaged, during recent years, in an explicit recognition of various types of risks. This practice at the SNG level is very spotty
	• Measurement of budget deficit	• Several standardized and non-standardized concepts are in use, leading to apprehensions about their practical utility

(Contd.)

(Table 8.1 Contd.)

	• Specification of areas for pursuit of economy and efficiency	• During periods of a fiscal squeeze, governments, including those at the sub-national level, may specify areas where economies are to be procured
Improved service delivery	Performance indicators and constraints	• A very selective beginning is being made to introduce performance indicators
Budget implementation	• Release of authority to spend amounts	• Systems may broadly be divided into those that are centralized and decentralized. Both are prevalent
	• Cash management	• This technique is still in its infancy in SNGs, contributing to problems in debt issue
	• Internal controls	• Most spending agencies have very little flexibility in the use of resources. Attempts are being made to empower them
Payment systems	• Carry-over of unspent amounts	• Although funds lapse at the end of the fiscal year, they are permitted to continue both legally and through the circumvention of law.
Accounting	• Cash disbursements, checks, electronic payments	• In most SNGs, cash is the common medium. Attempts are being made to introduce payroll and pension payment systems on an electronic basis
	• Centralized, decentralized	• Both these systems are prevalent in SNGs
	• Modified accrual system	• Most SNGs in developing countries operate cash based systems
	• Accrual system	• Accrual accounting, remains to be applied except for major projects
Financial reporting	• Monthly reporting	• Distinction needs to be made between reports that are made public and those intended for internal use. Reporting is more organized at the state level, while at the local level, given their size, reports take too long to be consolidated
	• Annual accounts	• In theory, these are required to be submitted. In practice, extended delays are common. In several cases, the reporting system is on a computerized basis. It is easier to administer them in local governments
Accountability	• Public assessment	• In some countries, particularly where SNGs are engaged in market borrowing, the quality

(Contd.)

(Table 8.1 Contd.)

		of public finances is rated by independent agencies
	• Legislative accountability	• Forms of accountability are specified in law and punitive action may be taken on those violating the law
	• Audit	• Forms of audit vary significantly within SNGs and among countries
Public participation	• Non-legislative user committees	• During recent years, a beginning has been made to co-opt the public, through user committees, to ensure more purposeful spending
		• During 2002, one state in India circulated a draft budget, for seeking the public's comments

ISSUES AND APPROACHES

The task of expenditure management is to deploy the instruments in a manner so to serve the strategic and contextual goals of the public authorities. Specifically, in the case of SNGs, this means addressing the structural problems as well as the issues in resource allocation, resource utilization, resource-use accounting, and in the management of the transition. Issues identified in all these areas and the ways in which they were addressed, either as a part of their own initiative or as a part of the structural adjustment lending programmes, are considered. The issues are several and only the more important ones are considered here.

Structural Problems

As noted at the outset, there has been deterioration in the quality of finances of SNGs. Even as cumulative problems were creating severe shortages of finances, new pressures are building up that contribute to higher expenditures. These pressures include (i) the accepted need, in most cases, to step up expenditures on health and education, and equally important, poverty alleviation programmes aimed at improving the standards of life. While there are inter-regional disparities in this regard, it is recognized that, in general, there is a need for more outlays in these areas; (ii) the reform of government through reduction of administrative staff and divestment of enterprises, would contribute to higher termination benefits in the short term and to higher expenditures, as well as higher budget deficits; and (iii) the need to provide minimum standards of basic services, as well as the need to increase maintenance outlays on existing infrastructure also exerts additional pressure. Moreover, during recent years, the level of investment expenditures in many SNGs has been, more or less stagnant or declining, reflecting the fiscal stress that they have been going through.

The approach taken, as a part of structural lending, has been to lay emphasis on reducing the staff levels, and divestment of public enterprises so that the expenditure increases could be moderate. Introduction of voluntary retirement schemes has met with mixed response, while the maintenance of surplus labour pool emerging from the divestment of enterprises and their training to acquire marketable skills, inevitably a gradual process, has yet to make its impact felt. Elsewhere, experience shows that many governments when confronted with fiscal stress took several measures, including the abandonment of programmes or pruning through fundamental reviews of expenditure. Relatively less emphasis has been placed, as a part of structural lending, on fundamental reviews.

Technical Aspects: Resource Allocation

Allocative Efficiency

There has been, for years, a general recognition of the need for improving allocative efficiency in public outlays. Apart from the microeconomic administrative practices contributing to wasteful spending, the programmes often overlapped, and the agency functions were not always clear and frequently there were many agencies addressing the same core area. Moreover, investment appraisal systems were deficient in several cases, and priorities were not observed in the allocation of resources to projects. As a result, the important and the productive as well as the unproductive but politically important received the same attention, and projects took more time to be completed, with the inevitable cost escalations. Besides, the costs of programmes were not always computed, and the draft of the current and continuing policies on the future was not clear and over-commitments were made, in turn contributing to the structural problem discussed earlier.

The approach towards capacity enhancement in this area stressed the importance of preparation of advance resource ceilings, introduction of capital projects appraisal, and the introduction of multi-year expenditure rolling plans. The formulation of advance resource ceilings and their communication to the spending agencies was expected to induce, apart from reflecting the commitment of the government at the highest level, a kind of priority planning within the agencies and to develop a heightened awareness of the resource constant. This change in the budgetary procedure, together with multi-year expenditure forecasts, has certainly created an improved awareness of resource limitation. Similarly, the introduction of investment appraisal techniques has contributed to an improved selection and management of the project portfolio. The multi-year forecasts were expected to clarify the future financial implications of current policies, and contribute to the determination of the policies to be continued and those that needed to be modified, to be within the resource limitations.

While the above efforts have contributed to an enhanced administrative capacity, several issues remain. The formulation of resource ceilings in SNGs has necessarily to take into account the financial transfers from the central government. The transfers cover a wide range, have different formulae for financing, and have different conditions. Sub-national governments may not be empowered to change the content of the programmes financed by the transfers. The programmes include those aimed at poverty alleviation, which are formulated on a national basis, with considerable impact on SNG finances but with little flexibility to change their content or to adapt them to their local situations (for a detailed discussion of how some of the financial populist programmes are formulated with nation-wide applicability, see Dornbusch and Edwards 1991). The resources to be transferred may not always be known to the SNGs. Consequently, the resource ceilings formulated tend to have the same uncertainty as before.

Even if the magnitude and components of the transfers are known (as is the case of budget support grants), there may be little flexibility for the SNGs to alter the content of the programmes.[1] To that extent, pressures on expenditures may continue unabated. Similarly, with

---

[1] In practice, there are always cases, including in developed industrial nations, where the SNGs may sometimes divert the money for other purposes. In such cases, there may be no penalties, and recourse may be taken to the issue of additional instructions. In most cases, the possibility of diversion arises from the passage of many separate programmes to deal with the same problem. For a discussion of the US experience in this regard, see Bok, 2001, p. 133.

respect to the MTEF experience, which varies widely, shows that, more often than not, they involve projections with reference to the baseline rather than being disaggregated cost estimates and related exercises to compute future requirements. Moreover, in the context of a dependent economy, expenditure forecasts tend to have limited utility except as a part of the multi-year fiscal framework that also includes an exercise in regard to the revenues. More significantly, resource forecasting at the SNG level needs to be reconciled with the resource forecasts of the centre in view of its dominant role.

Intent and Outcome

Experience shows that the formulation of budget estimates represents only a part of the problem, in that the degree of optimism shown, and the rosy scenarios assumed for the purpose, may contribute to increased budget deficits during the implementation stage. In many SNGs, the first budget submitted to the legislature may be viewed as a putative one that is subjected to constant revision, mostly upwards in so far as expenditures are concerned, during the year. Announcement of higher pay scales, introduction of new populist measures, supplementary budgets (in the case of British type administrative systems, these may be submitted thrice during the year) and related approaches contribute to widening deficits. The frequent resort to supplementary budgets may make the spending agencies underestimate their needs initially and resort to other methods during the year. These practices suggest that budgeting has become a year-round activity and with no hard constraints aimed at bringing financial discipline.

The above areas have so far not received much attention in the structural adjustment programmes other than the insistence that the initial budget should be viewed as a hard constraint and that greater emphasis should be laid on building up internal control mechanisms. Neither is adequate for ensuring budgetary outcome that is congruent with the intent, and to that extent destabilizing factors continue to operate within the system.

Inclusive Decision Making

A major problem associated with SNGs in the past was that there was not much information made available about the underlying assumptions of the budget and its linkages with the economy, or the computation of the deficit and its implications for macroeconomic stability or the fiscal sustainability of the government. While in several cases, extensive documentation was compiled primarily for the purpose of legislative passage of the budget, much of it was covered in archaic language that remained, for the most part, impenetrable to both the legislators and the lay public. Moreover, the extensive prevalence of extra-budgetary funds reduced the practical utility of the budget documents in view of their limited coverage. Also, in some cases, the classification of the budget left a good deal to be desired in that the purposes of outlays were not always rendered clear.

The primary need was two-fold—to prepare documentation in a way that made the budget more intelligible to the public, and to improve decision making within the executive wing of the SNG, to promote greater inclusiveness and participation. As a part of the first approach, SNGs in India, for example, to whom structural lending was extended, were enabled to prepare 'budget in brief' and related analytical documents that reduced the previous complexity, and presented more information on deficits and their financing. Similarly, the preparation of advance annual forecasts of the budget and medium-term expenditure plans, and their submission to the cabinet elicited a greater response from ministries and other civil servants. These two aspects reduced the fear associated with budgets, which was akin to the reaction of an adolescent about a visit to the dentist. Also, improved budget coverage and simplified budget classification reduced the barriers.

Austerity Management

The fiscal stress associated with SNGs contributed to budgets that promoted austere expenditure management approaches. Further, during the course of budget implementation, frequent revenue shortfalls in their own revenues as well as in devolved or shared revenues, contributed to additional doses of austere management. In most cases, austere management took the form of ad hoc uniform cuts throughout government, keeping staff positions vacant and reducing non-wage expenditure on items such as 'travel'. This uniform approach and the associated underfunding contributed to a severe decline in certain services (for example, health and education), stoppage of work on major projects (including irrigation), and frequently to the emergence of unpaid bills in several sectors. The extensive arrears in wages and pensions suggest a breakdown in financial discipline. In some cases, the political pressures were so extensive that closure of projects was not possible, forcing the authorities to 'lever' in external assistance from IFIs (for a very interesting case study at the level of a state in India, see Narayana 1999, pp. 106–21). However, as the external assistance was predicated on matched funding, the fiscal squeeze was accentuated, and the greater the assistance, the larger was the squeeze on non-assisted projects.

The approaches aimed at improvement placed emphasis on the formulation of priorities and the diversion of resources to core projects and programmes. Expenditures were to be treated unequally and cuts were to be made more judiciously. Furthermore, emphasis was also placed on an explicit recognition of payment arrears and their clearance in a phased way. Underfunding, it was recognized, was not a viable option. Despite this emphasis, austerity management in several cases remains a tactical operation based on knee-jerk reaction rather than on carefully formulated adjustment programmes. Pursuit of technical efficiency has not received the attention due.

Risk Management

Implementation of any budget is fraught with many risks. Risks may be macroeconomic or microeconomic in nature. In some cases, the impact of the risks arising from honouring the guarantees given by a state government may be very severe, and may contribute to prolonged fiscal crisis. At the municipal level, judicial verdicts or major failures may, in some countries, contribute to bankruptcy proceedings.[2]

To address this problem, two approaches have been adopted. First, efforts were made to compile full data on outstanding guarantees—accounts, purposes, and nature of contingent liability. Further, in several cases, as in India, state governments were encouraged to enact legislation governing the process of guarantee provision. These features enabled the SNGs to take into account, in the preparation of the annual budget, the guarantees that would need redemption. Improved

---

2. Chapter 9 of the United States Bankruptcy Code indicates that in these cases only the municipalities (not creditors) may commence proceedings and that the bankruptcy court may not interfere with the local government's political or governmental powers. It cannot be converted into a liquidation case. There may be similar procedures in other countries (for example, Indonesia, the Philippines, South Africa) where municipalities are empowered to borrow from the market.

housekeeping, through the maintenance of relevant records, is an important element of expenditure management and this enabled a better recognition of the problem. For other risks, a part of the expenditure totals computed as a part of the multi-year expenditure was treated as a contingency reserve. Practices vary considerably in this regard. In some cases, there may be no explicit reserve; more frequently, it may be notionally assumed in the layers of computations.

Resource Management

Four major issues were experienced in the process of the use of budgetary resources allocated to SNGs. To some extent, these are common with the central and federal government, but there is a fifth one, which is uniquely applicable to the SNG level. These relate to (i) cash management; (ii) internal financial controls; (iii) financial reporting on the end use of resources; and (iv) performance indicators. The fifth factor relates to the excessive administrative costs, as a share of programme costs, incurred in the process of administering a grant from the point of inception to the final point of utilization.

Cash management, which relates to the management of the seasonality of inflows and outflows and which facilitates coordination with the issue of debt, although a traditional instrument, has been in disuse in several governments. So much so, before payments were made, prior clearance had to be obtained from central agencies, leading to a lengthening of the administrative process and to delays. Under improved cash management, ceilings for specified periods, within which disbursements could be made were indicated to the spending departments. In one state (Andhra Pradesh), where new procedures were introduced as a part of structural lending, the spending agencies saw a reduction in administrative costs, and in the use of budgetary resources. The application of this technique, however, is yet to be extensively adopted in other SNGs.

Unlike the process of budget formulation, where inevitably, there is a greater role for central agencies such as the ministries of finance, resource-use is a phase where much is dependent on the spending agencies. Their capacity to plan and anticipate events, as well as to comply with laws, and to observe economy, can contribute to more effective management or to more problems. Traditionally, they had little stake in these matters, as financial management was a centralized process. The approaches towards improvement therefore stressed the importance of installing properly organized internal financial control systems in major spending agencies. Such a process, which is already underway in many central governments, is now being, albeit gradually, extended to the SNG levels.

Financial reporting assumes particular importance in the case of SNGs, as many of the conditional grants extended by the federal governments are released on the basis of the reports received from the SNGs. Experience shows that federal governments, in their zeal to control lower-level operations, tend to prescribe too many detailed reports, which while circumscribing the freedom of the lower levels, also lead to considerable delays in being submitted. In partial recognition of this, some federal governments (example, India) have been making attempts to reduce the coverage and complexity of these reports. Much progress remains to be made.

Both the public and governments are interested in the performance or the results obtained through the implementation of the budget. The traditional approach, which placed a good deal of emphasis on the line-item accounting of moneys spent and being accountable for that process, is being replaced by an expanded accountability system (for a detailed discussion of the evolution of public accountability, see Chapter 7 of this book). As a part of meeting this need, attempts are being made by SNGs to prescribe performance indicators. The specification of an agency's mission and the formulation of performance indicators that would reveal the heart and soul of its budget has not been an easy task.

The general experience in the administration of federal–state financial relationships reveals that in many cases, high transaction costs are being incurred in the administration of grants. In some cases, the grant may not reach the intended beneficiaries, or only a small amount may reach that level, putting the whole intent of the programme in jeopardy. An awareness of this aspect is making some SNGs (notably in Uganda), set up user councils to ensure that the grants reach the intended beneficiaries and are indeed used for the specified purpose. As with other areas, more progress remains to be made here too.

Resource Use Accounting

Four aspects of SNG level accounting merit specific recognition. These are (i) basis of accounting; (ii) foreign aid accounting; (iii) organizational aspects of accounting; and (iv) the growing application of electronic technology.

Following the general tradition, SNGs like their central counterparts are organized on a cash basis. This has proved to be restrictive because liabilities are not explicitly reckoned; and has resulted in myopic fiscal policies. To address this problem, the alternatives of accrual systems (with explicit provision for depreciation and capital charge) or modified accrual systems (without these provisions) are being explored. Their introduction, notwithstanding some commitments made by SNGs, (as for example, by Uttar Pradesh in India) however, has not made much headway partly because of lack of agreement on the benefits of accrual systems, and partly because of the continuing debate on whether these should selectively augment the cash system or replace it entirely. Meanwhile, as noted previously, a beginning has been made in compiling an inventory of liabilities such as guarantees.

Reliable accounts of foreign aid received continue to be problematic even at the level of the central governments. This is partly due to coverage differences between the donor and the receiving government, and partly, because of valuation differences. Aid extended to NGOs is not covered by governmental accounts; and, there are frequently differences in the value of aid recorded at the point of entry (customs), and at the point of utilization. These aspects are not significant at the SNG level as they have only recently begun to receive foreign aid directly from donors. This, however, represents an area where there are likely to be problems with further experience in the management of foreign aid.

The compilation of accounts at the SNG level may be organized, on a centralized or decentralized basis. The former approach, which is very common, locates the accounting responsibility in a central authority, usually an accountant general, who in turn is responsible for the compilation of SNG accounts. The accountant general may function under the aegis of the finance ministry, or as in India, as a part of a combined accounting and audit department managed by the federal government for all SNGs. Under the latter approach, the spending agencies are responsible for the compilation of initial and final accounts and their defence at the legislative level. The latter approach is viewed as important in generating policy-based accounts and in building up of internal financial management capability within the agencies. The process of decentralization or empowerment would be incomplete without responsibility for the compilation of accounts. Progress in decentralization has been slow.

Meanwhile, however, some of the interests of the spending agencies are aided by the process of computerization which is moving very fast at the SNG level. In the state of Andhra Pradesh (India), payrolls and pension payments have been computerized for the whole state. Similar efforts are being made by others. This, supplemented by the computerization of departments and agencies (as in Ghana), has up opened a new era where data are simultaneously available to the central and spending agencies. The cause of decentralization is considerably advanced by computerization.

Market Approaches

Efforts are also being made, notably in India, to develop non-administrative mechanisms, to evaluate the quality of public finances of state governments. In clear recognition of the limited success of administrative mechanisms to assess state finances, the initiatives taken in India have emphasized two approaches: one, rating by independent credit agencies, and second, self-evaluation in terms of the criteria evolved by a committee of state finance secretaries. The debt issued on behalf of state governments is still managed by the Reserve Bank (Central Bank) of India. Now, however, the market reactions are influenced to a large extent by annual ratings issued by the credit agencies. These agencies are, however, very few, and are commissioned by state governments. To that extent, their rating may not be as objective as desired. Second, the performance criteria evolved by the state finance secretaries are fairly detailed and thus provide an intra-state comparison. Both these developments have taken place outside the conditionality of structural lending programmes. Together, however, they offer additional mechanisms that are capable of inducing measures aimed at strengthening the expenditure management machinery.

Audit and Accountability

Audit plays an important role in evaluating the operations of the PEM machinery. The types of audit as well as the arrangements for conducting audit and the consideration of their reports differ among countries. The types of audit include administrative, financial, and performance audit. The last type of audit is still in its infancy in many countries, and requires, as a prerequisite, the existence of a performance-based budget system. In India, the audits undertaken by the Auditor General include studies of selected aspects of performance.

The Auditor General also undertakes investigative audit. In most cases, however, audit at the SNG level is limited to administrative and financial audit.

In a few countries, for example, India, audit is carried out at the level of the state governments by the combined audit and accounts department of the central government, which acts as a single audit agency for the whole government. Even in European countries, with the exception of Austria and Italy, the purview of the central audit does not extend to the SNGs. The lower levels make their own arrangements, while in the United Kingdom, the local government accounts are audited by auditors appointed by an audit commission, a statutory agency. The central audit is, however, empowered to follow the trail of money, where central transfers form a substantial share of total SNG revenues. The reports prepared by the audit agencies may be considered by committees appointed by the legislature (for example, in India) or through similar arrangements.

The above arrangements complete the cycle of financial operations and related accountability. But the patterns of audit and legislative review have not been subjected to serious improvement.

County and Municipal Governments

The financial management systems in operation at the level of county/district and municipal governments have not so far been a part of structural lending programmes except in cases where financial aid is extended directly to a municipality (for example World Bank loan to Kumbakonam municipality in the state of Tamil Nadu).

The techniques of budgeting, structures of budget classification, patterns of accounting and levels of computerization, as well as accountability arrangements vary among countries and within countries depending on the sources of revenue. In some cases, local governments' finances are evaluated periodically (for example, in India after the 73rd Amendment of the Constitution) by quasi-judicial commissions and arrangements made for devolution of resources. In a few cases, local and municipal governments receive funds directly both from central and regional/state governments (for example, India and Spain). Elsewhere, funds are channelled only through the state governments, and depending on the nature of financial transfer, accounting arrangements differ. In most cases, consolidated financial statements of this level of government remain to be compiled as there may be no single agency charged with this responsibility. The finance commissions in India have been publishing data on local finances during recent years but major progress remains to be made in their reliability.

As a greater share of work is proposed to be entrusted to these levels of government, as a part of decentralization endeavours, it would be necessary to gain a more detailed understanding of the working of their expenditure management machinery.

Continuity and Change

Achievement of macroeconomic stability and improved delivery of public services in an effective way are crucially dependent on the expenditure management machinery. The machinery needs to have an explicit strategy to manage the newly devolving tasks, and to restore the public's seriously eroded trust in governments. Improvements are of vital importance and are imperative. The structural lending programmes have enabled, both the lender and the recipient, to have a greater understanding of the current status of expenditure machinery in SNGs. Initiatives have been taken in selected areas but much progress remains to be made. The important task now is to carry forward the limited initiatives to their completion and to supplement these efforts with much-needed innovations in other areas. In undertaking this effort, the complementarity of the three levels of government has to be recognized and efforts made at all levels. Intensive efforts focused on one level are unlikely to bring enduring results in the absence of efforts at the other two levels. Some initiatives discussed earlier have focused on the second tier of government, but in the context of significant dependence on the central government, the changes needed in the nature of transfers and associated conditionality also need to be addressed. These tasks are yet to begin even as further progress is made in the initiatives already undertaken.

9. Preparing Annual Budgets
A Pragmatic Approach

STRENGTHENING EXPENDITURE MANAGEMENT

Some Preliminary Considerations

A continuing theme associated with public administration for more than a thousand years has been the management of finances—how they are raised, the purposes for which they are spent, and the benefits of spending. During recent years, particularly during the last three decades, growing attention has come to be paid to financial management in view of the widespread prevalence of several perceptions about governments and about the effectiveness of the fiscal machinery employed by them. Some common perceptions are that governments have not been very successful in adapting the fiscal machinery to meet the changing requirements of macroeconomic stability; that the delivery of services leaves a good deal to be desired even when budgets are in surplus; that the allocation of resources is dependent more on the strengths of the lobbies; that in practice there is no strategy to manage expenditures and that most policy responses are tactical; and that there is considerable waste of money in the activities of government, contributing to a poor quality of expenditures. These perceptions amount to a severe attack on the credibility of governmental management systems. Today's perceptions are tomorrow's political choices, and as such they need to be addressed as soon as possible. Such effort is not, by its very nature, a single step but involves constant attention and continuous adaptation. Tomorrow's problems may often be different from those of the past or of today.

Different Perspectives and Common Themes

The perceptions and the associated language of discussion tend to be different, depending on the analytical discipline of the individual. Although there are several legitimate groups which have their own well-articulated perceptions, for purposes of discussion, three groups are recognized here: economists, who are more concerned with the allocation and utilization of resources; financial managers, who tend to be more concerned with the instruments and thus with the formulation and implementation of the budget; and the community, which tends to be interested in the overall economic framework and with the benefits received from payments made by it.

In reality, however, the underlying themes are common, (as illustrated in Table 9.1). In the discussion here, a mix of the different perceptions is used.

Table 9.1
Different Perspectives and Common Themes

Broad objectives of government financial management	*Economists' perspective*	*Financial managers' perspective*	*Community's perspective*
Macroeconomic stability	Resource allocation • Aggregate resource allocation • Determination of sectoral strategies and related allocation of resources	Budget formulation	Sound economic framework
Delivery of services	Resource utilization • Utilization of budgetary resources for specified purposes	Budget implementation	Utilization of expenditure benefits
Pursuit of efficiency and economy in all operations	Resource accounting • Patterns in the actual use of resources	Accounting and reporting	Social accounting of contributions made to government and benefits received

Levels and Broad Instruments

Levels of Government: All governments are engaged in the provision of goods and services needed by the community. Such provision requires financial resources. The determination of the broad needs of the community and the determination of manpower, money, and materials required for meeting these needs are the main tasks of expenditure management. Provision of services is undertaken at various levels of government—central, regional, state, local, and state-owned enterprises and each level is engaged in planning its expenditures while coordinating with other levels so that there is no overlap. Allocation of expenditure responsibilities for each level is studied as a part of 'Federal Finance'. For analytical purposes, three levels are recognized—central government, general government, and the private sector. The range of broad instruments is, however, common to all governments and essentially involves three pairs of instruments, taxing and spending, lending and borrowing, and selling and buying.

Expenditure Instruments: Expenditures cover a wide range and the objectives that governments have for them may be achieved in more than one way—through direct and exhaustive expenditures; lending and acquisition of financial assets; provision of guarantees; pursuit of non-commercial objectives by state-owned enterprises; and quasi-fiscal activities carried out by government-owned financial institutions on

Table 9.2

Levels and Instruments of Public Finance

Levels of government	Broad instruments	Common instruments of expenditure
(a) Central government and its statutory organs (b) Regional/state provincial/local governments (c) State-owned enterprises	• Taxing* • Spending • Lending • Borrowing# • Selling • Buying	• Direct spending • Lending • Pursuit of non-commercial objectives specified by the government for state-owned enterprises • Guarantees and contingent liabilities • Quasi-fiscal activities carried out by banks and other financial institutions on behalf of the government

Notes: General Government (a + b), Public Sector (a+ b + c).

* Includes tax incentives, also known as tax expenditures, provided in support of specified fiscal objectives. The analytical framework of public expenditures does not include tax incentives although they are recognized instruments of public finance.

The determination of the overall level of borrowing is a part of fiscal policy while the determination of the instruments of borrowing, timing, and duration is deemed to be a part of monetary policy.

behalf of the government. The instruments have different degrees of substitutability, and together they aim at fulfilling the objectives of the government.

Expenditure management revolves around the use of these instruments, their assigned roles, their actual use, and the results obtained in the processes. The interrelationships between levels and instruments are illustrated in Table 9.2.

Management Structures and Styles

Governments being hierarchical organizations tend to organize themselves in terms of institutions, ministries, and agencies—each one assigned a specified responsibility and the necessary powers for carrying out the tasks inherent in that sphere. In turn, each institution devises its own systems to conduct operations within a framework of accountability. Expenditure management follows this general framework. There are organizations that have the responsibility for specified tasks. Most expenditure management tasks thus revolve around spending agencies, central agencies such as ministries of finance, payment and accounting organizations, and most of these organizations are common to countries. The actual working of these organizations may differ from one country to another, depending partly on structural features such as operational processes and the level of technology

Table 9.3
Management Structures, Styles, and Outcome

Structures		Styles		
• Institutions	• Systems	• Centralization	• Decentralization	Fiscal
• Organizations	• Operational processes and techniques	• Concentration	• De-concentration	Intent
	• Level of technology	• Issue of decrees	• Consultation with legislature and the community	↑
		• Emphasis on financial aspects only	• Emphasis on economic and financial performance and delivery of services	↓ Fiscal Outcome
		• Transparency		
		• Circumvention	• Opaqueness	

and partly on the management styles such as centralization or circumvention. Attention to institutions reveals only a part of the picture but the outcome both in terms of policy formulation and implementation is dependent on the fusion of formal structures and informal styles of working. To illustrate, the laws may specify several forms of control but if they are circumvented in the process of day-to-day working their effect would be different from what was expected.

The relationships between structures, styles and outcome are illustrated in Table 9.3. To assess the efficacy of expenditure management systems, structures and styles have to be examined together.

Structural Features of Expenditure Management

Constitution and Associated Laws

The expenditure management system of every government functions within the parameters of the constitution of the country and its associated laws. Most constitutions have separate sections that deal with the financial aspects of the working of governments (familiarly known as financial provisions). The provisions specify the tasks, powers, and responsibilities of governments in the financial sphere, and could be very broad and too detailed in nature. These provisions may also indicate the nexus between the executive and legislative wings and the relative roles of each. Thus, they may specify the fiscal year, the timing of submission of the budget (annual financial statement), the powers of the legislature, types of expenditures that require legislative approval and those that do not, arrangements to be made for the conduct of government business pending legislative deliberation and approval of the proposals made by the government, relationships with the central bank, powers for domestic and external borrowing, expenditure and revenue assignments to other levels of government, and a variety of other subjects.

There are no normative standards about the coverage of a constitution in regard to the management of finances. Much is dependent on the context in which the constitution was evolved and the political dilemmas it was expected to resolve. In reviewing the adequacy of the constitution for ensuring an effective expenditure management system, it is important to ascertain, in respects other than those specified below, whether the existing framework has any provision that tends to impede modernization efforts.

Delegated Spheres for Additional Legislation

The constitution of a country may specify, among others, that further legislation may be introduced, either on a permanent basis or with a sunset provision, that is, a cut-off period, or on an annual basis. For example, the Constitution of India indicates that further legislation would be enacted on the borrowing powers of government and guarantees given by it. This legislation remains to be enacted. It is quite likely that there are countries where similar indications have been given but are yet to be achieved. These delegated areas could be of crucial importance to the management of public expenditures. The review should, therefore, identify the areas where further legislation was indicated but which has not been carried out and the impact of the slippage on expenditure management.

Budget Coverage: The budget, or the annual financial statement, is the principal vehicle of the government to convey its fiscal policy intentions. The budget is also a tool of management in that the moneys needed for the provision of goods and services are appropriated by the legislature and need to be utilized in compliance with its wishes. It is also a tool of accountability in that the government, entrusted with the responsibility of implementing policies and programmes, informs the representative institutions of the progress made and the results secured.

In view of the above multiple dimensions of a budget, it is expected that all policies and programmes that have financial implications are included in the budget. In practice, however, the budget may be so organized that some transactions are excluded from it (example, oil coordination policies in India). In some other cases, either for reasons associated with managerial freedom or related considerations, some transactions may be carried out through extra-budgetary accounts (example, in Japan), that may be maintained outside the main budget. These accounts may not, in several cases, involve legislative consideration either before obtaining funds or after utilizing them. In some cases, task-oriented autonomous agencies may be established with operational freedom in the management of finances and they may be excluded from the budget even though all or most of their revenues are derived from transfers from the main budget. In a few cases, revenues may be earmarked for specific purposes and their utilization may be undertaken outside the ambit of the budget. Similarly, selected foreign aid inflows may be organized through tacit or explicit agreements between donors and receiving countries, outside the budget.

Both in principle and in practice the coverage of the budget should be comprehensive, encompassing all the financial transactions of the government. It is quite likely, however, that owing to the context in which the original legislation was enacted or the decree was issued, the scope of the budget, may be somewhat limited. It is, therefore, essential to distinguish a legal budget from an analytical budget. The latter should aim at being comprehensive where the laws tend to diminish the scope of the legal budget. An analytical budget should be a consolidated one, covering the activities of the central government, its budgetary transactions, the activities of the main autonomous agencies, the budgets of the state and local governments, and the net financial relationships with public enterprises (including the financing of their capital outlays). In some of the former centrally planned economics (for example, Uzbekistan), the law itself distinguishes between a state budget (covering central and local governments) and a consolidated budget, which includes, all extra-budgetary funds, in addition to the state budget.

The preparation of a consolidated analytical budget is considerably facilitated by the use of electronic technology. An important issue relates to the inclusion of autonomous agencies whose policies are funded and controlled by the government. Much is dependent on their role and functions. In each case, however, a careful and judicious review of budget coverage is indicated.

Fiscal Year: Government financial management represents, by its very nature, a continuum. The arrangement of that continuum into annual time slices was made to reflect the linkage between the budget and the national economy, on the one hand, and in some cases, legislative convenience, on the other. Thus, in most cases, the fiscal years were determined with reference to the agricultural cycle of operations so that forecasts of revenue could be made more accurately. In some cases, fiscal year was largely a matter of colonial legacy.

During recent years, however, the choice of the fiscal year has come up for renewed debate. First, the linkages between the agricultural operations and budget revenues tended to be less important with the gradual growth of the industrial base. Thus, the fundamental premise on which it had evolved came to be questioned. Second, in several countries that are dependent on foreign aid, it became more important, with a view to reduce uncertainty, to wait until donor budgets were approved in their respective countries. It was more convenient to plan budgets in the receiving countries in the light of firm indications from the donors. Thus, there was a need to change the fiscal year. Third, the possibilities of too many different years proved to be a needless complexity. In several countries, fiscal years of government were different from the tax years used to collect taxes, and both were different from the calendar year with reference to which National Income Accounts, (that exemplify the relationships between the budget and the economy) were prepared. Fourth, some categories of expenditure such as development or project outlays, did not lapse at the end of the fiscal year but were made available, without new legislative action, for the following year. In several cases, there was a rush of expenditure during the last part of the fiscal year aimed at avoiding lapse of funds. It is argued that the limitation of a fiscal year introduces avoidable behavioural oddities into the spending patterns and that much of this can be avoided with greater emphasis on medium-term planning of fiscal activities. In some countries, there are long liquidation periods during which the transactions of a year are permitted to be concluded. This contributes to delays in the compilation of annual accounts. Finally, in some countries, the fiscal year may start much ahead of the legislative timetable (for example, in China, where the fiscal year is the calendar year, and the People's Congress, the approving authority, generally meets in April) and resort has to be made to provisional legal arrangements.

In the light of the above discussion, the important issue is if there is a prima facie case for a review of the fiscal year. The answer is dependent on the problems arising from the existing fiscal year. If it contributes to more problems than to administrative convenience, it may be appropriate to change the fiscal year, as many countries have already done. Change will, in the immediate short term, contribute to statistical discontinuity and adequate arrangements need to be made for the transition. Associated issues of fiscal discipline such as a rush of expenditure or liquidation periods need to be addressed in different ways.

Experience shows that there is one major leakage in the process of compliance with the specification of the fiscal year. In the countries of the Indian subcontinent, there is a feature known as 'personal ledger accounts' under which funds may be transferred at the end of the year to avoid lapsing, from the budget account to the accounts of selected officials. Although the procedure was introduced a long time ago to address the problem of lack of rural branches of banks and treasury offices, and to facilitate the cash requirements of military officials at the front lines, it has come to be a widespread escape mechanism to avoid the rigidity of the fiscal year. These accounts, apart from being a violation of legislative accountability, overstate expenditures and present a misleading picture of the budget impact. Similar escape mechanisms may be prevalent in the form of deposit and uncleared suspense accounts. Their impact on the observances of the fiscal year and financial management needs to be investigated.

Basis of Budget

Traditionally, budgets and related accounts of government have been maintained in terms of cash, that is, when cash is received into or paid out from government funds. This system was considered convenient as it was easy to maintain accounts, to administer related expenditure controls, and to facilitate a link-up with monetary policy in terms of determining the magnitude of debt to be issued and its timing. Over the years, however, there has been a growing recognition of the limitations of the cash system. For example, it does not reveal the real financial picture of the government, nor does it permit the development of cost data. In terms of impact, the budget is important when decisions are made to commit or raise resources rather than the actual cash flow. Similarly, the recording of capital expenditure at the time of expensing is hardly indicative of the acquisition of a capital asset and its use. For these reasons, an accrual system is advocated for use in governments. Under this system, transactions are recorded when a commitment is made (and therefore a liability incurred) or when revenue is earned (when a receivable is recognized) regardless of when cash is received or paid out. The main distinction is that in a cash system, the recording of a transaction takes place when cash is paid or received regardless of the timing of the economic event giving rise to the payment, while in an accrual system, it is recorded when the economic event occurs regardless of the timing of payment and receipt of cash. In addition, the accrual system envisages the division of budgets into operational and investment, with the latter having a depreciation account. It will also have a capital charge revealing a payment for the use of an asset by user departments. Further, balance sheets and sources and uses of funds statements would show the diverse aspects of the financial health of government.

In applying accrual systems to government, selected features of experience may be noted. First, in some countries, a beginning is being made with the introduction of accrual accounting at the local level as an integral part of agreements reached with the World Bank. As an extension of this approach, a distinction is made between accrual budgeting and accounting as progress is made in applying the latter. Second, some countries, for example, Australia and New Zealand, have moved to full accrual systems covering budgeting, accounting, and reporting. Third, some countries, notably in Europe, have taken to the application of modified accrual systems, that is, without depreciation accounts and capital charges (which, it is argued, are more appropriate for the commercial sector). It is quite likely that the picture will change in the near future as regional organizations (for example, the EU) seek to achieve uniform standards in government budgeting and accounting. Moreover, international reporting (for example, government finance statistics) is also sought to be done on an accrual basis to permit greater transparency on the financial status of a country.

In the immediate short term, the question is whether efforts have to be initiated to introduce forms of accrual accounting so as to replace the cash system. The reality is that both systems have major attractive features. The cash system, while not reflecting the actual financial conditions, permits the effective use of traditional controls in government. The accrual system, while more reflective, involves a massive change in the management culture of government. Thus, the issue is not one of having one system to the exclusion of the other, but to have features of both. The use of electronic technology permits, without additional costs, use of programmes that capture data at different points of time in the budget process—when funds are committed and released, when invoices are received, when payments are made, when goods and services are received and when they are used. The more important step is to move towards that technology and to use the data for more effective decision making while providing for greater transparency and accountability.

An associated feature relates to the maintenance of budget and accounts on a gross or a net basis. In most governments, the gross basis is used to reflect the complete magnitude of a transaction. For reporting and analytical purposes, however, the transactions may be netted out. Thus, when special or extra-budgetary accounts are consolidated, intra-fund transactions are netted out. In some cases, expenditures may be appropriated net of offsets, that is, some revenue receipts that may be unique to a department. Such expenditure offsets may not fully reveal the fiscal picture, and it has to be ensured that estimates are always made on a gross basis. The importance of this comes into greater relief in the context of privatization of enterprises. Normally, a good deal of additional capital may be injected into these enterprises to make them attractive to investors. Maintaining these transactions on a gross basis enables a clear recognition of all the features of the transaction.

Budget Classification

This aspect refers to the ways in which government financial transactions are categorized in the budget and in the accounts. In analysing the adequacy of classification systems, it is appropriate to distinguish between purposes and practices. The purposes of classification are the following:

1. To indicate the broad activities on which government funds are spent, the types of the sources of revenue and the categories of all types of debt (formal and hidden), so as to facilitate the comprehension of the public; viz., the transparency function.
2. To facilitate the formulation of policies and the monitoring of their implementation in the spending and central agencies; viz., internal management function; and
3. To facilitate the consideration and enactment of the requisite annual budget and other legislation, including approval of appropriations by the legislatures; viz., the legislative function.

The classification approaches being as old as the budget have evolved over the years, both in precept and in practice. Tax revenues have been broadly classified traditionally by type as well as organization, such as taxes on income; customs and other taxes on international trade. This also reflected the organizational responsibilities in most cases, inland revenues, customs, etc. Expenditures were classified mostly in terms of organizations responsible for spending and in terms of the objects or line-items (hence the title, line-item budget) such as wages, travel, utilities, and purchases.

There has been a gradual recognition that this type of enumeration of items of expenditure was not particularly illuminating, although it served the traditional control approaches, as it did not show the purposes or activities on which the money was spent. To achieve this objective, a type of functional (all transactions were divided into functions—distinct services), programme (transactions grouped into homogeneous categories with major—end objectives), activity (that are more detailed categories of programmes) as well as economic (selected groups of objects of expenditure such as wages) classification was evolved. It was expected that these multiple dimensions would be reflected in expenditures. As for debt, the coverage, the range of instruments as well as importance have grown over the period, and it was expected that full information on the sources of debt would be provided as a part of the budget.

In practice, however, there appears to be a widespread diversity and consequently some problems stemming from an inadequate application of the principles. First, the revenue and receipts classification, in general, seems to be adequate although the categories of debt tend to be too aggregative. In expenditure, categories such as defence tend to be highly aggregative, contributing to opaqueness. In regard to other categories, in several countries, the classification follows the organizational lines, with little or no emphasis on programme or output orientation. Second, there is often a discrepancy between the classification followed in the development plans and the budget, requiring link-up arrangements. Moreover, the annual accounts may be prepared in a highly aggregative manner. Third, the distinctions between current and capital budgets are not strictly adhered to. Expenditures are frequently shifted from one category to another leading to analytical discontinuities. Some countries have equivalents of capital budgets in the form of investment, development, and construction budgets with the coverage varying over the years. As a consequence, the capital formation estimates needed for National Income Accounts are required to be calculated separately. And, finally, some countries have recently started to participate in the programme to publish government finance data in accordance with specified standards and some have even set up web sites so that there is greater transparency on government activities. These efforts are welcome from any point of view and are likely to be immensely facilitated if the original classification of the budget is organized along scientific lines.

Classification of government transactions is an evolving activity. Some of the republics of the former centrally planned economies have, taking the advantage of the latecomer, been revamping their classification systems. Similarly, efforts are indicated in other countries where for one reason or another classification may have become out-of-date and inadequate relative to the purposes it is expected to serve. Moreover, the introduction of accrual accounting would also involve the firm separation of transactions into operational and investment categories.

Areas for Review

Expenditure management is to fiscal policy what good sanitary arrangements are to the maintenance of reasonable health standards. They are the essential foundations and it is appropriate to periodically review the designs to ensure their adequacy to the changing requirements of the society and the government. The following structural elements are important in the review.

1. Financial provisions of the constitution—are they too restrictive? What changes are needed?
2. Delegated legislation. Have the constitutional intents been fulfilled? If not, what are the gaps?
3. Does the budget cover all financial aspects? If extra-budgetary accounts are organized, are there compensatory devices that would permit an overall perspective and facilitate fiscal policy formulation?
4. Is the fiscal year choice the right one?
5. Where budgets are predominantly cash oriented, how can they be strengthened to reveal the real use of economic resources and the financial status of governments?
6. Is the budgetary classification adequate to meet its diverse objectives? If not, how can it be improved?

Fiscal Policy, Fiscal Discipline, and Fiscal Responsibility: A Legal Framework

Fiscal policy, which is dependent on the economic climate, involves the pursuit of several objectives. Important among these, as noted in the previous sections, are: (i) pursuit of economic stability, in which the role of expenditure management is to assist in the determination of the size of annual budget deficit or surplus, and once determined, to ensure that the annual targets are adhered to; (ii) delivery of services, which is primarily a function of the spending agencies but the role of expenditure management is to assist in the determination of magnitude of moneys needed to achieve specified levels of services in conformity with the priorities within a framework of targets relating to time, costs, and quality. Equally important, expenditure management has to ensure that the intended benefits from expenditure programmes are actually reaped by the targeted groups; and (iii) pursuit of economy and efficiency; where the role of expenditure management is to devise approaches that would be conducive to efficient management while internalizing the risks in each area.

Experience shows that there have been many slippages in the fulfilment of these objectives. In addition to the recognition of this failure, there has also been a recognition of the fact that most policies need to be evolved and implemented over a medium term, and that with a view to achieving political consensus it might be more appropriate to specify some objectives as a part of legislation. Such legislation (usually called fiscal policy and responsibility legislation) may provide clarity in the overarching themes, while contributing to transparent functioning and thus moving towards the restoration of fiscal credibility of the country.

Towards this end, countries such as Australia and New Zealand have enacted legislation indicating the broad fiscal policy goals, the levels of deficit, and the levels of outstanding debt. Elsewhere, countries in Latin America, for example, Argentina and Brazil, have enacted similar legislation. In some ways the legislation in Brazil is far more comprehensive as it includes provisions that are generally included in the budget law. In considering the need for new laws, it is useful to distinguish the common law tradition from the civil law. In the former, there is greater reliance on executive orders, while in the latter, there is more emphasis on specifying all aspects in the form of a law. It is generally felt that to ensure the conduct of governmental affairs within a framework of law, it may be prudent to enact a budget law, either independent of the fiscal policy and responsibility law or as a part of omnibus legislation covering all budgetary aspects. Some former republics of the Soviet Union have since enacted (or are in the process of enacting) comprehensive budgetary laws.

The budget laws, in general, deal with three aspects, organizational, transparency, and accountability. In terms of the organizational function, the laws may specify the coverage, basis, budget calendar, budget implementation, accounting, internal and external audit, role of central and spending agencies, role of local governments, and related aspects. In fulfilling the transparency function, the contours of the government sector, nature, sources and periodicity of fiscal information, and observance of relevant internal or international standards may be specified. From an accountability point of view, it may specify the levels and types of vertical and horizontal accountability and the role of oversight bodies and their functioning. The enumeration of the contents here is illustrative rather than exhaustive. In addition, the machinery established to deal with fraud and corruption may be specified.

It is expected that legislation of the above types could promote greater cohesion and fiscal responsibility.

Areas for Review

The need for additional legislation is dependent on the existing legal tradition and the adequacy of existing legislation. It would be useful to review the existing laws, and the current and future policy needs to determine the direction and content of future legal changes.

RESOURCE ALLOCATION: POLICY FRAMEWORK

Medium-term Fiscal Planning: Role of Expenditure Planning

Nature of Policy Planning

A key component of PEM is the allocation of resources in a manner consistent with policy priorities (strategic allocation). Implicit in this statement is a long process in which the government is engaged in the formulation of policies aimed at meeting the needs of society. All policies have financial implications which have to be recognized for the duration of the proposed policies. The collective implications of the policies are evaluated in terms of the resources likely to be available. In light of that evaluation, priorities are formulated. This entire process has three dimensions: (i) structural aspects dealing with the formulation of goals, objectives, and policies in terms of decision packages; (ii) analytical aspects or the application of objective criteria with reference to which the proposals are evaluated (both for the costs and benefits and formulated priorities); and (iii) informational aspects dealing with the monitoring of the progress made in the implementation of policies. These aspects are applicable to expenditure management and are exemplified in the budgetary process of every government.

The budgetary process does not, however, function in an independent or autonomous fashion but is viewed as an integral part of the overall management of the economy. The management of the economy requires, as an essential prerequisite, the internalization of the structural characteristics of the economy and its sensitivity to external and internal volatilities. With the increase in globalization, the explicit reckoning of these vulnerabilities gains added importance. In advanced and industrialized countries, the availability of automatic stabilizers lessens the dimensions of the problem. In most developing countries, the absence of well-organized social security systems makes the governments potentially weaker in responding to changing economic fortunes. In some cases, governments may even reduce their spending to adjust to the declining revenues, thus worsening the cycle. In countries that have unemployment funds (for example, former republics of the Soviet Union and now independent countries) they may be subject to rules that are independent of the annual budget policies and may contribute to 'enclave mentality' and diverse approaches to tackling the problem.

Some countries have organized stabilization funds, social funds, and reserve stabilization funds to meet diverse needs. Stabilization funds seek to provide a kind of insurance when the external prices of export products are too low to be remunerative. Social funds are intended (for example, post-Asian crisis after 1998) to provide assistance to low-income and vulnerable groups. Reserve arrangements refer to the short-term flows into the country when the level of reserves is low. The measures intended to be deployed in the context of various phases of the business are of importance in the management of the economy. While they are not always integral parts of expenditure management, as is the case with reserve maintenance arrangements, some elements could be very prominent (for example, automatic stabilizers and social funds) and therefore have to be internalized at each stage. The extent to which this is done is a matter for additional review.

Budget Expenditures and Types of Budgets

Financial planning involves a closer examination of the links between the stated objectives and the available instruments. The links may be direct in some cases and indirect in others. The broad categories of expenditures utilized for the achievement of fiscal objectives have already been identified. For purposes of discussion here, they may be regrouped into three broad categories. (1) Maintenance or continuing outlays or expenditures needed for the continuation of existing or approved policies. This involves the payment of wages for the approved personnel, associated outlays on the purchase of goods and services needed for the continued implementation of policies, transfers to individuals, organizations, and other levels of government already approved and firmly entrenched in law, debt servicing, and capital expenditures. In the absence of specific efforts aimed at reducing these proposed outlays, they are considered, to all intents and purposes, as unavoidable or mandatory. (2) Outlays where magnitudes are determined by the economic climate, for example, subsidies. The nature of subsidies may be specified in law or in policy, but the actual outlay is determined by the difference between procurement and sale prices. To the extent that the former is higher than the latter, the outlays in this area tend to grow. (3) Those that are intended to influence the functioning of the economy (example, in Korea after the crisis in 1997 and Japan during the last few years). Where governments are expected to provide stimulus, more expenditures may be incurred. The budgets may contain substantial stimulus packages, and when these are not deemed to be adequate, supplementary budgets providing for additional stimulus may be planned and implemented. It is important to note that the new outlays may be incurred in the form of additions to existing services or totally new services.

Traditionally, for purposes of control, a distinction is made between 'new items' and 'new services'. In parliamentary systems of the Whitehall type, expenditure on a new service cannot be incurred except with the approval of the legislature. New items are technically viewed as additions to existing services which, while requiring legislative approval, provide the executive with a little more flexibility than is the case with new services. When new outlays are proposed, they are expected to be subjected to the same rigorous examination from a cost–benefit point of view, as is the case with other outlays and are included in the budget only after successfully meeting the specified criteria.

Before the advent of the dirigist approach to economic development and the formulation of medium-term or annual development plans, these new services were considered in an ad hoc manner. After the introduction of development planning, however, plans came to be viewed as the basic framework through which additional services were provided and additional expenditures incurred. But new activities or outlays may not always be 'developmental' in character. While all outlays are to be incurred only through one budget, the continuing outlays were analysed within the realm of the annual budget process, and the developmental outlays came to be concluded through the 'plan' process. This brought about a separation between planning and budgeting, a feature that continues to be prevalent in several countries. With the decline of the importance of development plans during recent years, medium-term expenditure planning on a rolling basis has come to be adopted as the new framework. Development plans were viewed as somewhat rigid, while the rolling expenditure plans (considered in detail in the following section) were viewed as more flexible. Both these approaches permit a detailed analysis of the problem, the desired policy response, and implementation of the proposed policy.

The conversion of the policy response into a budgetary package is dependent on the type of the budget system of the country. The line item or the conventional budget permits the use of all three types of expenditures but requires the packages to be broken down into input items. They can also be processed through a performance type. Here the packages are converted into desired impact categories. The policy proposals, both existing and new, may need to be thoroughly re-examined when a country is passing through a fiscal crisis. In this context, ZBB may be used. (These linkages are illustrated in Table 9.4)

Table 9.4
Types of Expenditures

Types of Budgets	Types of Expenditures		
	Maintenance or continuous outlays	Outlays determined by economic conditions	Outlays intended to influence the functioning of the economy
Budgets or strategies intended for more than a year			
Development Plans	Takes into account these categories	Takes into account these categories	Takes into account these categories
MTEF on a rolling basis	As above	As above	As above
Budget Systems in terms of their orientation			
Line-item budget	As above	As above	As above
	(These are required to be converted into input categories)		
Performance/ output budget systems	These systems do not distinguish between the above types of expenditures but are amenable to include these three groups and performance indicators can be specified. Performance budgets are supply driven, therefore, expenditures may not lend themselves to reduction when these systems are in use		
ZBB	All varieties of expenditures are subject to review under a very strict regime		

Medium Term Fiscal Framework

Expenditure forecasting beyond the fiscal year was undertaken, periodically, by some governments to illustrate the future financial implications of current and continuing policies. Since the early 1970s, however, medium-term expenditure planning has come to be taken up by several governments in the industrial and developing worlds. Several reasons contributed to this practice. First, in those countries that formulated formal development plans there was a recognition that the scope of the plans was, in general, restricted to government investment outlays and that the estimates included in the plan were often treated as firm and inviolate. In reality, such rigidity contributed to several distortions. Second, there was a recognition that expenditure adjustments and related implementation of fiscal policies could only be envisaged over the medium term. In addition to the massive capital projects whose implementation was spread over several fiscal years, there were areas such as poverty alleviation, modernization of defence forces, development of partnerships with the private sector, and adjustment for previous fiscal follies could only be envisaged over the medium term. Third, IFIs engaged in lending advocated the introduction of rolling public investment planning so that the investment programme could be formally linked to the annual budget and the lending programmes of the institutions. Finally, the medium-term forecasts illustrated the continuing financial implications of existing policies, their draft on future resources, and thus illustrated the leeway available for further expansion or contraction. In due course, it was felt more appropriate to extend the exercise to cover all types of expenditures.

As more experience was gained with expenditure planning and forecasting, there was widespread recognition that the exercise had limited utility in the absence of an explicit recognition of the resource constraints. Thus, the medium-term fiscal framework (MTFF), covering resources and outlays and affording an annual opportunity to update the estimates on a rolling basis, came to the fore. Increasingly, it was felt that the sustainability, flexibility, and vulnerability of fiscal policy over the medium term were of paramount importance. The MTFF is now viewed as a policy instrument that seeks to inform the public, the market agents, and government agencies, and thus provides ample transparency, clarity, and to the extent possible, a stable environment for more detailed policy making. In its endeavour to reduce uncertainty, it assists all economic agents to make their own decisions in the context of MTFF. The MTFF is different from the MTEF in that the latter is a component of the former and is as vast as fiscal policy itself.

The formulation of the estimates included in the MTFF may involve the use of extensive econometric methodology. In a simpler formating, it could involve, in some cases baseline projections or formulation of estimates taking into account the buoyancy and elasticity factors affecting revenues, and the past autonomous rates of growth of expenditures. Projections from a base year have limited usefulness and it is for this reason that practice has yielded place to rolling estimates. Each year, estimates are made for the following two or three years and the formulation of the annual budget provides an opportunity to revisit the estimates and to revise them in the light of changing economic variables. Both MTFF and MTEF are essentially auxiliary devices that provide support to the formal, legal budget approved by the legislature.

An important analytical component of the MTFF is the deficit or surplus emerging from the exercises. A surplus may imply a potential for reduction in future tax rates, while the persistence of deficits would imply the need for a comprehensive fiscal strategy aimed at reducing the levels over the medium term, thus improving the prospects of fiscal sustainability. The use of the concept of the deficit is not uniform, however, and much is dependent on the underlying intent of analytical use. There are at least fifteen concepts of deficit, each one illustrating a particular aspect. For example, a deficit calculated on the basis of intergenerational accounts may illustrate the phase in a distant future that may not be of immediate relevance. Hence, sufficient care has to be extended in the choice of the analytical concept as policy implications emerge from it. These aspects are of particular relevance to countries that are experiencing severe fiscal stress. It becomes important for them to formulate medium-term policies towards moderation of the rate of growth of current expenditure clearance of accumulated arrears, and to focus more on capital formulation.

Organizational Aspects

The organizational aspects essentially cover three areas (illustrated in Figure 9.1): (i) features of the MTEF; (ii) linkages with the MTFF; and (iii) the way in which the content of MTEF and MTFF is converted into day-to-day action. The MTEF should have a coverage that is comprehensive in that it should include the budget, extra-budgetary

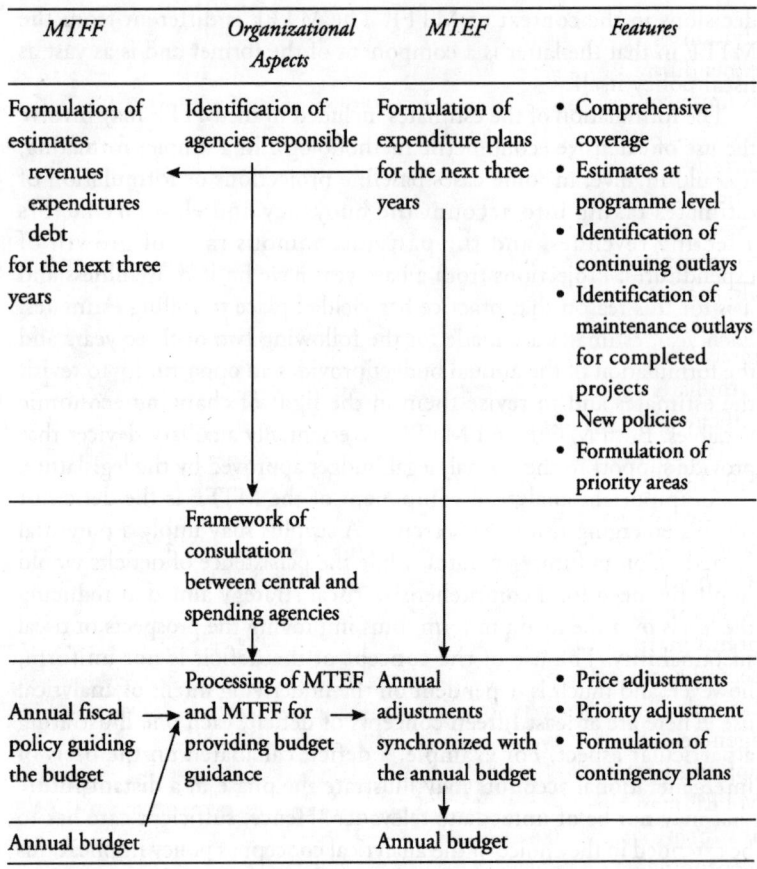

Figure 9.1: Medium-term Fiscal Framework and Medium-term Expenditure Framework

accounts, and should be perceived at a national level. The coverage should also include potential contingent liabilities as these have a tendency to shock the adjustment process. They should therefore be carefully estimated and internalized. Similarly, if the government faces a situation of accumulated arrears, the manner in which those arrears would be cleared needs to be addressed as a part of the MTEF. Alternatively, if it is a stimulus package, that should be covered as well. The exercise should not be too aggregative, as may be done in an econometric model. Rather, the intent of MTEF is to analyse the medium-term behaviour of each programme, how its internal expenditure dynamics is going to impact on the programme and on the total expenditure. In contrast, the MTFF may be at an aggregate level as it is more concerned with the direction of fiscal policy. The programme level analysis should explicitly include the continuing outlays on policies already approved, the new maintenance levels that will be needed for already completed projects, and any major changes in policies expected to be made. As an integral part of this exercise, effort should also be made to formulate priorities, so that in the event of a resource shortfall, alternative policies are available. The intent of the MTEF is not to enumerate but to facilitate further intensive planning in the light of the total picture. It is important to recognize that if the policies are not properly formulated, then the implementation would be rendered considerably difficult and the whole intent of policy formulation is likely to be defeated.

The relationship between MTEF and MTFF is a reciprocal one, each influencing as well as strengthening the other. The MTFF needs the knowledge of firm expenditure requirements, just as the MTEF has to have a firm estimate of the resource availability. The annual adjustments, which set the scenario for the formulation of the annual budget, are common to both. As such, the calendar of activities, such as the preliminary preparation of estimates by the spending agencies and central agencies, needs to be specified with care. In some countries (for example, Australia), the forward estimates are prepared by the central agencies, viz., finance, and the spending agencies are afforded an opportunity to comment on and to revise them. In other countries, the MTEF may reflect a bottom–up exercise in that the rolling estimates are formulated by the spending agencies and then consolidated. Depending on the approach taken, the steps involved in the process of consultation should be specified and should preferably be transparent.

The eventual intent of MTEF and MTFF is to strengthen the policy formulation processes. Therefore, the information processed and the conclusions reached through these analytical devices have to be considered by the various policy-making bodies in the countries. Thus, the extent of use of these techniques by the central agencies in the formulation of annual budgets, their consideration by the cabinet, and finally deliberation and approval by the legislature, illustrate the effective utilization of these techniques. In some countries, these two techniques may go through all the above phases, while in others, the results of MTEF and MTFF may be presented as a part of the budget documents, more for information than for effective use in decision making. These aspects, therefore, merit a judicious review.

Issues

Notwithstanding the inherent attractiveness of the above techniques, several issues have arisen in their implementation. In considering the next steps, it is essential that these issues are considered and the alternatives explored. First, experience shows that the formulation of forecasts has not been followed by the adoption of the much-needed risk management strategies. Inherently, some forecasts cover areas that tend to be volatile. Revenues tend to experience shortfalls: outlays on entitlement programmes could be higher. Several transactions may be decided on considerations other than merits. Some categories of expenditures may not always reveal the true characteristics. For example, loans given by governments are renegotiated in several cases, to the point that they may be written off. Meanwhile, as they are shown as possible recoveries, they provide a misleading picture. In addition, the contingent liabilities arising from internal and external guarantees are generally ignored until it is too late. These aspects require a risk management strategy, which is in general not available. Second, the forecasts are often restricted to the central government, and in several cases, are too aggregative and mostly in the nature of baseline projections rather than reflecting the expenditure dynamics of the categories. These methodological shortcomings are not insurmountable and improvements can be undertaken with ease. In undertaking such improvements, it has to be recognized that the preparation of a forecast by itself would be of little use, unless the end uses are explicitly recognized and these features are built into the system. Third, in countries that are mostly dependent on foreign aid, the forecasts have not proved to be very valuable as the final levels of outlays are dependent on the aid received than on the needs. This illustrates the need for a more detailed dialogue with the donors. Fourth, the general experience reveals that once forecasts are made, the spending agencies tend to view them as floor levels for obtaining resources. In some cases, given the dependence of the central agencies on the estimates provided by the spending agencies, they have little opportunity to scrutinize the estimates in detail. Fifth, in some cases, the resource constraints are not internalized as the forecasts are limited to outlays and do not include revenue forecasts. And, finally, the forecasts do not explore the alternative approaches to service delivery (for example, public–private financial partnerships). In view of these shortcomings, the legislatures and the public do not appear to view them as credible. In at lease one case (India), the experiment of running medium-term forecasts was abandoned, as it was felt that it was contributing to a lowered importance of the established developmental planning machinery.

These issues need to be addressed frontally and properly if the systems have to gain credibility. The point of review is to identify the gaps that need to be filled.

Macroeconomic Framework and the Annual Budget

Proceeding from a properly prepared MTFF, the formulation of an annual budget should be an easy and a normal step. In reality, however, the annual budget exercise could be different, not in nature, but in terms of the changes that have taken place or are likely to take place in the national economy. Adjustments from the MTFF could involve two steps: (i) an evaluation of the changes that have taken place in the economy and the proposed policy responses; and (ii) addressing the unresolved dilemmas in the MTFF. The former could involve, depending on the situation, a sudden reversal in the policy direction and revisiting the policy debates previously faced. Where no MTFF or MTEF are formulated, annual budget-making would involve an assessment of the national economy, its likely impact on the budget categories, and the desired influence proposed for next year's budget.

The general framework of objectives, range of instruments available, and their applicability are summarized, for facility of discussion, in Table 9.5. The most important consideration relates to the determination of the size of the fiscal deficit (surplus) in the light of the estimated changes in the magnitudes of revenues and expenditures. These are generally estimated in terms of the expected changes in the GDP. Notwithstanding a considerable amount of progress made in the computation of GDP, in several countries they remain, for the most part, tentative and are revised several times during the year. The revisions reflect problems of coverage and classification, both with profound impact on the budget categories. Further, the use of a GDP deflator may not fully reveal the likely changes in the expenditure magnitudes of some categories, for example, defence. Each major category of government expenditure is likely to be more affected by the price index of that sector and to that extent, the calculations made on the basis of GDP deflator may prove to be underestimations.

The consideration of needed adjustments is undertaken simultaneously for revenues and expenditures (and debt). These aspects are illustrated

Table 9.5

Objectives and Instruments of Expenditure Management

Objectives	Instruments	Remarks
Macroeconomic stability	• Medium-term fiscal policy • Medium-term rolling expenditure planning • Development plans • Specific strategies aimed at containing deficits or increasing them • Fundamental expenditure reviews • ZBB • Output budget systems • Target-based budgeting • Accrual-based budgeting system	• By far the most successful approach has been 'specific strategies' including strict limits on budget deficits. As such, the benefits may not be of an enduring type • Most developing countries have very little experience with output or accrual based systems
Service provision	• Performance or output budget system • Cost standards • Evaluation to ensure that the intended benefits have been utilized	• Standards remain, for the most part, entrenched to measure effort and not results or performance
Economy and efficiency, prevention of waste of resources	• Internal evaluation of programmes and projects • Re-engineering of work processes • Market tests and competitive tendering and bidding • Application of electronic data processing (EDP) technology to reduce processing costs	• The programmes in all of the areas may be too limited to have any significant impact on the growth of expenditure or avoidance of waste

in Table 9.6. It has to be noted, however, that in countries which are substantially dependent on foreign aid, much is dependent on the dialogue with donors. In both cases, it is of utmost importance to resist the impulse to engage in the formulation of a rosy scenario as optimism in the early stages could lead to a series of problems at a later stage. As for expenditures, a distinction is made between discretionary and non-discretionary types, but the distinction may actually be overstating the flexibility available to government, for what is available in theory

Table 9.6
Estimating Changes in Revenue and Expenditure

Revenues			Expenditures	
Changes in the tax base	Changes in tax rates and exemptions	Changes due to vigorous enforcement	Discretionary expenditures • Wages • Subsidies • Expenditure on government services	Non-discretionary expenditures • Public debt • Contingent liabilities • Judicial verdicts • Entitlements
		Arrears clearance	• Capital expenditures • Loans	• Legally determined transfers
Elasticity of tax revenues	Changes in tax revenues			
	Total revenues		Total expenditures	Deficit/Surplus

may be constrained by political factors, for example, wages and subsidies may not lend themselves to quick adjustment as the community's expectation may be in the opposite direction. The approaches of economists and finance managers tend to be different to expenditures. Economists view the situation, (as illustrated in Table 9.1) in terms of objects of expenditure, while the latter view them in terms of programmes and projects. From the point of delivery of services, it is the programmes that are important. Ideally, expenditure adjustments are best viewed in terms of programme costs and the possible approaches towards their reduction. In practice, however, many governments do not have the requisite cost data and where such data are compiled, they reflect cash flows more than the accrued cost of resource use. Strategic choices required to be made are in terms of programmes, which also implies that all expenditures should not be treated as equal. For policy purposes, they are unequal and should be so considered. From the macroeconomic point of view, the total level of expenditure is an important policy variable. From the point of service delivery, it is the programme which is the focal point and these macro and micro aspects are expected to be reconciled during the annual rite of policy making.

Another important area that merits recognition relates to the performance during previous and current years. As noted above, between intent and reality, there are several shadows, some creeping and others explicit. These administrative factors are as important as the economic ones. Identification of these slippages and consideration of the factors contributing to the slippages requires up-to-date reporting systems. Lags in reporting contribute to distortions in policy making.

Areas for Review

1. Policy formulation: adequacy of structural, analytical, and informational aspects
2. Economy and business cycle: Adequacy of existing mechanisms and their impact on budgets
3. Policy responses and adequacy of budgetary instruments
   (a) Types of expenditures
4. Features of MTEF and MTFF
5. Adequacy of the organizational process to internalize the results of MTEF and MTFF
6. Attention paid to issues
   (a) Formulation of strategy
   (b) Assessment of risk
   (c) Consultations with donors
   (d) Dialogue between central and spending agencies
   (e) Exploration of service delivery
7. Macroeconomic framework and annual budget
   (a) Identification of linkages
   (b) Use of GDP deflator and other indices
   (c) Adjustments in revenue and expenditure items: different approaches and their usefulness
   (d) Formulation of policies and choice of instruments; issues in their effective use

BUDGET MANAGEMENT

Budget Formulation

Scope and Importance

The formal expression of annual policy making described in the preceding sections is in the formulation of an annual budget. As noted already, policy formulation is a continuing activity and the preparation of an annual budget, as distinct from other policy planning instruments, involves the compression of a continuum into a highly focused process that has the aim of producing a document for the consideration of the pubic and the approval by the legislature or its equivalents. Such a budget has several purposes.

1. It serves as a report on the status of government finances.
2. It is an assessment of the current and expected economic situation of the country and an indication of what the government expects to do during the course of the next fiscal year.
3. It is a document that seeks to inform the public about the benefits that may be expected (including the measures aimed at poverty alleviation) and the sacrifices that may be needed to be made by the community.
4. It is a financial expression of the various sectoral policies that are being pursued and are likely to be continued during the next fiscal year.
5. It is a financial action plan for the activities of all government agencies.
6. It is a signal to markets about the range of borrowing that may be undertaken by the government.
7. It is the document that serves as the basis for annual financial legislation.
8. It is the main instrument for public financial accountability.

In view of the above multiple dimensions, preparation of the annual budget forms the very heart of expenditure management. The budget is larger than an expenditure plan in that it includes revenue resources and the amounts to be borrowed during the year. A government budget is different from the practices of the corporate sector. The corporate sector may have annual strategy but no explicit budget with the same procedural trappings as in the public sector. The distinctiveness of the government arises for two reasons. First, in government, it is the size of expenditures which determines the amount of resources to be raised, while in the corporate sector, a major part of the activities is determined by the income. Second, the plans of government have macroeconomic importance in that they seek to influence the direction in which the national economy is moving. The activities of the corporate sector are determined by the national economy. It is for these reasons that greater transparency is urged in the activities of government—what it does? why is it doing whatever it is doing? what are the costs of government activities? and the like.

Approaches to Budget

Broadly, the annual budget involves the preparation of estimates of expenditure requirements for all the activities of government. These include ongoing activities, proposed new activities, and the abandonment of existing policies that have not proved effective. The preparation, review, and consolidation of estimates of expenditures follows, broadly, two approaches—bottom–up and top–down. To some extent, this division into two categories, for analytical purposes, involves oversimplification and some governments may follow both approaches depending on the types of expenditures.

Essentially, the bottom–up approach, which is also known as the conventional approach, (illustrated in Figure 9.2), involves the

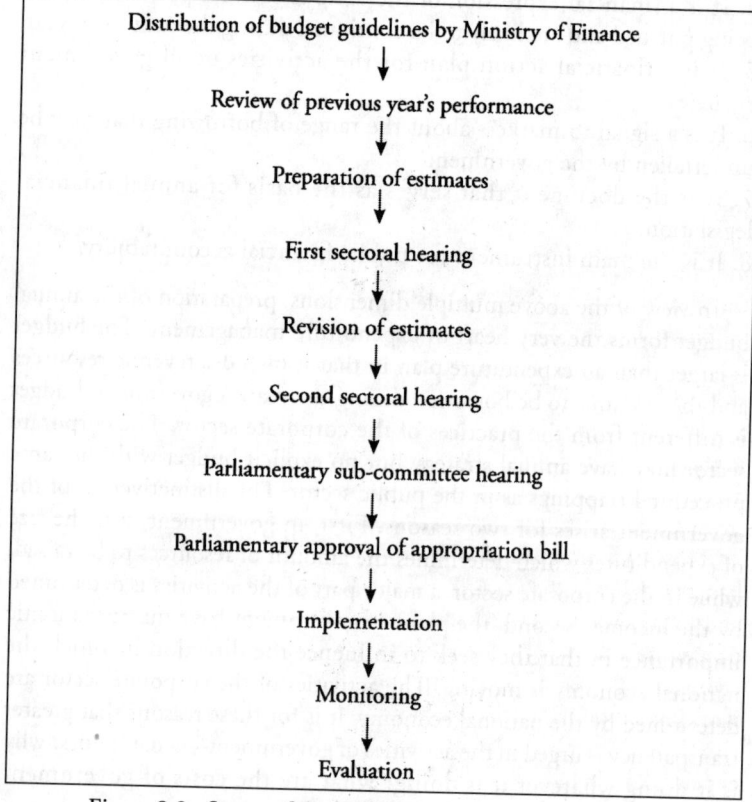

Figure 9.2: Stages of the Budget—Conventional Approaches

preparation of estimates by the various agencies, of the financial resources needed to implement the existing policies and any new policies. These estimates involve detailed calculations of manpower requirements, the associated administrative expenditure (example, consumption of utilities and travel), and materials and equipment (including replacements) needed. In addition, attention is paid to the amounts to be transferred to other levels of governments, and the amounts needed for the servicing of debt, and for the continuation of the financial portfolio. Estimates are first prepared by the agencies and are processed upwards to the ministries and central agencies. Eventually, they are finalized and are included in the draft budget. The process is an iterative one, and notwithstanding its extensive use over the years, is considered as having several weaknesses. As a starter, the spending agencies may not have any idea of the resource constraint, and when finally the draft bids are added up, they tend to be considerably larger than the resources available. So, a process of adjustment at various levels becomes imperative, but inasmuch as the draft estimates acquire legitimacy as the reflections of the demands of the agencies, adjustment ends up as a game in which decisions are made, not with reference to priorities but more on considerations of who thumps the table harder. Intense politicization of the debate makes policy making harder and turbulent. When the legislature enters the fray, the process becomes even more extended, and estimates of revenue tend to be manipulated to suit the requirements. For these reasons, it was felt that the process should be changed to a top–down approach, where the central agencies responsible for macroeconomic management determine the policies and strategies to be implemented during the next fiscal year in the light of available resources. To that extent, the resource constraint is internalized in the approaches and in the processes of decision-making. Each of these aspects is further facilitated in the context of a rolling MTFF. The stages involved in this approach are illustrated in Figure 9.3.

The determination of the ceilings is itself a formidable process. It has its origins in the years of fiscal stress experienced during the 1980s and 1990s and in the heightened awareness of the potential implications of a widened fiscal deficit and its adverse consequences, on the economy. The ceilings, for the most part, are derived in a process of working backwards from the potential level of deficit. Working from this level, the ceilings may be expressed as a rate of change for expenditure (where the rate of growth of expenditure is sought to be moderated, the estimated rate could often be lower than the rate of

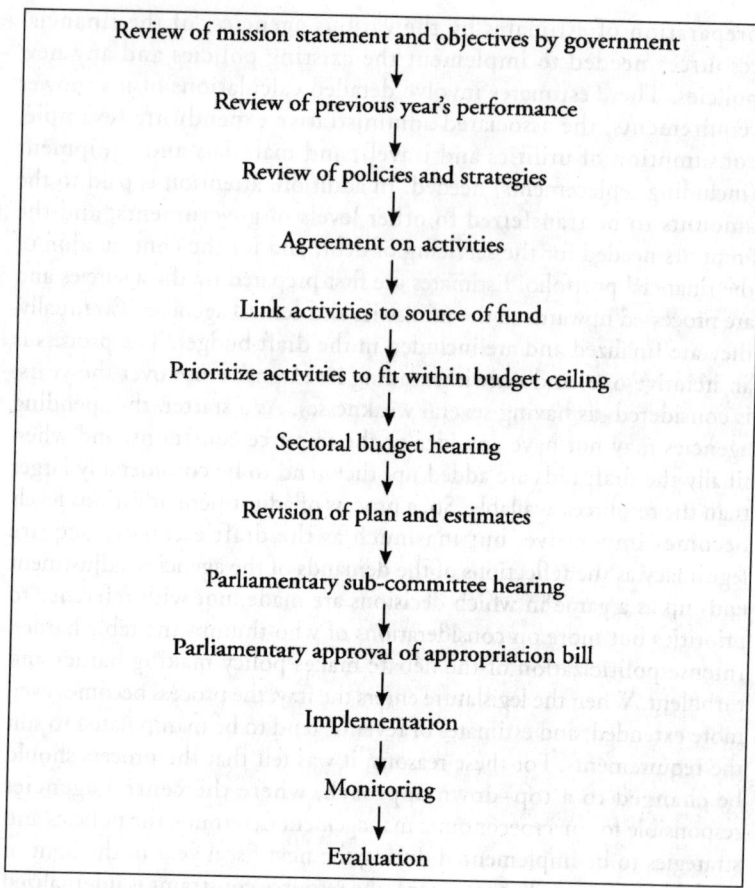

Figure 9.3: Stages of the Budget—Recent Approaches

growth witnessed during previous years) or as an absolute value for the policy variable in nominal terms. Thus, the ceilings, as illustrated in Figure 9.4, may be on total expenditure, or some categories of expenditure (plan and non-plan, or where defence is an important category, defence and non-defence), or for different portfolios (for broader clusters of expenditure, such as social, economic, administrative) and thus move progressively to more specific categories (for example, travel, consumption of utilities) and others. It should be noted that these ceilings may also apply, in heavily indebted countries, to the conventionally centrally determined outlays such as public debt.

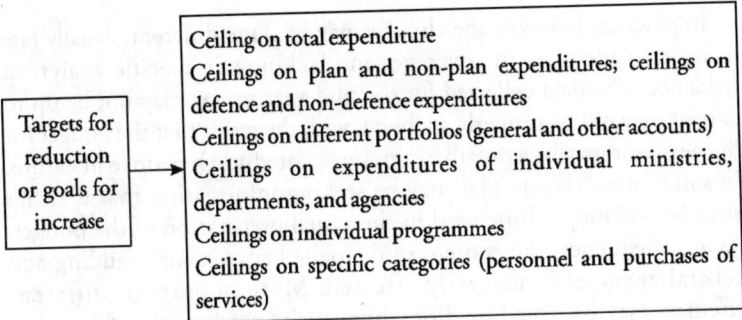

Figure 9.4: Types of Ceilings

The calculations that underpin the determination of ceilings are themselves derived from assumptions on GDP growth, price level, and exchange rates and are therefore liable to change. Such changes need to be absorbed or anticipated in the determination of the total level of expenditure, so that there is adequate margin or latitude. Towards this end, a global reserve may be maintained. Alternatively, the changes may be absorbed by giving up existing programmes so that the ceilings can be maintained. Country practices, however, differ widely in this regard and it would be useful to review their adequacy.

The budget activities for the next year start with the issue of a budget circular, which is the primary instrument of communication to the numerous agencies of the government. It is used, depending on the choice of above approaches, to facilitate budget planning and is expected, in theory, to include a general review of the economic situation and the goals set for the next budget, a review of the trends in the current budget, and an indication of the ceilings within which the spending agencies are required to formulate their estimates. In addition, the circular is expected to identify the high-risk areas that can have a potential impact on the budget outcome; and following from the diversity of objectives, emphasize the needed improvements in the delivery of services as well as areas where more economy and efficiency are to be pursued. Moreover, the circular is expected to be unified (comprising all aspects regardless of whether they are included in the budget or other accounts) and to contain the potential contingent liabilities. Further, it is expected to be issued early on so that the agencies have time to internalize the constraints. In a context where moderation in the rate of growth of expenditure is indicated, it is expected to reveal the strategy and the ways and means of framework available for achieving that objective.

In practice, however, the circular may be quite different, usually late in issue, inadequate in coverage, and lacking any specific analytical guidance. The data collected for the mid-year review may not be up to date or may not be properly analysed, with the result that the budget for the next year may be a putative exercise updated and repetitive in nature. In some cases, the circular may be seeking information that is either already available or little used in the actual preparation of the budget. As a consequence, the content of dialogue between the spending and central agencies is adversely affected. More important, different circulars may be issued by different agencies concerned with parts of the budget. The circulars in regard to the developmental budget may be issued by the planning agency while the circular in regard to current budget may be issued by the ministry of finance. Each may specify a different timetable and follow different approaches, thus providing opportunities to the agencies to play one central agency against another. Further, the circulars may not identify the risk areas or the improvements in the delivery of services or the areas where economy is called for. These critical areas, if not properly addressed, tend to reduce the value of the circular and erode the very credibility of the guidance sought to be provided. In turn, these aspects may reflect the more fundamental problems affecting financial planning in general. For these reasons, it is important to review the adequacy of the circular in detail.

Formulation of Estimates

Expenditure estimates and associated issues are best considered in terms of three levels: (i) new and continuing outlays, (ii) estimates for various objects or categories of expenditures, and (iii) estimates at the programme level.

As noted earlier, a distinction is made between new and continuing outlays to facilitate decision making at various levels. The information compiled for this purpose may not find its way into the budget in the same form as it covers diverse aspects and looks beyond the next fiscal year. In taking decisions about the budget eligibility of a new policy, the recurring and non-recurring financial implications need to be carefully estimated for both programme and project outlays. Similarly, data are needed on the continuing outlays too. Justifications are required to indicate that they need to be continued in the future (public interest test), that they need to be provided by the government (role of government test), and that their provision may take place in partnership with the corporate and voluntary sectors. Traditionally, the consideration of these aspects was more implicit than explicit. Recent emphasis on transparency, however, requires that these considerations be made explicit. These aspects are illustrated in Table 9.7.

Formulation of detailed expenditure estimates following the stages of consideration, analysis, and policy formulation, involves a detailed examination of the financial requirements of each category of expenditure. In turn, economic, technical, and policy factors need to be taken into account and an integrated approach formulated.

Table 9.7

Formulation of Expenditure Estimates (Preliminary Considerations)

New Expenditures	1st Year	2nd Year	3rd Year	Annual Outlay in Future Years
Programme Outlays				
• Recurring outlays				
Manpower				
Others				
• Non-recurring Outlays				
Project Outlays				
Pre-feasibility Study*				
Feasibility Study#				
Engineering analysis				
Economic analysis				
Financial analysis				
Environmental analysis				
Managerial analysis				
Social impact analysis				
Project Outlays				
Recurring				
Non-recurring				
Continuing Expenditures				
• Impact of policy changes				
• Impact of price factors				
• Impact of economy and efficiency measures				
• Public interest test				
• Role of government test				
• Partnership test				

Notes: * Outlays on these aspects are incurred prior to the inclusion of the project in the budget.
Mostly outlays in this regard are incurred prior to the inclusion of the project in the budget

The expenditure estimates included in the budget may be in terms of objects of expenditure (conventional item-wise classification) or in terms of programmes that reflect the transactions of each agency and to that extent, tend to be different from one agency to another. The estimated expenditure of each programme is dependent on its integral components, such as manpower, machinery, and money transfers. The combination of these parts and their relative roles tend to be different among programmes and the dynamics of their movement during the next year need to be carefully estimated. In most countries, however, the focal point continues to be the object categories and not programme categories. The growing emphasis on the delivery of services and the pursuit of economy and efficiency require that the imbalance in the day-to-day approaches be addressed.

Review of Estimates

Draft budget estimates formulated by all agencies are processed through various administrative stages before their final inclusion in the draft budget submitted to the legislature. The stages differ from one country to another but involve a hierarchy of steps discussed in the following section. Broadly, however, the review involves several approaches of scrutiny including a detailed sectoral analysis to assess the needs of the individual sectors of the economy and to determine the investment priorities in the sector as well as to evaluate the capacity of the institutions involved. As a part of this scrutiny, the opportunities for partnerships with the private sector may be explored. These steps are likely to be considered as a part of MTFF or as a part of a development plan. To that extent, priority listings may be drawn from these plans. The determination of the annual outlay is somewhat narrower in focus in that it has to ascertain the actual progress made so that the lags in implementation are taken into account. As an extension, it may be prudent to compile lists of projects and programmes that may be considered for deferral or further scaling down in the context of unforeseen resource shortfalls. The zero-base approach may be used in the event of a severe fiscal crisis. In practice, all the techniques may not be used; rather, a combination of approaches may be adapted.

The success of the review depends on two factors: the quality of information, and the prevailing approaches towards analysis. In most cases, information is generally weak in regard to the expenditure profiles of programmes, as well as in timeliness. (The latter aspect is being addressed through the application of electronic technology.) Decision making is inevitably affected by the information shortages and lags. As for approaches, two types need specific recognition. In several countries, outlays on defence are not subjected to intense scrutiny by the central agencies and greater freedom is permitted to the defence agencies for making internal allotments. In some countries, outlays on running costs are permitted a rate of growth that is in accord with the expected rate of growth of GDP and a detailed analysis is avoided to save time. In all these stages, the endeavour is to arrive at estimates that are reasonably firm while fully reflecting the fiscal strategy. Firm estimates are viewed as hard constraints; if the estimates are viewed as putative, then hard constraints become soft, in the process sending wrong signals to the spending agencies and to the community.

Practices in this area reveal some common problem areas. First, the review takes place in a tight time squeeze with the result that some aspects are either glossed over or are deferred to a more detailed analysis during the fiscal year. The latter approach has the effect of extending the budgetary process to the whole year while conclusively indicating the tentative nature of the budget. Second, procedures may be either suspended or undermined. The review adds a dimension of legitimacy that is not dependent on the economic fortunes of a country. Third, several agencies, particularly those that are perceived to have political clout, may get around the opposition or review by central agencies and prevent further review, and proposals may be included in the estimates without rigorous examination, contributing to potential risks. These aspects merit review.

Processing of the Draft Budget

The draft estimates prepared by each agency are reviewed at the next higher level, for example, a department or a ministry, to ensure conformity with the budget guidelines. These are then further reviewed by the central agencies, such as the civil service commission for personnel, ministries of finance, and planning commissions. These reviews may take quite some time and some of the new initiates as well as ongoing activities may get allocations lower than those proposed. Disagreements between the central agencies and the spending agencies may be resolved at the senior civil services or ministerial levels or may even end up with the cabinet for final resolution. In some countries, the offices of the prime minister or the cabinet may play very active roles and new additions may be proposed by them to the budget. This may be applicable particularly to foreign aided projects.

The draft expenditure estimates may then, in some countries, be discussed either as a part of the total budget package or independently, with the standing committees of the legislature. In some countries (example, Malaysia), broad consultations may be held with the representatives of the corporate sectors, mostly regarding tax issues than about expenditures. Consultations with outside bodies about the specifics of the budget are often governed by the privileges of the legislature and a good deal of secrecy may be attached to the draft expenditure proposals.

Increasingly, however, avenues are being explored to hold discussions with the stakeholders and the stockholders so that the expenditure estimates broadly reflect a consensus.

Organizational Aspects

The unique feature of preparation of budget estimates is that the process brings together the activities of all branches of government to a common wavelength for a brief period. The review and consolidation of expenditure estimates takes place at several points depending on the functional orientation of agencies in a government. Table 9.8 illustrates a general division of work in governments. It is quite likely that personnel budgets are reviewed by the civil service agencies, while public debt and pension estimates may be reviewed or consolidated by the central banks (where these transactions are managed by them)

Table 9.8

Fragmentation of Expenditure Control

Expenditures	Reviewing Agency
Personnel expenditure	Civil service commissions
Public debt	Central bank or ministries of finance
Subsidies	Quasi-governmental commissions
Development expenditure	Planning agencies
Defence	Defence agencies
Construction	Public works agencies
Foreign aid	Departments of economic coordination
Foreign currency outlays	Ministries of finance or central banks
Pension payments	Pension organization
State and local transfers	Departments of local governments

or autonomous organizations. Foreign aid may be coordinated by other agencies and there may be similar arrangements for other spheres.

In the absence of firm budgetary guidance, there is a potential danger that these agencies may work at cross purposes, may not have a uniform approach to expenditure determination or may believe in exercising excessive, repetitive control over the agencies. Avoidance of these aspects is dependent on the quality of information specification of the role and tasks of each agency, and the actual processes of day-to-day working. Areas for review are the coordination between the finance and planning agencies and between the finance and civil service commissions.

Issues

The formulation of the budget is a vast area and, inevitably, a number of problems are experienced by governments. Some of the more common ones are indicated here.

Coordination Issues: From an organizational point, issues of coordination are experienced in regard to revenue and expenditure planning, personnel planning and formulation of budget ceilings, current and investment budgets, and in the management of aid. Experience shows that, in general, revenue planning is undertaken as a separate exercise with inputs into the budget process at the penultimate stage, when it is too late to undertake expenditure adjustments except in broad terms. In several cases, personnel planning and related determination of staff strength for agencies also proceeds as a separate exercise based on work load factors, rather than on resource ceilings. An inevitable consequence is the discrepancy between the level of posts agreed to with the civil service agencies, and the actual level funded in the budget. Moreover, the investment budgets are formulated separately in several countries, and the coordination with the current budget is minimal. As a consequence, attention to the financial requirements of future years, evaluation of budgetary performance, analysis of policy alternatives, computation and budgetary provision for completed development projects, tend to be minimal. In the area of aid management, experience shows that spending agencies bypass the central agencies and engage in direct consultations with donors. In addition, problems are also experienced in the provision of counterpart funds.

Consultations and Hearings: Spending agencies in many countries tend, to take the view that consultations with the central agencies leave a good deal to be desired. It is their perception that adequate budget guidance is not provided, that there is inadequate understanding of the importance of the programmes, that the determination of budgetary allocations is arbitrary, and that too much control is exercised by central agencies in all the phases. As a consequence, spending agencies resort to escape mechanisms such as leasing rather than purchasing, underestimation of financial requirements, earmarking and establishment of extra-budgetary accounts, unbundling approaches to avoid funding ceilings, and ghost employees. The alternatives lie in the improvement of technical areas (discussed earlier) and in strengthening the formal process of consultations with agencies.

Reserves and Special Accounts: In some countries, allotment of general account transactions follows the rates of growth of GDP, while allotments from the budgetary reserves and special accounts become the main issues of negotiation between the central and spending agencies. In some ways, this shifts attention from the main to the side shows largely because the size of the budgetary reserve or special accounts is significant. The alternative consists of formulating an integrated framework covering all the areas.

Underfunding and Performance Aspects: When confronted with resource shortfalls, governments may engage in explicit or implicit underfunding without specifying alternative procedures for service delivery. In the absence of changes in programmes and projects, agencies are confronted with hard choices and may pursue soft constraints, such as incurring arrears in payment, in order to maintain service levels. Underfunding is a false choice, and it is appropriate that attention is paid to high-risk areas throughout the process. Similarly, it is also important to pay explicit attention to performance and to the pursuit of economy and efficiency.

Areas for Review

The adequacy of technical instruments goes a long way in ensuring that appropriate policies and budgets are formulated. Given the importance of the budget, the following areas merit regular reviews.

1. Adequacy of the approaches to the formulation of budgets.

Regardless of whether the approach is top–down or bottom–up, it is essential to ascertain that the resource constraint is internalized and that specific attention is paid to the three important objectives of stability, service delivery, and pursuit of economy.

2. Adequacy of the process in facilitating explicit recognition of the linkages with the major trends and determinants of the economy.

3. Formulation of ceilings: methodology and different areas for which they are determined and their linkages to macroeconomic policies.

4. Adequacy of the guidance provided through the budget circular and the focus on sectoral strategies, high-risk areas, and fall-back management procedures.

5. Technical bases and their adequacy in the formulation of budget estimates.

6. Procedures for review and dialogue with spending agencies.

7. Procedures for processing the budget.

8. Fragmentation of expenditure control and procedures for coordination.

9. Attention to the issues generally experienced in the phase of the budgetary process.

Budget Calendar

The experience of many countries shows that the preparation of the budget may take anywhere from four to sixteen months. The period essentially reflects the time spent in compiling initial estimates by revenue and spending agencies, their review by state, and the printing of documents for submission to the legislature. These procedures are not, however, common to all countries as a good deal depends on the framework and administrative tradition.

As a checklist, an illustrative calendar is provided in Table 9.9. This shows the desirable elements in a calendar and when applied to a country, shows the possible directions for strengthening. For example in countries that are dependent on foreign aid, the framework should provide for adequate consultations with the donors.

Table 9.9
Budget Calendar (an illustration)

Activity	Medium-term Financial Projections	Projections for Next Year	Tentative Ceilings Formulated	Issuance of a Budget Circular	Preparation of Detailed Estimates	Review of New Proposals and Hearings	Draft Budget	Budget
Central agencies								
Revenues and spending agencies								
Internal coordination committees								
Cabinet								
Legislative consultative committees								
Legislature								

Expenditure Control: Nature and Process

Nature

Expenditure control, as a concept and as an administrative framework, has not been free from ambiguity and is, therefore, subject to different interpretations. Essentially, it refers to an administrative process designed to ensure that the overall objectives of government expenditures are achieved. Thus, it includes the formulation of policy, and the subsequent process entrusted with the task of implementing it. That process, in turn, includes verification to ensure that the existing laws are complied with and that there is a framework of financial discipline which is transparent and provides, at a minimum, for financial accountability, so that the public may be assured, in the absence of market tests, that efforts are being made to secure value for money. In a more narrow way, it refers to the process of verification. (In some European languages, for example, French, there is no equivalent to the term control, except as a verification process.) Here the term is defined in a broad way.

Process

Expenditure control, in the broad interpretation, comprises policy controls, process controls, and efficiency controls illustrated earlier.

These stages cover resource allocation, resource utilization, and resource-use accounting. In the allocation phase, it permits the determination of the specific role to be played by governments in arranging public services (who will carry out what), their financing, and specifying organizational responsibilities. In the utilization phase, the task is to provide services (or to arrange to provide services) within specified costs, quality, and time framework. In the last phase, it is to ensure that there is adequate public information (accounts) about the financial transactions. The exercise of these controls is dependent to a very large degree on the portfolio of a government's expenditures.

Implications of Portfolios

The portfolio of expenditures differs from one country to another. (In a federal set-up—as in India, Indonesia, and Malaysia—substantial sections of the budget may involve transfers to other levels of government. In unitary governments too, there could be major transfers to local levels of government but as a share of total outlays could be less than that in the federal types of governments. These transfers may be determined by law, or in several cases, on the basis of formulae devised through political agreements; these may not be revised annually.) Similarly, transfers to autonomous agencies of government, and entitlement programmes to individuals may be governed by laws enacted for the purpose. In these cases where the policies and the underlying controls are determined by law, the scope of expenditure control is somewhat narrow in that its influence on policy is to be internalized at the stage when laws were formulated. During annual operations, expenditure control is, for the most part, limited to the process controls illustrated above.

In regard to the other types of expenditure, for example, direct outlays and subsidies to public and private enterprises, there is greater scope for the system of expenditure control to influence all the four phases. This portfolio illustrates the annual flexibility that a government has, in theory, in manipulating the size and content of outlays. Even that flexibility may be constricted by annual legislation, previous commitments, and the difficulties in going counter to the expectations of the public (Figure 9.5).

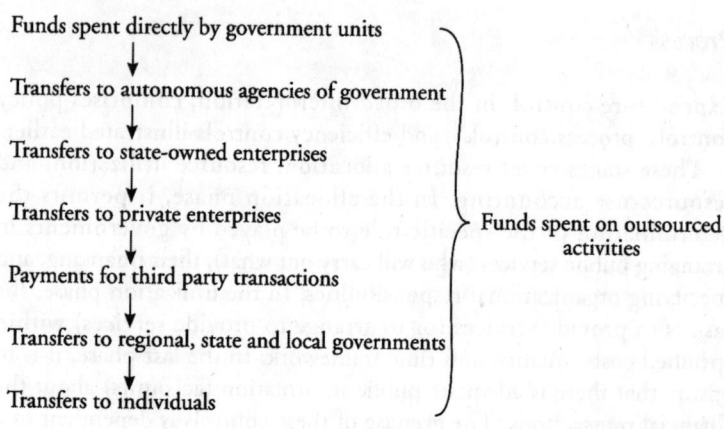

Figure 9.5: Portfolio of Government Expenditures

Public–Private Partnerships

The partnerships between government and the corporate (or private, including voluntary organizations and NGOs) sectors cover a wide area, including the government as a buyer of goods and services, as a funding agency, as a coordinator, and as a regulator. From the point of expenditure control, it is the first two roles, viz. as a buyer and as a funding agency, that are important. As a buyer, governments undertake advance planning (with careful estimates of financial implications) followed by annual or multi-year budgets, determine the conditions for the award of contracts, fund contracts, monitor the implementation of contracts, and evaluate contract performance before the expiry of the warranty. There is, however, a major distinction between the roles, in that it is the government which is the immediate consumer or beneficiary as a buyer, whereas in the case of the latter, services are provided to the public from government funds by agencies that have been contracted for the purpose. These agencies are, to all intents and purposes, outside the government and the only leverage that the government has is through provisions included in the contract. If the services provided by the contractor are not up to the expectations of the public, then the latter would blame the government as it is the funding agency.

The separation of funding from provision of services poses several tricky issues to the government. Its only means of control is the contract. Even so, in several cases, governments or their audit agencies do not have the power to inspect the financial records of the contractors or any other machinery to ensure that the financial management practices of the contractors are in conformity with generally accepted standards. These standards, if any, are set up by the corporate sector which, in most cases, may not be applicable to NGOs. Further, it is often difficult to specify the quality of services (example, child care), or to make alternative arrangements in the event of a failure on the part of a contractor. Expenditure control seeks value for money through competitive bidding but may be less than adequate in ensuring the provision of services where that task is entrusted to non-governmental agencies. It is essential to review the adequacy of the machinery, in particular in the area of risk management, in view of the growing share of outlays on contractually provided services.

Areas for Review

The following areas are candidates for review.

1. Adequacy of budget calendar.
2. Adequacy of expenditure control in policy matters, processes, regulatory tasks and in securing performance and efficiency.
3. Assessment of expenditure portfolio and evaluation of the scope of flexibility.
4. Review of contractual agreements with the corporate sector in the provision of services.

Budget Implementation and Resource Utilization

Implementation and resource utilization is the most important phase as the political fortunes of a government are dependent, amongst others, on the fulfilment of the promises held out in the budget. From a macroeconomic point of view, while it is necessary to have the requisite flexibility to adapt to the changing requirements, the budget outcome should, to a very large extent, be congruent with the intent. Major slippages could contribute to a widening of the size of the deficit and to the generation of inflationary impulses. From the point of service delivery, it is equally essential that services are provided in time and in an efficient manner. Perceptions of waste and imprudent fiscal behaviour are bound to have an adverse impact on the fiscal credibility of governments. These dimensions add more to the importance, indeed the crucial nature, of this phase.

Tasks

Budget implementation is organizationally quite different from the formulation phase, in that unlike the latter, the former involves thousands of decision-making centres, and actions by numerous officials that need to be synchronized if service delivery schedules are to be met. Thus the first task is to convert the budget into meaningful decision packages and administrative processes. In most civic societies, these tasks have to be undertaken in a transparent way to meet the oversight requirements of the legislature and the public. The tasks may be undertaken, each in its own way, by the central (in particular, the ministries of finance) and spending agencies. The underlying core or substance is however identical in that the purpose is to ensure prudent budget implementation. These tasks are illustrated in Table 9.10.

Table 9.10
Budget Execution—Role of Ministry of Finance and Spending Agencies

Category	Ministry of Finance	Spending Agencies
Policy controls	• Oversight on flow of expenditure • Management of cash • Revision of policies where needed • Diversion of funds to needy areas • Assessment of supplementary budget needs	• Plans for regular flow of expenditures and implementation of programmes and projects • Revision of policies • Analysis of variations • Assessment of additional needs • Diversion of funds to needy areas
Process controls	• Release of funds on a time slice basis • Oversight on payments to and from government where these are centralized • Oversight on total and asset management • Matching of resources with additional demands	• Release of funds • Making arrangements for contracts • Making commitments • Verification of documents and arrangement of payments • Arrangements for hiring of personnel • Procurement and construction arrangements • Contingent liability management

(Contd.)

(Table 9.10 Contd.)

		• Asset and liability management • Internal evaluation • Matching financial and physical progress • Compilation of periodic accounts • Avoidance of shortfalls and excess and rush of expenditures toward the end the year • Timely surrender of funds or processing requests for more funds
Regulatory tasks	• Promulgation of uniform accounting standards • Specification of competitive bidding and tendering procedures • Promotion of competition in the economy and diversification of service providers • Oversight on the functioning of internal control systems	• Oversight on the contracting systems of subordinate agencies • Oversight on internal control systems in agencies
Efficiency controls	• Specification of performance standards • Standards for economy in expenditures	• Regular monitoring and observance of performance goals • Detailed specification of economy measures
Transparency	• Specification of transparency standards	• Observance of transparency standards
Accountability	• Regular review of accountability channels • Ensuring that regular evaluations are carried out	• Observance of accountability specification • Periodic internal evaluation

The role of policy controls during budget execution needs to be noted here (other aspects are discussed, in detail, further on). In a number of countries (example, the Commonwealth countries), proposals and policy initiatives may be included in the budget on the condition that they will be considered in more detail after the approval of the budget and during the fiscal year. To ensure legislative approval (approval in principle) a token grant may be provided in the estimates. Where the size of the token grants is small, the impact on the budget may be minimal. But where these 'prior approval' cases are large, they tend to have the effect of prolonging the budgetary process into the following year with probable adverse consequences on the policy stances. This aspect needs a detailed review in evaluating the adequacy of the budget system.

The implementation process involves the pursuit of two tracks at the same time. The concern of the spending agencies is to complete the administrative actions needed to secure finances provided for in the budget. The concern of the central agencies is to ensure that there is adequate and timely provision of funds, to enable the spending agencies to conduct their operations in a smooth way. Thus, these two tracks have to be conducted concurrently.

Release of Budgetary Authority and Commitment Management

The first step in budget implementation is to have an orderly and time-sliced release of budgetary authority. The need for funds is not uniform throughout the fiscal year and there is considerable seasonality in both revenue and expenditure flows. Thus, spending agencies may prepare advance plans at the beginning of the fiscal year, showing their requirements by each month or quarter and submit them to the central agencies. The practices in this regard vary from one country to another. Broadly, two types of practices are evident. First, in some countries, spending agencies have the freedom to spend the amounts soon after the appropriation process is completed by the legislature. In some cases, warrants may need to be issued by the ministry of finance but these may be conducted more as a formality than as a substantive control. Thus, the warrants needed for the whole year may be issued in a single bunch. Second, in some countries (including the former centrally planned economies), spending agencies prepare advance action plans indicating the budgetary requirements for each month/quarter, which are then reviewed and approved by the central agencies. In the first type, spending agencies have greater freedom, while in the second type, they are subjected to continued control by the central agencies. The release by the central agencies may take two forms—release of budgetary authority, that is, power to commit and spend; and release of budgetary authority and the requisite funds to the agency. In the latter case, the funds would be at the disposal of the agency, in a liquid form.

In general, with growing emphasis on ensuring organized cash management, it is believed to be preferable to have a quarterly system of release of budgetary authority (apportionment) that reflects, on the one hand, the seasonality of requirements, and on the other, seasonality of receipt inflows.

The first step, from the point of view of spending agencies, is to place orders for the goods and services that they require in order to provide services. When these orders are firm, they are considered commitments—a sort of explicit contractual understanding to honour the consequential financial implications. For the most part, particularly with continuing expenditures, these commitments are of a continuing type. Thus salaries (to a very substantial extent), utility payments, entitlements, legally specified transfers, and interest repayment of debt belong to this category. With regard to new major purchases, implementation of new turnkey projects, and similar capital projects, commitments may be needed afresh. These commitments may be entered into by the spending agencies in decentralized management systems, while in centrally managed systems, they might need prior approvals by the ministries of finance which would then also engage in the verification of documentation at a later stage but prior to payment, and finally in the payment itself.

These commitments, once formalized, are taken into account in the time-sliced release of budgetary authority. In countries that are extensively dependent on foreign aid, the releases may be made by the planning ministries separately from the releases made for current expenditures. In several cases, they are issued on an ad hoc basis and reveal no specific periodicity.

Within the above framework, at least three types of common problems are discernible. First, the need for spending agencies to refer the matter to the central agencies to obtain approval of commitment has proved to be a contentious issue. It is argued, from the viewpoint of spending agencies, that during periods of fiscal squeeze, expenditures have been pared to the minimal levels and that most of them relate to continuing activities which would have been scrutinized several times. As such, a fresh consideration is at best a new wrinkle, and an irritation without any substantial effect. The central agencies aver that in the context of budget fragility, utmost care should be taken to review matters. This is an area where there may be scope for additional delegation of financial powers; and spending agencies may be made more responsible for entering into commitments within specified limits. Further, if there is an electronic recording and reporting system permitting instant access to information, the central agencies would have the opportunity to be aware of new commitments. Second, the spending agencies that are the ones with the task of providing government services seek continuity and certainty in the release of funds. In cash-strapped countries, where significant revenue shortfalls are experienced, the releases may be made on a monthly basis, and in some cases, even on a daily basis. In these countries, an important task for the finance ministries is to monitor inflows daily and regulate outflows within the magnitude of revenues received. The result is often chaotic and frequently there is a pile-up in the arrears. In addition, continuous underfunding implies that a budget different from the one approved is being implemented. This changes the very tone of financial management whose main purpose is to achieve a smooth implementation of the budget. And third, in some countries where the release of budgetary authority is accompanied by the actual release of cash, the procedure implies that there are, in the short term, cash surpluses with the spending agencies, which some (particularly at the local level) may even reinvest in government paper to make money. In turn, this leads to an anomalous situation in that the government may be facing deficits while its units are cash-rich. Notwithstanding all the care taken in the formulation of time–slices, the large-scale rush of expenditures towards the end of the fiscal year experienced in some countries, and the carry-over permitted in some countries (to carry forward unspent amounts at the end of the fiscal year) illustrate that the administration of the system leaves a good deal to be desired. These aspects merit a more in-depth review.

Contract Management

Increasingly, as greater reliance is placed on contracting out services (see earlier discussion on separation of funding from provision), in addition to the conventional procurement of goods and services for internal consumption, contract management has become an important area in expenditure management. The objectives of the government in this phase are essentially to secure cost savings through promotion of competitive forces, and to ensure that there is proper delivery of services. To secure these objectives, governments engage in a good deal of pre-tender activity and in the review of bids. The pre-tender activity includes the determination of the relationship between the proposed contract and organizational goals, timing of the supply, and an analysis of the financial implications. This is followed by the coordination of tenders, issue of tenders, review of received tenders, and the final award of the contract. These activities, which are considered to be specialized in nature, may be undertaken either by separate organizations (central tender boards) or through decentralized arrangements. In selected cases of foreign aid, donors may also be co-opted before determining the final award of the contract.

From an expenditure control point of view, the most important considerations are the prices paid, and the quality of the service provided. Contracts may have a fixed-price, or cost-plus-fixed-fee basis, or a combination of these two features with an incentive provision. In a cost-plus-fixed-fee contract, the contractor may have little incentive to procure economies or efficiency. In general, experience shows that the final cost is a multiple of the initial estimate, reflecting in part the frequent changes made in project design. Further, in regard to the services provided, there are very few cost standards either insisted upon or provided. It is also the experience that little attention is paid in government to costs of procurement, costs of shortage, process costs, and holding (or inventory maintenance) costs. Moreover, when procurement is made either through other governmental agencies or through public enterprises, the procedures may be less rigorous, and frequently there may be no competitive bidding at all. In regard to activities and services organized by the NGOs, particularly in the social sector, the specification of quality is often too general to hold anyone accountable for failure in service provision. All these aspects require review with a view to strengthening the expenditure management processes.

Cash Management

Cash management in governments or in the commercial sector has the major objective of reducing the costs of money or cash being used in the entity without adversely affecting the scale of its activities or exposing the entity to risks in meeting its obligations. Underlying this practice is the recognition that money has alternative uses and shall not be left in a liquid state without earning its dues. Reinforcing this approach, the legislatures in some countries introduced a system of exchequer control (establishment of an authority that would work on behalf of the legislature and issue periodic warrants to implement the budget) or the appropriations were so devised legally as to indicate the ceilings that were to be adhered to during the year.

Cash management has acquired additional importance during recent years in the context of stabilization programmes that have either evolved on the own initiatives of governments or as a part of the agreements reached with international organizations. Cash management is undertaken with a view to ensuring a smooth implementation (to the extent possible) of the budget while avoiding uneconomic transactions stemming from immobilization of resources and borrowing more resources than needed. It arises to meet the seasonality in the collection of revenues and in expenditure outflows. In countries that have surplus budgets, it is intended to facilitate the utilization of surpluses so that the maximum return may be obtained. Cash management involves two contrary elements, viz., acceleration in revenue collections and moderating the disbursement of funds, without adversely affecting the scale of operations of agencies. Further, it is intended to formulate a common framework with reference to which the central bank, where it is involved, may prepare its plans for ensuring sufficient liquidity in the economy. Cash management is not a substitute for a budget nor is it intended to be an instrument to arbitrarily reduce budgetary outlays, in the name of pursuit of macroeconomic stability.

In practice, cash management recognizes that there may be lags in the receipt of revenues. In particular, three types of floats are commonly noticed. Revenue collection agencies may reveal a processing float in that a lag is experienced in depositing the taxes paid by the public. In some cases, a mail-float may be experienced indicating the lag between the mailing of a cheque and its receipt and inclusion in the consolidated funds of the government and, finally, a clearing float may be experienced, revealing the time taken in the cheque clearing system. In addition, government agencies may have short-term cash deposits in the banking system pending payment for commitments already entered into. In this context, governments may be borrowing even when they have resources available internally.

Cash management involves a cooperative working partnership between the central and spending agencies. The latter (which admittedly do not have information on the seasonality of revenues) have a better understanding of the seasonality in expenditure flows and of the lumpiness in payments. As a first step, therefore, agencies prepare draft plans indicating cash requirements for meeting their expenditure needs. These are then assessed in the light of revenue availability, and borrowing capacity and ceilings are communicated to the agencies within which they are required to manage their finances. These ceilings ensure that there is government-wide observance of fiscal discipline, which may be further reinforced when banks also observe these ceilings. In formulating the ceilings, the entire gamut of transactions of government are considered excluding non-cash transactions that arise from foreign aid and intra-government transactions. If the gap between the resource needs and availability is too large, governments have the option to either accelerate revenue collections, reimburse pending foreign aid collections, or to provisionally defer some expenditures. Arrears reflect a failure of budget implementation and should not be resorted to. The adequacy of existing procedures of cash management should be periodically reviewed to ensure that they are serving the purposes for which they were originally designed.

Payment System and Arrears

Traditionally, the payments made to the government and by it were conducted by a treasury that was also a part of the ministries of finance or their equivalents during periods of monarchy. The primary emphasis during those periods was the safe custody of money and good bookkeeping so that the King's wealth was not subjected to pilferage and defalcation. With the emergence of democratic forms of government, the same form continued and reliance of the treasury system was considered necessary in the absence of a banking system with branches in rural areas. With the gradual growth of the banking system, however, the importance of the treasury system came to be reduced.

In general, however, the experience of many countries, including industrial countries, shows two distinct approaches towards payment, which for purposes of convenience may be termed as centralized and decentralized. In the centralized system (such as in France), all commitments made by agencies are subject to prior approval by the treasury. Later, the documents relating to payment are reviewed by them and arrangements made for payment through cash or cheque. Detailed accounts are compiled by the agencies, but the treasury has direct up-to-date knowledge of the cash flows. Even after computerization, these procedures continue, largely because of the mainframe operations, which were located in the ministries of finance. In the decentralized systems (for example, UK, Sweden) there is a sliced release of budget authority within which agencies have the power to make commitments, to spend the money, and to account for it as well as be accountable for the total management of finances of the agency to the legislative oversight bodies. The underlying approach is that a central agency cannot keep an oversight on all transactions and that this responsibility is best left to the agencies so that a conducive and responsible behaviour is promoted for heightened financial conscience in the agencies.

The need for a centralized treasury system came to be considered again during the 1990s in the context of modernizing the financial management systems in the former centrally planned countries. Some countries in this bloc installed a treasury system under which the existing functions of the ministry of finance were separated and established as a treasury to facilitate budget implementation. The framework of relations between the finance ministry and the agencies in some of these republics is illustrated in Table 9.11. It shows that there are adequate safeguards for the ministry of finance to ensure prudent fiscal behaviour by the agencies. The treasury system contributed to a consolidation of all accounts into a single account and, in several cases, became an agency for verification. But because of the increased network, it contributed to greater expenses, without commensurate benefits. Arguably, it also contributed to avoidable centralization.

In the context of application of computer technology, substantial sections of payments are conducted through centralized and decentralized methods. In several cases, payrolls are organized on a centralized basis (although big agencies have their own payrolls), and pensions and public debt payments are also centralized while all other

Table 9.11

Nexus between Ministry of Finance and Spending Agencies

Area	Ministry of Finance	Spending Agency	Central Bank
Time-sliced release of budget authority	X		
Commitment		X	
Pre-commitment approval	X		
Preparation of payment schedule		X	
Approval of payment schedule	X		
Release of money supporting payment schedule	X		
Issue of cheques or payment of cash		X	
Recording of primary transactions		X	
Delivery of services		X	
Daily balance sheet (aggregate)			X
Monthly reports		X	
Review of next quarter needs	X		

payments are made by agencies or by a centralized treasury. The importance of the treasury as a focal point has, however, been reduced with an independent computerized system of payments and simultaneous access to information.

The second aspect of payments relates to the instruments of payments. The traditional payment of cash continues to be the most dominant form in most countries, followed by cheques (or payment authority) and electronic transfers. Experience shows that the processing of cash payments is labour-intensive and expensive while electronic payments are quick and less expensive, and facilitate a quick compilation of accounts. More significantly, necessary investment may be made by the corporate banking sector than by the government. Increasingly, more governments are moving to electronic payments, as it is economical.

The third aspect of payments relates to arrangements with the banking system. In most cases, these arrangements are made with the central bank or with commercial banks (some of them owned by the government). Some arrangements may not always be transparent and in several cases, short-term advances may be made by the banking system routinely without charges. (On the other hand, government deposits may not also receive interest.) In view of the proposed independence of the central bank, the relationships between the government and the banking system should be reviewed and made more transparent while extending the market discipline to government transactions.

Payment controls have in recent years also contributed to the accumulation of arrears in payment. Many governments faced by resource shortages do not honour their own pledges to pay, inevitably contributing to arrears. When arrears are anticipated, the vendor internalizes them and includes them in the prices quoted. More importantly, arrears represent an involuntary, zero-rate lending by the public to the government. As a control, arrears reflect a failure of the system and are, therefore, best avoided. But where they arise and are accumulated, it is important to have complete data on the age profile of arrears and to formulate a strategy for their clearance and for avoiding their recurrence.

It is, therefore, important to review the existing payment arrangements, the instruments of payment, the arrangements with the banking system and the arrears, and to explore the alternatives, including the progressive application of computer technology.

Financial Reporting

Financial reporting has several facets and different end uses. For purposes of expenditure management, end users comprise two distinct groups—internal and external. The internal group, in turn, comprises spending or administrative agencies, central agencies, for example, ministries of finance and planning ministries. The external group comprises the legislature, the public, and the IFIs as well as donors. Although the end-use intent in each case is different, the source of information needed by all is the same, viz., accounting system. From an organizational point of view, it is necessary to review as to how the basic data are compiled, the frequency with which they are compiled, and the coverage of the material.

From the point of view of agencies, their primary interests lie in ascertaining the current budgetary status—the extent to which budgetary authority has been committed, authority available for new commitments, and payments that remain to be made. These data may be maintained either by a central agency responsible for compiling accounts or in a decentralized system by the agencies themselves. In the former case, experience shows that there may be long lags in the compilation of data and to that extent the immediate needs of monitoring may not be met by the system. In such cases, reliance may be placed on daily data furnished by the central bank. Such data are too aggregative in nature and may not be of much use to the spending agencies, although they illustrate the overall financial status for the central agencies. The spending agencies have an intent in ascertaining the physical progress, or issues in the delivery of services, in areas which are of strategic importance to them. Toward this purpose many agencies have set up, to reflect their interests, management information system. In countries where EDP systems have been introduced, financial information, including the analysis of budgetary variations, has become routine and any standard off-the-shelf software can provide such data.

The interests of the central agencies could be more generic. For example, the ministry of finance would be interested in monitoring the broad trends in budget implementation, in the levels of borrowing, and in the flexibility needed for the remainder of the fiscal year. The needs of planning agencies could be both macro and micro in nature. From a macro angle, their interests would be to ascertain the progress made in the implementation of the development plan and from a micro point, the status of key projects that would have a vital impact on the overall out-turn.

The external users include the legislature, the public, and the IFIs. In some countries, depending on the legal provisions, periodic data are submitted to the legislatures. In countries that are dependent on borrowing, monthly information is published, including by the central banks, on government finances. In countries that are more technologically oriented, governments provide data on an up-to-date basis. Many countries also observe international standards in the dissemination of financial information and to that extent considerable progress has been made in making government finances more transparent.

Notwithstanding the rapid progress, four aspects remain to be addressed. First, in several countries, data on foreign aid reveal problems of coverage, valuation, and timeliness. Second, data on finances during the intra-year period may reveal a trend that may not be sustained through the year as year-end adjustments (which tend to be massive in some countries) may change the picture. These factors underline the importance of reviewing financial information with caution. Third, most of the data are on a cash basis and to that extent provide only a partial picture, as liabilities are excluded. To address this issue, some countries (for example, New Zealand) have taken to accrual accounting and to the publication of balance sheets at six-monthly intervals. Fourth, the information published is addressed mostly to the investing public, than to the general public, whose interests may be less financial and more related to the delivery of services and expenditure benefits.

Budget Revision

Although the intent is to secure congruence between budget intent and outcome, it is also necessary to endow the system with a degree of flexibility as rigidity could contribute to a triumph of process over purpose. Towards this end, three techniques are utilized. These are virement or re-appropriation, supplementary or mini-budgets, and surrender of savings or provision for carryovers.

Virement is essentially intended to empower spending agencies, within overall budgetary limits, to shift proposed outlays from low-priority to high-priority areas. In some cases, these powers may be administered by the agencies while in a few cases, prior consultation with central agencies may be required. The intent in placing limits on this technique is to minimize departures from the purposes approved by the legislature.

The movements in the economy may not always adhere to the predicted paths. Growth rates of GDP may be lower than those forecast and inflation rates may be higher than anticipated. Besides, policy changes may be needed. All of these, in turn, necessitate changes in the budget. For this purpose, supplementary budgets seeking additional allocations may be proposed. In countries that follow Commonwealth traditions, supplementary budgets may be submitted to the legislatures thrice a year (the timetables of the legislatures provide for this). In some cases, where more fundamental changes are indicated, mini, mid-term budgets may be prepared. In general, however, a greater reliance on supplementary budgets sends wrong signals on the viability and credibility of the annual budget.

Experience also shows that vast amounts may remain unspent at the end of the fiscal year. As underspending in one year, according to the perceptions of spending agencies, may lead to reduced allocations in future years, efforts may be made to engage in spree spending on low-priority areas. To avoid this and to promote orderly management, some countries have permitted selective carryovers to future years. This could, in principle, contribute to the implementation of parallel budgets—one for the current year and another comprising carryovers from previous years.

In evaluating the need for revisions, it is essential to distinguish between policy changes and changes in assumptions about national aggregates and technical factors.

Performance Orientation

During recent years, there has been a growing recognition of the need to balance the emphasis of control by shifting somewhat from compliance to rules to improved productivity, performance, and effectiveness. Towards this end, forms of performance budgeting were tried in various countries (for example, Australia, India, Malaysia, the Philippines, and Sri Lanka). Performance-oriented budgets have some common ingredients.

1. Performance objectives—a statement of measurable objectives that are proposed to be achieved with the annual budget outlays.
2. A performance-oriented classification that seeks to link proposed objectives with the transactions of the agency.

3. A set of performance measures or indicators to show how the objectives have been achieved. Measures are deemed to be the quantitative expressions of outputs or results, while indicators are proxies for outputs or results. Indicators are usually provided where there are substantial difficulties in the measurement of outputs.
4. A system of performance-oriented reporting that goes beyond the financial reports and covers the distinctive features of the activities.
5. A system of performance-oriented audit.

The system, which has been evolving over the years, seeks to provide a window of opportunity to indicate efficiency through three approaches: (i) target vs actual, where the targets are associated with the objectives sought to be achieved; (ii) historical series of data on performance, selective data such as cost or workload factors may be presented to illustrate the progress made by the agency; and (iii) through appropriate benchmarking with comparable activities in the corporate or other sectors. Through these measures, the system serves to provide a framework for a possible performance-based contract between the agency and the legislature or the public.

Performance-based budgets pose their own quota of problems. Government services being somewhat unique may not lend themselves to easy measurement. Some measures, such as costs, require several changes in the supporting infrastructure. Further, performance-oriented budgets contribute to supply-driven expenditures in that once a bridge or a norm is established between desired objectives, provision of complementary financial resources becomes obligatory. Its particular appeal lies in shifting the emphasis from inputs to results and in providing links to the delivery of services. Where such services are provided by contractors, it provides an improved empirical basis to link outlays with results.

The introduction of variants of this approach, despite inherent appeal, has not made much headway, and where implemented, such approaches have not replaced the traditional system. At the same time, there is a recognition that this dimension is too important to be ignored, particularly in a context where making public organizations more efficient has become an imperative, not an option, of the times. The progress made in this regard needs an in-depth review.

Pursuit of Economy

Budgetary practice makes a distinction between economy and efficiency, the former reflecting a more economical use of given resources and the latter concerned with greater than scheduled achievement using the given resources. Both these firmly belong to the managerial realm during the phase of budget implementation.

In envisaging economy and efficiency, a goal that is shared without any qualifications by all, three factors need to be explicitly considered: (i) the nature of economies, (ii) the mechanism for securing them, and (iii) the incentive structure for the agencies to pursue them. In many cases, economies tend to be ad hoc with minimal life duration. The annual calls for reducing utility consumption, purchase of office equipment, and deferral of salary increments belong to this type. Economies, to the extent secured, have at best, a contribution for that fiscal year and tend to catch up in later years. Real economies should be more durable and should seek improved or alternative ways of service delivery at a lower cost. The second type requires a mechanism, such as evaluation. Evaluation seeks to improve agency and programme effectiveness through a review of the rationale of programmes, identification of the strengths and weaknesses and deriving lessons for improvement. In order to be effective, there should be links between the budgetary process and evaluation. An advance programme of evaluation, reflecting the priorities and high-risk areas of the budget, needs to be formulated annually. A separate organization for the purpose may add to the objectivity; if undertaken by agencies, the technique may be used to support their own agendas than to secure an optimal mix of programmes and activities.

The agencies may have little incentive to seek economies if such efforts lead to reduced future budget allocations. In some countries, for example Australia, agencies are permitted to retain half of the moneys saved (to be utilized on agreed projects). Similar incentives may be needed to make the search for economies a regular budgetary mechanism.

Areas for Review

1. Contract management: centralized or decentralized; management of controls: service delivery.
2. Cash management; adequacy and its contribution to total budget management.
3. Relative roles of policy, process, regulatory and efficiency controls in the process, and the balance in emphasis.

4. Delineation of tasks between central and spending agencies and their implications for centralization and decentralization.
5. Adequacy of procedures for time-sliced release of budget authority and monitoring of commitments.
6. Payment systems; authority for issue of cheques; use of different instruments; application of technology; accumulation of arrears and their implications.
7. Financial reporting; forms, content, bases and periodicity and end use.
8. Budget revision; procedures and their impact.
9. Performance orientation; current practices and future plans.
10. Pursuit of economy; present practices and plans for improvement.

Project Implementation and Expenditure Control

From an expenditure management point of view, there are three distinct phases in the implementation of projects. Apart from the pre-budget stage and associated appraisal, annual expenditure management involves the link of public investment plans with the medium-term plans, payments for the work completed and their implications for cost controls, and where relevant, for foreign aid, and reaping benefits from projects. To facilitate these tasks, many governments have compiled detailed project profiles and specification of milestones for completion. In the payment phase, an important distinction is discernible from other payments. For the bulk of non-project payments, the task of verification of documentation is part of the responsibilities of the accounting staff. For projects, all payments are subject to a detailed review, (prior to payment) by the engineering staff and the role of the accounting staff is relatively minor.

MTEF and PIP: Role of Spending Agencies

As noted previously, some governments have been engaged, during recent years, in the preparation of MTEF and medium-term public investment plans (PIPs) as well as annual plans. The experience in this regard provides, as yet, a mixed picture revealing the need for considerable progress to be made. In several cases, spending agencies do not appear to have the capacity to undertake these plans. In some cases, the approach continues to be one of compiling shopping lists uninfluenced by the resource picture with the result that the annual review becomes a long and contentious process. To that extent, the procedural conveniences of instruments such as the MTEF are not fully exploited in practice. Moreover, the political forces and the need for inclusion of projects to gain benefits of visibility appear to dominate the technical and financial considerations.

Cost Management

The role of expenditure management is significant in the course of project implementation and experience shows that in this area also it has been a major failure. In several cases, the completed cost is vastly different from the estimated or contracted cost, largely due to initial underestimation, frequent design changes, incorrect assumptions on technical matters such as exchange rate and prolonged delays in implementation. Delays are partly due to administrative reasons and partly due to financial factors. Experience shows that in some countries, delays are extensive in the procurement of sites for construction. To minimize this impact, some governments have been trying to include projects in budgets only after sites have been acquired. In other cases, routine underfunding of projects has contributed to further delays. It appears more prudent to make estimates of completed costs that are more realistic. The accounting system should shift its emphasis from routine compliance of rules to the management of costs. Revisions of costs make cost recovery a more difficult exercise.

Pace of Aid Utilization and Implications

Most projects as defined by governments, are funded by donors or from loans obtained from IFIs. Here again, experience shows that the pace of utilization, reflecting the general pattern, is remarkably lower than that forecast. Such slow utilization has a different, and frequently costly, impact on the finances of a country. Most loans have commitment charges that have to be paid even if the funds are not utilized. Such payments to the donors and IFIs could, in some years, be higher than the aggregate inflows from these sources, contributing to an overall negative flow. The slow utilization could be the result of both administrative and financial factors (already described). An overall negative flow does not help the political situation and progress an adverse image of the expenditure management system.

Contract Management

Implementation of projects involves regular contact with contractors and monitoring of their activities. Experience shows that there is a major difference in the approaches of the contractee and the contractor. The contractee has to keep, in view of the enormous implications, one eye on the aggregate fiscal picture; the contractor is, however, more narrow in his perspective in that the task for him is to complete the job at hand and move on to other jobs, and to that extent may follow a divergent path in spending than the ceiling-constricted approaches of governments. In turn, this requires calculation of cash ceilings (where indicated) with one eye on the aggregate picture and the other on the links with the physical stages of project work. This is a complex task, and if not performed effectively, it can contribute to arrears in payment.

Areas for Review

1. The capacity and approaches of spending agencies for integrating annual plans with medium-term rolling forecasts.
2. Cost systems and identification of factors (and their controllability) contributing to cost overruns.
3. Foreign-aided projects and measures that can contribute to enhanced pace of utilization.
4. Relationships with contractors so that there is an improved understanding in the determination of cash ceilings

Management of Fiscal Crisis

Fiscal crisis can be a medium-term or a short-term issue that arises during a fiscal year. The reference here is to the latter. Several issues reflecting the developments in the economy arise during the implementation of the budget in a fiscal year. These developments, to the extent not anticipated, could involve changes in the directions of budgetary policy and a budget outcome different from the intent. The economy could experience sudden and severe shortfalls in revenues; or in countries dependent on foreign aid, changes in the plans of donors might in turn require substantial changes in the budget. How are these crises managed? What has been the response of the expenditure management machinery in dealing with this type of fiscal crisis? What are the lessons to be learnt from the experience?

Measures Taken

Experience shows that governments take a range of actions aimed at containing fiscal crisis. The underlying rationale behind these efforts is to ensure, as far as possible, that the size of the budget deficit has not widened as a result of revenue shortfalls. Broadly, the following measures are taken to limit expenditures or to reduce them to reflect the changing revenue resources during the year: (i) as a short-term economy measure, unfilled personnel positions may be deferred, held in abeyance, or even abolished; (ii) in several cases, limits are also placed on some elements of running costs—utility consumption, foreign travel; (iii) frequently, across-the-board cuts are imposed on all budgetary activities in the form of percentage reductions from the approved appropriations; (iv) major capital projects, which have not yet made significant progress, may be deferred; (v) during recent years, distinctions have come to be made between essential or core and non-core expenditures, and budgetary payments may be limited to essentials such as wages, debt payments, and other selected categories of expenditures; and (vi) in several cases, substantial payment arrears may be incurred.

Programme Effectiveness

The above approaches reveal several problem areas that have a vital impact on the credibility and effectiveness of the proposed programmes. These issues have their roots in the systemic aspects of expenditure management. First, experience shows that the approaches to crisis management suffer from severe handicaps. There is little anticipation of the impending crisis and consequently little preparation in the formulation of the contingent programmes. The delays in the identification of the problems contribute to delays in policy formulation and there is, in general, little consultation with the spending agencies. Second, most reductions sought have become, in several cases, hardy perennials (for example, continuing exhortations to reduce personnel and other outlays) with the result that the spending agencies seek to provide slack in their budget estimates to overcome the short-term reductions. Third, most measures are aimed at object categories without an assessment of the expenditure profiles of programmes or their impact on programmes. The result is that the delivery of services is severely affected while full payments are being made for wages. Fourth, the accumulation of payment arrears has severely eroded the credibility of governments. And fifth, in countries with complex legal provisions, limiting or reducing approved budget estimates requires prior legislative approval, and this has often been a tortuous exercise. Overall, the working of the machinery shows that there is little anticipation and when a crisis occurs, the policy package is ineffective.

Risk Management

Given the mutual reinforcing mechanisms between the budget and the economy and in view of the inherent vulnerabilities of the economy, it is prudent, as the recent experience of some governments shows, that efforts are made to install risk management as a feature of the expenditure management machinery. Risk management involves the recognition, and consequent preparedness, to deal with three types of risks—macroeconomic, programme, and financial. Macroeconomic risks deal with the major vulnerabilities of the budget and how they may be addressed. This, in turn, could involve the establishment of notional contingency reserves that could be invoked in the event of unexpected slack or changes in the exchange rate. In the event of a major resource shortfall, this could imply the formulation of policy packages aimed at containing or reducing outlays in terms of programmes in the light of full assessment of the impact of proposed reductions in outlays on delivery of services. These efforts have to be made both at the level of administrative agencies and the central agencies, and in planning for risks, the known, presumed, and as yet not fully known factors have to be taken into account and internalized at the programme level. Financial risks are associated with the acquisition and management of financial assets and contingent liabilities. As a part of this approach, the factors affecting the provision for loans, and contingent risks stemming from guarantees have to be considered and alternatives explored. These approaches have the potential of substantially augmenting the capacity of governments to face mid-year fiscal crisis.

Areas for Review

1. Availability of information to anticipate fiscal crisis.
2. Process of formulating action packages and a review of their adequacy.
3. Consultation between central and spending agencies in the above process.

4. Procedures for identifying and dealing with macroeconomic programme, and financial risks.

Resource Use Accounting

Although accounting is considered by many to be a single and unified field, in practice, government accounting has developed over the years, as a separate field. It has gone through a good deal of evolution, and it is safe to assert that it is still evolving in several countries. The crucial issue today is whether governments should move over to accrual accounting. The discussion here relates to the other aspects of accounting which are summarized in Table 9.12.

Table 9.12

Resource-use Accounting

Purposes	Features	End Users
To serve as a window on government finances	• Single entry/double entry • Cash/accrual system • Comprehensive coverage • Budget classification • Links with national income accounts • Links with performance reports	Internal • Budget management • Pursuit of economy and efficiency External • Status of assets and liabilities
To aid budget management	• Analysis of variations in budget appropriations • Measurement of costs • Develop activity-based costing	• Spending agencies • Central agencies • Legislative oversight bodies
To provide standards on the data reported	• Specification of accounting standards • Guidance on inflation adjustments.	• Ensuring the quality of information which will also aid decision making
To be effective organizationally	• Centralized/decentralized working • Manual/electronic	• Orientation is different in centralized systems • Advances in electronic technology have reduced operational costs

Features

Government accounting continues, in several cases, to be based on single-entry bookkeeping method, and is cash oriented. The primary purpose of accounting is to record the budget transactions as they take place and to compile appropriation accounts that are rendered to the audit agency for its scrutiny. To a large extent, therefore, the classification followed is mostly identical to the budget system. Through a systematic compilation of data, it enables budget management at each and every stage. It also assists in the compilation of National Income Accounts. Until recently, there were few efforts to develop costing except in regard to major projects, but owing to the imperatives of the fiscal situation, attempts are being made to develop costing methods, either as an integral part of the accounting system or on a supplementary basis.

Issues and Areas for Review

Although in principle the system should function effectively because of its simple design, yet in practice several common issues are explained. First, organizationally, it is found that the compilation of accounts takes a long time and there are inordinate delays in the submission of intra-year and year-end accounts. As a consequence, decisions that are to be made are rendered difficult and the implementation of the budget suffers as a consequence. In part, this may be due to the centralization of accounts in a single organization, set apart from the spending agencies. It is argued that separation of accounting from the spending agencies has contributed to a reduced financial consciousness in the agencies. In part, the year-end accounts may be delayed due to the extended complementary or liquidation periods. Second, government accounts lack, for the most part, standards that specify the treatment of the items, and that are in accord with the generally accepted accounting principles (GAAP). As a result, in analysing historical series, considerable attention has to be paid to the inflation factors. Third, the links with performance reports, where available, remain tenuous, and activity-based costing remains a distant and elusive goal. Fourth, the final accounts may be too brief or too summarized to be of much use to the spending agencies or to the public at large. Because of the continuing cash orientation and lack of inflation adjustment, the picture of assets and liabilities can be incomplete and misleading.

To address many of the above issues, vigorous efforts are being made to investment in the application of electronic technology and to that extent, a transition is being experienced in several countries. In order to assess the current status and the future directions of government accounting, the following areas need to be reviewed.

1. Current status of the basis and where it is cash, efforts made to complement it with elements of accrual accounting.
2. Compilation of detailed accounts to assist in budget monitoring, efforts made to install costing methods.
3. Efforts being made to develop accounting standards.
4. Organizational factors contributing to delays in the compilation of accounts.

Internal Audit and Evaluation

Distinctions

Internal audit and evaluation reflect, in some measure, the concluding stages of expenditure management within the executive. The former is intended to ensure compliance with the relevant laws. It consists of a systematic review of all operations of an agency so that the interrelationships between inputs, activities, and outputs can be looked at afresh and the agency management advised about the findings. It is generally organized as a part of the office of the head of the agency and its role is a concurrent one, in that it undertakes reviews even as the activities are being undertaken. Internal audit is interpreted in some quarters in a narrower way as consisting of verification of vouchers before payment. This routine function is sustained in the payment process discussed earlier. In this section, internal audit is interpreted in its broad connotation.

Evaluation, unlike internal audit, is done mostly at the conclusion of a programme or a project and is more concerned with the impact of resources used and the benefits generated. It seeks to provide useful data to the management, on securing an approach that has the potential to improved cost management. More specifically, it seeks to stimulate an awareness of the issues in policy formulation, implementation, and impact. As a result, information is provided to those interested on the effectiveness of the organizations, their methods and procedures, and the schedules followed. Organizationally, it may be undertaken by the agencies themselves or by a separate agency. Each year, an agenda may be developed, reflecting the concerns of the public, the executive, and the legislature, comprising areas that may be evaluated, and a design may be either a sample survey, a case study approach, a field experiment, or the use of already available data.

Areas for Review

In view of the growing importance of financial accountability and the need for pursuing economical and efficient ways of programme and policy delivery, it would be prudent to review the existing facilities available for the purpose. It may be noted that most governments have yet to make a beginning in this respect and as such, where there is no existing machinery, the plans and intents of governments may be ascertained. More specifically: (i) the functional effectiveness of internal audit; and (ii) the scope, functioning, and impact of the evaluation machinery on policy and programme delivery need to be reviewed.

Intergovernmental Fiscal Management

Intergovernmental fiscal management is technically viewed as an integral part of federal finance, but is considered here for two reasons. First, macroeconomic stability requires the pursuit of fiscal goals by the central and other levels of government. Fiscal perversity or major fiscal slippages may, by widening the size of the fiscal deficit, have an adverse impact on macroeconomic stability. Second, in several countries, many services which are funded by transfers from the central budget are actually provided by the regional, state, and local governments. The effectiveness of service delivery is dependent, among others, on the conditionality specified and on the capacity of the local administrative machinery.

Grant Management

Transfers from the federal or central government essentially take the following forms: devolution of taxes; specification of subventions (which, among others, may be for purposes of budgetary management) in permanent or annual law and associated transfers; discretionary grants, and loans including re-lent funds from donors and IFIs. In addition, central governments may provide guarantees (with associated contingent liabilities) to the lower levels of government.

From an expenditure point of view, there is little control that can be exercised with regard to devolutionary transfers and statutory subventions. These transfers take place routinely, and in some of the former centrally planned economies, the shares of the lower levels of government are automatically retained in the banking system. The system of expenditure management has a role primarily in regard to the determination of bulk grants or specific conditional grants, and in some cases, contributions by the lower levels of government. Traditionally, the pattern was to specify the conditions for the use of grants in extensive detail. During recent years, however, there has been a trend towards bulk grants and empowering the lower levels of government to use their flexibility keeping in view the general goals. Moreover, there may be cases where general mandates (for example, road safety and, environmental standards) may be issued by the central government without provision of funds. In these cases, funding the mandates creates additional demands on the resources lower levels of government.

Experience shows that broadly two issues are encountered in the management of grants. First, grants may not be released in time. More specifically, when central governments experience fiscal stress, they tend to underfund the transfers. This contributes to a good deal of uncertainty at the lower levels and contributes to major problems in service delivery. On the other hand, it is argued that the lower levels of government cannot be immune from the general fiscal stress and that sacrifices should be common for all levels of government. Second, from the grantor's point of view, the only machinery available for ensuring that the purposes of grants are met is to rely on the system of financial reporting and occasional inspections. Neither has proved to be sufficient in this respect.

Lending and Contingent Liabilities

Governments at the central level also extend loans to lower levels of government. In some cases (example, India), funds received from IFIs may be re-lent to lower levels of government at different rates of interest and amortization schedules to compensate for the assumption of risk. Re-lending takes place because of the restrictions on the local governments to borrow from foreign resources. Moreover, guarantees are also offered.

From an expenditure point of view, two considerations are important. First, the loans, which technically constitute financial assets for the central governments, may be converted to grants and thus a hard constraint may become a soft one. This also changes the composition of the financial portfolio of the central government. Second, in the absence of proper arrangements, when the lower levels of government default on the loans, the repayment liability may be taken over by the central government with the inevitable consequence of a widened fiscal deficit.

Areas for Review

Given the importance of the role played by lower levels of government, it is appropriate to review the following.

1. The existing arrangements for grant determination, conditions associated with them and the adequacy of the machinery to ensure their fulfilment.
2. Arrangements for extending loans and guarantees and their management.

Debt and Contingent Liability Management

Debt management is appropriately considered to be a part of the conduct of monetary policy. During recent years, however, the responsibilities of the central bank as the debt manager of the government are being reduced and returned to the government. The scope of discussion here is limited to the more technical aspects of organization of repayment funds and the maintenance of public debt registers, regardless of the agency responsible for its maintenance.

Sinking Fund

Until the end of the Second World War a distinction was made between unfunded debt and funded debt. The former usually consisted of funds held by the government in a trust capacity and utilized for financing budget needs without the issue of formal instruments of debt. These funds, usually called public account or trust funds, were quite substantial in size and frequently consisted of provident funds, employee retirement funds and, contractors' deposits. These were termed as 'unfunded' largely for the reason that there were no amortization schedules and no sinking funds to fund their repayment, rather they were organized on the principle of inflows financing the outflows. Parts of these amounts are paid interest and some parts such as contractors' deposits may not be paid any. In the interest of proper discipline, however, it is appropriate that this segment is recognized as public debt (only the part utilized by the government).

In most countries, public debt is treated in a separate chapter in the budget and is conducted on a centralized basis, usually by the ministries of finance or autonomous agencies set up for the purpose. Where it is managed by the latter, it may not be adequately shown in the budget at all. A major feature of a separate chapter is that the costs of the debt service are not recognized by the spending agencies that use the loan proceeds (the proceeds do not have a separate identity once they enter the stream of consolidated funds of the government). Some countries (for example, Chile) have started showing the project loans and associated debt servicing as a part of the outlays of the spending agency concerned in the hope that this will promote a heightened awareness of the costs of debt servicing.

To enable repayment for recognized loans, many countries organized sinking funds (funded debt) and contributions were made into the sinking funds based on the amortization schedule of the loan. Repayments, when due, were made from these funds. Sinking funds, however, fell into disuse after the Second World War largely reflecting the view that the magnitude of debt was too high (larger than GDP in some cases) and that the credibility of the government was to be seen not in terms of the size and procedures of sinking funds but in terms of the overall macroeconomic policies. During recent years, however, there has been an advocacy for the revival of these funds on the ground that they may be helpful in shoring up the credibility of governments in the markets.

As noted earlier, governments are also engaged in re-lending to other levels of government. The proceeds of loans in a few countries (for example, Indonesia) are organized into separate funds, which are then used as sources for short-term financing of the central budget. The scope for the use of these funds arises largely because of the differences in the amortization schedules between those from the primary and secondary lenders.

An equally significant aspect relates to the guarantees and to the maintenance of contingent liabilities. Some countries have enacted laws governing the issue and terms of guarantees and the arrangements for the recognition of contingent liabilities. In others, however, these are recognized only when the liability is invoked, in turn contributing to budgetary volatility.

Record Maintenance

Considerable progress has been made, over the years, in the maintenance of external debt records and reporting of data in conformity with international standards. With regard to domestic debt, however, the maintenance of the debt register reveals that there are long lags between the purchase of instruments and their accrual recording. These lags have, in some cases, contributed to the development of secondary markets (that are also informal). Selective progress has been made in the computerization of these records but, admittedly, more remains to be done.

Areas for Review

It is appropriate to review the following areas.

1. The arrangements for the unrecognized debt.
2. Arrangements for showing the costs of public debt for projects in terms of users.
3. Organization of sinking funds and other amortization funds.
4. Procedures relating to guarantees and contingent liabilities.
5. Procedures for the maintenance of national debt registers.

Post-Budget Control: Audit and Legislative Control

Audit, like other aspects of government financial management, is considered to be of vital importance for securing accountability in a civic society. In recognition of this, many countries, including the former centrally planned economies, have established offices of audit on an independent basis. In many countries, the office of the audit, established under separate legislation, is usually endowed with a lot of independence so as to secure unbiased assessment of the government's financial performance.

The scope of audit remit differs from one country to another. The broad range is illustrated in Table 9.13. In many countries, the audit may be limited to the central government. (In India, the Auditor General audits the accounts of state governments in addition to compiling accounts; the separation of accounts is limited to the central government.) In a few countries, the scope of audit may also involve supplementary audit of state-owned enterprises by the audit office. The powers of the audit office to review the accounts of organizations and contractors receiving funds from government may be very limited. To overcome legislative restrictions, audit agencies may be asked to look into the books as a part of conditionality attached to the transfers from government. These arrangements are somewhat ad hoc in nature.

Table 9.13
Scope of Audit

Audit Remit	Types of Audit	Consideration of Audit Reports
Central government	A priori audit	Committees of the
Regional government	Concurrent audit	legislature
State/provincial government	A post-priori audit	Whole house
Local government	• Judicial	Regional/local level
State enterprises	• Financial	legislative bodies
Other public bodies	• Performance	Audited bodies and
NGOs which receive funds from government	Investigative audit	government
Records of contractors that work with governments		

Types of Audit

Audit is generally viewed as an activity that takes place largely after the completion of the fiscal year. In reality, however, practices differ and there is audit on an a priori basis, a concurrent basis and a post-priori basis. Although a priori audit is not common, it still takes place in some industrial countries (for example, Italy). This audit involves participation in the financial control process and transactions are reviewed by the audit agency before they take place. Concurrent audit takes place even as the financial transactions are being concluded and to that extent the views of audit may be taken into account in making decisions. For the most part, however, audit is conducted after the action is completed. This audit comprises, broadly, three elements. The judicial audit, which is less common, puts the agency in a quasi-judicial status in that the audit agency is responsible not only for the audit of accounts, but also for identifying and passing judgements on delinquent officials. Financial audit (which includes administrative and appropriation audit) includes an examination of whether operations were carried out in compliance with existing laws and regulations, whether expenditures were contained within appropriations (and in case of excesses, they are regularized ex-post facto by the legislature on the recommendations of the audit agency), and whether the broad purposes of the legislature were met. Performance audit, of relatively recent origin, involves the examination of the pursuit of economy, efficiency, and effectiveness and whether more value could have been obtained. In addition, audit agencies may also undertake, mostly at the behest of the legislature, special or investigative audit of specific areas or transactions. This may involve scrutiny of selected policies introduced by governments prior to elections (example, in New Zealand).

Legislative Considerations

Audit is generally viewed as an organization aimed at assisting the legislatures in the conduct of financial affairs of the country. It is for this reason that audit reports are considered by the legislatures and action proposed. In the absence of such action, audit reports would have reduced value, servicing only the transparency function. Accountability implies that the reports are considered by an oversight body. Procedures in this regard differ among countries. In the Commonwealth type of countries, audit reports are first examined by the PAC (a committee of the legislature) and its findings are submitted to the whole House. In all these cases, however, the reports are first considered by the audited bodies and by the government.

Issues in Effectiveness

Although audit is an important and a venerable function, some contend that its effectiveness is limited (for the following reasons). First, audit is precluded, in most cases, from reviewing policy aspects. Limiting attention only to the financial transaction does not enable a complete perspective on the financial viability of policies. Second, in a context where a greater share of transactions is being carried out by autonomous agencies, NGOs and contractors, the limited remit of the audit agency and its lack of access to their records limits the scope of audit. Third, performance audit remains, for the most part, at an early stage and more progress remains to be made. Finally, the overall purpose of audit is to bring about a more effective financial management system but the improvements brought about as a result of audit are few and far between.

Areas for Review

The following areas merit review.

1. Organization of the audit agency, its independence, and statutory powers.
2. Remit of the audit agency and complementary efforts by others to complete the audit of all levels.
3. Emphasis on the type of audit and plans to undertake performance audit.
4. Links between legislative committees and the audit agency and adequacy of arrangements to ensure action.
5. Overall impact of the audit work on the financial management system.

SUPPORTING INFRASTRUCTURE

Organizing Finance Ministries and Internal Financial Management Capability in Spending Agencies

No organization is perfect but each one tries, in its own way, to adapt to the changing needs and to serve the purposes for which it was originally designed. Ministries of finance and other central agencies, as well as spending agencies are no exceptions to this general experience. What distinguishes them from others is the nature of their tasks and the pace of adaptation.

Changes in Philosophy

During recent years, as a part of the application of new management philosophy and establishment of task-related agencies with functional autonomy and specified accountability, there has been a focus on the organization of finance ministries and on the ways in which they can be made more effective. The impetus for such a focus is derived largely from the following approaches that are today dominating discussion in management philosophy. There is the emphasis that organizations should basically recognize their core tasks and address them. It is pointed out that over the years, organizations gather—largely due to the stress of the situation and what appears, at the moment, to be a convenient approach—several tasks for which they may not be best equipped. Focus on core tasks enables the organizations to discard the excess load and assists them in renewing themselves for higher performance. This process involves five steps: (i) identification of core competencies, (ii) establishing a core competence agenda, (iii) building core competence, (iv) deploying core competencies, and (v) defending core competencies. It is recognized now that central agencies should primarily engage in 'steering' and that the 'rowing' should be left to the spending agencies; and there should be greater and renewed emphasis on decentralization so that the agencies would have the freedom, incentive, and supporting infrastructure to help them achieve their objectives.

As a result of these approaches, some countries (for example, the United Kindgom) have carried out fundamental reviews of the central agencies and established reorganized central agencies. The central agency for finance (whether called a treasury or ministry of finance) would have some broad clusters of activities such as: policy analysis and management; budget review and formulation of annual budget; output and outcome management; procurement and contracting guidance; guidance on financial management in spending agencies; management of financial information; public debt management and legislative liaison. As a part of this approach, some traditional tasks, such as payments, have been contracted out to the corporate sector.

It should be noted that all governments cannot have a uniform model in this regard; rather, the opportunity of review should be utilized to ascertain what is important and to discard areas that have a low priority.

Subsidiary Principle

The application of this principle to financial management requires that those tasks that are best done by the lower levels of organizations or levels of government be left to them and not be administered, as distinct from providing guidance and stimulus, on a day-to-day basis, by the higher levels or central agencies. The functional relationships in budget management, as discussed in the previous sections, reflect a complex web in which the spending agencies end up spending a major part of the time in processing approvals from the central agencies than on the actual provision of services. This has often contributed to overdependence and to the loss of financial consciousness (as a result of the command and control structure) in the spending agencies.

Increasingly, however, it is recognized that the command and control structure in the relationship between central agencies and spending agencies should be replaced by partnership for improved collaboration. The emphasis on partnerships requires, as a first stage, delineation of the areas where more tasks, powers, and responsibilities can be delegated, within a framework of accountability, to the spending agencies. In the determination of these areas, avenues for greater coordination that promote the pursuit of macroeconomic stability should be identified and strengthened.

Hierarchy vs Teams

Traditionally, the structures in government are designed in a pyramidical style with a large base and a narrow top. In between, there are several layers that are engaged, as a part of supervisory duties, in a daily review and verification of the work done by the lower levels. It is now suggested that this approach should, to the extent possible, be undertaken by specified teams (reflecting the core clusters). Teams promote greater coordination while being less expensive. Even in the existing systems, several ad hoc teams are set up from time to time for specialized tasks. In the proposed approach, teams would replace the hierarchy and be somewhat more durable.

Internal Financial Management Capability in Spending Agencies

Delegation of greater responsibility to spending agencies requires, as a condition precedent, efforts for strengthening their financial management capability. In general, experience shows that in many governments major spending agencies have budget and accounting units engaged in the routine tasks of preparing budgets and implementing them. It is now suggested that there should be an adequate internal control system that ensures, effective and efficient operations in addition to compliance with regulations. To achieve this objective, there should be an explicit commitment by the management for the promotion of a financial culture oriented to efficient results, identification of risks and associated plans, and supporting information systems.

It is suggested that this internal control system be reviewed, by the audit agency and an annual assessment provided as in the corporate sector. It is further suggested that the internal system be preferably headed by a comptroller who would be responsible for advancing stewardship and accountability, while maintaining the internal control system on an efficient basis. These ideas remain, for the most part, to be implemented in many countries.

Areas for Review

The following areas lend themselves to review.

1. Review of the tasks of central agencies and ensuring that they concentrate on core competencies.
2. Review of the framework of relationships between central and spending agencies and exploration of avenues for renewed partnership through greater decentralization.
3. Review of the continuing need of multiple layers of hierarchy and the possibility of introducing enduring teams.
4. Review of the internal control systems in spending agencies and exploration of channels for strengthening them.

Financial Management and Technology

The application of technology to the daily tasks performed by governments is bringing benefits that could not have been imagined a couple of decades ago. As an extension, it is also revealing some problem areas that were not anticipated. The experience of government financial management confirms both these aspects. Both the benefits and problems are dependent on the extent of application of computer technology and these aspects are discussed here.

Improved Work Processes

The application of computer technology to government financial management shows improved, and less expensive, work processes in the following areas.

1. In a few governments, the compilation of budget draft estimates, their submission to and review by the spending agencies are performed

electronically and paperwork has been mostly eliminated. It has also enabled a reduction in the time spent in the process.

2. The preparation of the medium-term expenditure planning as well as the annual budget scenarios are undertaken electronically.

3. During the phase of budget implementation, the available software permits simultaneous access to data both for central and spending agencies and the need for additional reporting has been largely eliminated.

4. The existing facilities permit a regular window to ascertain the status of the commitments made, payments made, services received, and resources utilized.

5. In several cases, payments for payroll, pensions, and debt are processed electronically; the scope of extending the coverage of electronic payments further is being regularly explored.

6. The compilation of annual accounts has been considerably facilitated with the result that they are available within a month after the close of the fiscal year.

Information Storage

The above benefits have their origins in the data storage capabilities of the computers—whether of mainframe or other types. Most significantly, electronic processing has enabled the recording of transactions and the compilation of accounts to be up-to-date. In addition, through the storage of data, the machinery permits the maintenance of an inventory of vendors, while alerting the finance managers about the payments due. The composition of government accounts, reflecting the size of operations (by far the largest) has been rendered substantially easier. It has also permitted greater transparency of government operations to the public (where they are permitted access through the web sites).

The machinery has also enabled the smooth functioning of the many large projects undertaken by governments through their capacity for storage and quick retrieval of data.

Problem Areas

Although the application of technology differs widely across countries and the developing countries are slowly moving forward in deriving benefits, some common problem areas are becoming evident.

First, the application of electronic technology was expected to yield an abridged and leaner civil service and reduced work processes. In several cases, this has not been realized as the technology is being used for data processing rather than as an effective substitute for manpower.

Second, experience also reveals that the new systems were introduced rather suddenly, and the previous manual systems were given up immediately thereafter. This proved problematic when the new systems developed glitches, and there were no manual records to fall back upon.

Third, far too many types of software are used (for example, payroll) with the result that interchange of data within governments has been rendered difficult.

Fourth, the excessive dependence on technology has brought its own quota of problems. Admittedly, the types of problems that emerge are dependent on the extent of application of technology in governments.

Areas for Review

The areas for review are mostly dependent on the existing level of application and the plans for future extension, including the transition from a mainframe to a network of personal computers. It is prudent to review the following area.

1. To which areas has technology been applied and what were the benefits?
2. What are the plans for future applications?
3. What are the improvements in financial management as a result of technology application?

Looking Ahead: Managing for the Future

It is becoming increasingly clear that the management of government finances would become more complex and that managers would have to deal with more uncertainties. That alone is reason enough to review the existing expenditure management systems and to keep them ready to address the changing tasks and needs of the community. A review (on the lines suggested in the preceding sections) has the potential of revealing the numerous problem areas that need to be addressed. Some of these may be perceived to be major and some minor. Some may need immediate attention, while others may be deferred. Some may pose fundamental challenges while quite a few could be of a routine nature.

In analysing these aspects, a combination of three mindsets is indicated. As in the field of art, it requires the combination of skills of a landscape artist as well as those of a miniature artist. As in the field of sports, particularly karate, it requires the mindset of a Mu-shin, that is, absorbing all the minutiae but keeping the mind uncluttered, about the goal. As in the field of medicine, it requires the application of a triage—to separate those requiring immediate attention from those who can wait a little longer.

An explicit recognition of the above, and an effort to gather support for the needed changes is the primary task of managing for the future.

References

Allan, Percy (2003), 'Australia's Experience with State-level Reforms' in Ashok K. Lahiri and Nicolas Stern (eds), *State-level Reform in India: Towards More Effective Government*, Delhi: Macmillan India.

Anderson, Lisa (2003), *Pursuing Truth, Exercising Power: Social Science and Public Policy in the 21st Century*, New York: Columbia University Press.

Banca d'Italia (2001), *Fiscal Rules*, Rome: Central Bank of Italy.

——, (2001), *The Impact of Fiscal Policy*, Rome: Central Bank of Italy.

Barnard, Cherster I. (1938), *The Functions of the Executive*, Cambridge, MA: Harvard University Press.

Beder, Sharon (2003), *Power Play: The Fight to Control World's Electricity*, New York: The New Press.

Bok, Derek (2001), *The Trouble with Government*, Cambridge, MA: Harvard University Press.

Brewer, J. (1989), *The Sinews of Power: War, Money and the English State 1688–1783*, New York: Alfred A. Knopf.

Caiden, Naomi and Aaron Wildavsky (1980), *Planning and Budgeting in Poor Countries*, New Brunswick, NJ: Transaction Books.

Carr, E.H. (1961), *What is History*, New York: Alfred A. Knopf.

Collyns, Charles and Russel Kincaid (2003), *Managing Financial Crisis and Lessons from Latin America*, Washington: International Monetary Fund, occasional paper 217.

Crick, Bernard (2002), *Democracy: A Very Short Introduction*, Oxford: Oxford University Press.

Danziger, Sheldon H., Gary D. Sandefur, and Daniel H. Weinberg (eds.) (1994) *Confronting Poverty*, Cambridge, MA: Harvard University Press.

Davies, A.C.L. (2001) *Accountability: A Public Law Analysis of Government by Contract*, Oxford: Oxford University Press.

Day, Patricia and Rudolf Klein (1987), *Accountabilities*, London: Tavistock.

Donovan, Nicholas and David Halpern (2002), *Life Satisfaction: The State of Knowledge and Implications for Government*, Cabinet Office, London.

Dornbusch, Rudiger and Sebastian Edwards (eds) (1991), *The Macroeconomics of Populism in Latin America*, Chicago: University of Chicago Press.

Dunn, John (2000), *The Cunning of Unreason: Making Sense of Politics*, New York: Basic Books.

Farson, Richard (1996), *Managing of the Absurd: Paradoxes in Leadership*, Simon & New York.

Ferguson, Niall (2001), *The Cash Nexus: Money and Power in the Modern World, 1700–2000*, New York: Basic Books.

Feldstein, Martin (1994), *American Economic Policy in the 1980s*, Chicago: University of Chicago Press.

Flyvbjerg, Bent, Nils Bruzalein, and Werner Rothengatter (2003), *Mega Porjects and Risk: An Anatomy of Ambition*, Cambridge: Cambridge University Press.

Foster, Christopher D. and Francis J. Plowden (1996), *The State Under Stress*, Buckingham, UK: Open University Press.

Friend, Thedore (2003), *Indonesian Destinies*, Cambridge, MA: Harvard University Press.

Geertz, Clifford (1995), *After the Fact*, Cambridge, MA: Harvard University Press.

Glazer, Amitai and Lawrence S. Rothenburg (2001), *Why Government Succeeds and Why it Fails*, Cambridge, MA: Harvard University Press.

Government of Karnataka (2003), *White Paper on State Finances*, Bangalore.

Government of Kerala (2001), *White Paper on State Finances*, Thiruvananthapuram.

Government of Punjab (2000), *White Paper on State Finances*, Chandigarh.

Greenberg, Daniel S. (2001), *Science, Money and Politics: Political Triumphs and Ethical Erosion*, Chicago: University of Chicago Press.

Hayek, Frederick A. (1960), *The Constitution of Liberty*, Chicago: University of Chicago Press.

Heinz, John P., Edwardo Laumann, Robert E. Nelson, and Robert H. Salisbury (1993), *The Hollow Core: Private Interests in National Policy Making*, Cambridge, MA: Harvard University Press.

Hundert, Edward M. (1995), *Lessons from Optical Illusion on Nature and Nurture, Knowledge and Values*, Cambridge: Harvard University Press.

IMF (1998), *Code of Good Practices of Fiscal Transparency: Declaration of Principles*, Washington, DC.

___ (2000), *World Economic Outlook, Focus on Transition Economics*.

___ (2001a), *Code of Good Practices on Fiscal Transparency*, Washington, DC.

___ (2001b), *Manual on Fiscal Transparency*, Washington, DC.

___ (2003a), Fiscal Adjustment in IMF-supported Programmes, an evaluation Report, Washington, DC.

___ (2003b), *World Economic Outlook* (Annual) Various years.

Ingram, Helen and Rathgeb Smith Stephen (eds.) (1993), *Public Policy for Democracy*, Washington, DC: Brookings Institution.

Jouvenel, Bertrand de (1993), *On Power: The Natural History of Growth*, Indianapolis: Liberty Fund.

Kautilya (1992), *The Arthashastra*, New Delhi: Penguin Books.

Kay, John (1995), *Why Firms Succeed*, New York: Oxford University Press.

Kitcher, Philip (2001), *Science, Truth and Democracy*, New York: Oxford University Press.

Lindblom, Charles F. (2001), *The Market System*, New Haven: Yale University Press.

Lukes, Steven (ed.) (1986 and 1992), *Power: Readings in Social and Political Theory*, New York: New York University Press.

Macdonald, James (2003), *A Free Nation Deep in Debt: The Financial Roots of Democracy*, New York: Farrar, Strauss and Giroux.

Maier, Karl (2000), *The House Has Fallen*, Cambridge, MA: Westview Press.

Marquand, David (2004), *Decline of the Public: The Hollowing out of Citizenship*, London: Polity Press.

Meyers, Roy T. (ed.) (1999), *Handbook of Government Budgeting*, San Francisco: Jossey Bass.

Moss, David A. (2002), *When All Else Fails: Government as the Ultimate Risk Manager*, Cambridge, MA: Harvard University Press.

Narayana, D. (1999), 'Public Expenditure Reform without Policy Change: Infrastructure Investment and Healthcare Provision under Fiscal Squeeze in Kerala' in Maureen Mackintosh and Rathin Roy (eds), *Economic Decentralization and Management Reform*, Cheltenham: Edward Elgar.

OECD (1987), *The Control and Management of Public Expenditure*, OECD, Paris.
Petrei, Humberto (1988), *Budget and Control: Reforming the Public Sector in Latin America*, Inter-American Development Bank, Washington, DC.
Premchand, A. (1983), *Government Budgeting and Expenditure Controls*, International Monetary Fund, Washington, DC.
_____ (1993), *Public Expenditure Management*, International Monetary Fund, Washington, DC.
_____ (1995), *Effective Government Accounting*, International Monetary Fund, Washington, DC.
_____ (2000), *Control of Public Money*, New Delhi:Oxford University Press.
Putnam, Robert D. (1993), *Making Democracy Work*, Princeton: Princeton University Press.
Remington, Thomas F. (2001), *The Russian Parliament: Institutional Evolution in a Transitional Time 1989–1999*, New Haven: Yale University Press.
Reserve Bank of India (2000), *Finances of State Government*, Mumbai.
Sampson, Anthony (2004), *Who Runs the Place: The Anatomy of Britain in 21st Century*, London: John Murrray.
Schauer, Frederick (1991), *Playing by the Rules: A Philosophical Examination of Rule-based Decision Making in Law and Life*, Oxford: Clarendon Press.
Schiavo-Campo, Salvatore and Daniel Tomasi (1999), *Managing Government Expenditure*, Asian Development Bank, Manila.
Schiavo-Campo, Salvatore ed. (1999), *Governance, Corruption and Public Financial Management*, Asian Development Bank, Manila.
Simon, Herbert A. (1997), *Administrative Behavior*, New York: The Free Press.
Thapar, Romila (2002), *Early India*, New Delhi: Penguin Books.
Tocqueville, Alexis de (2000), *Democracy in America*, Chicago: University of Chicago Press.
Wade, Robert (1990), *Governing the Market: Economic Theory and the Role of Government in East Asian Industrialization*, Princeton: Princeton University Press.
Wilson, James Q. (1989), *Bureaucracy: What Government Agencies Do and Why they Do it?* New York: Basic Books.

364 Index

Alexander, invasion through Central Asia 26
Allied power 34
allocation of resources, between different levels of government and departments 148–53
    ceilings on 162
    cuts in 24
    and expenditure instruments 154
allocative mechanism 4
    efficiency in 171, 265–7
    and rigidity 144–56
America(an), democracy
    see also United States
American War of Independence 34
Anderson, Lisa 23
Andhra Pradesh, computerization in 273
annual budget 9, 39, 51, 103, 171, 214
    and contract with community 180
    forecasts of 54
    funds for 147
    as a law 51
    manipulation of estimates of 147, 176
    policy, determination of 260
    preparation of 55, 56, 246, 262, 276–356
    spending of 178
    see also budgets
anti-corruption bureaus 86
Antwerp, as financial centre 31
a post-priori audit 344
a priori audit 348
Argentina 47, 50
    economic crisis in 184
    financial crisis in 49
    legislation of fiscal policy in 289
    no-deficit rule in 127, 184
    zero-deficit legislation in 49
Aristotle 176, 191
Asia 10, 44
    conflicts in, and expenditure control framework in 123
Asian economies, financial crisis in 60, 117, 147, 231
Asian Development Bank 2
asset and liability, and borrowing 72
audit 12, 90, 264
    and accounting function 35
    and financial control process 24
    of government accounts 203
    reports, 218, 226
        examination of, by PAC 349
        scope of 348
    at sub-national government level 273–4
    system, review of 14
    types of 348–9
audit office/agency 32, 130, 221–2, 229, 232, 347, 348
    accountability and 221–2
    establishment of 192, 231
    organization of 350
auditor, role of 28
Auditor General 273, 274, 347
Australia 32, 47, 48
    accrual budgeting in 70, 285
    'envelope budgeting' in 56
    fiscal responsibility legislation in 261
    making of forecasts in 54
    on performance measures 66–7
    resource allocation between different levels of government in 149–50

Index

accountability 5, 13, 38, 42, 89, 132, 204
  budget and 321
  concept of 86, 210
  evolution and practice of 206–11
  framework 13
  horizontal 230
  at local level 263–4
  machinery for 227, 232
  management of 207
  objective of 205
  in sub-national governments 271
  transparency and 20–1, 23, 83–7, 95
accountants 27, 28
  in the Treasury 30
accounts/accounting 5, 32, 42, 213, 231, 331
  compilation of 341
  organization 90
  records 28
  and reporting system 202
  standards 9, 10
  system, development of 28, 29
  at sub-national governments level 271, 172
accounting and auditing offices, establishment of 35
accrual accounting system 3, 5, 42, 90, 188, 189, 245, 263, 272, 284–5, 287
  introduction of 207
  misuse of 72
accrual budgets/budgeting 68–73, 199, 300
  and accounting 94, 187
  and balance sheet 71
  introduction of 188, 189
across-the-board cuts 56, 158–9
administration, checks and balances in 206
  costs, reduction in 5
  infrastructure, changes in supporting 201
  reports 203
  role of 26
  system 169
advanced economics, payment of benefits in 17
African countries, conflicts in, and expenditure control framework in 123
African Peer Review Mechanism (APRM) 129
aged population, costs of maintaining 17, 142
agency relationship, in government 109
Agency Theory 108, 109
agricultural labour, predominance of 242

World Bank (2000), *Reforming Public Institutions and Strengthening Governance: A World Bank Strategy*, Washington, DC.
___ (2002a), *Building Institutions for Markets: World Development Report*, Washington.
___ (2002b), *Transition: The First Ten years*, Washington, DC.
___ (2004) *Making Services Work for the Poor People*, Washington, DC.

austerity management, by sub-national governments 268–9
Axis powers 34

balanced budgets 46, 50, 127, 137, 184
balance sheet 72, 213, 284
banking/financial standards 60
system, and payment system 327, 329
bankruptcy laws 59
Barnard, Chester 96, 209, 229
Baumol 139
Benefit-providing organizations 237
biennial budgets of 262
advantages of 119
'binding rules,' introduction of 46
Bismark 169
book adjustment 73
bonds, taxable and tax-free, in the United States 80
borrowings 35
Brazil 47, 81
fiscal responsibility legislation in 261
British Treasury 192
budget/budgetary 4, 107, 246
agencies, independent 90, 201
allocations 140
approaches to 304–8
authority, and commitment management 322–4
budget, . . .
basis of 284–6
calendar 315–16
constraints 50, 150, 157
conventional approach to 304–5
cycle, changes in 119

deficits 61, 141, 249
measurement of 262
estimates 250, 305, 312
for sub-national government 267
execution of 116, 320–1
expenditures, and types of budget 291–93
forecasts 268, 298
implementation of 4, 5, 115, 202, 216, 263
laws 47
information on 119
issues arising in 298–9
laws 289
and macroeconomic stability 124
policy, objectives of 224
post-budget control 347–50
preparation of annual 55–6, 246, 276–356
publication of 253
role of 34
secrecy of 84
transfers, to autonomous bodies of government 317
from central to other levels of government 317
Budget Enforcement Act, United States 136
budgetary reserves, and special accounts 314
bureaucracy 46, 121
and accountability 233
and decision-making 189
growth in 74
and legislature, and financial control 103
and provision of services 252
responsive 78

role of 116
strengthening of 106
buyer-provider, of services, relationship between 108–9

Cameralist school of accounting 30, 191
Canada, contraction out in 179
'envelope budgeting' in 56
system, recording of 284
capital budget, introduction of 35
capital projects, appraisals 266
cash, and accrual budgeting 69
based budgeting 68–9 188
disbursement, in sub-national governments 263
system, traditional controls in 285
catastrophic risks 59
ceilings, fiscal deficit and types of 305–7
central bank, data on financial status with 330
and financial institutions, and fiscal transparency 197
as regulatory agency 117–18
central government, loans to lower levels of governments 252, 260, 344–5
centralization, of authority 22, 45
centralize treasury system, need for 328
China, allocation of power in 111
audit office in 90
and financial accountability 225–6
participation 82, 122
civil society, concept of 186
client group, and budgetary implementation 81–2

colonial legacy, financial management under 4
Commission of Audit 192
company/county bail-outs 59
computer/electronic technology, use in financial management 6, 21, 94, 113, 353–5
in payment system 328–9
use at sub-national government level 273
Congressional system, entitlement programmes in 116
consolidated budget 199, 282
Constitution of India 169n
and associated laws 280–1
legislation on public expenditure 281
consultative legislative committees 118, 214, 222
contingency liabilities 59, 61, 69, 85, 262, 346–7
contingency plan 54
contract management, and expenditure management 324–5, 337
contraction out, of service 6, 9, 42–3, 73–8, 94, 155, 160, 324–5
and budget implementation 179–80
remuneration for contractors in 76–7
control structures, types of, for financial management 7
core competencies 351
core projects, resources for 269
corporate sectors 5, 14
annual strategy of 303
government and, and fiscal transparency 197

Index 367

as partners of government 34
on research and development 37
standards for 60
successful 43
Costa Rica, resource allocation in 151
cost(s), and benefits programme 4, 13
 project implementation and 366
 standards 300
country, and municipal governments, financial management systems in 274–5
Crick, Bernard 103
current, expenditure, financing 19
 and investment expenditures, impact of 133

Davies, Anne 179
debt, and contingent liability management 345–7
 financing 39–40, 140
 information in, in budget 287
 management 6, 33, 144, 201
 outstanding, domestic/external 73
 and public finance 26
 as source of financing 30
decision-making, in democracy 105, 131
 approaches on fiscal policies 172, 194
decentralization 42, 45, 127, 162, 273, 275
 and empowerment 83, 95
democracy, and expenditure management 102–24
 meaning of 103–4
 governments in 104

 public policy management in 121
democratic institutions, maintenance of 103
Dekker, Marcel 2
developing countries, absence of social security in 132
 capital spending in 133
 development plans in 7
 differences between industrial countries and 242–3
 expenditures in 11
 financial management in 4, 11–12
 fiscal information and innovative payment systems in 257
 performance budgeting in 10
 resource allocation and IFIs norms on 152
 risk burden in 60
 social safety nets in 238
development, budget, circular for 308
 outlays 141, 292
 plans 38, 213, 231, 292–3, 300
devolutionary budgeting 106
Directive Principles of State Policy 169n
disaster relief 59
discretionary grants 343
discretionary transfers 149–50
domestic credit, ceilings on 9
donor(s), budgets 282
 and foreign aid 215
 monitoring by 219
draft budget 305
 estimates, review of 310–12
 processing of 311–12

'e'-governance 45

economic development, dirigist
    approach to 292
  plans 208
economic and fiscal policies,
    instruments of 4
economic stability 39, 146, 288
economy, and efficiency, in
    budgetary practice 333–4
  and programme performance,
    measurement of 233
Ecuador, appropriation in 111
electronic technology, application of
    5, 21, 26, 43–4, 243, 271,
    273, 285, 300
Elgar, Edward 2
empire-building foreign policy 33
employment, government support
    to 239–40, 242
empowerment 78–83, 127
enclaves, reforms and establishment
    of 101
England, debt in Hanoverian
    rule in 30
  introduction of financial
    accountability in 208
  power of legislature in 30
  taxation in 30
  see also United Kingdom
Enron affair 60, 72
Entitlement programmes
    153
'envelope budgeting' 56
environment, liability 59
estate, management 208
  preservation 207
European Bank of Reconstruction
    and Development (EBRD)
    92
European Community, disbursing
    of power in 223
    financial accountability in
        227–8
European kingdoms, management
    of finances in 31
European Organization of Systems
    Audit Authorities 231
Exchequer and Audit Act of 1866,
    England 31–2
Exchequer control, in cash
    management 325
executive, decision making by 20
  functions of 209
  powers of 116
  role in financial matters 12, 31,
    226
expenditure, allocation 155, 177
  benefits, utilization of 66
  estimates 171–72, 215,
    308–10
  forecasting 294
  management 1–3, 11, 38–9, 41,
    63, 88–9, 93–5, 143, 160,
    251, 279, 300, 339
    democracy and 102–24
    instruments of 259–64,
      278–9, 335
    and life support programmes
      237–54
    reforms in 98, 100
    structural features of 280–8
  plans 88
  policies 13, 177
  portfolios, implementation of
    317–18
  reduction in 136
  review of 300
  types of 293
extra-budgetary accounts/activities
    198, 220, 225, 262, 268,
    282, 295–6

federal system, financial relations 68
　and sub-national governments
　　78, 271
Ferguson, Niall 139
finance commissions 275
finance managers, perspective of
　　277, 301
finance ministries 90–1
　authority of 22, 157
　and spending agencies 83, 350
financial accountability 204–36
　citizens and 225–6
　conventional and enhanced
　　207–9
　instruments of 213–19
　recent developments in 228–32
financial audit 348–9
financial crisis 173, 249
financial institutions, domestic,
　　bankruptcy of 18
　reforms in 100
　role and activities of 93
financial management 4–14
　instruments and techniques of
　　8, 12
　performance-oriented 10
　reforms in 4, 23, 234
　and technology 323–5
financial markets 31, 154
financial portfolio 305
financial powers, decentralization of
　　79
financial reporting 263, 270–1,
　　330–1
financial responsibility, between
　　legislature and executive 32
financial transfers, between
　　government, donors and IFIs
　　219
fiscal, balances 97

crisis 56, 157, 192–3, 337–40
deficits 4, 15–16, 40, 299,
　　305–7
information, instruments and
　　features of 186–7, 194,
　　196–203
responsibility legislation 47, 81,
　　83, 106, 183, 261, 288
rules 47, 184
slippages 39, 127
surplus 15–16
stability 2, 51, 88–9, 138
sustainability 20, 89
transparency 1, 84, 107, 155,
　　185, 191–203
　and accountability 182,
　　186–7
　history of 191–3
　objectives of 193–4
　year 282–4
Fiscal Responsibility Legislation,
　　New Zealand 47
foreign-aid 6, 261, 331
　accounting by sub-national
　　governments 271–2
　dependence on 298, 323
　developing countries dependence
　　on 10–11
　projects with 11, 54
France, medium-term fiscal plans in
　　53
fraud, and corruption 289
　and waste 252–3
　and provision of services 318–19
　release from central government
　　324

Game Theory, third-party
　　enforcement in 107–8
Gandhi, Mahatma 165n

General Accounting Office 90
general pool, resource allocation from 151
Germany 49
Gladstone, Prime Minister of England 31
Gladstone reforms, of exchequer management 208
Gore Commission on Reinvention of Government 119
government(s),
    expenditure control in 15–87
    financial management process in 243–4
    financial relationship with non-governmental organizations (NGOs) 223
    funded programmes 6
    institutions, information on role of 25–6
    as lending institutions 37
    operation and expenditure growth 139–40
    organizational shortcomings in 43
    principal–agent relationships in 51
    provision of goods and services by all levels of 277–8
    retrenchment programme by 40
    review of spending estimates 55–8, 94
    structures hierarchies vs team 353
    transaction, classification of 286–7
    see also federal system, sub-national government
Gramm-Rudman-Hollings legislation, in United States 136
grants, determination of 345
    extended 35
    in-aid 153, 258
    to sub-national governments 261
Great Depression, effect on role of the budget 34
gross domestic product (GDP) 38–9, 64, 140, 299, 307, 311, 314
guarantees,
    outstanding, at sub-national level 269

Hart, H.L.A. 173
health, and education, expenditure on, in sub-national level 264
    regulated 59
    services, funds for 147
    improved 16
Herodotus 172
human factors, and expenditure management 131

Iceland, accrual budgeting in 70
incentives 32, 131, 334
indebtedness 150
India, audit function in 273–4
    consultative committees in 118
    empowering local governments in 257–8
    legislators' appropriation in 111
    performance indicators in 67
    risk management in government in 60–1
    users' association in 82
individual responsibility, concept of 209–10
Indonesia, market borrowing by local governments in 81
industries/industrial, government investments in 37
industrial countries 53

developing countries and 5–7, 242–3
and entitle payments 54
welfare benefits in 237
inflation rate 53, 56, 59, 143, 156
asymmetries 193, 204
information,
technology, application of 5, 13, 45
infrastructure/infrastructural, facilities 13
government support to 239, 241
institutions/institutional, changing ideas and 88–91, 137
and expenditure management 125–32
hurdles, portfolio management and 156–63
reforms 98–102
insurance guarantees funds 59
interest groups, role in formulation of forecasts 54–5
role in policy making 168–9
interest rates 49, 59, 142
intergovernmental fiscal management 343–5
international audit, and evaluation of expenditure management 342–3
international financial institutions (IFIs) 2, 6, 18, 41, 45, 55, 61, 63, 92, 100, 142, 152, 215
advice on policy making 170
'alternative proposal' by 167
and fiscal transparency 84
loans from 164, 336, 343
and medium-term expenditure framework 188
monitoring of programmes by 219
and new public management philosophy 116, 179
and transparency and accountability 186, 230
International Monetary Fund (IMF) 97
on 'best practices' 128–9
on fiscal transparency 84, 92
on institutional reforms, in developing countries 128
on macroeconomic stability 63
investment, appraisal techniques 266
lags 134
plans, medium-term 6, 36
in sub-national governments 262
see also medium-term plans
Iraq, invasion of 37
Israel, establishment of treasury by 29
Italy, agreement with IMF 128
fiscal adjustment policies in 128
legislative functioning in 115

Japan, policy packages in 134
Jefferson, 31
judicial audit 348

Kant 167
Kautilya 28
On accounting and audit 206–7
and *Arthasastra* on management of finance 26–7
on bureaucracy 206
Kennedy, John F. 166
Keynes, J.M. 2, 151
Korea 15
Korean War 37

labour, development and
functioning of 147
land revenue 27
Latin America 10, 44, 49, 110
accounting and auditing offices
in 35
crisis in 117
market borrowing by local
governments 80
law and order, cost of maintenance
of 17
legislature/legislative 20
committees and audit agencies 350
decision making during war
periods 36
decline in power of 189
and executive, and public policy
making 168–9
and expenditure management
110–14, 117
and financial accountability 227
financial control by 103
on fiscal responsibility 47–9
institutions, development of 192
review of government accounts
by 203
role and functions of 103, 246
and society 42
tradition, growth of 29–33
liabilities, contingent 344–5
of government 71, 94, 232
liberalization 81
'life satisfaction' 16, 165–6
life support programmes 59, 148,
239–42, 246
expenditure management and
237–54
liquidation 27
loan, from central to local
government 261

from donors/IIFs 343
provision of 133–4, 154
repayment of 14, 347
lobbies 117
local governments, borrowing from
markets 80–1
empowerment of 79
London, as financial centre 31

Maastricht Treaty, European Union
48–9, 93, 136
Macdonald, James 26
Machiavelli 104, 162
Madison, James 126
macroeconomic framework, and
annual budget 200,
299–302
macroeconomic stability 13, 59, 63,
121, 171, 238, 275, 277,
300, 343
Malaysia, biennial budgets in 119,
178–9
management, culture, public
involvement in 235
philosophy, new 37, 117
reforms 1, 5
managerial class, and accountability
211
role of 117, 228
market, borrowings by local
governments 80–1, 273
and economic growth 125, 146
functioning 105
oriented policies 15, 60
medical care/services, government
expenditure on 17, 239,
251
medium-term expenditure
framework (MTEF) 187–8,
260, 295–7, 299, 305

Index 373

public investment plans and 335–6
medium-term fiscal framework (MTFF) 7, 260, 294–5, 299, 305
and medium-term framework 295, 302
medium-term plans/planning/policy 101, 213
expenditure 10–11, 55, 136, 143, 268, 293–4, 300
fiscal 40, 47, 51–5, 62, 94, 122, 188, 197, 213, 231, 290–300
Mexico, local–central government financial nexus in 80
Middle Ages 28, 30
Middle East, legislature's role in 111
Mill, J.S. 104
modernity 91
monetary policies 49
and preparation of national accounts 69
Monteiro, Arthur 3
multi-year expenditure rolling budget/plans 198, 266
municipal/county level, of governments 257

national accounts, monetary policy and 69
national expenditure commissions 57
national income 56
National Health Service, UK 82
National Income Accounts 39, 70, 283, 287, 341
National Institute of Public Finance and Policy 2

Netherlands, fiscal adjustment policies in 128
New Deal policy 237
New Partnership for African Development (NEPAD) 129
New Zealand 48
accrual budgeting in 70, 285
application on depreciation in 70
financial management reform in 109
fiscal responsibility legislation in 183, 261, 289
reforms on public economies and corporate practice 99
The Nicomachean Ethics 176
Nolan Commission, UK 166
non-governmental organizations (NGOs), delivery services by 6, 21, 74, 77, 220, 252
non-performing assets 18
Nordic countries 35
North American Treaty Organization (NATO), information a defence costs by 195
Norway, risk sharing in 61

occupational safety 59
Office of Comptroller General 90
Office of Inspector General 90
oligarchy 105
omnibus legislation 118, 289
One-size-fits-all approach, to expenditure 12
'original sins' 172
output budget systems 300

Paris, as financial centre 31
Parliamentary Commission, scrutiny of government accounts 31

parliamentary system, consultative
    committees of 118
  passing of money bills in 168
partnerships, private and public in
    providing services 16, 352
payment system, contracting out 351
  in governments 21
  strengthening of 90
payroll, management 14
  system 44
pensions, benefits, reduction in 135
  payment of 14
  regulation 59
  system, liabilities on governments
    142
performance, agreements, revisions
    in 143-4
  appraisal/audit 66, 85-6, 348-9
  budgeting 10, 63-6, 99, 293,
    300, 332-3
  contracts 217, 223-4, 229
  indicators 67, 224, 270
  measurement 63-8, 94, 201,
    332-3
personal computers, introduction of
    45
personal, ceiling on 11
'personal ledger accounts' 179, 283
Peru 48
Philippines, appropriation in 111
  market borrowing by local
    governments 81
plans/planning, medium-term 51-5
Plato 105
policy, controls and budget
    execution 132, 320-1
  functioning and evaluation of
    343
  instruments, choice of 138
  making and implementation 38,
    68, 125, 164, 169, 200
  management and financial
    management 248-50
  research organizations 22-3
  role of private interests in making
    166, 168-9
Popper Karl 102
portfolio management, and
    institutional hurdles 156-63
poverty, alleviation, expenditure on
    18
  problems of 254
  programmes 133
  in sub-national governments
    264
price, distortions, minimizing 148
  indices 143
principles, and protocols 171-2
privatization, budget deficit and
    135
project, contracts with contractors
    337
  financing, allocation for 151-2
  implementation, and
    expenditure control 335
'project, categories of expenditure'
    152-3
protocols, principles and 171-2
'prudent management' 48, 183,
    209, 219
Public Accounts Committee (PAC)
    31, 86
Public Choice theory 42, 47,
    106-8, 110, 182
public debt 30, 70, 142, 215, 220,
    306, 346
  and financing government
    expenditure 144
public expenditure management
    (PEM) 290

alternative proposal for 181–9
computerization of 187–8
manipulation of 181
measures to restrain growth of 135–7
public finance, instruments of 277–9
public investments plans, MTEF and 335–6
reduction in 136
public policy 20, 120–1, 167–81, 195
public–private partnership 147, 318–19
public sector, management of 5, 97
public service commissions 157
public services, allocation for 248–9
contracts 109
delivery of 23, 243, 251–2, 277
and expenditure management 288
improved 63–4, 91, 275
underfunding of 250–1
public works programme,
governments' role in 34–5, 240
Putnam, Robert D. 96

ratchet effect, expenditure management and 134
'real water content' 134
receipt planning 261
'red tape' 21
reform programmes 2, 41–3, 46
content and discontent 45–51
evaluation of 92
regional developmental banks 55
regulatory tasks/framework 8–9, 58, 132
budget and 321

Reserve Bank of India 80, 273
reserve stabilization funds 291
resource, allocation 5, 25, 65, 88, 108, 156, 172–7, 244, 246, 265–70, 290–302, 317
ceilings, in sub-national governments 83, 265–6
constraints 298
management, in sub-national governments 270–1
stewardship of 171–2
use accounting 5, 172, 180–1, 244–5, 271–3, 317, 340–2
utilization 5, 172, 178–80, 244–5, 317
retirement, programmes, and benefits 17
compulsory/voluntary 157
retrenchment, personnel 132
revenue, collection agencies 326
estimates, and inflation 174
growth and expenditure growth 9
review, and evaluation measures 158, 136–9
of expenditure management 355
risk identification, budget and 182, 185–6
risk management 58–63, 94, 185, 298, 339
at sub-national government levels 269–70
rolling plans/planning 6, 13, 52–3, 143
royalty/royal court, and expenses 27–8
serving 26–9
and treasury 162

rule of law 42, 182
  and fiscal responsibility
    legislation 182–5
  and responsibility legislation 93
Russel, Bertrand 161
Russia, reforms in local governments
    in 79–80
Russian Federation 44
  market borrowing by local
    governments in 81
  reserve allocation in 152

safety laws 60
safety nets, provision of 58
Samuelson, 166
sanctions, imposition of 48, 233
Savings and Loan debacle 60
Schiavo-Campo, Marcel 2
science and technology,
    governments' role in research
    and development 37
secrecy, centralization and, in
    government decision making
    177
Security and Exchange Commission,
    functioning of 60
Simon's system, of values 210
single-entry bookkeeping method,
    of accounting 341
sinking funds 345–7
social insurance programme,
    compulsory 239
social safety nets, in developing
    countries 17, 133, 148, 238
social security system 17, 132, 239,
    242, 291
social service, investments by
    government, corporates and
    NGOs 18, 147
  lobby 248

South Africa, market borrowing by
    local governments in 81
Soviet bloc countries, economic
    planning in 35–6
Spain, accrual budgeting in 70
spending agencies, budgetary
    requirements of 322–3
  coordination with donors
    313–14
  funds for 216, 324
  internal control system in 352–3
  internal finance management in
    352–3
  and medium-term expenditure
    plans 11
  ministry of finance and 83, 350
  responsibilities of 129–30
  role of 33
stabilization, funds 291
  programmes, cash management
    and 325
staff, complements, mandatory
    ceilings on 50
  wages/salaries, expenditure on
    156–8
state, budget and consolidated
    budget 282
  owned enterprises, divestment
    and sale of 15, 41
  policies on reducing the role of
    165
Stigler, George 118
structural and institutional reforms
    98
structural lending programmes 268,
    275
structural problems, in sub-national
    governments 264–5
structural reforms, advancing
    88–163

sub-national governments,
   allocations from centre to
      149, 258–9
   control of 78
   finances of 79, 264
   liabilities of 272
   white paper on fiscal state of
      256
subsidiary principle, to financial
   management 351–2
subsidies, government 37, 148
   for subsistence sectors 241
subventions, statutory 343–4
supplementary budgets 217, 267,
   292
supranational government 21
surplus budget 295
Sweden 33
triennial review system in 57

target-based budgeting 300
task-oriented agencies, creation of
   223
tax/taxation,
   administration 193
   budget deficit and higher 135
   collection 14, 27–8, 30
   devolution of 342
   expenditure 85, 154
   proposals 225
   revenues, classification of 286
   secrecy in 195
   transparency in 187
technology, application 95, 131
   changes and growth in
      expenditure 139
   in defence and expenses on
      government 141–2
Thailand 15
Theory of the Second Best 183

Theory of Transaction Costs 108
'third party payments' 243
Tocqueville, Alexis de 42, 78, 104,
   225
'token' provision, in budget
   preparation 56
Transaction Theory 43
transition economies, weak public
   sector management in 97
transparency, and accountability, of
   government policies 20–1,
   23, 42, 83–7, 95,
   244–5, 253–4
   budget and 309, 321
Transparency International 187
treasury, colonization of 30
   control 27
   formulation and management of
      budget by 31
   maintenance of 28–9
   and payment system 327–9
trigger mechanisms, for financing
   public benefits 249
trust funds 345
Tsarist system of finance 33

Uganda, financial programmes in 80
underdeveloped countries 38
underfunding, of public services/
   projects 178, 180, 268–9,
   314, 366
Unit Trust of India (UTI), losses in
   60
unitary type of governments 255
United Kingdom 32–3, 47–8
   accrual budgeting in 70
   auditing in 274
   borrowing requirements of
      central and local
      governments 80

378 *Index*

citizen groups in 82
citizen' rights in 106
decentralization of financial powers in 35
economic management in 64, 128
expenditure management system in local governments in 256–7
green paper on government proposals 177
parliamentary consultative committees in 118
review in 57
waste in government services in 22
United Nations 2
United States of America,
appropriation committees in 118
biennial budgets in 119
budgetary appropriation 70
borrowings for national and local governments in 80
Bureau of Budget in 35
debt repayment in 33
expenditure management in local governments in 256
finances during wars 37
General Accounting Office 35
incentives for retirement in 40
investigative audit in 229
legislature functioning in 115
performance-based annual reports in 66
Perjury Act in 77
users' associations, at local levels 82
user charges 16

value system, public policy and 167–8

Vietnam War 37
voluntary retirement schemes 264

wage, bill reduction 135
freeze 135
Wagner 16
war finance, demands of 31
'Washington concensus' 182
welfare state 36, 40, 166, 169
and scrutiny of public transactions 208
Westminister type of democracy, legislature and executive in 110, 111, 116
legislature's control of expenditure 112–15
Wilson, President of United States 170–1
World Bank 52, 55, 63, 74, 97, 99–100, 127, 285
'best fits' of 128
on fiscal adjustments 127, 128
on institutional reforms, in developing countries 128
loans from 47–8, 81
and public expenditure reforms 92
structural loan adjustments by 67
World Conference on Governance 2
World War(s), rehabilitation and reconstruction in post- 36
and management of economy 34

zero-based approach, fiscal crisis and 310
zero-based budgeting (ZBB) 56–7, 137, 261, 293